A GRAPHIC NOVEL BY
DAVID J. DESJARDIN

HEAVY WEAPON

PRECURSOR OF WAR

South Vietnam
September 4, 1968

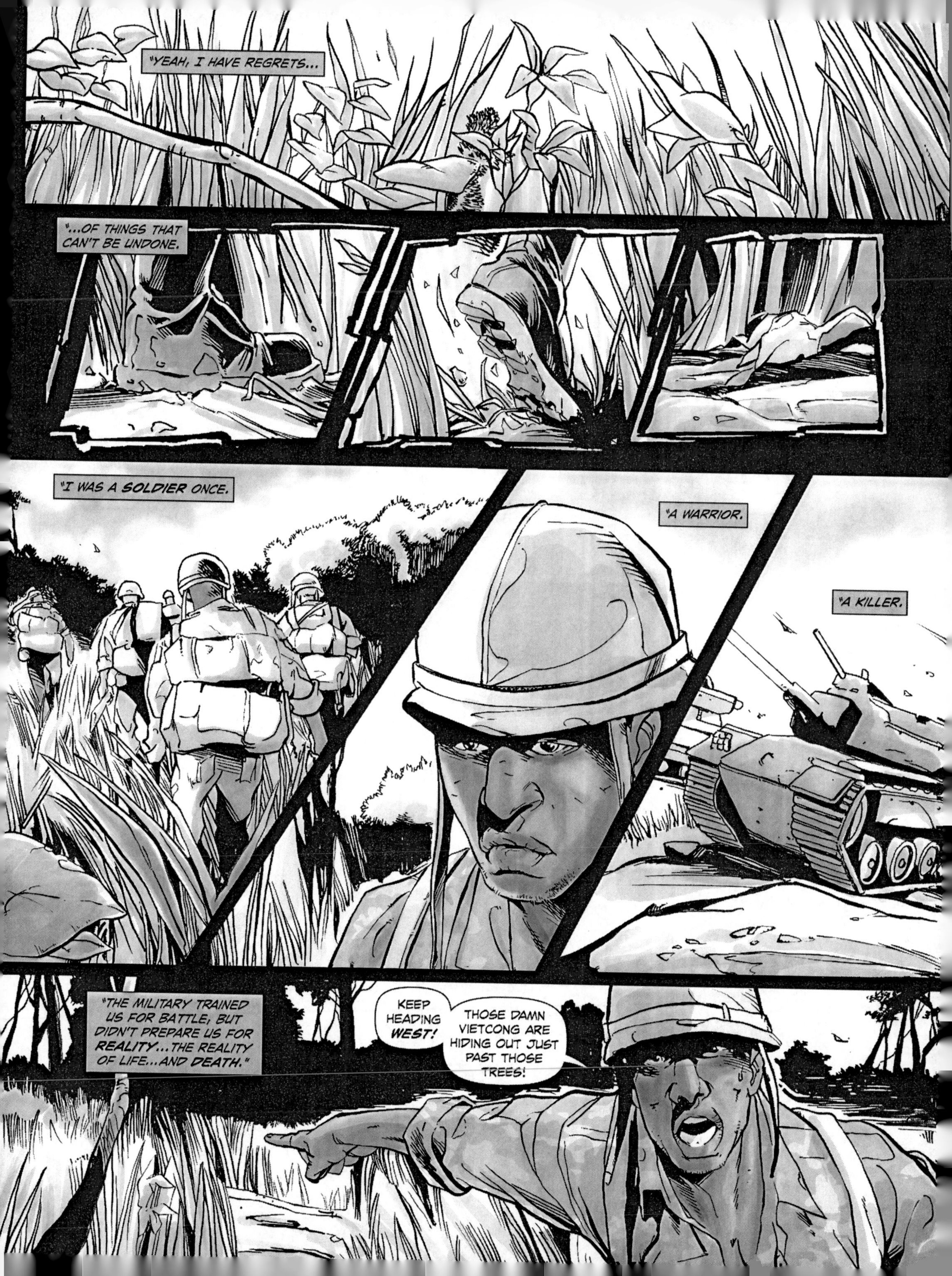
"YEAH, I HAVE REGRETS...
"...OF THINGS THAT CAN'T BE UNDONE.
"I WAS A SOLDIER ONCE.
"A WARRIOR.
"A KILLER.
"THE MILITARY TRAINED US FOR BATTLE, BUT DIDN'T PREPARE US FOR REALITY...THE REALITY OF LIFE...AND DEATH."
KEEP HEADING WEST!
THOSE DAMN VIETCONG ARE HIDING OUT JUST PAST THOSE TREES!

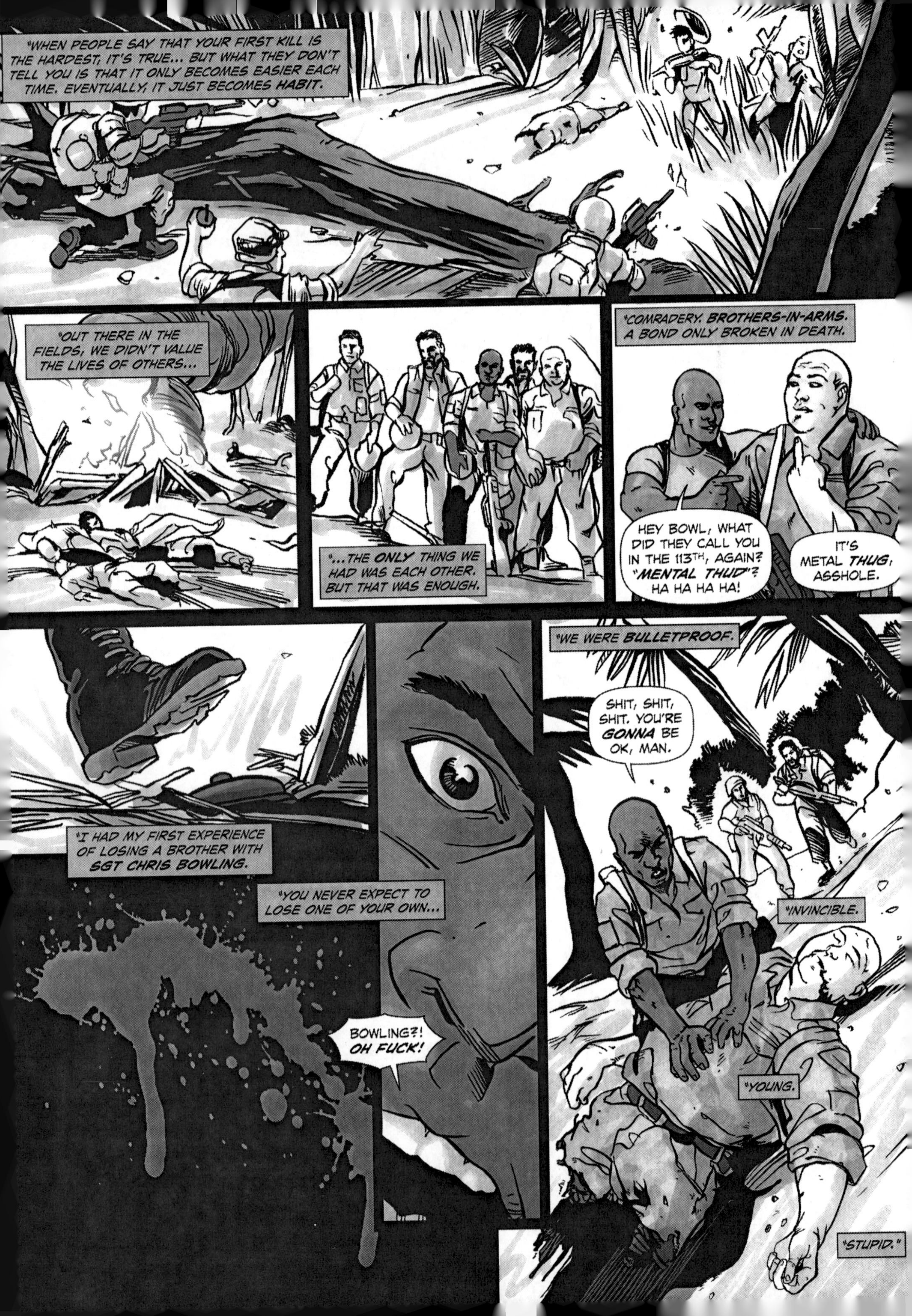
"WHEN PEOPLE SAY THAT YOUR FIRST KILL IS THE HARDEST, IT'S TRUE... BUT WHAT THEY DON'T TELL YOU IS THAT IT ONLY BECOMES EASIER EACH TIME. EVENTUALLY, IT JUST BECOMES HABIT.
"OUT THERE IN THE FIELDS, WE DIDN'T VALUE THE LIVES OF OTHERS...
"...THE ONLY THING WE HAD WAS EACH OTHER. BUT THAT WAS ENOUGH.
"COMRADERY. BROTHERS-IN-ARMS. A BOND ONLY BROKEN IN DEATH.
HEY BOWL, WHAT DID THEY CALL YOU IN THE 113TH, AGAIN? "MENTAL THUD"? HA HA HA HA!
IT'S METAL THUG, ASSHOLE.
"I HAD MY FIRST EXPERIENCE OF LOSING A BROTHER WITH SGT CHRIS BOWLING.
"YOU NEVER EXPECT TO LOSE ONE OF YOUR OWN...
BOWLING?! OH FUCK!
"WE WERE BULLETPROOF.
SHIT, SHIT, SHIT. YOU'RE GONNA BE OK, MAN.
"INVINCIBLE.
"YOUNG.
"STUPID."

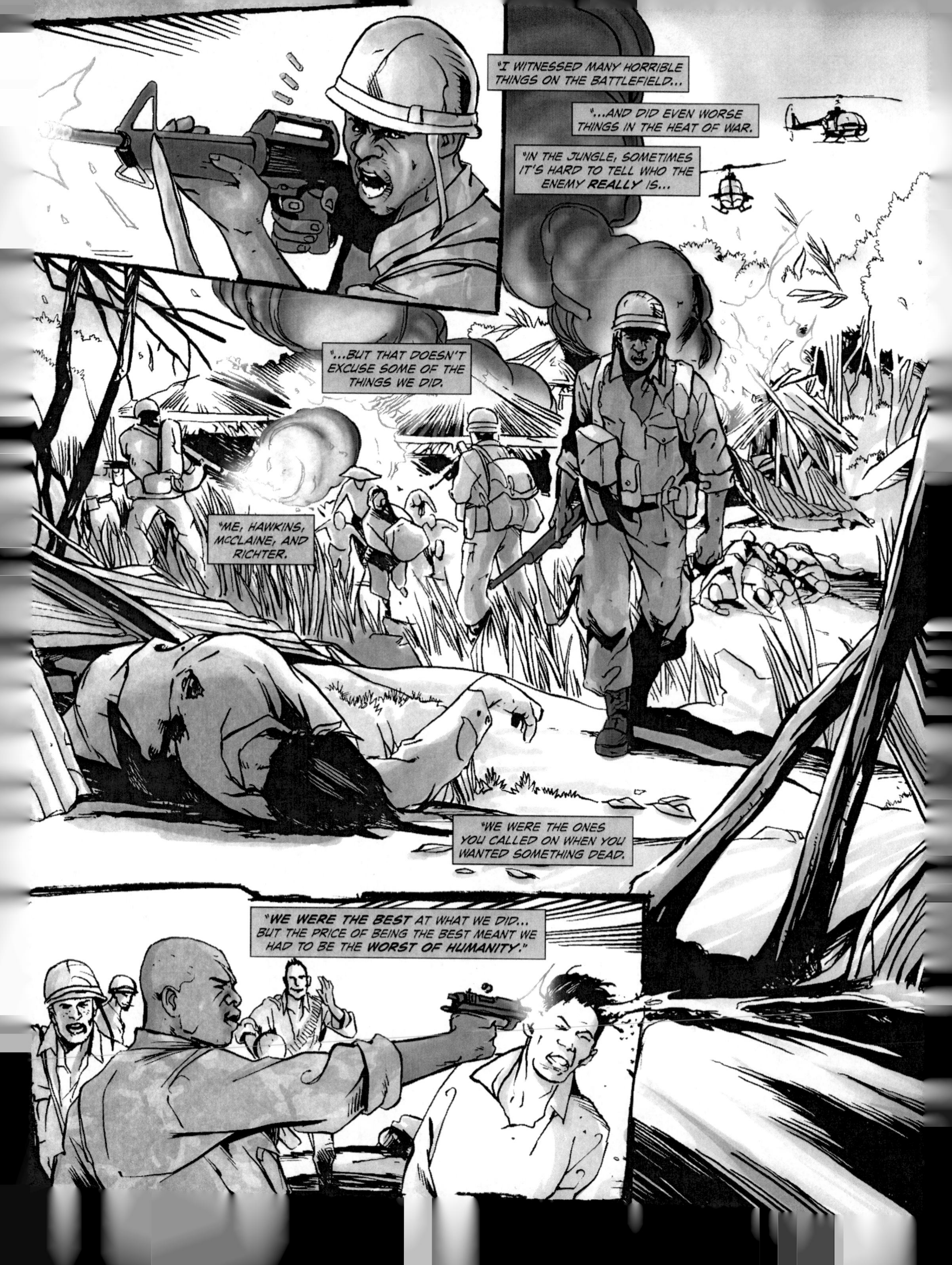
"I WITNESSED MANY HORRIBLE THINGS ON THE BATTLEFIELD...
"...AND DID EVEN WORSE THINGS IN THE HEAT OF WAR.
"IN THE JUNGLE, SOMETIMES IT'S HARD TO TELL WHO THE ENEMY REALLY IS...
"...BUT THAT DOESN'T EXCUSE SOME OF THE THINGS WE DID.
"ME, HAWKINS, McCLAINE, AND RICHTER.
"WE WERE THE ONES YOU CALLED ON WHEN YOU WANTED SOMETHING DEAD.
"WE WERE THE BEST AT WHAT WE DID... BUT THE PRICE OF BEING THE BEST MEANT WE HAD TO BE THE WORST OF HUMANITY."

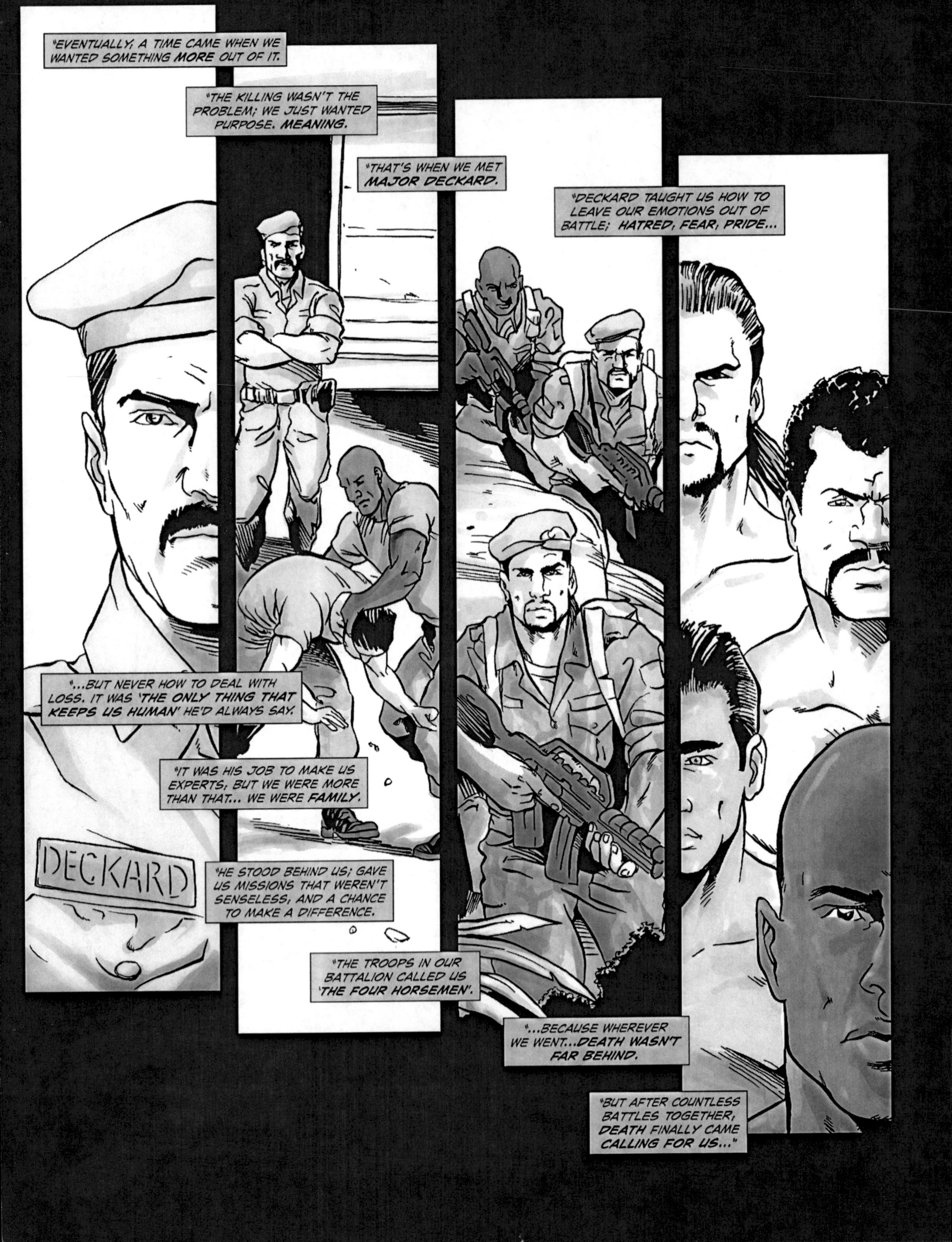
"EVENTUALLY, A TIME CAME WHEN WE WANTED SOMETHING MORE OUT OF IT.
"THE KILLING WASN'T THE PROBLEM; WE JUST WANTED PURPOSE. MEANING.
"THAT'S WHEN WE MET MAJOR DECKARD.
"DECKARD TAUGHT US HOW TO LEAVE OUR EMOTIONS OUT OF BATTLE; HATRED, FEAR, PRIDE...
"...BUT NEVER HOW TO DEAL WITH LOSS. IT WAS 'THE ONLY THING THAT KEEPS US HUMAN' HE'D ALWAYS SAY.
"IT WAS HIS JOB TO MAKE US EXPERTS, BUT WE WERE MORE THAN THAT... WE WERE FAMILY.
DECKARD
"HE STOOD BEHIND US; GAVE US MISSIONS THAT WEREN'T SENSELESS, AND A CHANCE TO MAKE A DIFFERENCE.
"THE TROOPS IN OUR BATTALION CALLED US 'THE FOUR HORSEMEN'.
"...BECAUSE WHEREVER WE WENT...DEATH WASN'T FAR BEHIND.
"BUT AFTER COUNTLESS BATTLES TOGETHER, DEATH FINALLY CAME CALLING FOR US..."

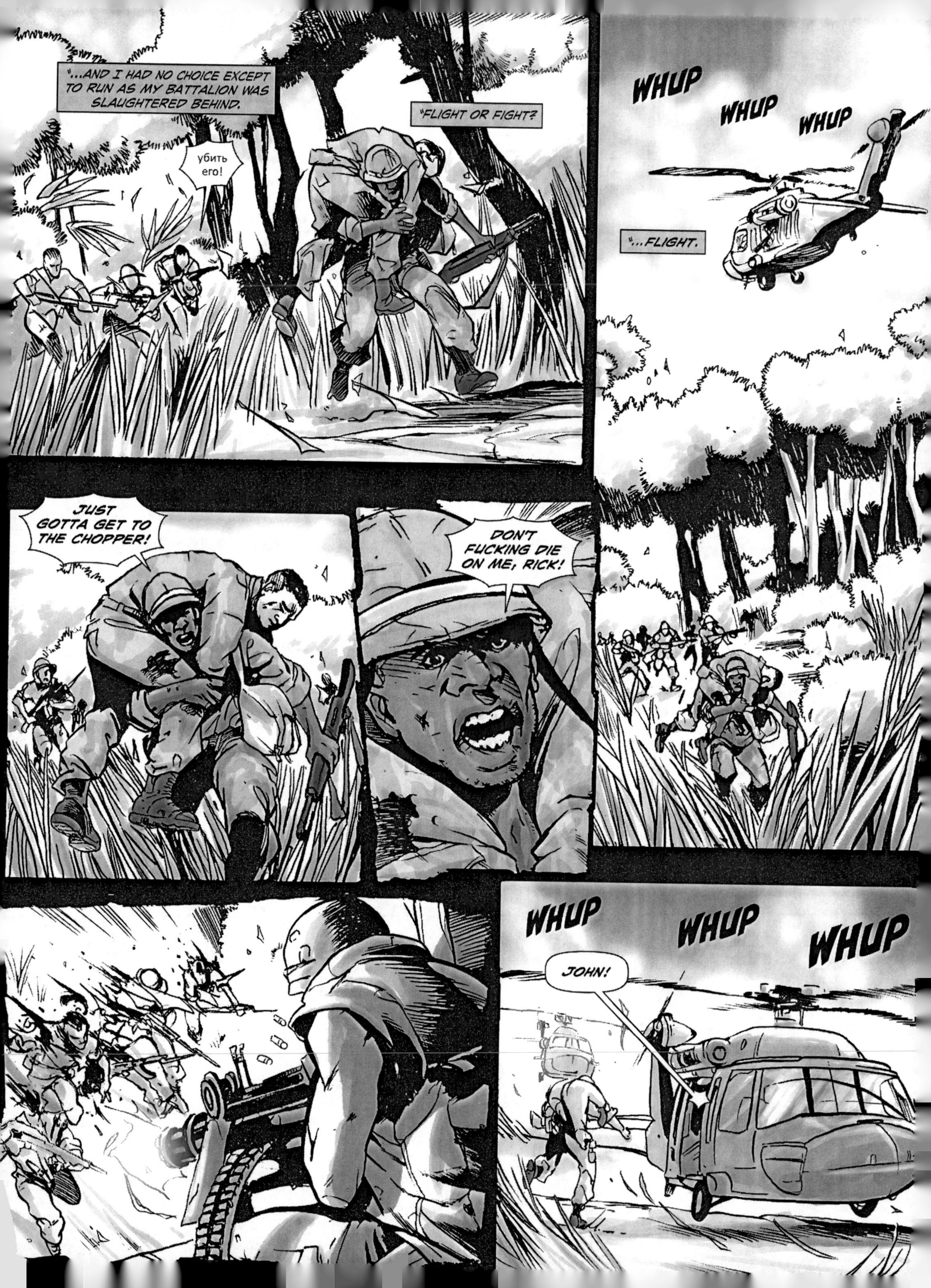
"...AND I HAD NO CHOICE EXCEPT TO RUN AS MY BATTALION WAS SLAUGHTERED BEHIND.
убить его!
"FLIGHT OR FIGHT?
WHUP
WHUP
WHUP
"...FLIGHT.
JUST GOTTA GET TO THE CHOPPER!
DON'T FUCKING DIE ON ME, RICK!
WHUP
WHUP
WHUP
JOHN!

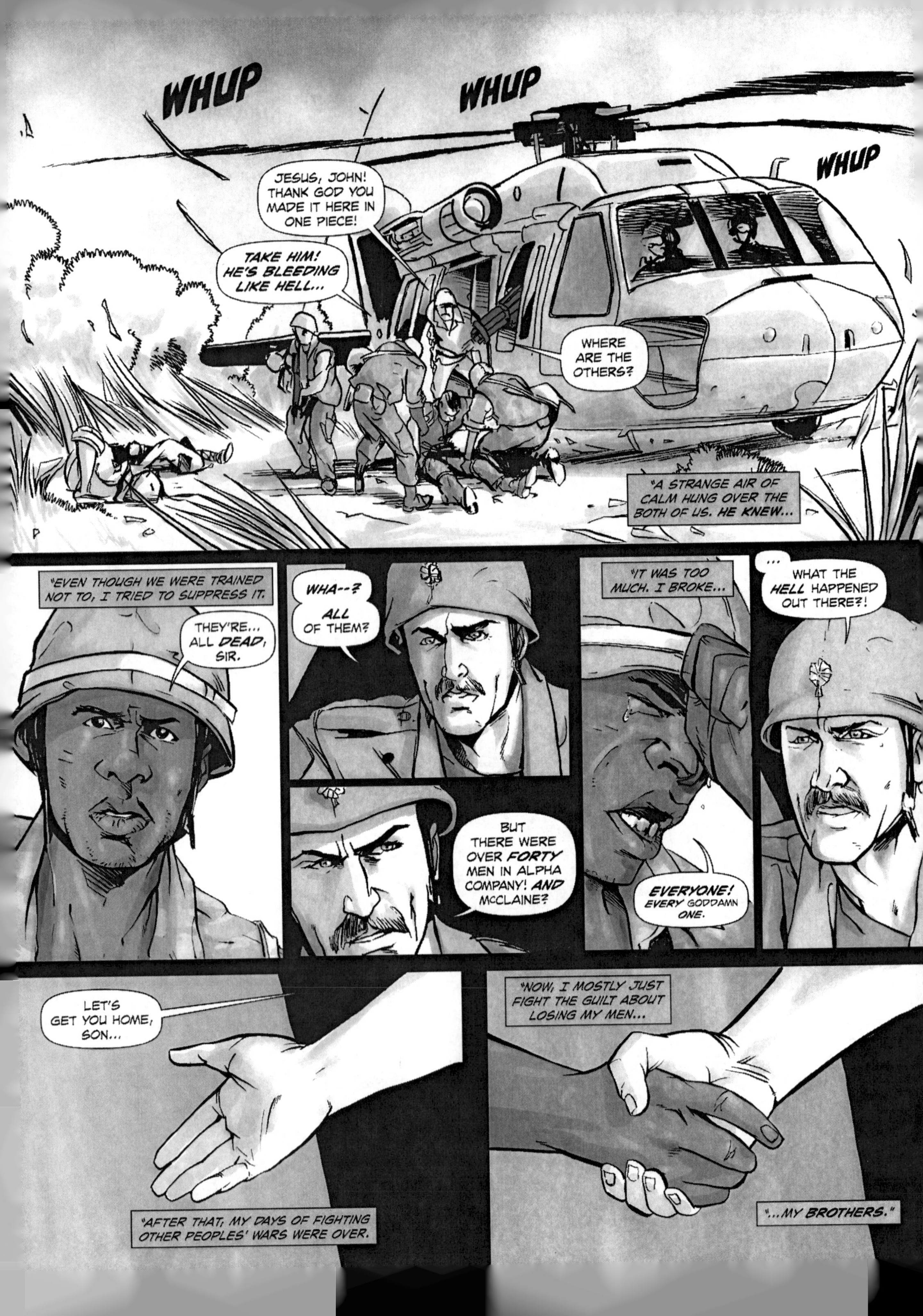
WHUP
WHUP
WHUP
JESUS, JOHN! THANK GOD YOU MADE IT HERE IN ONE PIECE!
TAKE HIM! HE'S BLEEDING LIKE HELL...
WHERE ARE THE OTHERS?
"A STRANGE AIR OF CALM HUNG OVER THE BOTH OF US. HE KNEW...
"EVEN THOUGH WE WERE TRAINED NOT TO, I TRIED TO SUPPRESS IT.
THEY'RE... ALL DEAD, SIR.
WHA--? ALL OF THEM?
BUT THERE WERE OVER FORTY MEN IN ALPHA COMPANY! AND McCLAINE?
"IT WAS TOO MUCH. I BROKE...
EVERYONE! EVERY GODDAMN ONE.
... WHAT THE HELL HAPPENED OUT THERE?!
LET'S GET YOU HOME, SON...
"AFTER THAT, MY DAYS OF FIGHTING OTHER PEOPLES' WARS WERE OVER.
"NOW, I MOSTLY JUST FIGHT THE GUILT ABOUT LOSING MY MEN...
"...MY BROTHERS."

"I MAY HAVE SAVED RICHTER, BUT I HAD TO LEAVE McCLAINE, HAWKINS, AND THE OTHERS BEHIND.

"I STILL FEEL LIKE I COULD HAVE DONE SOMETHING MORE...

"...SOMETHING TO SAVE THEM.

WHUP
WHUP
WHUP
WHUP

WHUP
WHUP

"I'VE KILLED A LOT OF MEN... BUT I'D KILL MANY MORE TO SAVE ONE OF MY OWN..."

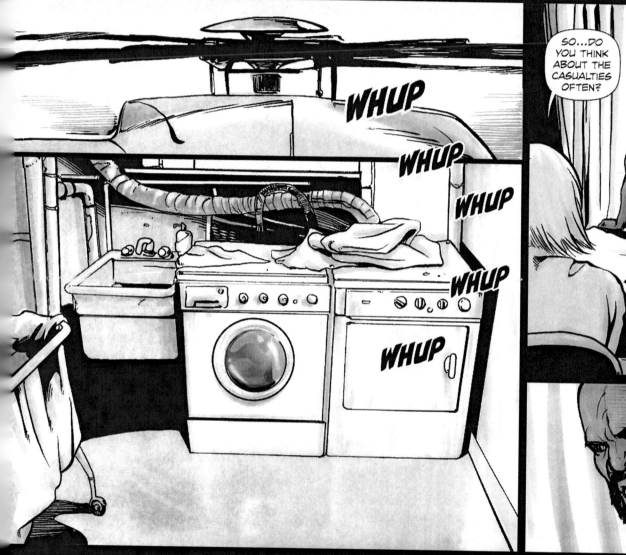

WHUP
WHUP
WHUP
WHUP
WHUP

SO...DO YOU THINK ABOUT THE CASUALTIES OFTEN?

TAP
TAP
TAP

...WELL? DO YOU?

≈SIGH≈ ARE WE DONE HERE?

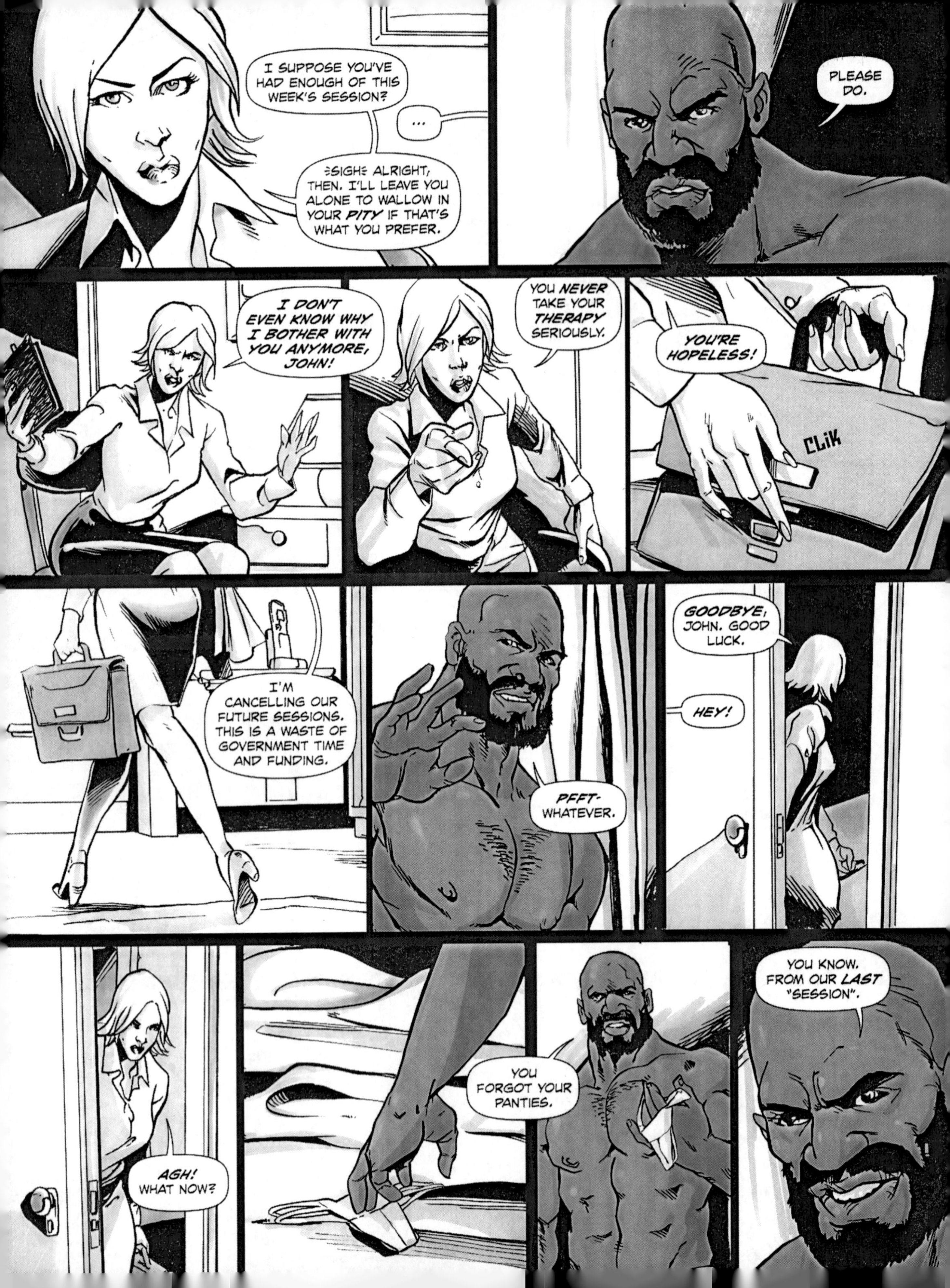
I SUPPOSE YOU'VE HAD ENOUGH OF THIS WEEK'S SESSION?
...
=SIGH= ALRIGHT, THEN. I'LL LEAVE YOU ALONE TO WALLOW IN YOUR PITY IF THAT'S WHAT YOU PREFER.
PLEASE DO.
I DON'T EVEN KNOW WHY I BOTHER WITH YOU ANYMORE, JOHN!
YOU NEVER TAKE YOUR THERAPY SERIOUSLY.
YOU'RE HOPELESS!
CLiK
I'M CANCELLING OUR FUTURE SESSIONS. THIS IS A WASTE OF GOVERNMENT TIME AND FUNDING.
PFFT- WHATEVER.
GOODBYE, JOHN. GOOD LUCK.
HEY!
AGH! WHAT NOW?
YOU FORGOT YOUR PANTIES.
YOU KNOW. FROM OUR LAST "SESSION".

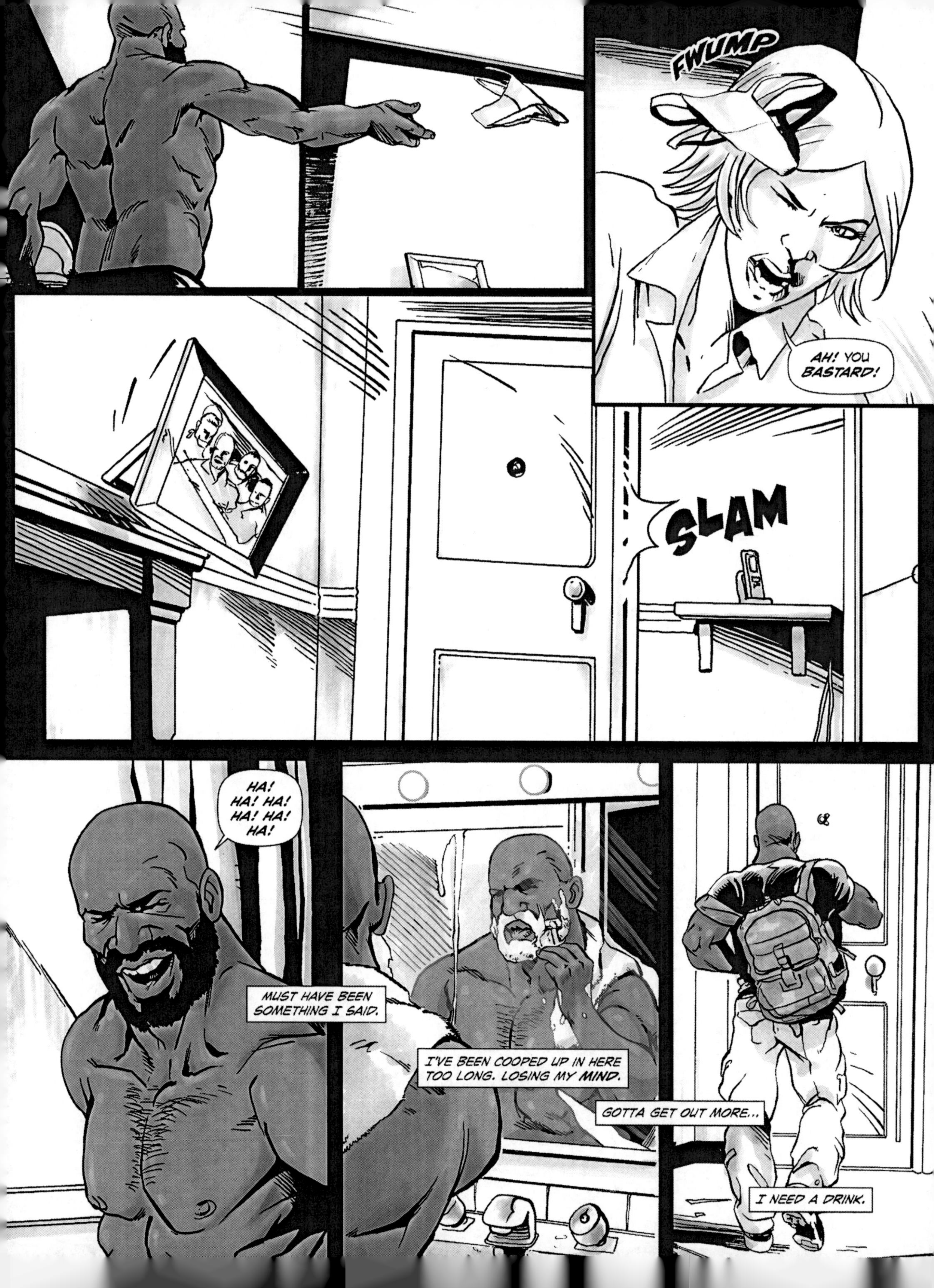
FWUMP
AH! YOU BASTARD!
SLAM
HA! HA! HA! HA! HA! HA!
MUST HAVE BEEN SOMETHING I SAID.
I'VE BEEN COOPED UP IN HERE TOO LONG. LOSING MY MIND.
GOTTA GET OUT MORE...
I NEED A DRINK.

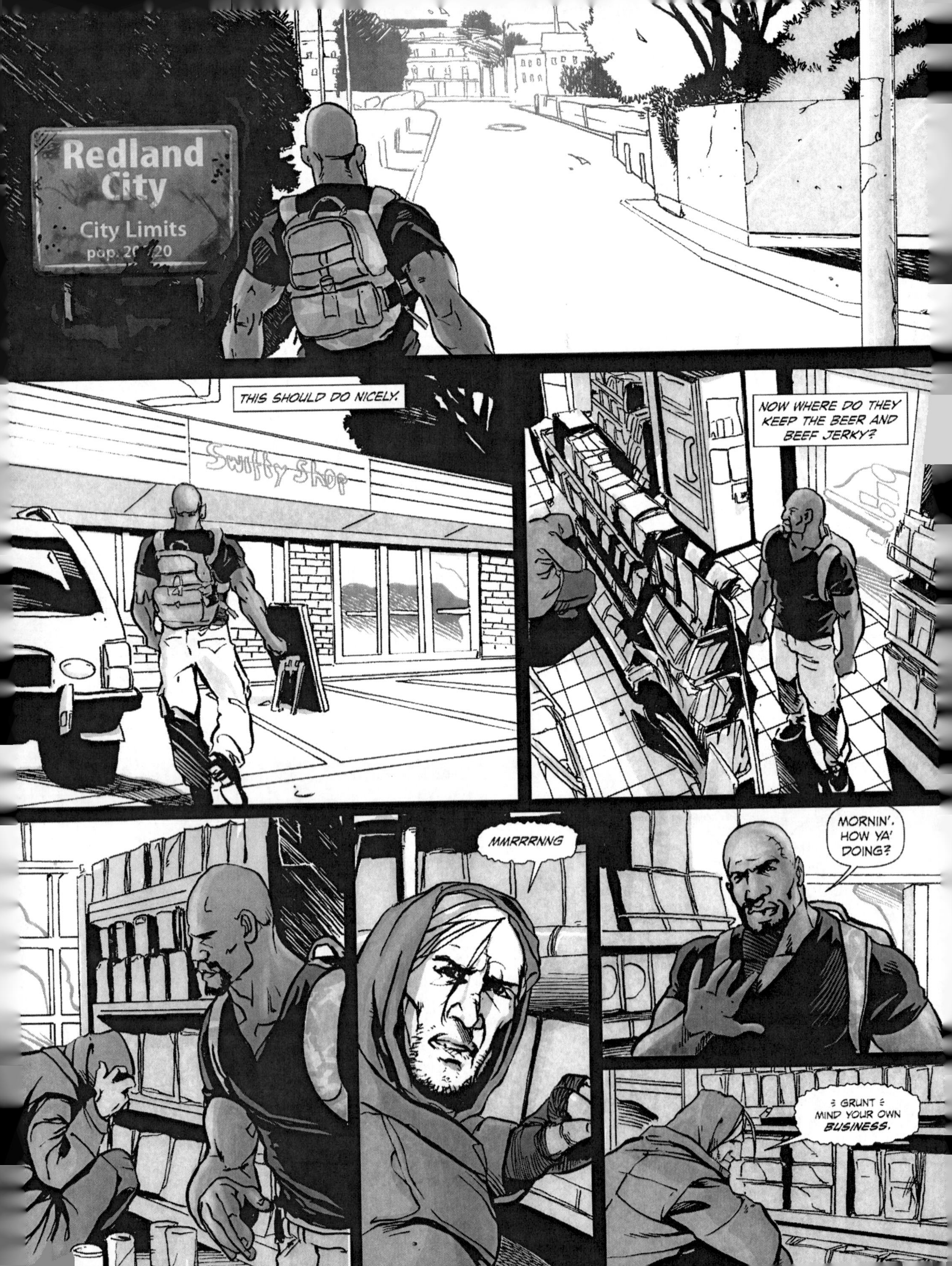
Redland City
City Limits
THIS SHOULD DO NICELY.
Swifty Shop
NOW WHERE DO THEY KEEP THE BEER AND BEEF JERKY?
MMRRRNNG
MORNIN'. HOW YA' DOING?
GRUNT
MIND YOUR OWN BUSINESS.

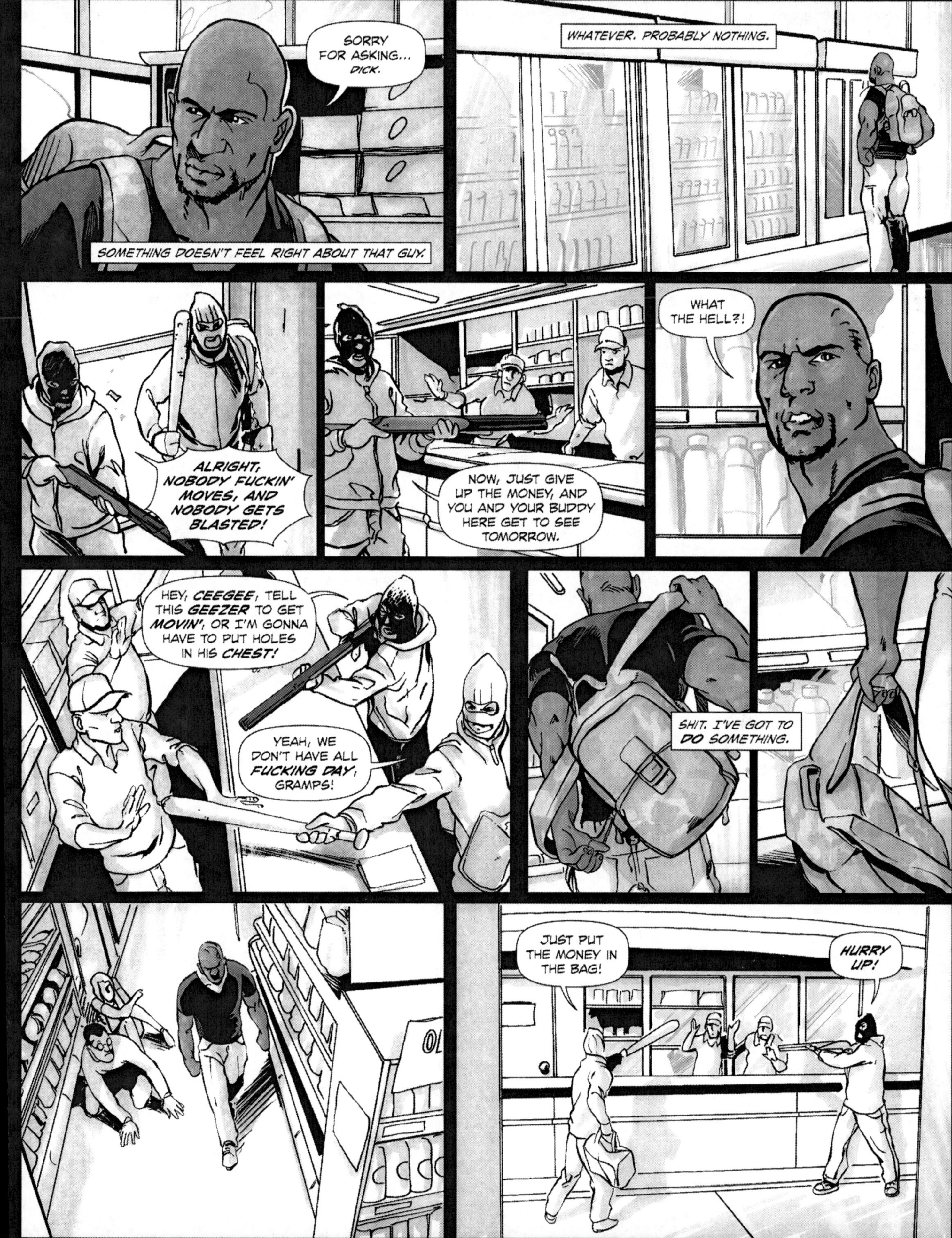
SORRY FOR ASKING... DICK.
SOMETHING DOESN'T FEEL RIGHT ABOUT THAT GUY.
WHATEVER. PROBABLY NOTHING.
ALRIGHT, NOBODY FUCKIN' MOVES, AND NOBODY GETS BLASTED!
NOW, JUST GIVE UP THE MONEY, AND YOU AND YOUR BUDDY HERE GET TO SEE TOMORROW.
WHAT THE HELL?!
HEY, CEEGEE, TELL THIS GEEZER TO GET MOVIN', OR I'M GONNA HAVE TO PUT HOLES IN HIS CHEST!
YEAH, WE DON'T HAVE ALL FUCKING DAY, GRAMPS!
SHIT. I'VE GOT TO DO SOMETHING.
JUST PUT THE MONEY IN THE BAG!
HURRY UP!

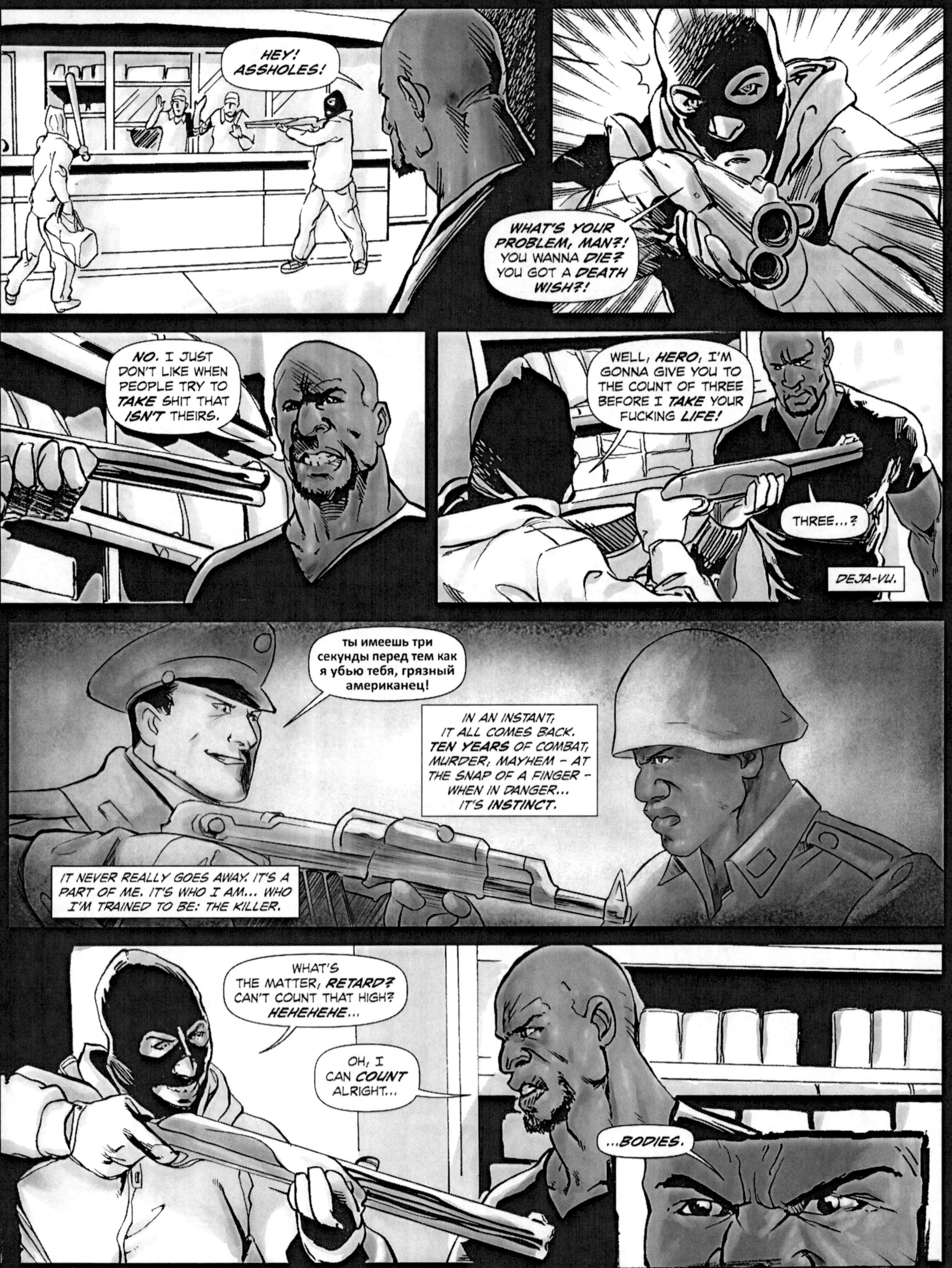
HEY! ASSHOLES!
WHAT'S YOUR PROBLEM, MAN?! YOU WANNA DIE? YOU GOT A DEATH WISH?!
NO. I JUST DON'T LIKE WHEN PEOPLE TRY TO TAKE SHIT THAT ISN'T THEIRS.
WELL, HERO, I'M GONNA GIVE YOU TO THE COUNT OF THREE BEFORE I TAKE YOUR FUCKING LIFE!
THREE...?
DEJA-VU.
ты имеешь три секунды перед тем как я убью тебя, грязный американец!
IN AN INSTANT, IT ALL COMES BACK. TEN YEARS OF COMBAT, MURDER, MAYHEM – AT THE SNAP OF A FINGER – WHEN IN DANGER... IT'S INSTINCT.
IT NEVER REALLY GOES AWAY. IT'S A PART OF ME. IT'S WHO I AM... WHO I'M TRAINED TO BE: THE KILLER.
WHAT'S THE MATTER, RETARD? CAN'T COUNT THAT HIGH? HEHEHEHE...
OH, I CAN COUNT ALRIGHT...
...BODIES.

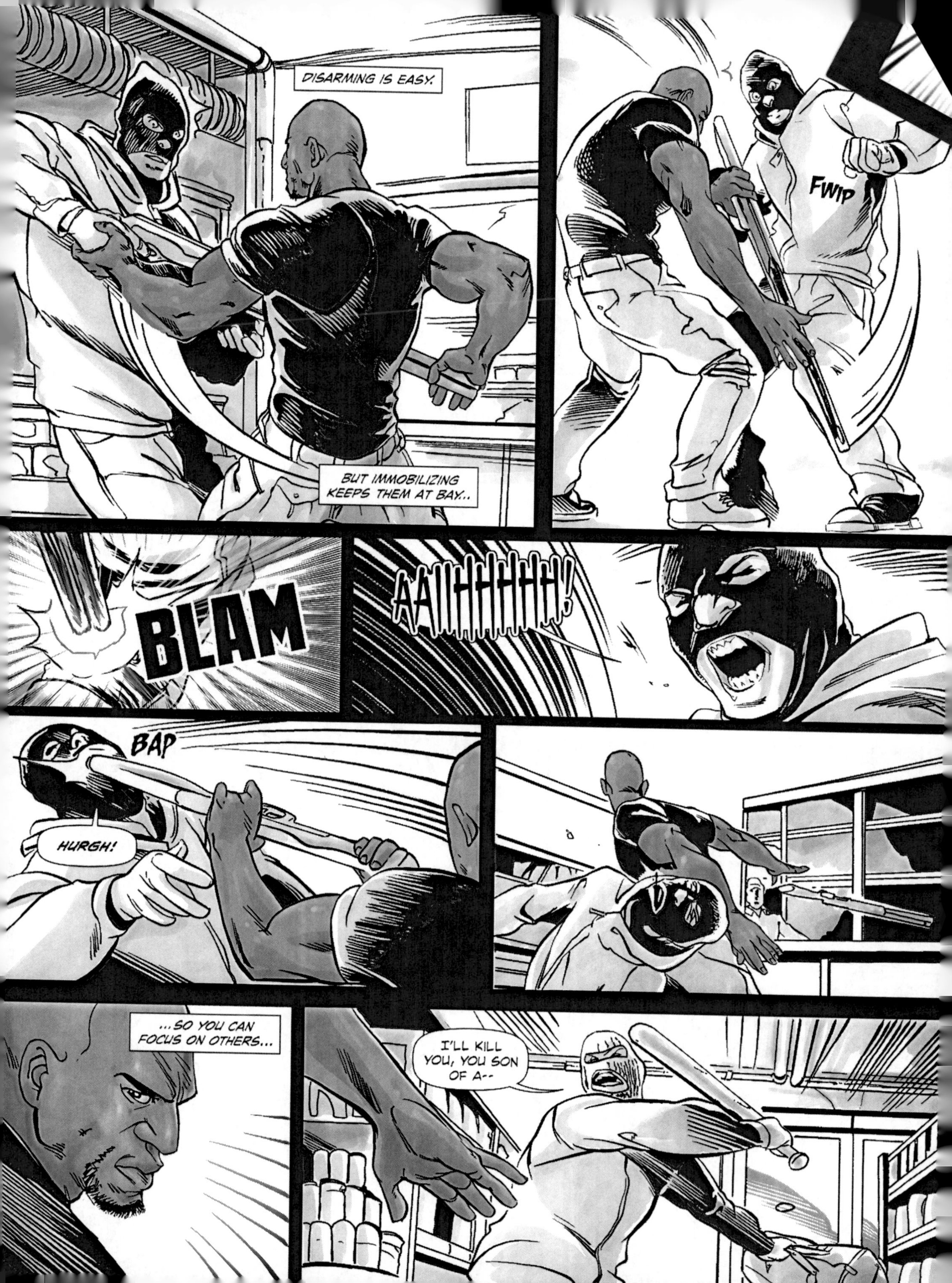
DISARMING IS EASY.
BUT IMMOBILIZING KEEPS THEM AT BAY...
FWIP
BLAM
AAIIIHHHHH!
BAP
HURGH!
...SO YOU CAN FOCUS ON OTHERS...
I'LL KILL YOU, YOU SON OF A--

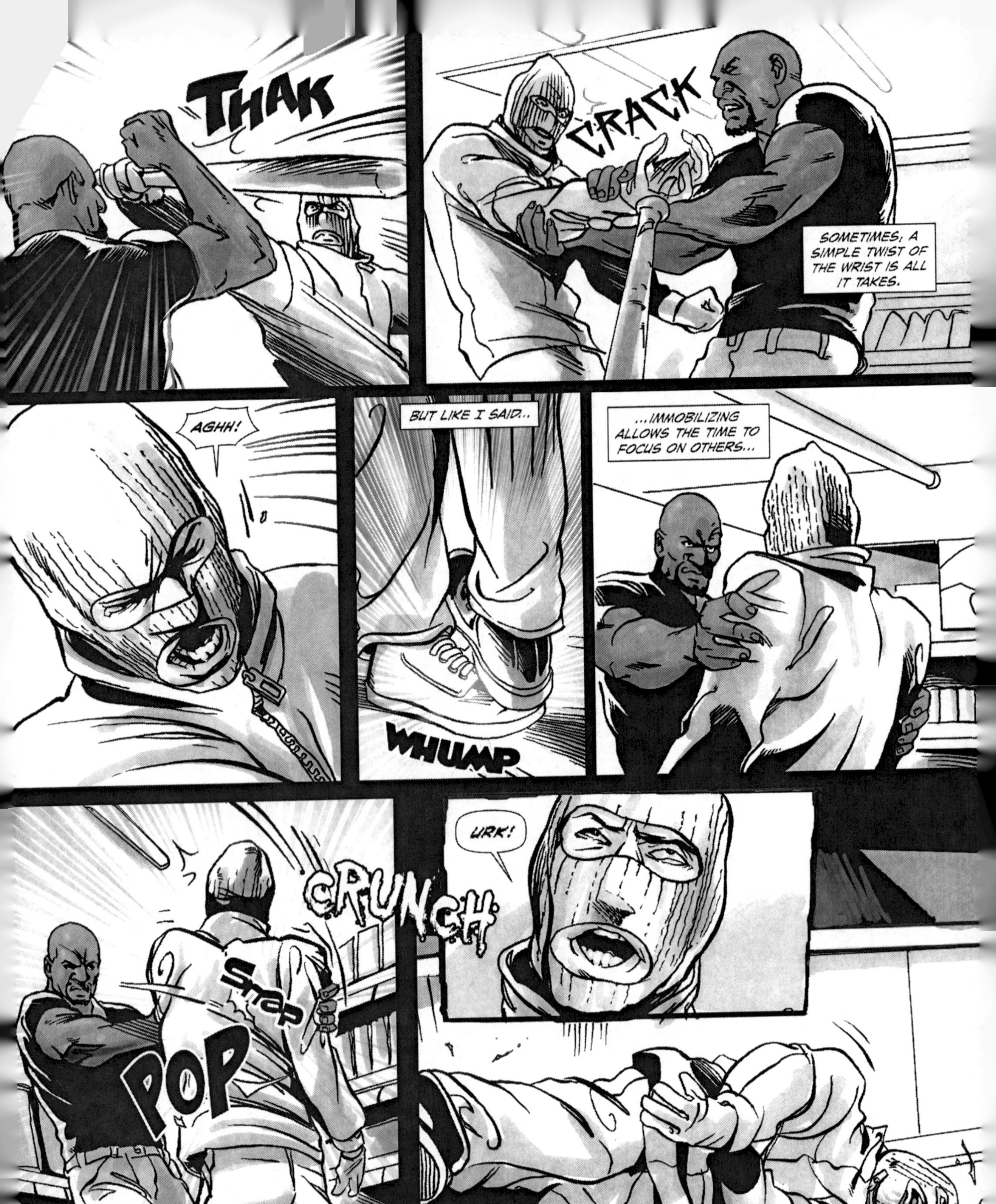
THAK
CRACK
SOMETIMES, A SIMPLE TWIST OF THE WRIST IS ALL IT TAKES.
AGHH!
BUT LIKE I SAID...
WHUMP
...IMMOBILIZING ALLOWS THE TIME TO FOCUS ON OTHERS...
CRUNCH
Snap
POP
URK!
THUD

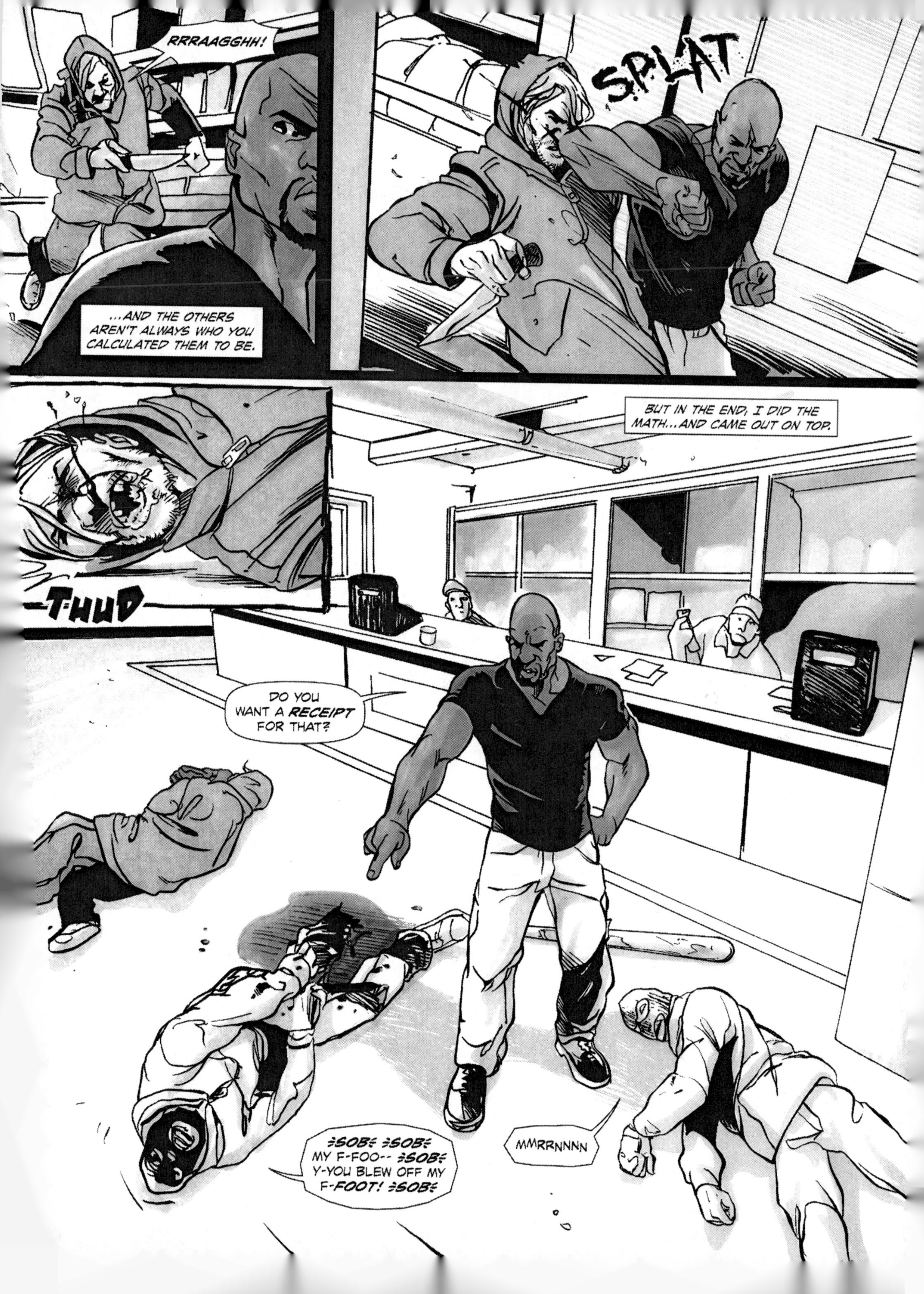
RRRAAGGHH!
...AND THE OTHERS AREN'T ALWAYS WHO YOU CALCULATED THEM TO BE.
SPLAT
THUD
BUT IN THE END, I DID THE MATH...AND CAME OUT ON TOP.
DO YOU WANT A RECEIPT FOR THAT?
SOB SOB MY F-FOO-- SOB Y-YOU BLEW OFF MY F-FOOT! SOB
MMRRNNNN

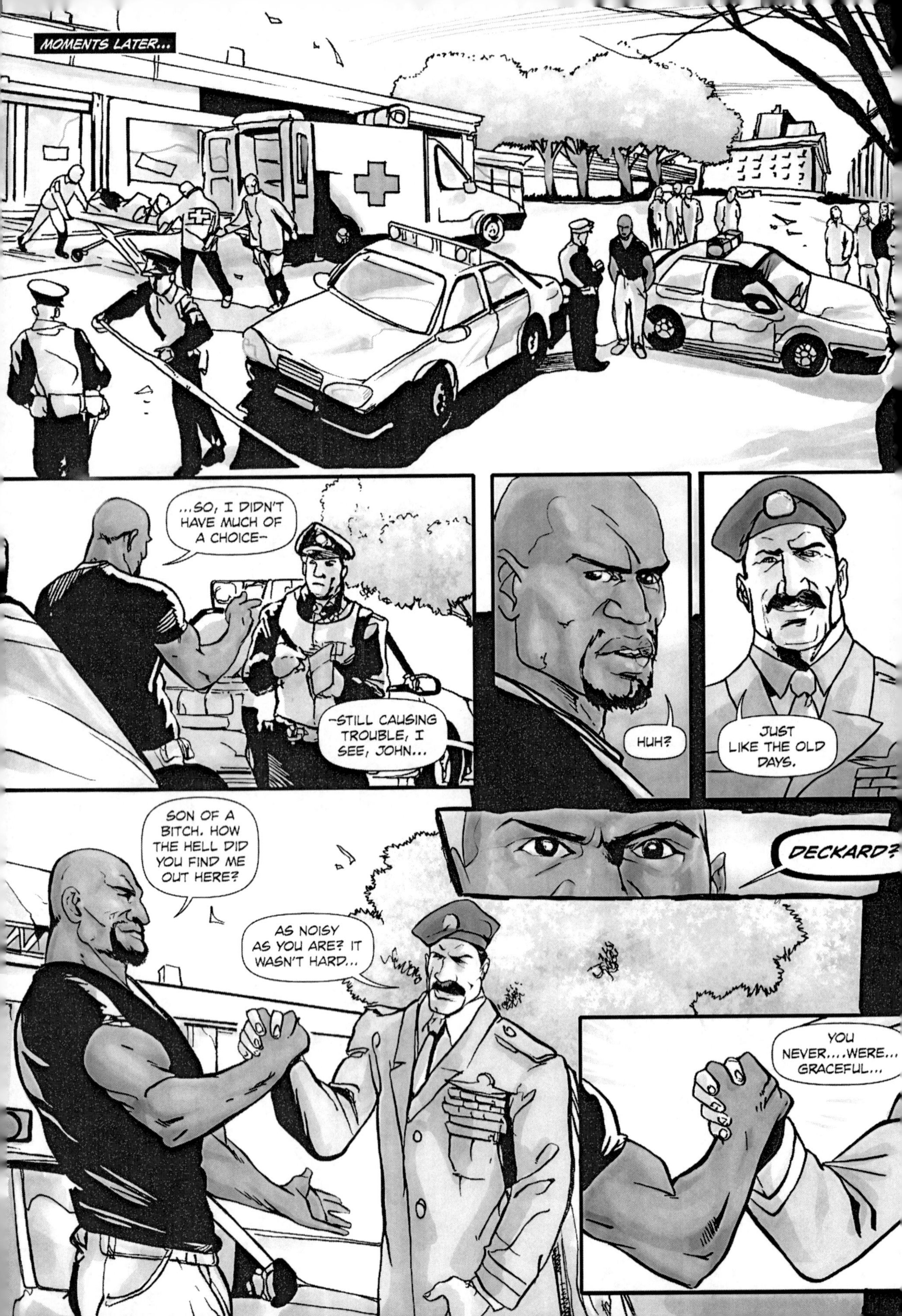
MOMENTS LATER...
...SO, I DIDN'T HAVE MUCH OF A CHOICE-
-STILL CAUSING TROUBLE, I SEE, JOHN...
HUH?
JUST LIKE THE OLD DAYS.
DECKARD?
SON OF A BITCH. HOW THE HELL DID YOU FIND ME OUT HERE?
AS NOISY AS YOU ARE? IT WASN'T HARD...
YOU NEVER....WERE... GRACEFUL...

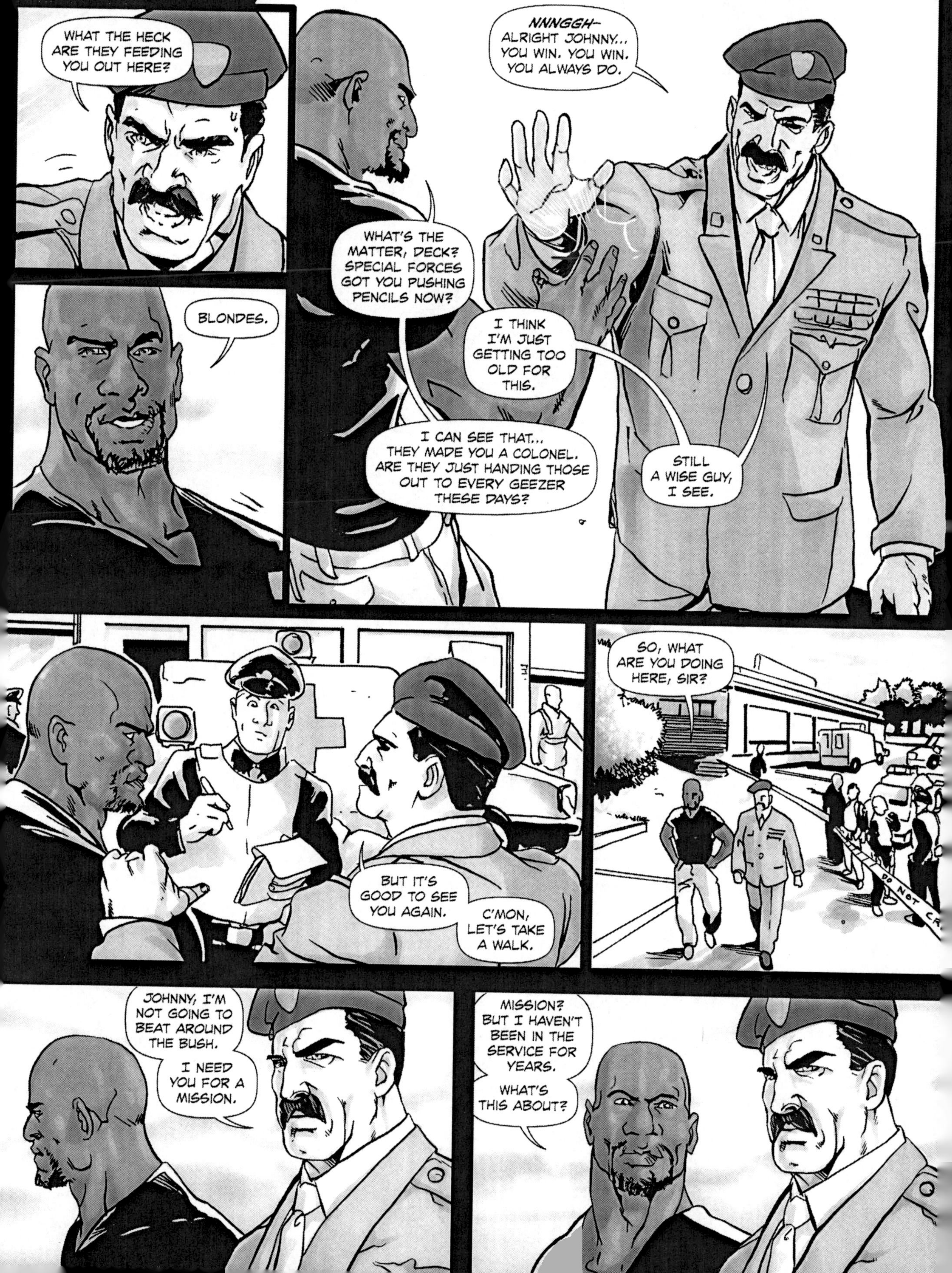
WHAT THE HECK ARE THEY FEEDING YOU OUT HERE?
BLONDES.
WHAT'S THE MATTER, DECK? SPECIAL FORCES GOT YOU PUSHING PENCILS NOW?
NNNGGH— ALRIGHT JOHNNY... YOU WIN. YOU WIN. YOU ALWAYS DO.
I THINK I'M JUST GETTING TOO OLD FOR THIS.
I CAN SEE THAT... THEY MADE YOU A COLONEL. ARE THEY JUST HANDING THOSE OUT TO EVERY GEEZER THESE DAYS?
STILL A WISE GUY, I SEE.
BUT IT'S GOOD TO SEE YOU AGAIN.
C'MON, LET'S TAKE A WALK.
SO, WHAT ARE YOU DOING HERE, SIR?
DO NOT CR
JOHNNY, I'M NOT GOING TO BEAT AROUND THE BUSH.
I NEED YOU FOR A MISSION.
MISSION? BUT I HAVEN'T BEEN IN THE SERVICE FOR YEARS.
WHAT'S THIS ABOUT?

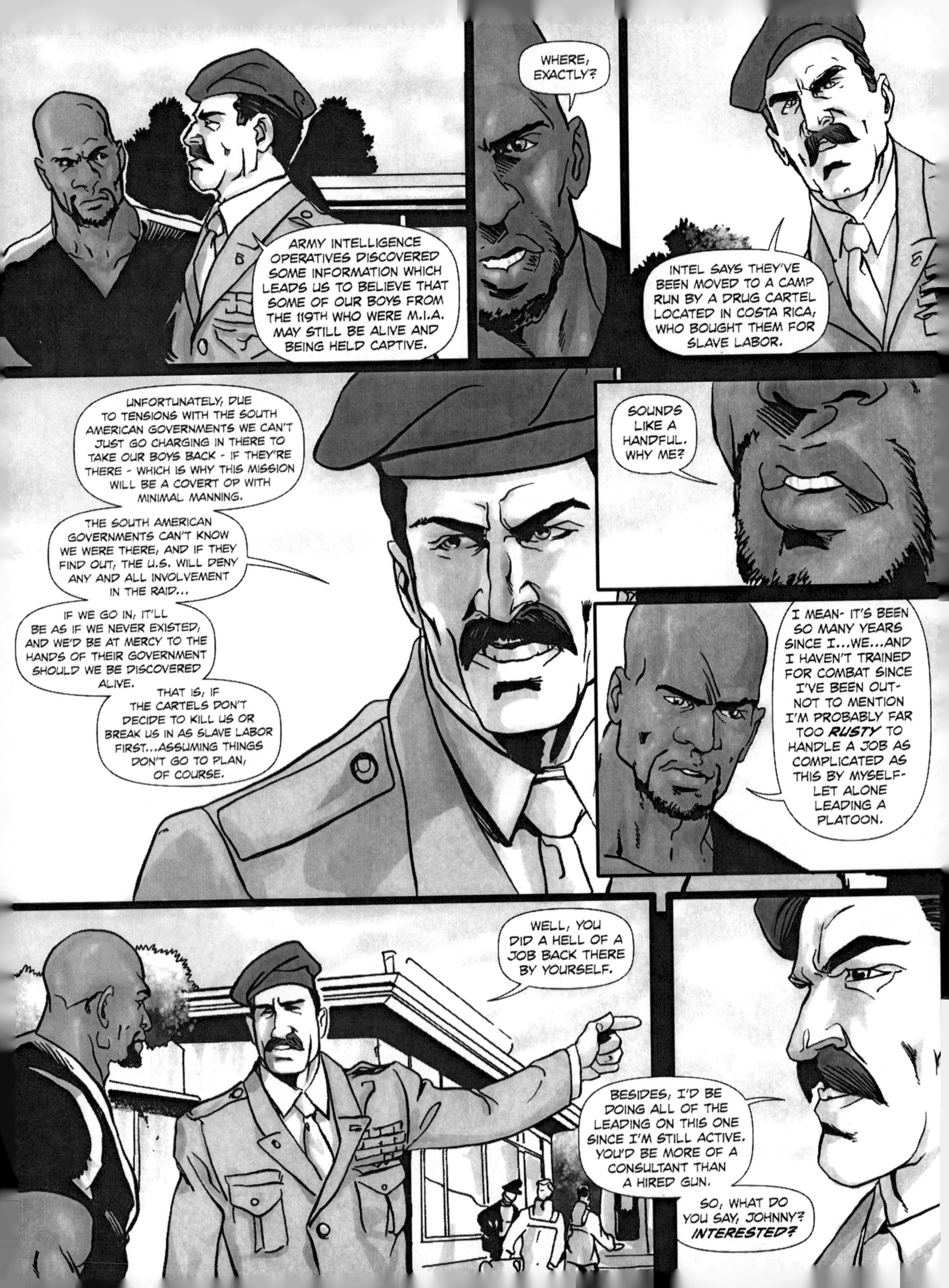
ARMY INTELLIGENCE OPERATIVES DISCOVERED SOME INFORMATION WHICH LEADS US TO BELIEVE THAT SOME OF OUR BOYS FROM THE 119TH WHO WERE M.I.A. MAY STILL BE ALIVE AND BEING HELD CAPTIVE.
WHERE, EXACTLY?
INTEL SAYS THEY'VE BEEN MOVED TO A CAMP RUN BY A DRUG CARTEL LOCATED IN COSTA RICA, WHO BOUGHT THEM FOR SLAVE LABOR.
UNFORTUNATELY, DUE TO TENSIONS WITH THE SOUTH AMERICAN GOVERNMENTS WE CAN'T JUST GO CHARGING IN THERE TO TAKE OUR BOYS BACK - IF THEY'RE THERE - WHICH IS WHY THIS MISSION WILL BE A COVERT OP WITH MINIMAL MANNING.
THE SOUTH AMERICAN GOVERNMENTS CAN'T KNOW WE WERE THERE, AND IF THEY FIND OUT, THE U.S. WILL DENY ANY AND ALL INVOLVEMENT IN THE RAID...
IF WE GO IN, IT'LL BE AS IF WE NEVER EXISTED, AND WE'D BE AT MERCY TO THE HANDS OF THEIR GOVERNMENT SHOULD WE BE DISCOVERED ALIVE.
THAT IS, IF THE CARTELS DON'T DECIDE TO KILL US OR BREAK US IN AS SLAVE LABOR FIRST...ASSUMING THINGS DON'T GO TO PLAN, OF COURSE.
SOUNDS LIKE A HANDFUL. WHY ME?
I MEAN- IT'S BEEN SO MANY YEARS SINCE I...WE...AND I HAVEN'T TRAINED FOR COMBAT SINCE I'VE BEEN OUT- NOT TO MENTION I'M PROBABLY FAR TOO RUSTY TO HANDLE A JOB AS COMPLICATED AS THIS BY MYSELF- LET ALONE LEADING A PLATOON.
WELL, YOU DID A HELL OF A JOB BACK THERE BY YOURSELF.
BESIDES, I'D BE DOING ALL OF THE LEADING ON THIS ONE SINCE I'M STILL ACTIVE. YOU'D BE MORE OF A CONSULTANT THAN A HIRED GUN.
SO, WHAT DO YOU SAY, JOHNNY? INTERESTED?

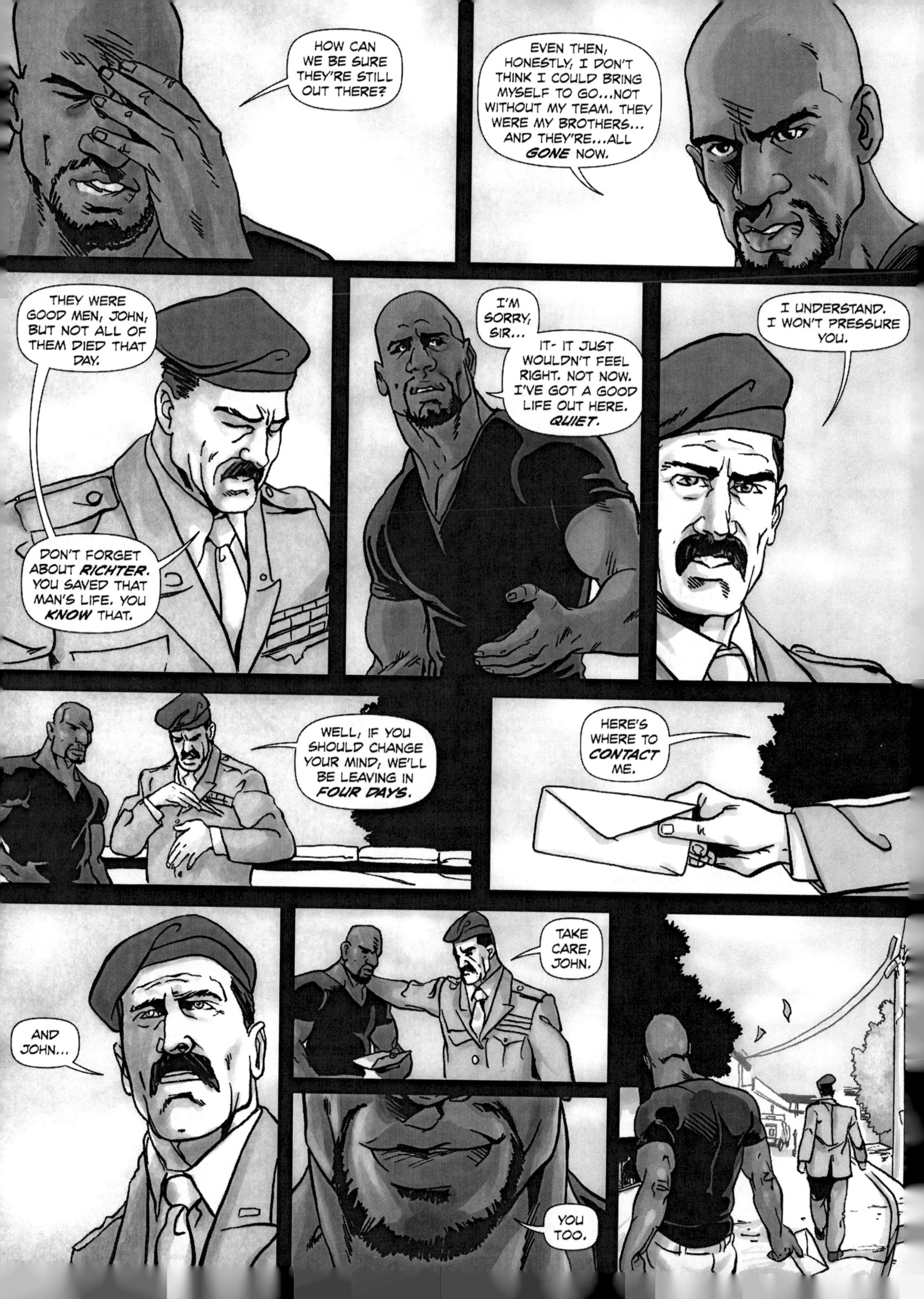
HOW CAN WE BE SURE THEY'RE STILL OUT THERE?
EVEN THEN, HONESTLY, I DON'T THINK I COULD BRING MYSELF TO GO...NOT WITHOUT MY TEAM. THEY WERE MY BROTHERS... AND THEY'RE...ALL GONE NOW.
THEY WERE GOOD MEN, JOHN, BUT NOT ALL OF THEM DIED THAT DAY.
DON'T FORGET ABOUT RICHTER. YOU SAVED THAT MAN'S LIFE. YOU KNOW THAT.
I'M SORRY, SIR...
IT- IT JUST WOULDN'T FEEL RIGHT. NOT NOW. I'VE GOT A GOOD LIFE OUT HERE. QUIET.
I UNDERSTAND. I WON'T PRESSURE YOU.
WELL, IF YOU SHOULD CHANGE YOUR MIND, WE'LL BE LEAVING IN FOUR DAYS.
HERE'S WHERE TO CONTACT ME.
AND JOHN...
TAKE CARE, JOHN.
YOU TOO.

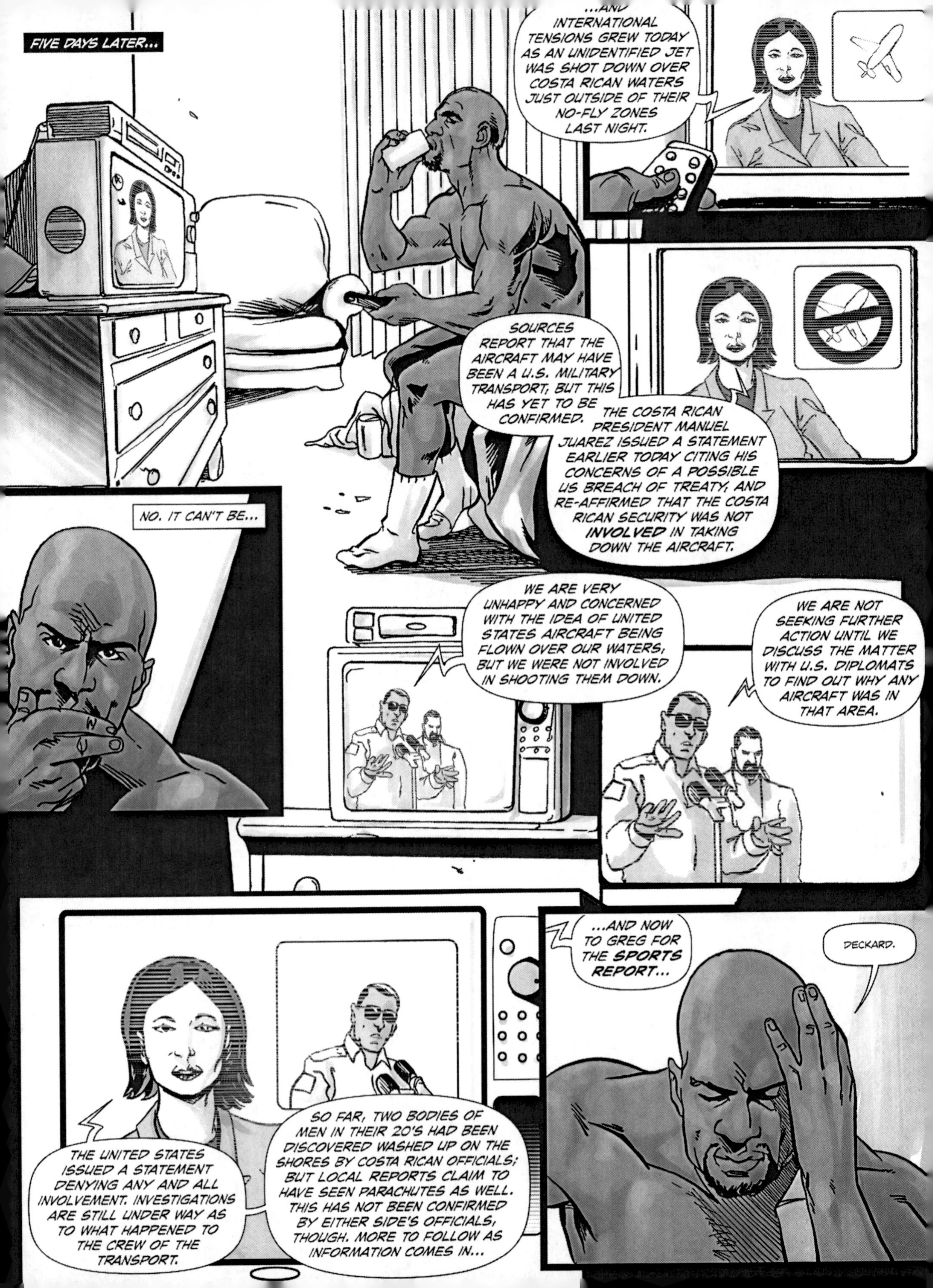
FIVE DAYS LATER...
...AND INTERNATIONAL TENSIONS GREW TODAY AS AN UNIDENTIFIED JET WAS SHOT DOWN OVER COSTA RICAN WATERS JUST OUTSIDE OF THEIR NO-FLY ZONES LAST NIGHT.
SOURCES REPORT THAT THE AIRCRAFT MAY HAVE BEEN A U.S. MILITARY TRANSPORT, BUT THIS HAS YET TO BE CONFIRMED.
THE COSTA RICAN PRESIDENT MANUEL JUAREZ ISSUED A STATEMENT EARLIER TODAY CITING HIS CONCERNS OF A POSSIBLE US BREACH OF TREATY; AND RE-AFFIRMED THAT THE COSTA RICAN SECURITY WAS NOT INVOLVED IN TAKING DOWN THE AIRCRAFT.
NO. IT CAN'T BE...
WE ARE VERY UNHAPPY AND CONCERNED WITH THE IDEA OF UNITED STATES AIRCRAFT BEING FLOWN OVER OUR WATERS, BUT WE WERE NOT INVOLVED IN SHOOTING THEM DOWN.
WE ARE NOT SEEKING FURTHER ACTION UNTIL WE DISCUSS THE MATTER WITH U.S. DIPLOMATS TO FIND OUT WHY ANY AIRCRAFT WAS IN THAT AREA.
THE UNITED STATES ISSUED A STATEMENT DENYING ANY AND ALL INVOLVEMENT. INVESTIGATIONS ARE STILL UNDER WAY AS TO WHAT HAPPENED TO THE CREW OF THE TRANSPORT.
SO FAR, TWO BODIES OF MEN IN THEIR 20'S HAD BEEN DISCOVERED WASHED UP ON THE SHORES BY COSTA RICAN OFFICIALS; BUT LOCAL REPORTS CLAIM TO HAVE SEEN PARACHUTES AS WELL. THIS HAS NOT BEEN CONFIRMED BY EITHER SIDE'S OFFICIALS, THOUGH. MORE TO FOLLOW AS INFORMATION COMES IN...
...AND NOW TO GREG FOR THE SPORTS REPORT...
DECKARD.

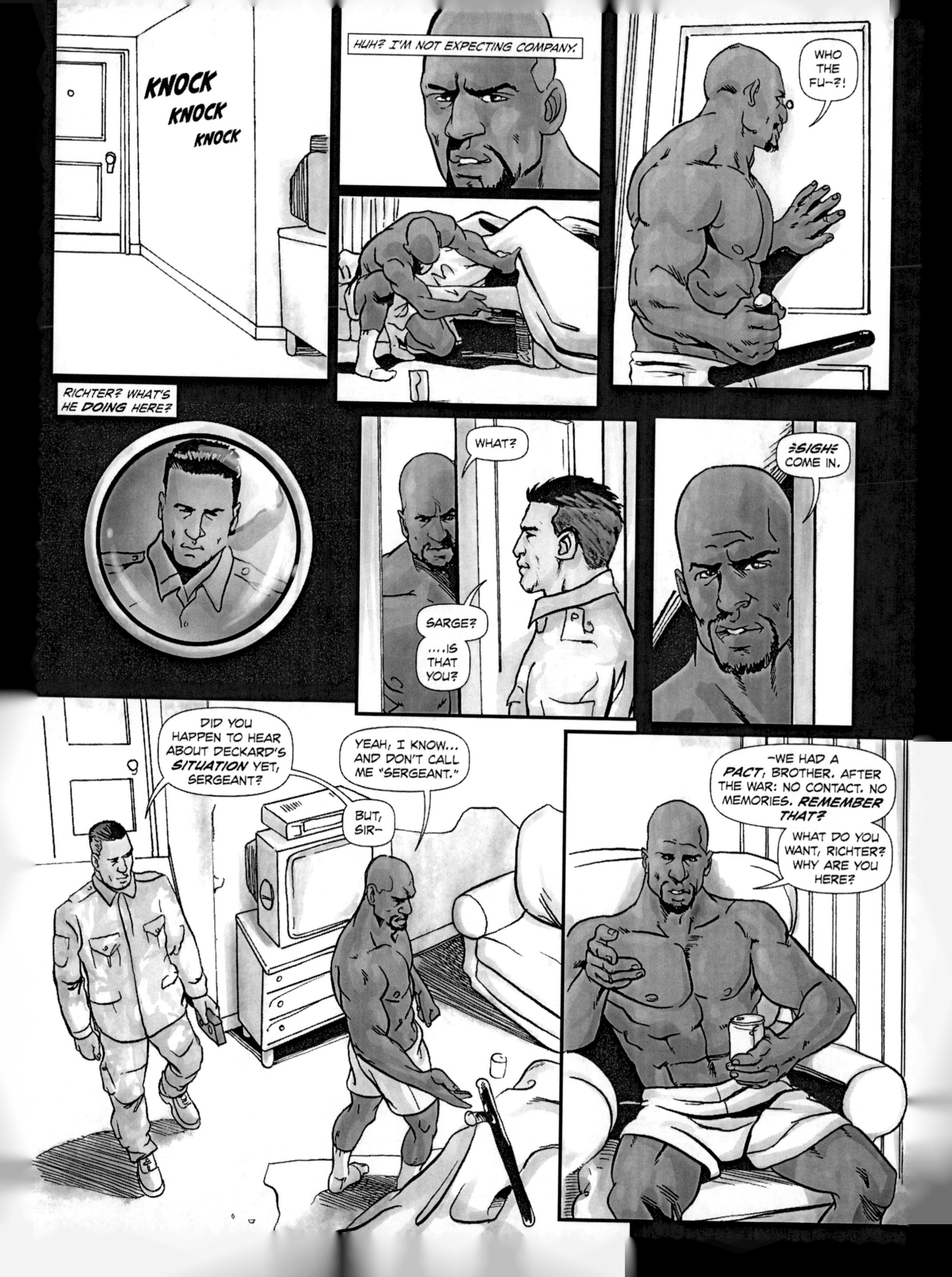
KNOCK
KNOCK
KNOCK
HUH? I'M NOT EXPECTING COMPANY.
WHO THE FU--?!
RICHTER? WHAT'S HE DOING HERE?
WHAT?
SARGE?
....IS THAT YOU?
SIGH COME IN.
DID YOU HAPPEN TO HEAR ABOUT DECKARD'S SITUATION YET, SERGEANT?
YEAH, I KNOW... AND DON'T CALL ME "SERGEANT."
BUT, SIR-
-WE HAD A PACT, BROTHER. AFTER THE WAR: NO CONTACT. NO MEMORIES. REMEMBER THAT?
WHAT DO YOU WANT, RICHTER? WHY ARE YOU HERE?

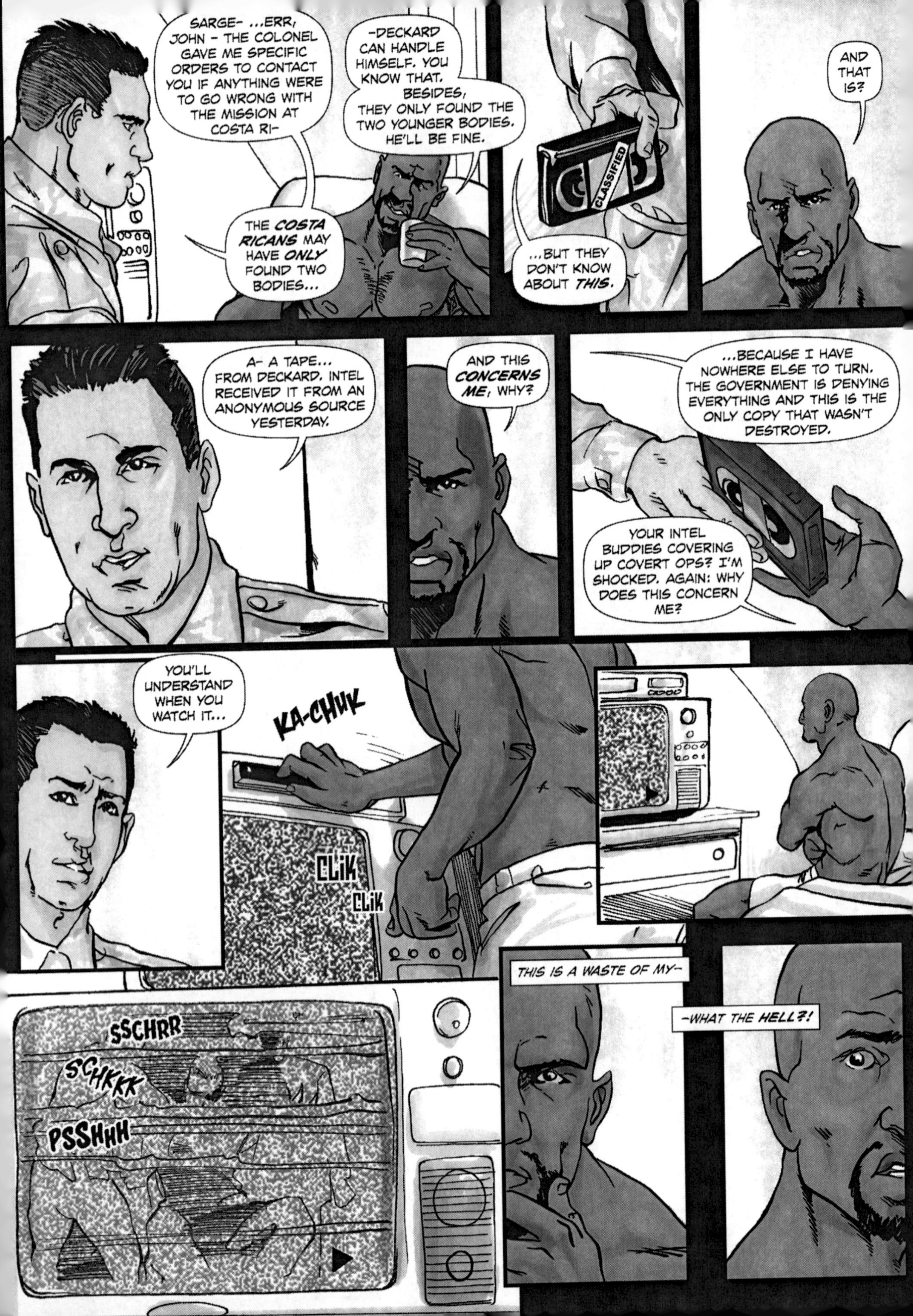
SARGE- ...ERR, JOHN - THE COLONEL GAVE ME SPECIFIC ORDERS TO CONTACT YOU IF ANYTHING WERE TO GO WRONG WITH THE MISSION AT COSTA RI-
-DECKARD CAN HANDLE HIMSELF. YOU KNOW THAT.
BESIDES, THEY ONLY FOUND THE TWO YOUNGER BODIES. HE'LL BE FINE.
THE COSTA RICANS MAY HAVE ONLY FOUND TWO BODIES...
CLASSIFIED
...BUT THEY DON'T KNOW ABOUT THIS.
AND THAT IS?
A- A TAPE... FROM DECKARD. INTEL RECEIVED IT FROM AN ANONYMOUS SOURCE YESTERDAY.
AND THIS CONCERNS ME; WHY?
...BECAUSE I HAVE NOWHERE ELSE TO TURN. THE GOVERNMENT IS DENYING EVERYTHING AND THIS IS THE ONLY COPY THAT WASN'T DESTROYED.
YOUR INTEL BUDDIES COVERING UP COVERT OPS? I'M SHOCKED. AGAIN: WHY DOES THIS CONCERN ME?
YOU'LL UNDERSTAND WHEN YOU WATCH IT...
KA-CHUK
CLIK
CLIK
SSCHRR
SCHKKK
PSSHHH
THIS IS A WASTE OF MY-
-WHAT THE HELL?!

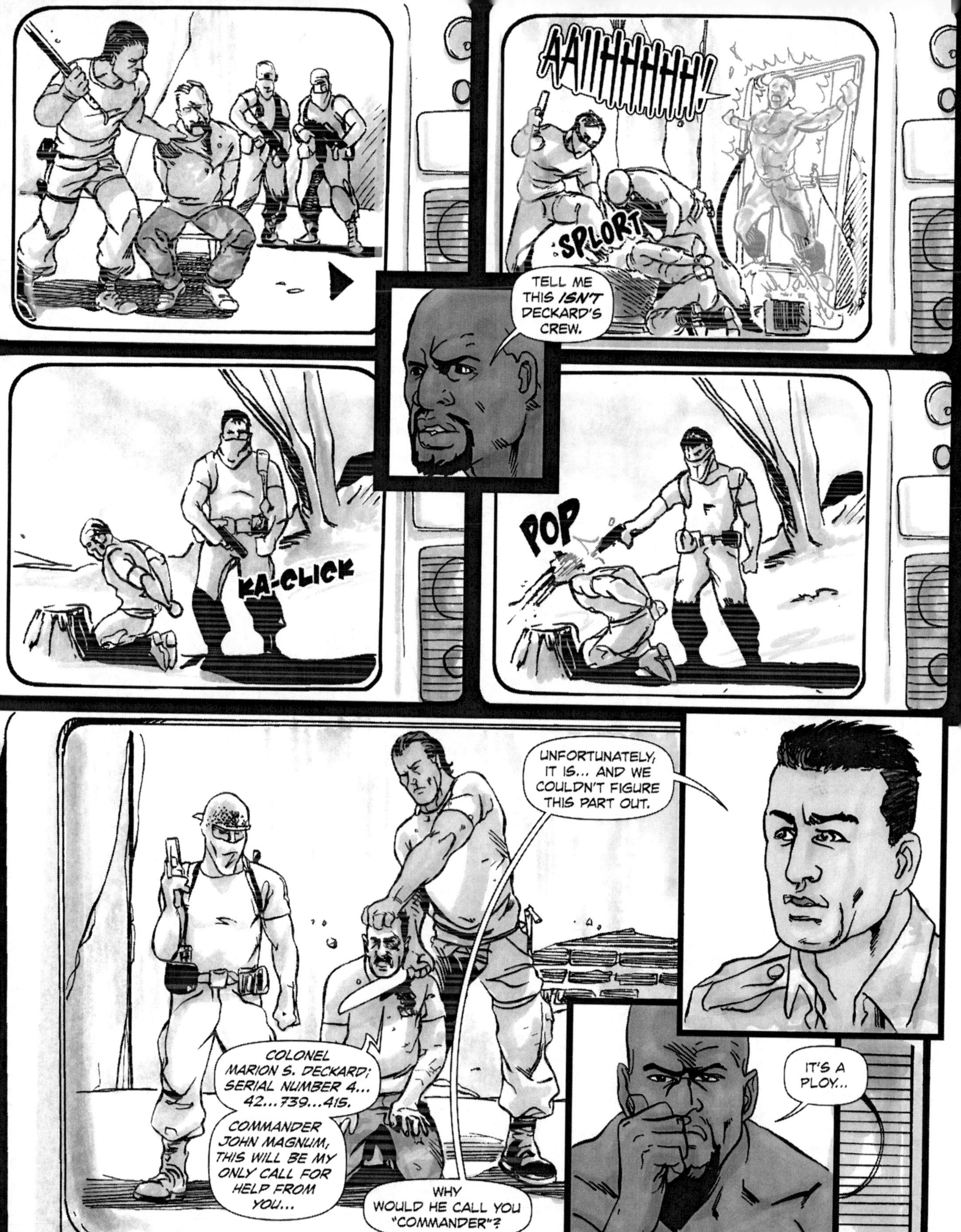
AAIIHHHHH!
SPLORT
TELL ME THIS ISN'T DECKARD'S CREW.
KA-CLICK
POP
UNFORTUNATELY, IT IS... AND WE COULDN'T FIGURE THIS PART OUT.
COLONEL MARION S. DECKARD; SERIAL NUMBER 4... 42...739...415.
COMMANDER JOHN MAGNUM, THIS WILL BE MY ONLY CALL FOR HELP FROM YOU...
WHY WOULD HE CALL YOU "COMMANDER"?
IT'S A PLOY...

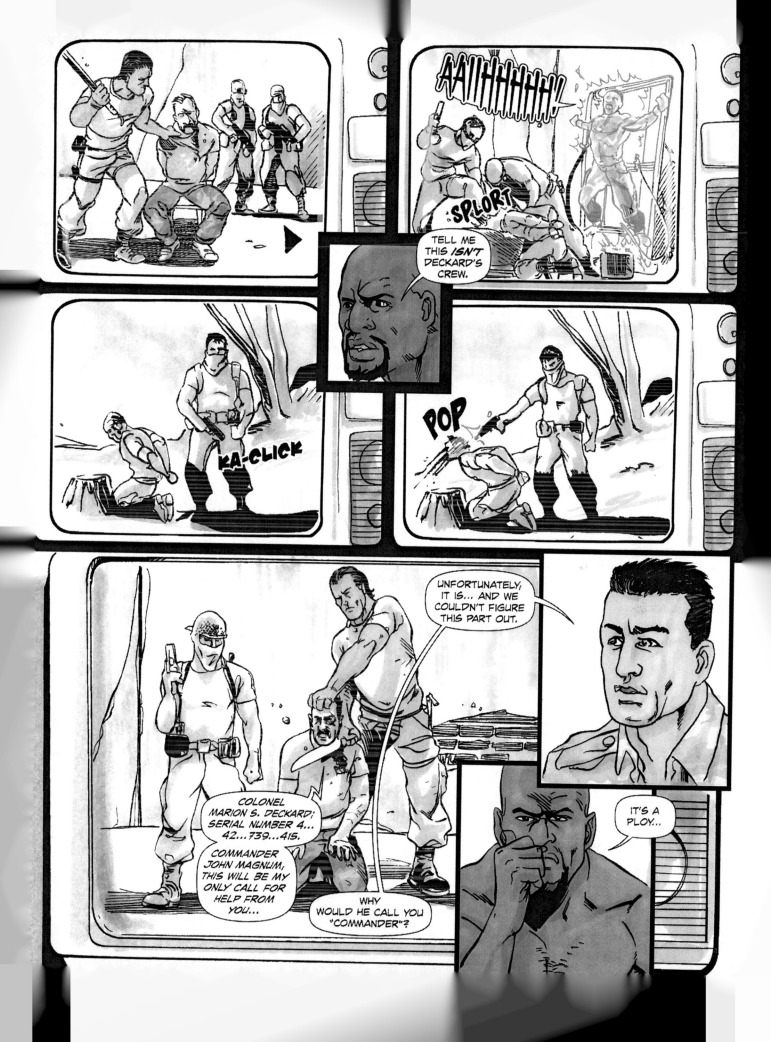

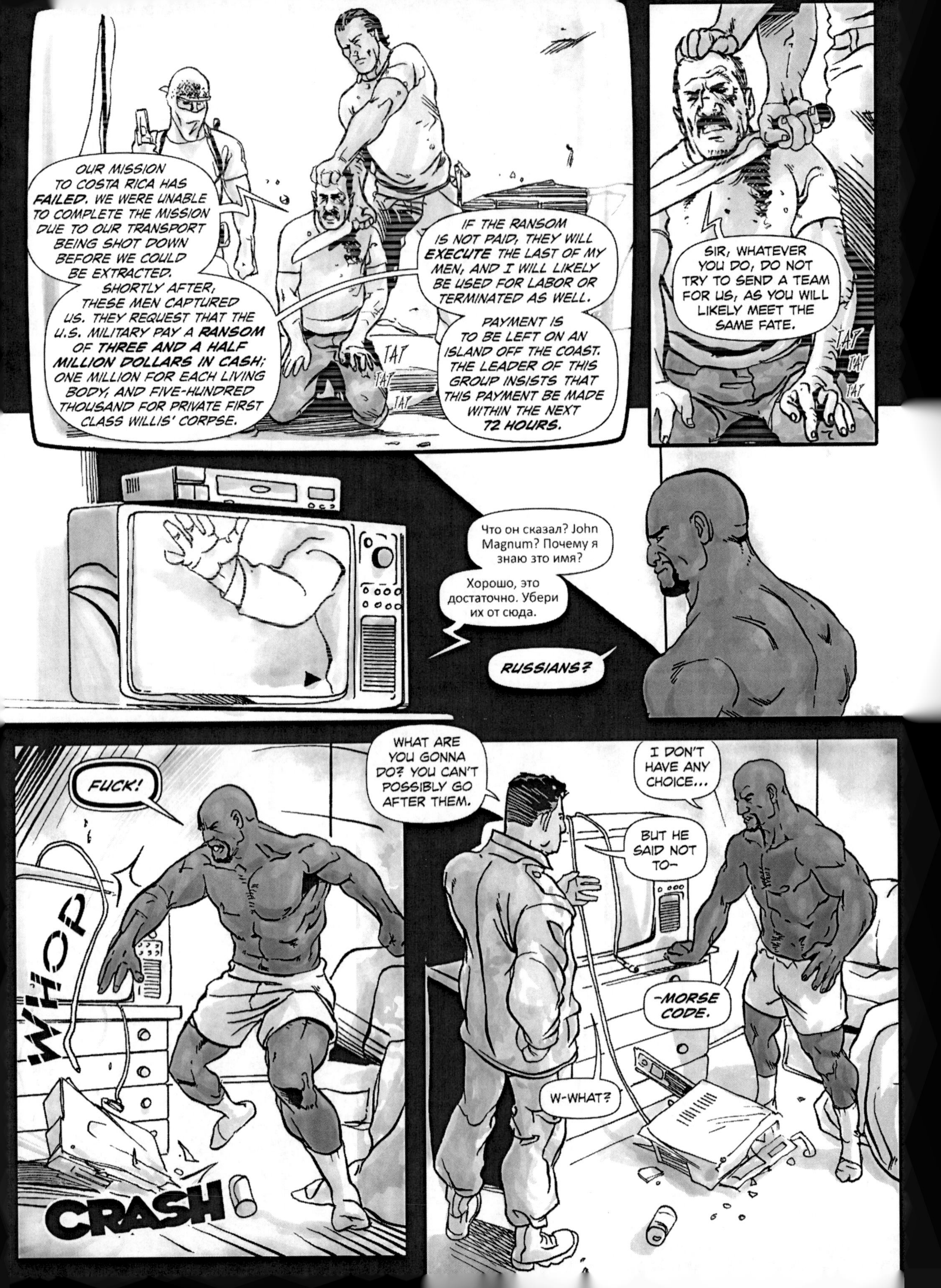
OUR MISSION TO COSTA RICA HAS **FAILED**. WE WERE UNABLE TO COMPLETE THE MISSION DUE TO OUR TRANSPORT BEING SHOT DOWN BEFORE WE COULD BE EXTRACTED.
SHORTLY AFTER, THESE MEN CAPTURED US. THEY REQUEST THAT THE U.S. MILITARY PAY A **RANSOM** OF **THREE AND A HALF MILLION DOLLARS IN CASH**; ONE MILLION FOR EACH LIVING BODY, AND FIVE-HUNDRED THOUSAND FOR PRIVATE FIRST CLASS WILLIS' CORPSE.
IF THE RANSOM IS NOT PAID, THEY WILL **EXECUTE** THE LAST OF MY MEN, AND I WILL LIKELY BE USED FOR LABOR OR TERMINATED AS WELL.
PAYMENT IS TO BE LEFT ON AN ISLAND OFF THE COAST. THE LEADER OF THIS GROUP INSISTS THAT THIS PAYMENT BE MADE WITHIN THE NEXT **72 HOURS.**
TAP
TAP
TAP
SIR, WHATEVER YOU DO, DO NOT TRY TO SEND A TEAM FOR US, AS YOU WILL LIKELY MEET THE SAME FATE.
TAP
TAP
TAP
Что он сказал? John Magnum? Почему я знаю зто имя?
Хорошо, это достаточно. Убери их от сюда.
RUSSIANS?
FUCK!
WHOP
CRASH
WHAT ARE YOU GONNA DO? YOU CAN'T POSSIBLY GO AFTER THEM.
I DON'T HAVE ANY CHOICE...
BUT HE SAID NOT TO–
–MORSE CODE.
W-WHAT?

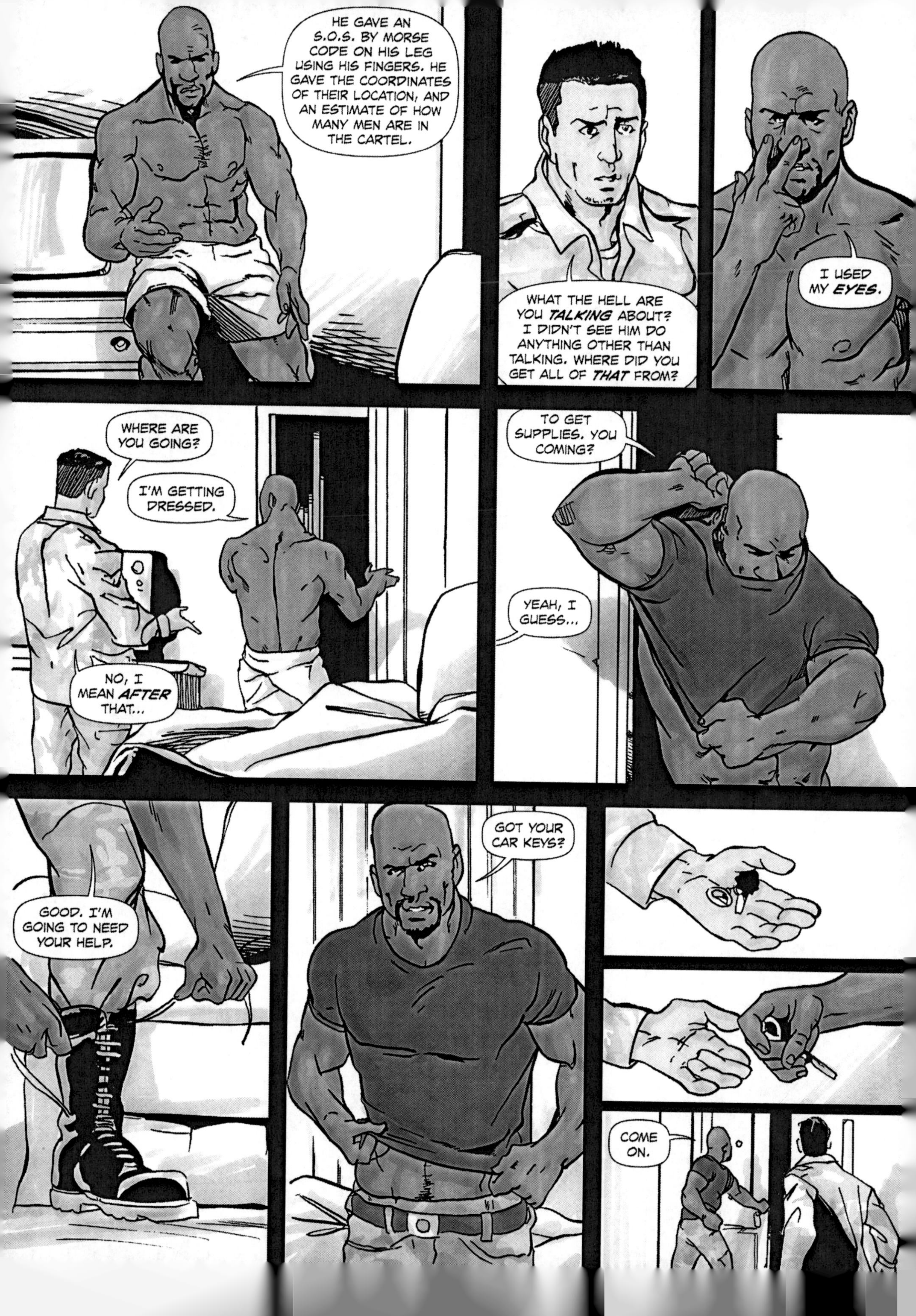
HE GAVE AN S.O.S. BY MORSE CODE ON HIS LEG USING HIS FINGERS. HE GAVE THE COORDINATES OF THEIR LOCATION, AND AN ESTIMATE OF HOW MANY MEN ARE IN THE CARTEL.
WHAT THE HELL ARE YOU *TALKING* ABOUT? I DIDN'T SEE HIM DO ANYTHING OTHER THAN TALKING. WHERE DID YOU GET ALL OF *THAT* FROM?
I USED MY *EYES*.
WHERE ARE YOU GOING?
I'M GETTING DRESSED.
NO, I MEAN *AFTER* THAT...
TO GET SUPPLIES. YOU COMING?
YEAH, I GUESS...
GOOD. I'M GOING TO NEED YOUR HELP.
GOT YOUR CAR KEYS?
COME ON.

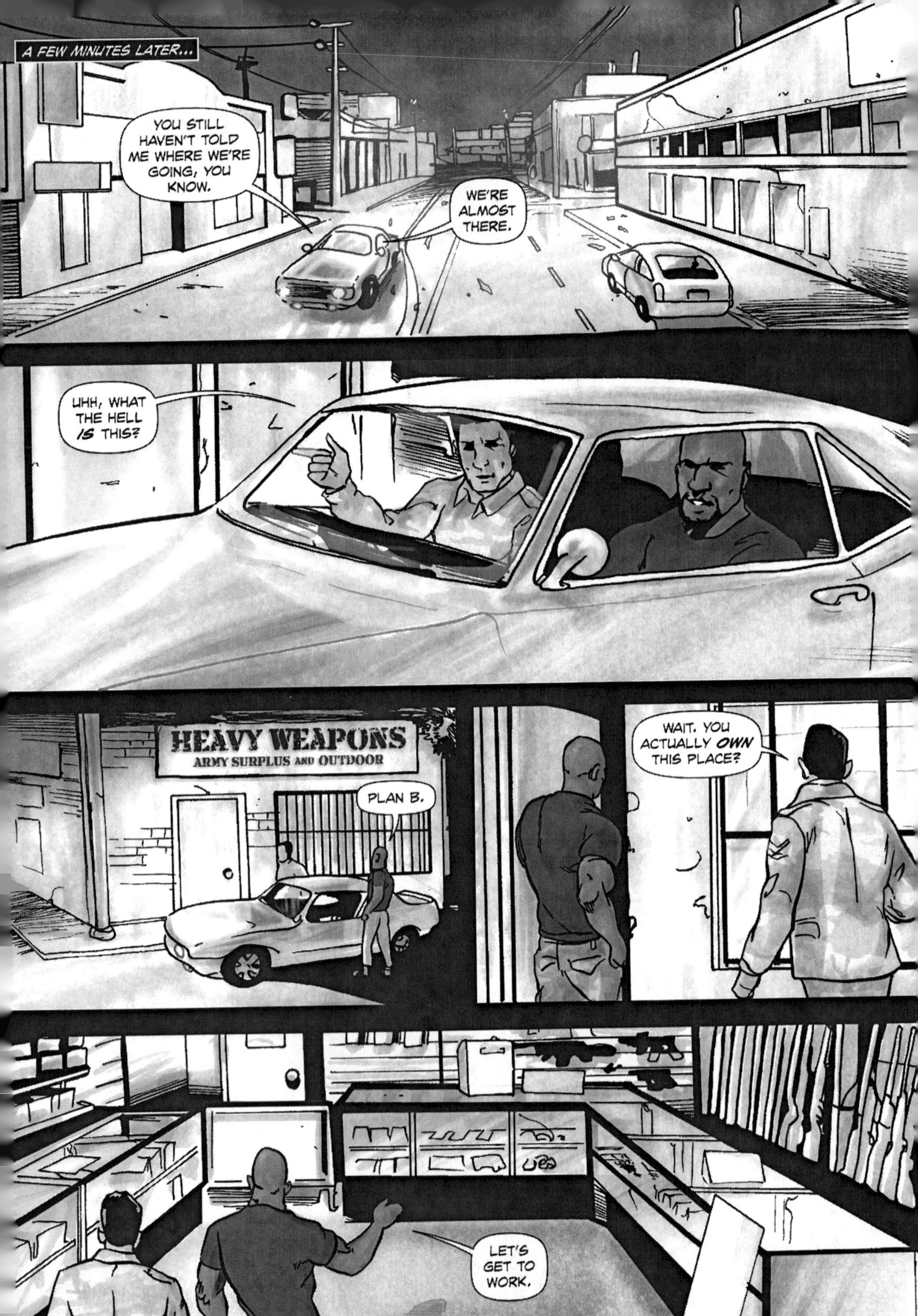
A FEW MINUTES LATER...
YOU STILL HAVEN'T TOLD ME WHERE WE'RE GOING, YOU KNOW.
WE'RE ALMOST THERE.
UHH, WHAT THE HELL *IS* THIS?
HEAVY WEAPONS
ARMY SURPLUS AND OUTDOOR
PLAN B.
WAIT. YOU ACTUALLY *OWN* THIS PLACE?
LET'S GET TO WORK.

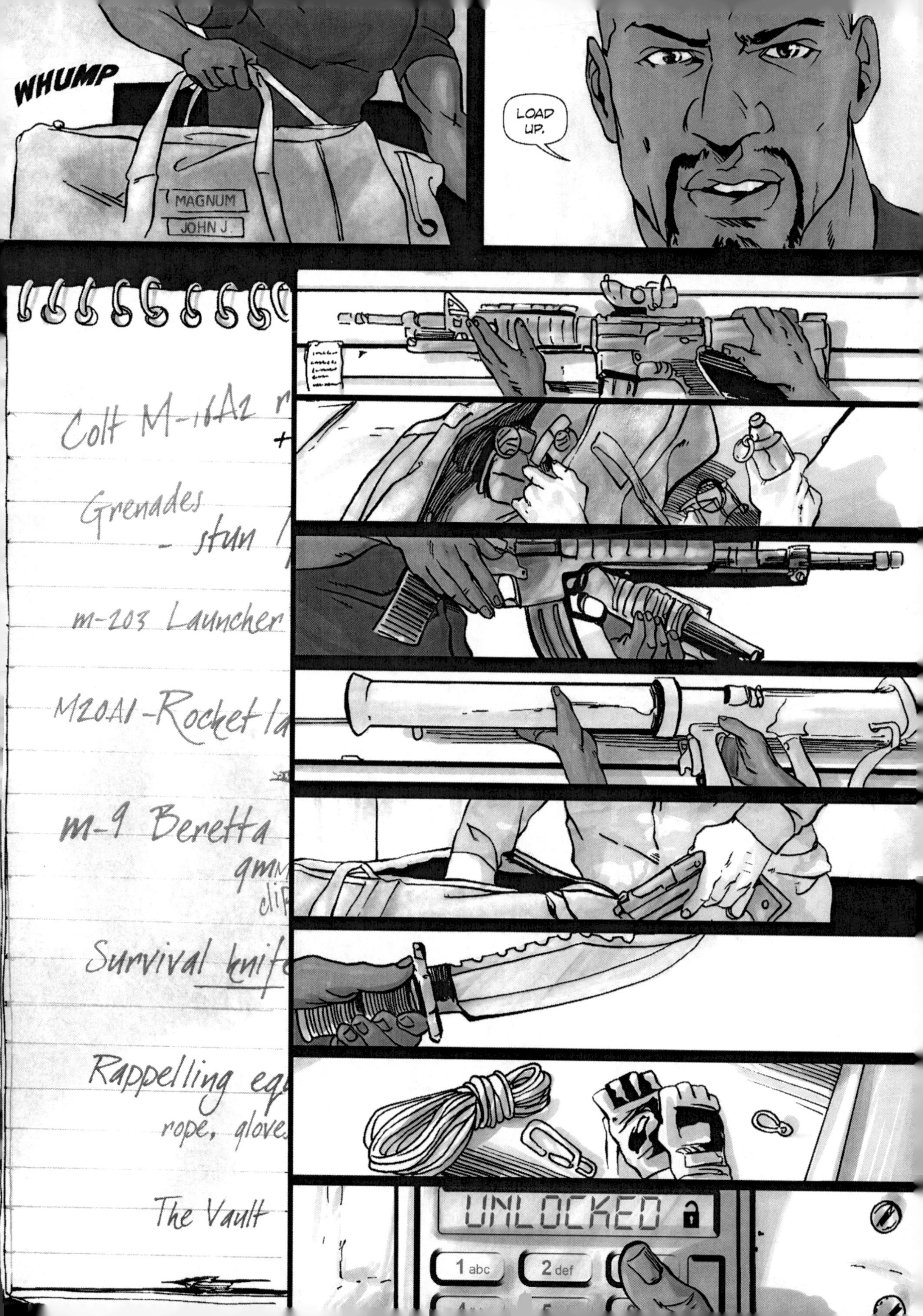
WHUMP
MAGNUM
JOHN J.
LOAD UP.
Colt M-16A2
Grenades
- stun
m-203 Launcher
M20A1-Rocket la
m-9 Beretta
9mm
clip
Survival knif
Rappelling eq
rope, gloves
The Vault
UNLOCKED
1 abc
2 def

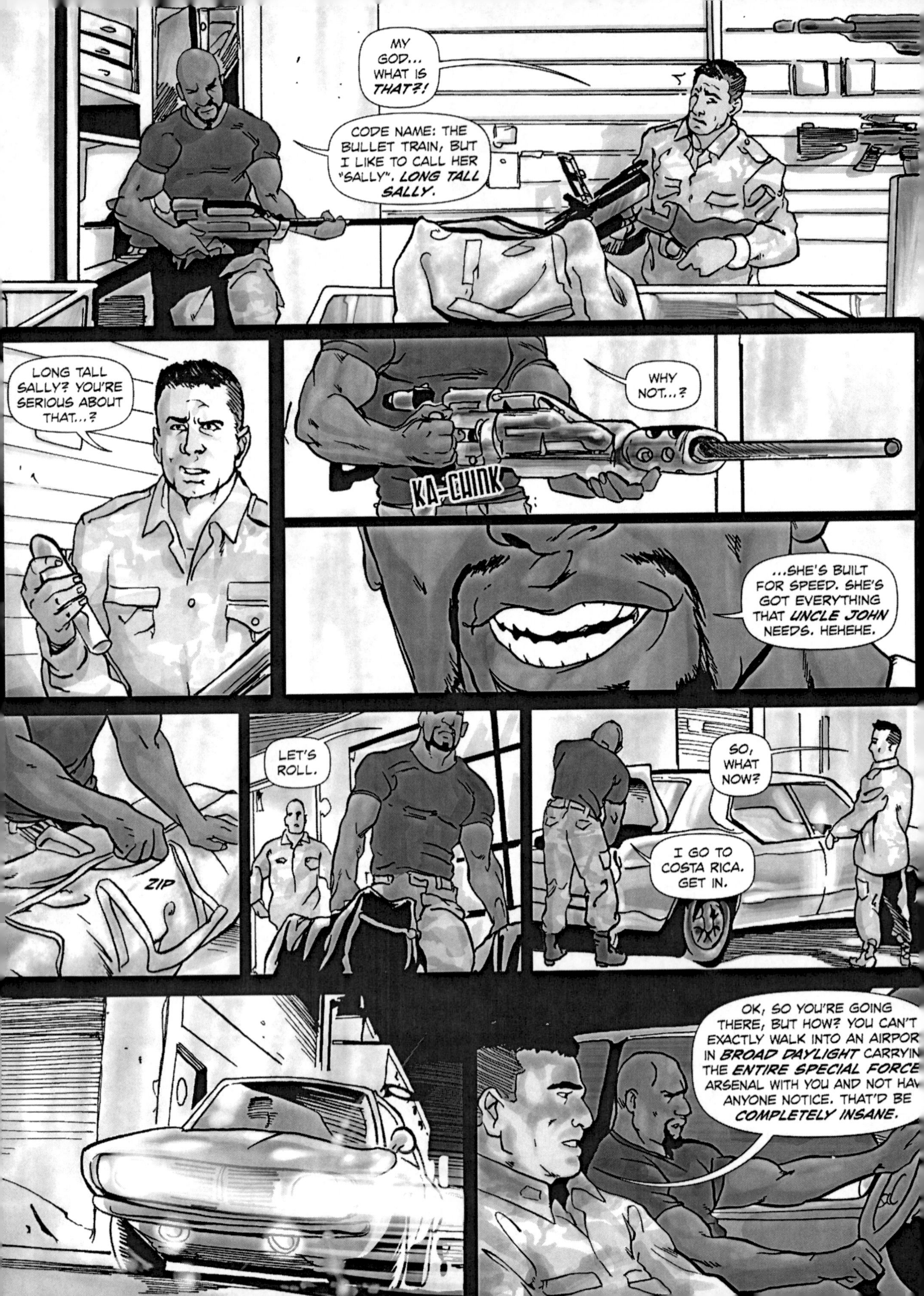
MY GOD... WHAT IS THAT?!
CODE NAME: THE BULLET TRAIN, BUT I LIKE TO CALL HER "SALLY". LONG TALL SALLY.
LONG TALL SALLY? YOU'RE SERIOUS ABOUT THAT...?
WHY NOT...?
KA-CHINK
...SHE'S BUILT FOR SPEED. SHE'S GOT EVERYTHING THAT UNCLE JOHN NEEDS. HEHEHE.
ZIP
LET'S ROLL.
SO, WHAT NOW?
I GO TO COSTA RICA. GET IN.
OK, SO YOU'RE GOING THERE, BUT HOW? YOU CAN'T EXACTLY WALK INTO AN AIRPOR IN BROAD DAYLIGHT CARRYIN THE ENTIRE SPECIAL FORCE ARSENAL WITH YOU AND NOT HAV ANYONE NOTICE. THAT'D BE COMPLETELY INSANE.

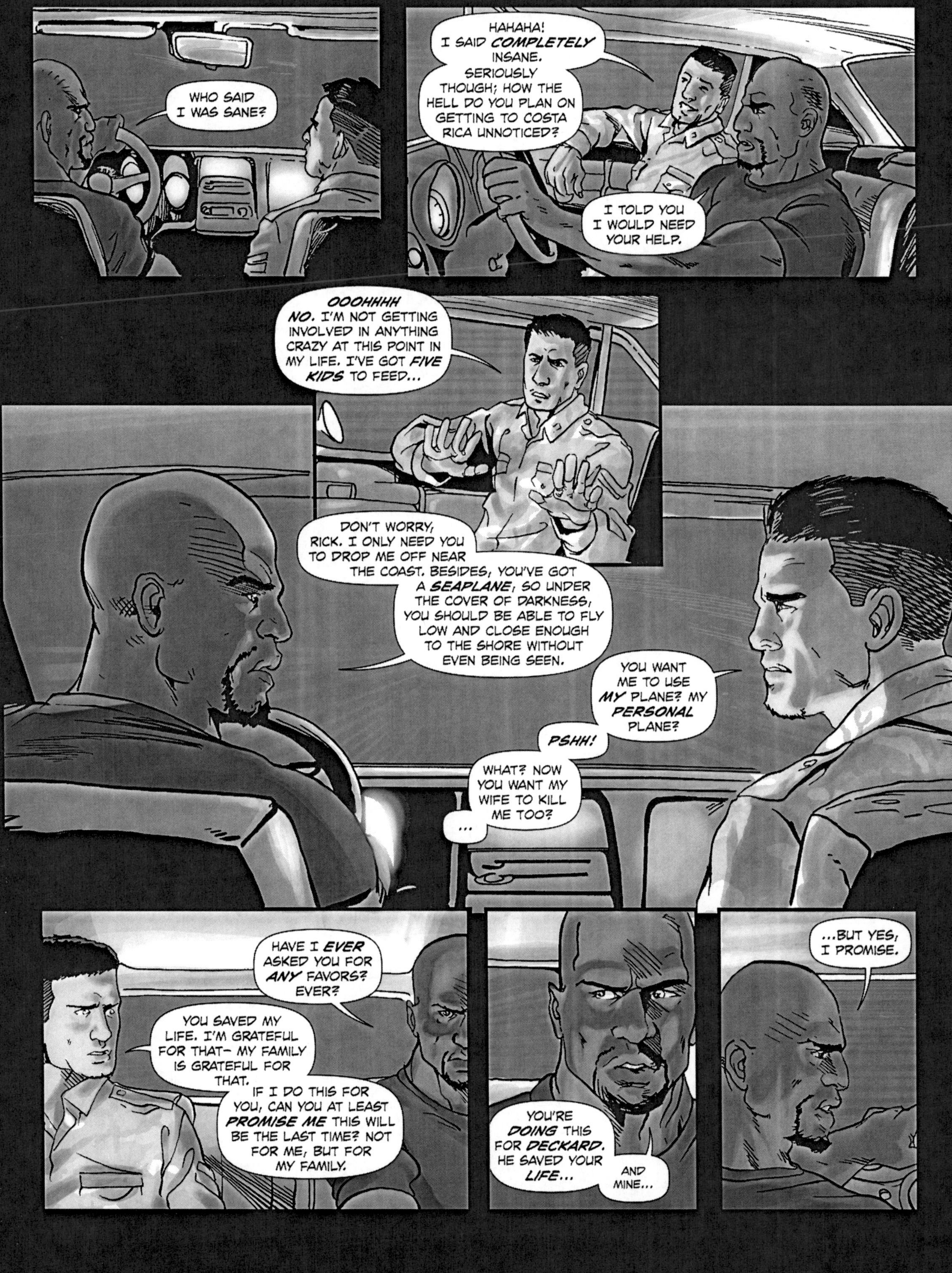
WHO SAID I WAS SANE?
HAHAHA! I SAID COMPLETELY INSANE.
SERIOUSLY THOUGH; HOW THE HELL DO YOU PLAN ON GETTING TO COSTA RICA UNNOTICED?
I TOLD YOU I WOULD NEED YOUR HELP.
OOOHHHH NO. I'M NOT GETTING INVOLVED IN ANYTHING CRAZY AT THIS POINT IN MY LIFE. I'VE GOT FIVE KIDS TO FEED...
DON'T WORRY, RICK. I ONLY NEED YOU TO DROP ME OFF NEAR THE COAST. BESIDES, YOU'VE GOT A SEAPLANE, SO UNDER THE COVER OF DARKNESS, YOU SHOULD BE ABLE TO FLY LOW AND CLOSE ENOUGH TO THE SHORE WITHOUT EVEN BEING SEEN.
YOU WANT ME TO USE MY PLANE? MY PERSONAL PLANE?
PSHH!
WHAT? NOW YOU WANT MY WIFE TO KILL ME TOO?
...
HAVE I EVER ASKED YOU FOR ANY FAVORS? EVER?
YOU SAVED MY LIFE. I'M GRATEFUL FOR THAT- MY FAMILY IS GRATEFUL FOR THAT.
IF I DO THIS FOR YOU, CAN YOU AT LEAST PROMISE ME THIS WILL BE THE LAST TIME? NOT FOR ME, BUT FOR MY FAMILY.
YOU'RE DOING THIS FOR DECKARD. HE SAVED YOUR LIFE...
AND MINE...
...BUT YES, I PROMISE.

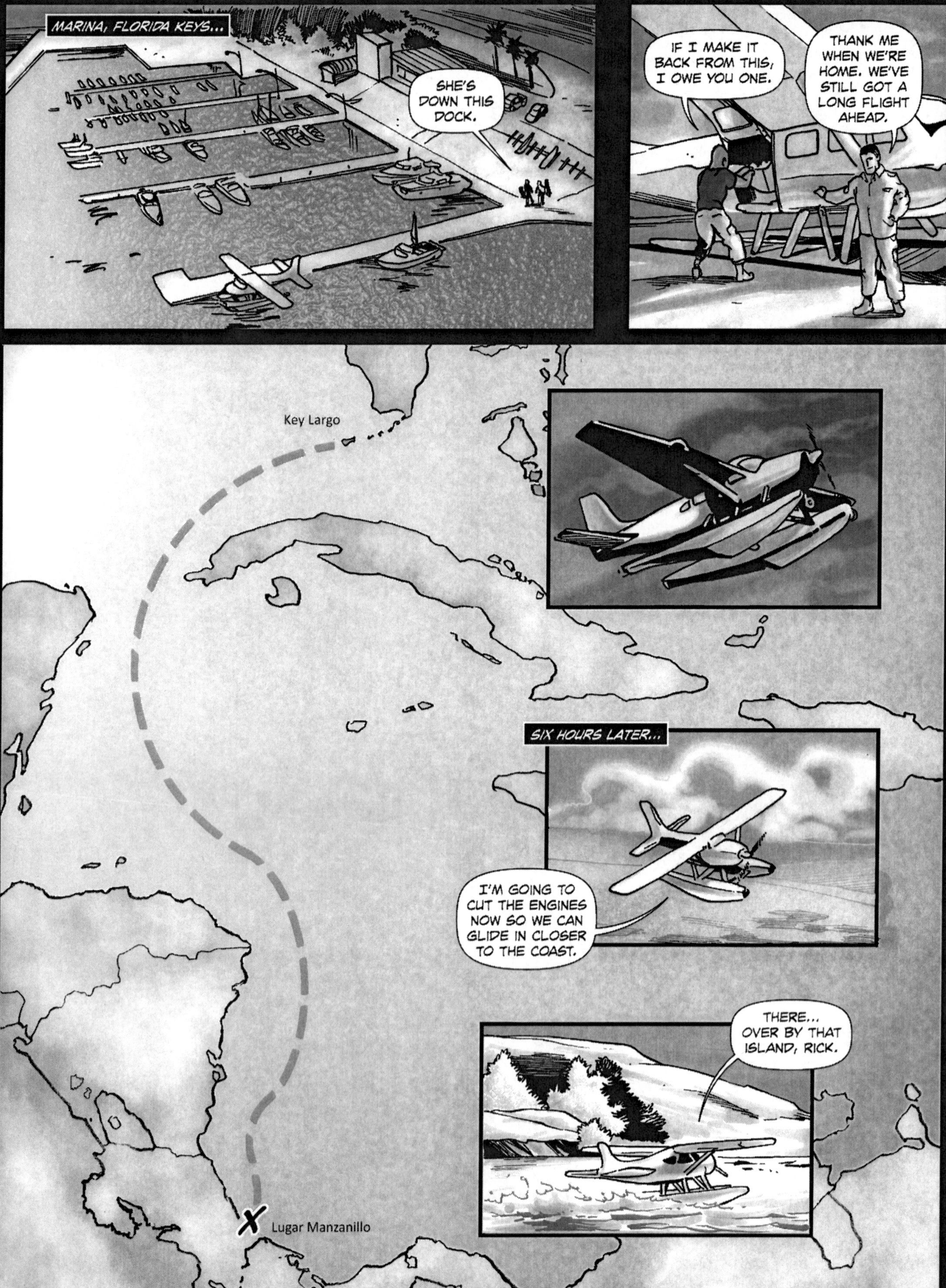
MARINA, FLORIDA KEYS...
SHE'S DOWN THIS DOCK.
IF I MAKE IT BACK FROM THIS, I OWE YOU ONE.
THANK ME WHEN WE'RE HOME. WE'VE STILL GOT A LONG FLIGHT AHEAD.
Key Largo
SIX HOURS LATER...
I'M GOING TO CUT THE ENGINES NOW SO WE CAN GLIDE IN CLOSER TO THE COAST.
THERE... OVER BY THAT ISLAND, RICK.
Lugar Manzanillo

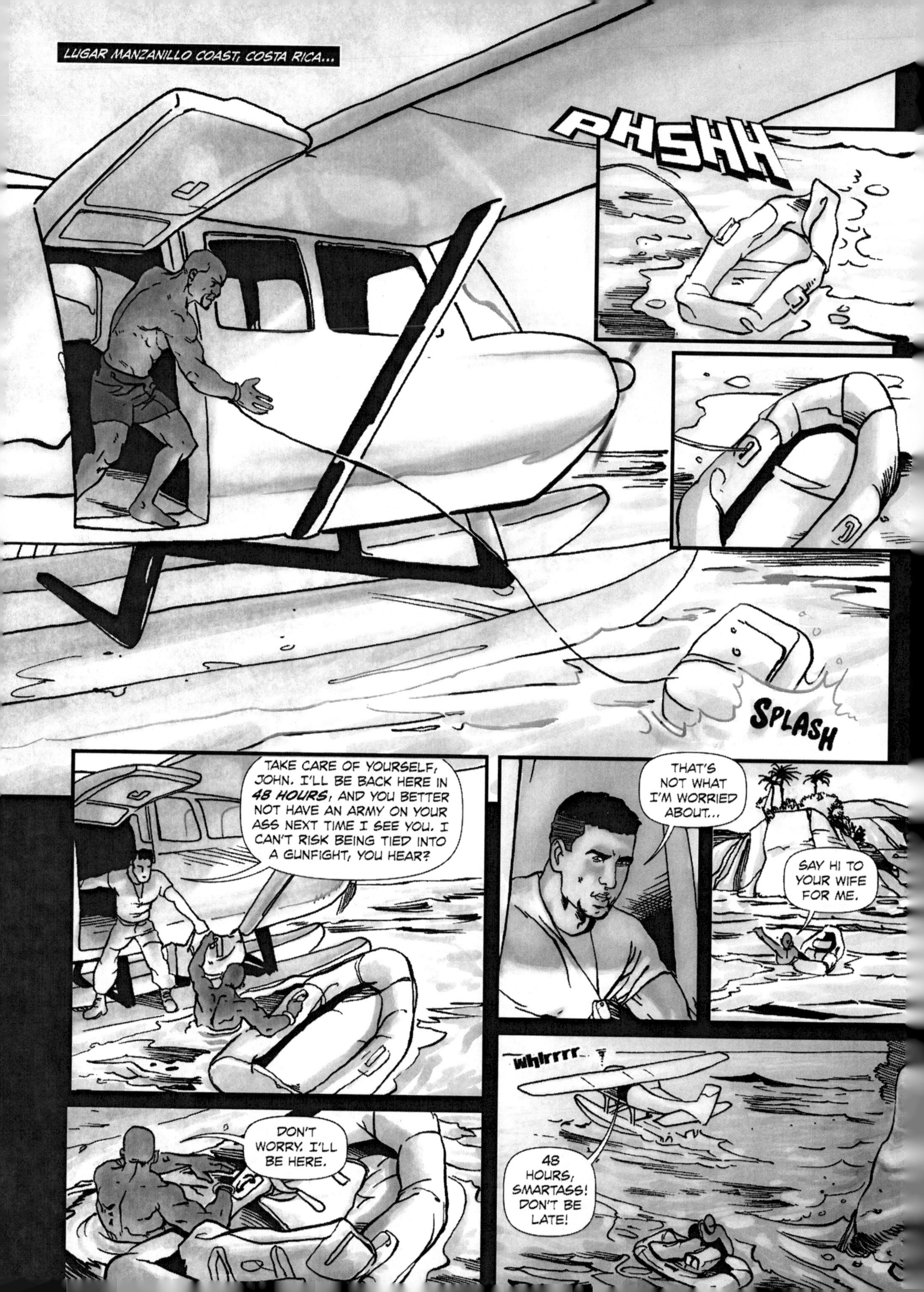
LUGAR MANZANILLO COAST, COSTA RICA...
PHSHH
SPLASH
TAKE CARE OF YOURSELF, JOHN. I'LL BE BACK HERE IN 48 HOURS, AND YOU BETTER NOT HAVE AN ARMY ON YOUR ASS NEXT TIME I SEE YOU. I CAN'T RISK BEING TIED INTO A GUNFIGHT, YOU HEAR?
THAT'S NOT WHAT I'M WORRIED ABOUT...
SAY HI TO YOUR WIFE FOR ME.
DON'T WORRY. I'LL BE HERE.
whIrrrr
48 HOURS, SMARTASS! DON'T BE LATE!

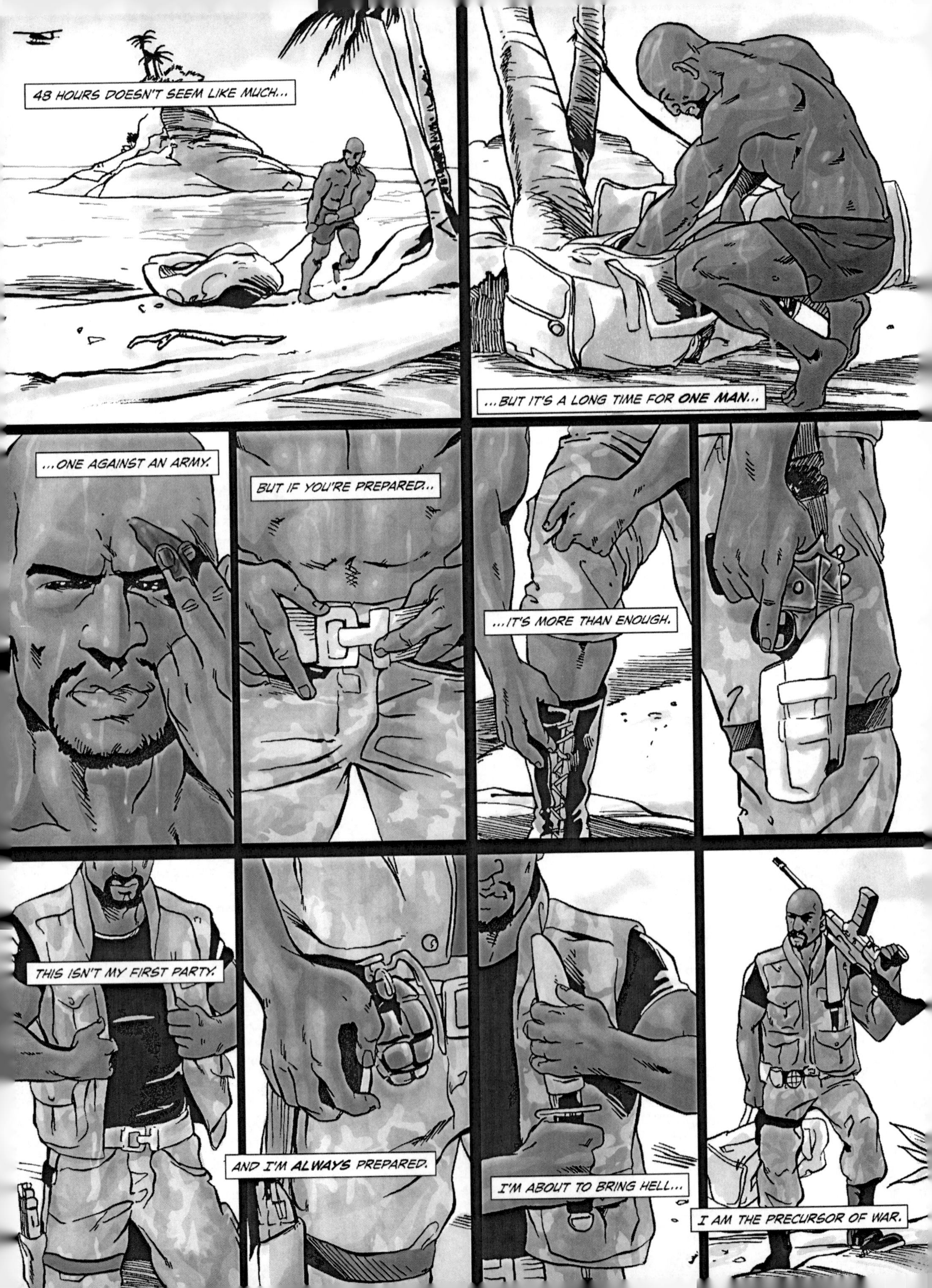
48 HOURS DOESN'T SEEM LIKE MUCH...
...BUT IT'S A LONG TIME FOR ONE MAN...
...ONE AGAINST AN ARMY.
BUT IF YOU'RE PREPARED...
...IT'S MORE THAN ENOUGH.
THIS ISN'T MY FIRST PARTY.
AND I'M ALWAYS PREPARED.
I'M ABOUT TO BRING HELL...
I AM THE PRECURSOR OF WAR.

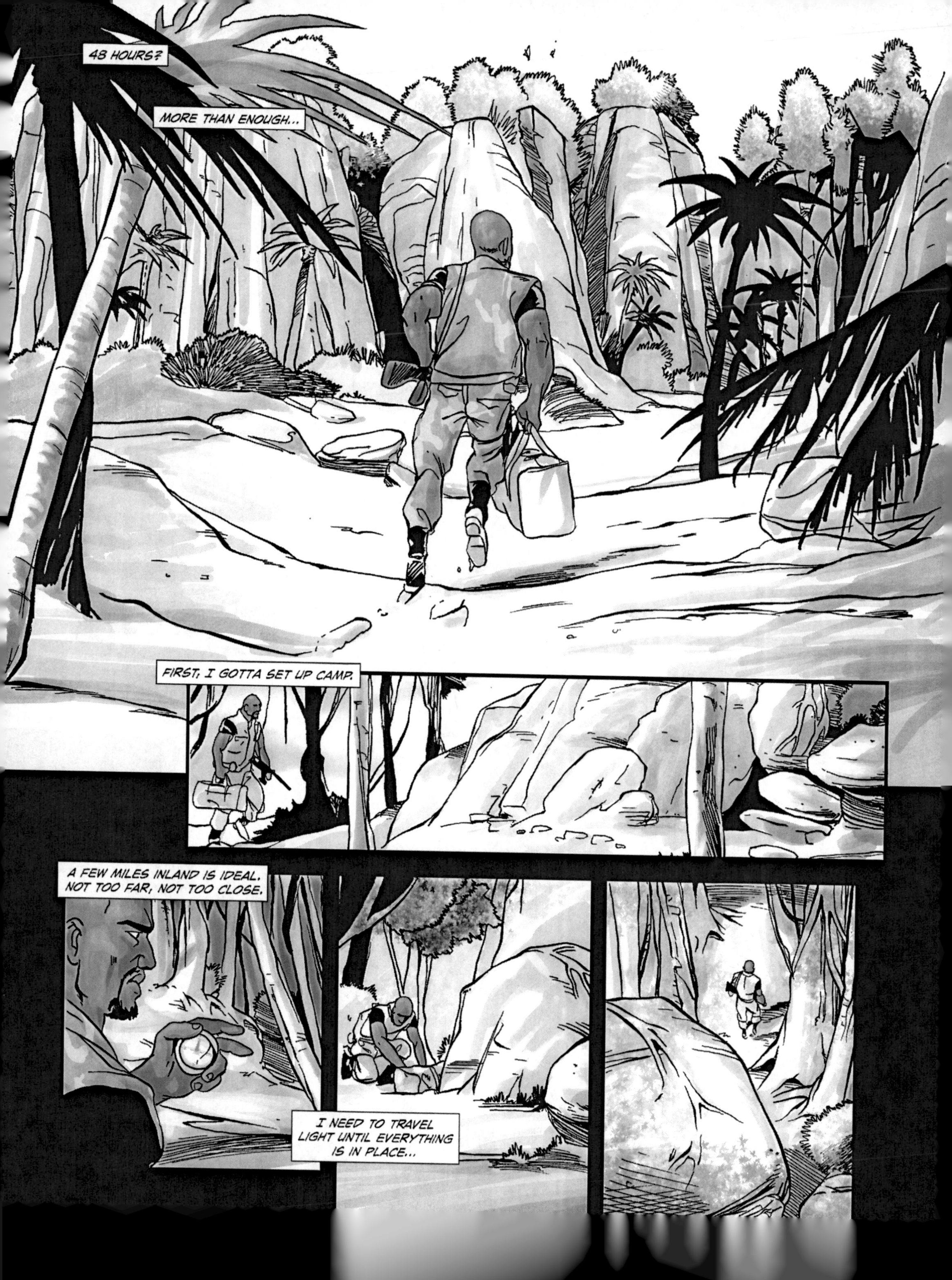
48 HOURS?
MORE THAN ENOUGH...
FIRST, I GOTTA SET UP CAMP.
A FEW MILES INLAND IS IDEAL. NOT TOO FAR, NOT TOO CLOSE.
I NEED TO TRAVEL LIGHT UNTIL EVERYTHING IS IN PLACE...

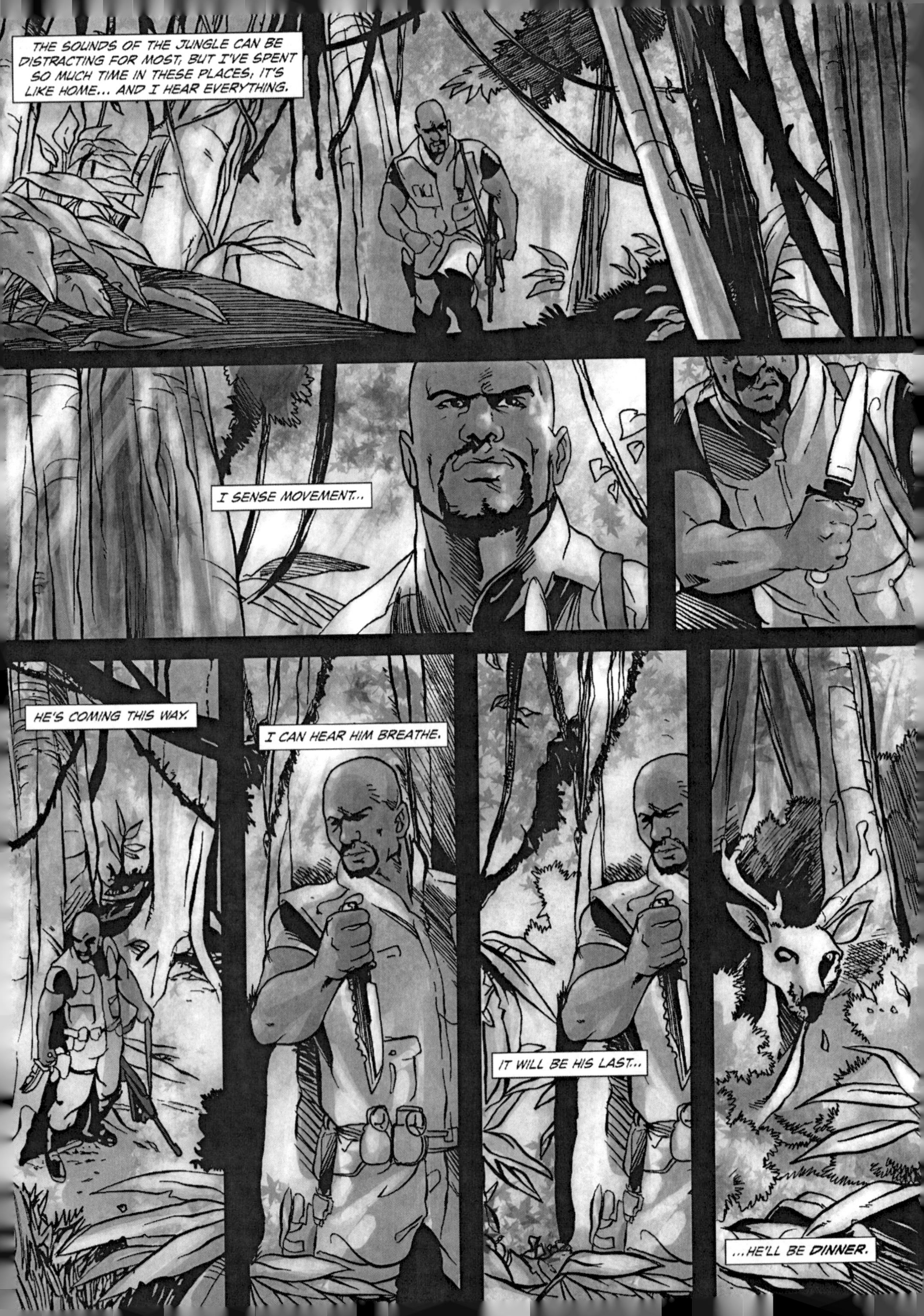
THE SOUNDS OF THE JUNGLE CAN BE DISTRACTING FOR MOST, BUT I'VE SPENT SO MUCH TIME IN THESE PLACES, IT'S LIKE HOME... AND I HEAR EVERYTHING.
I SENSE MOVEMENT...
HE'S COMING THIS WAY.
I CAN HEAR HIM BREATHE.
IT WILL BE HIS LAST...
...HE'LL BE DINNER.

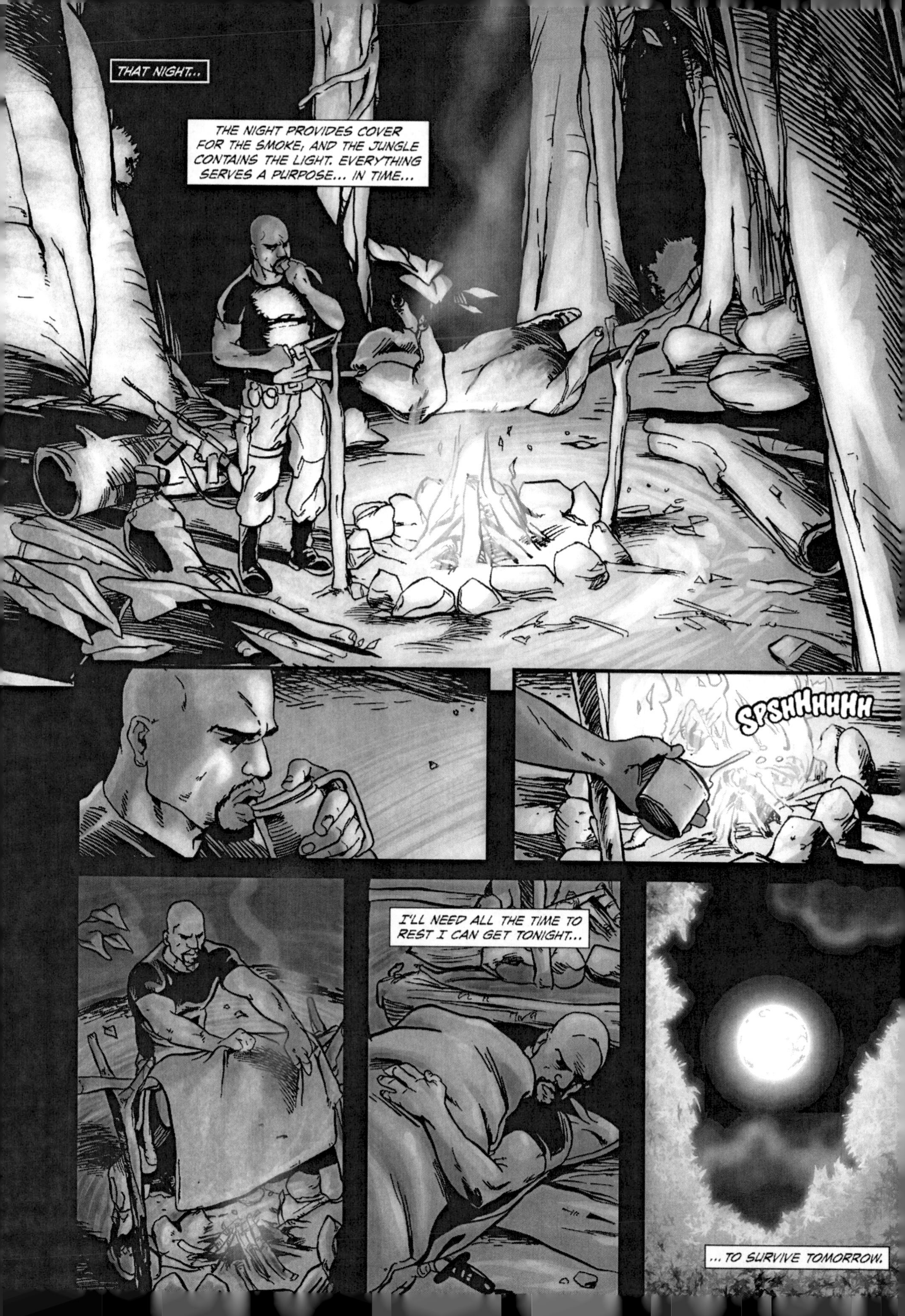
THAT NIGHT...
THE NIGHT PROVIDES COVER FOR THE SMOKE; AND THE JUNGLE CONTAINS THE LIGHT. EVERYTHING SERVES A PURPOSE... IN TIME...
SPSHHHHHH
I'LL NEED ALL THE TIME TO REST I CAN GET TONIGHT...
...TO SURVIVE TOMORROW.

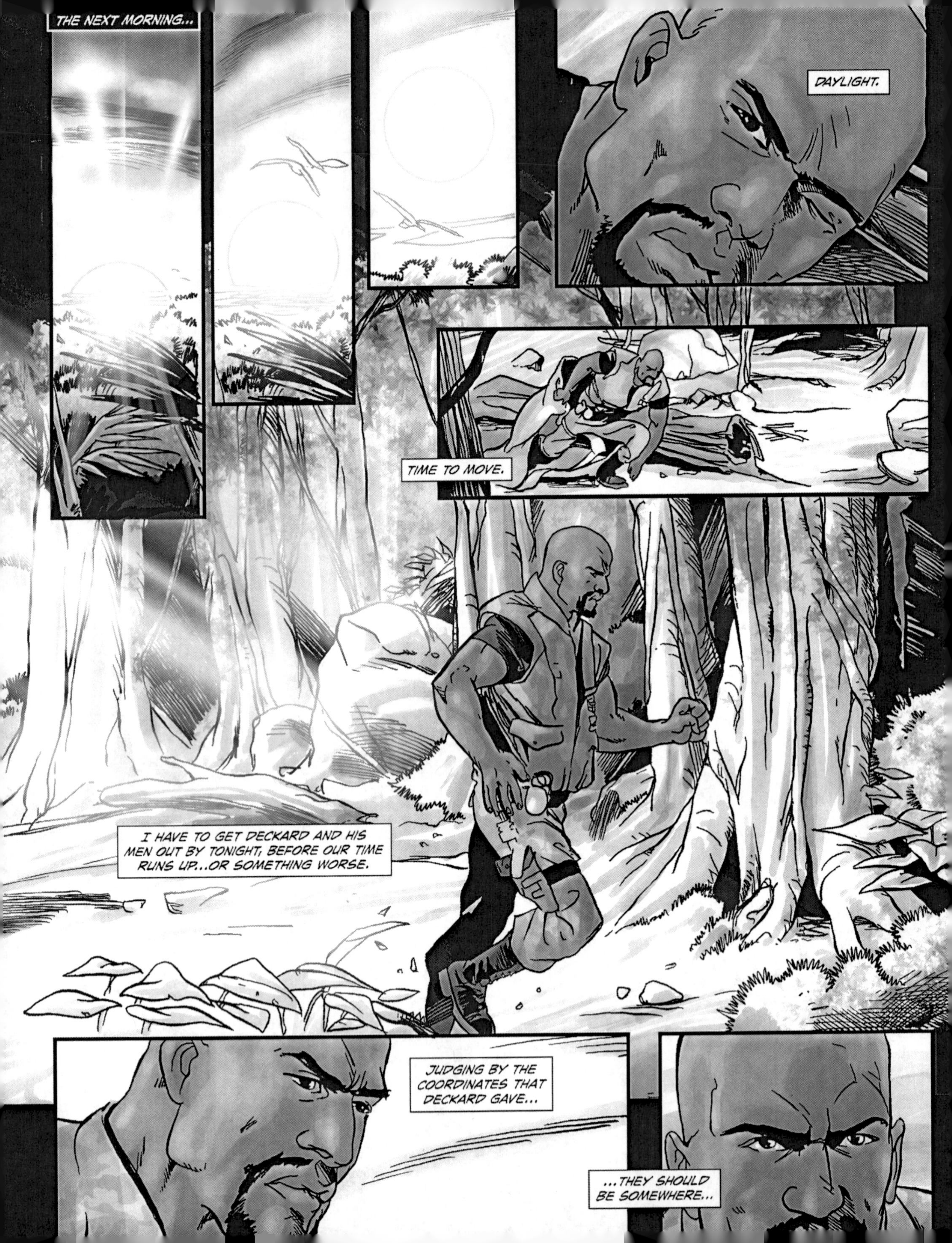
THE NEXT MORNING...
DAYLIGHT.
TIME TO MOVE.
I HAVE TO GET DECKARD AND HIS MEN OUT BY TONIGHT, BEFORE OUR TIME RUNS UP...OR SOMETHING WORSE.
JUDGING BY THE COORDINATES THAT DECKARD GAVE...
...THEY SHOULD BE SOMEWHERE...

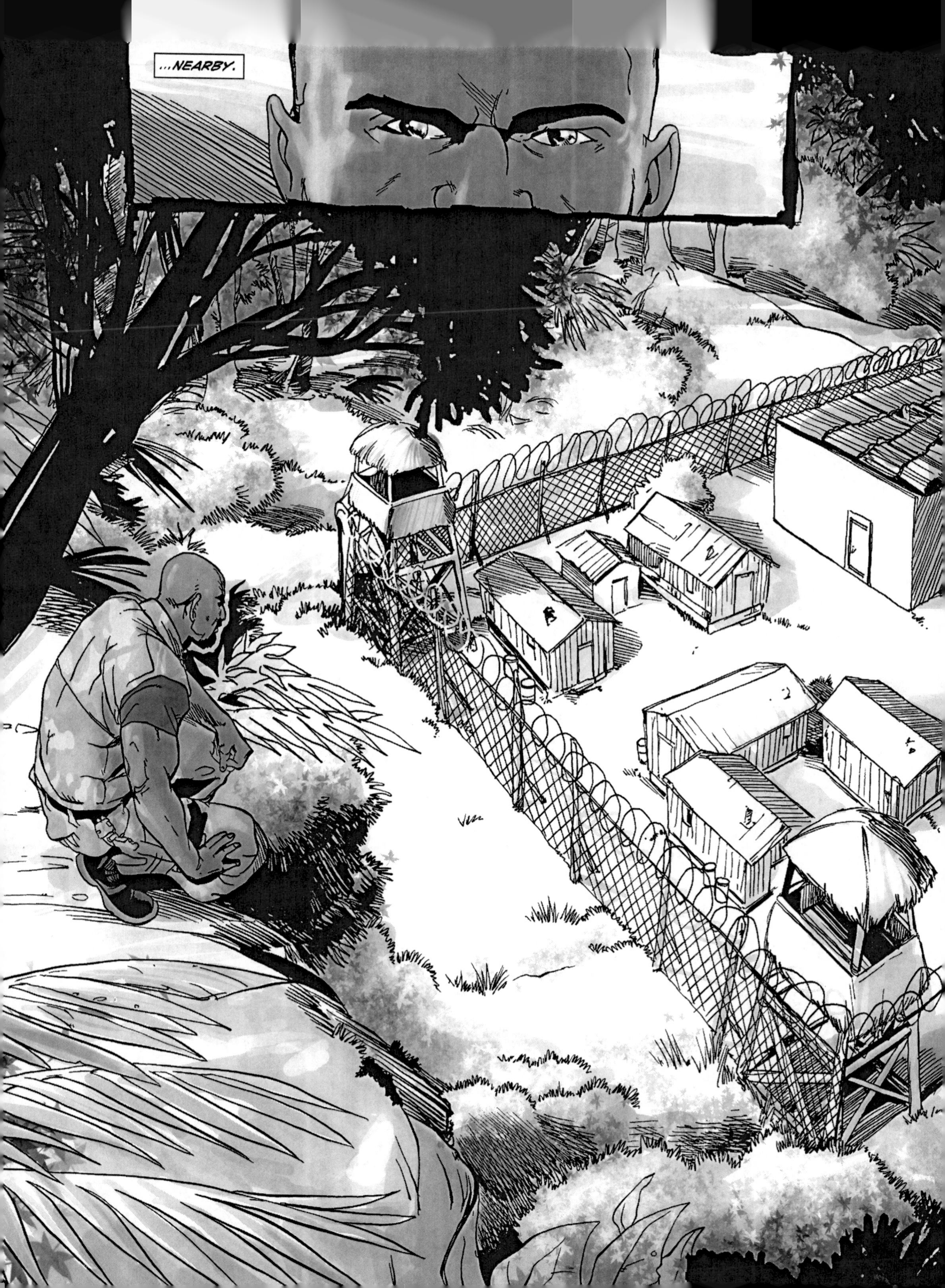
...NEARBY.

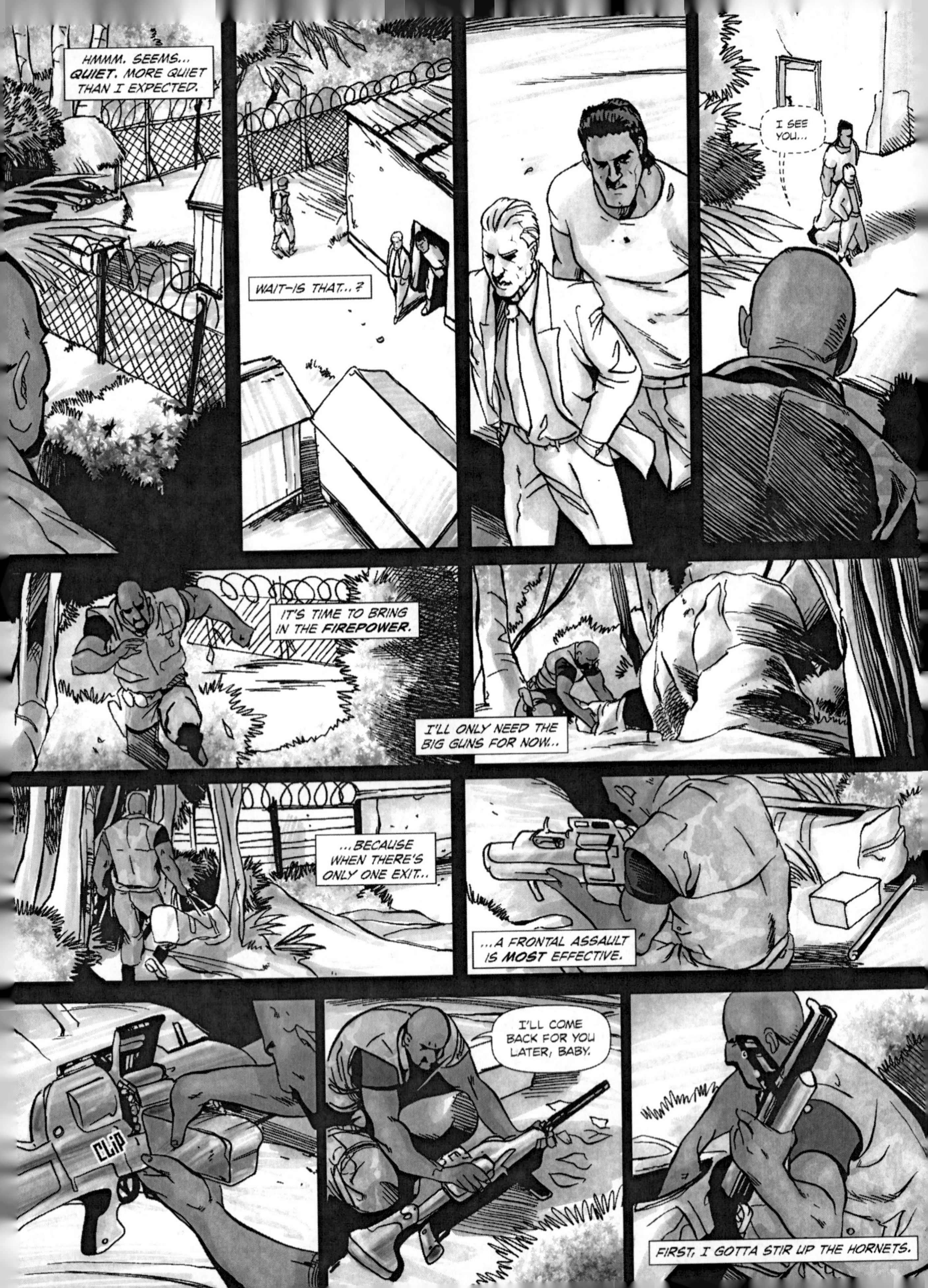
HMMM. SEEMS... QUIET. MORE QUIET THAN I EXPECTED.
WAIT–IS THAT...?
I SEE YOU...
IT'S TIME TO BRING IN THE FIREPOWER.
I'LL ONLY NEED THE BIG GUNS FOR NOW...
...BECAUSE WHEN THERE'S ONLY ONE EXIT...
...A FRONTAL ASSAULT IS MOST EFFECTIVE.
CLIP
I'LL COME BACK FOR YOU LATER, BABY.
FIRST, I GOTTA STIR UP THE HORNETS.

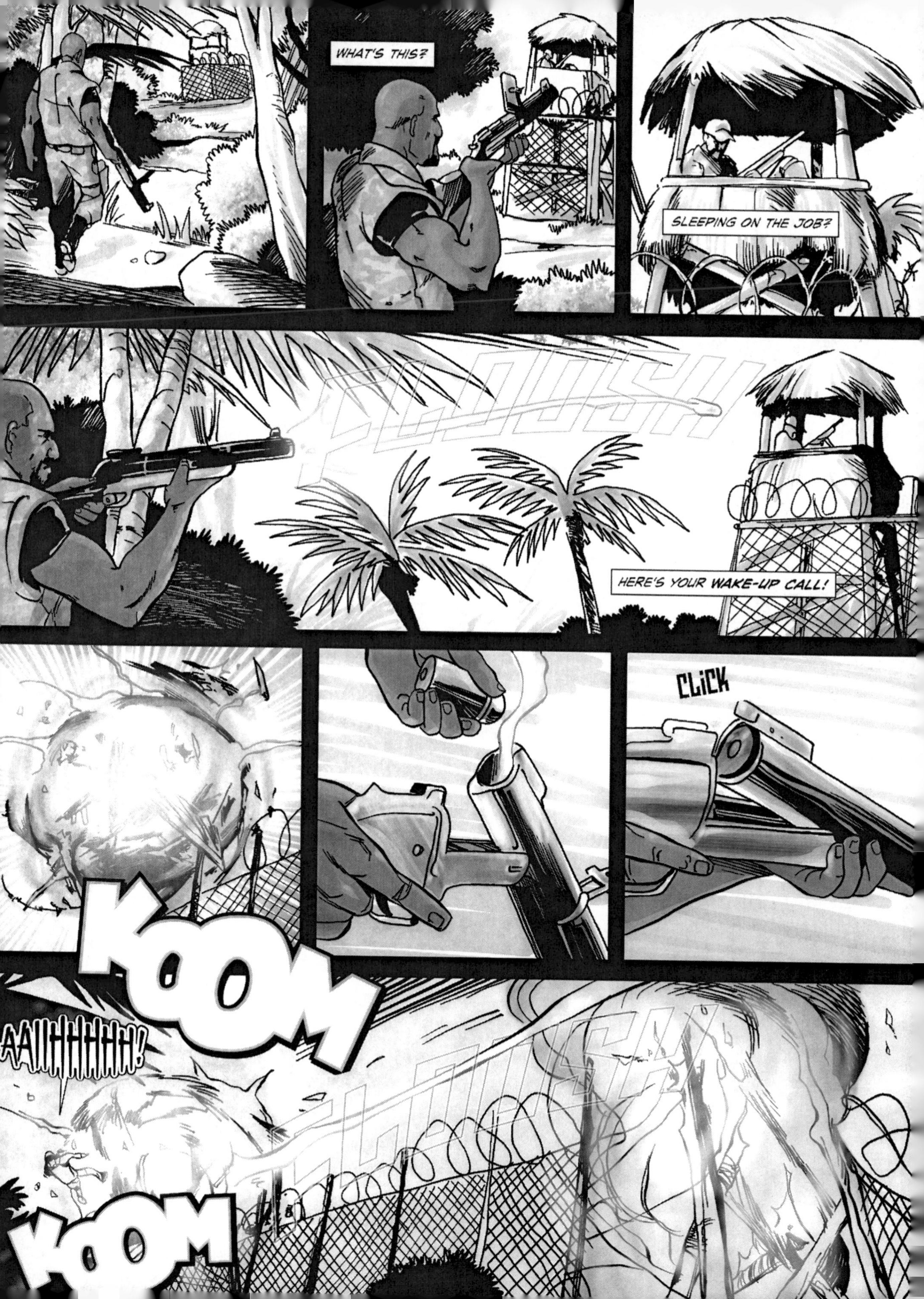
WHAT'S THIS?
SLEEPING ON THE JOB?
HERE'S YOUR WAKE-UP CALL!
CLICK
KOOM
AAIIHHHHH!
KOOM

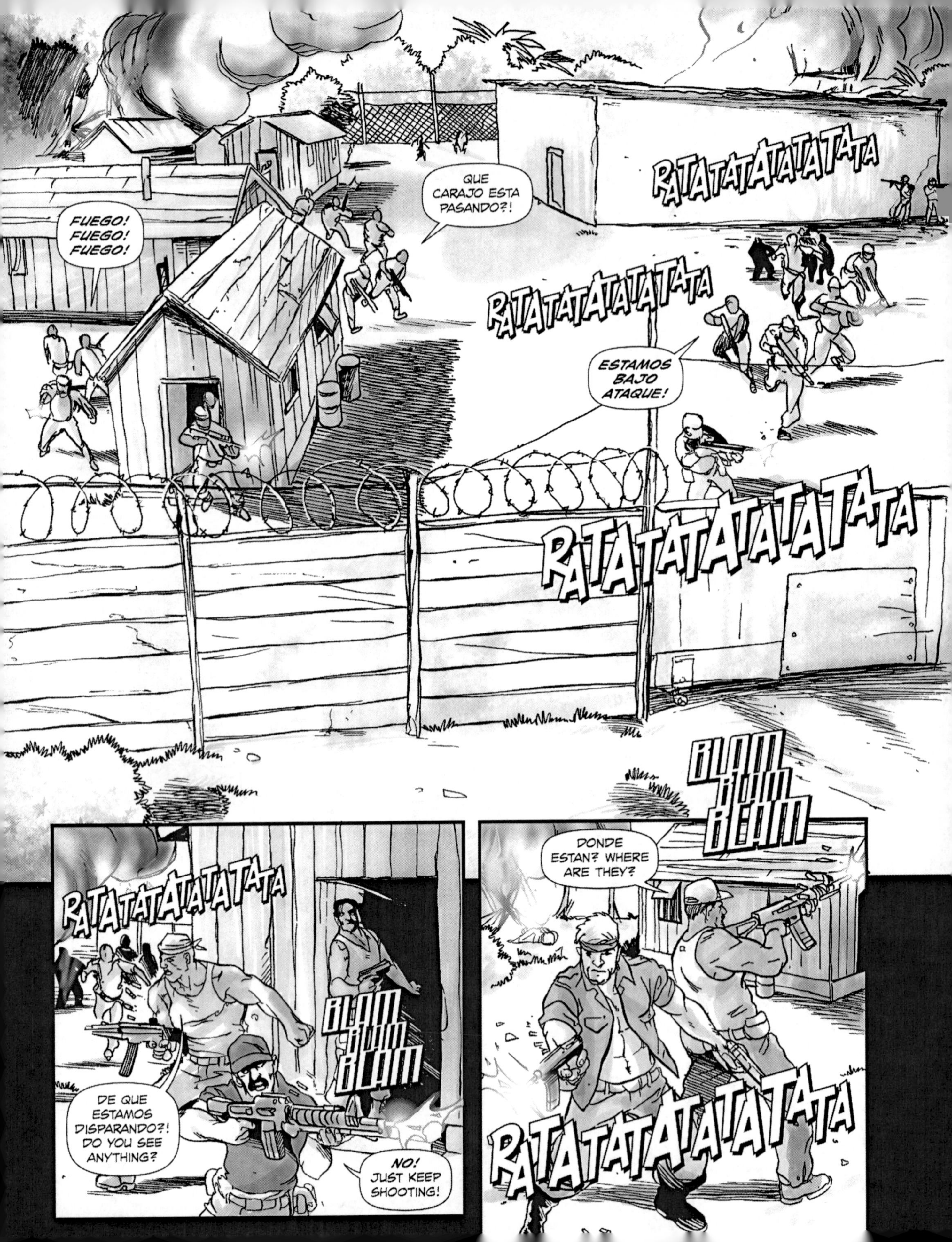
FUEGO! FUEGO! FUEGO!
QUE CARAJO ESTA PASANDO?!
RATATATATATATATA
RATATATATATATATA
ESTAMOS BAJO ATAQUE!
RATATATATATATATA
BLAM BLAM BLAM
RATATATATATATATA
BLAM BLAM BLAM
DE QUE ESTAMOS DISPARANDO?! DO YOU SEE ANYTHING?
NO! JUST KEEP SHOOTING!
DONDE ESTAN? WHERE ARE THEY?
RATATATATATATATA

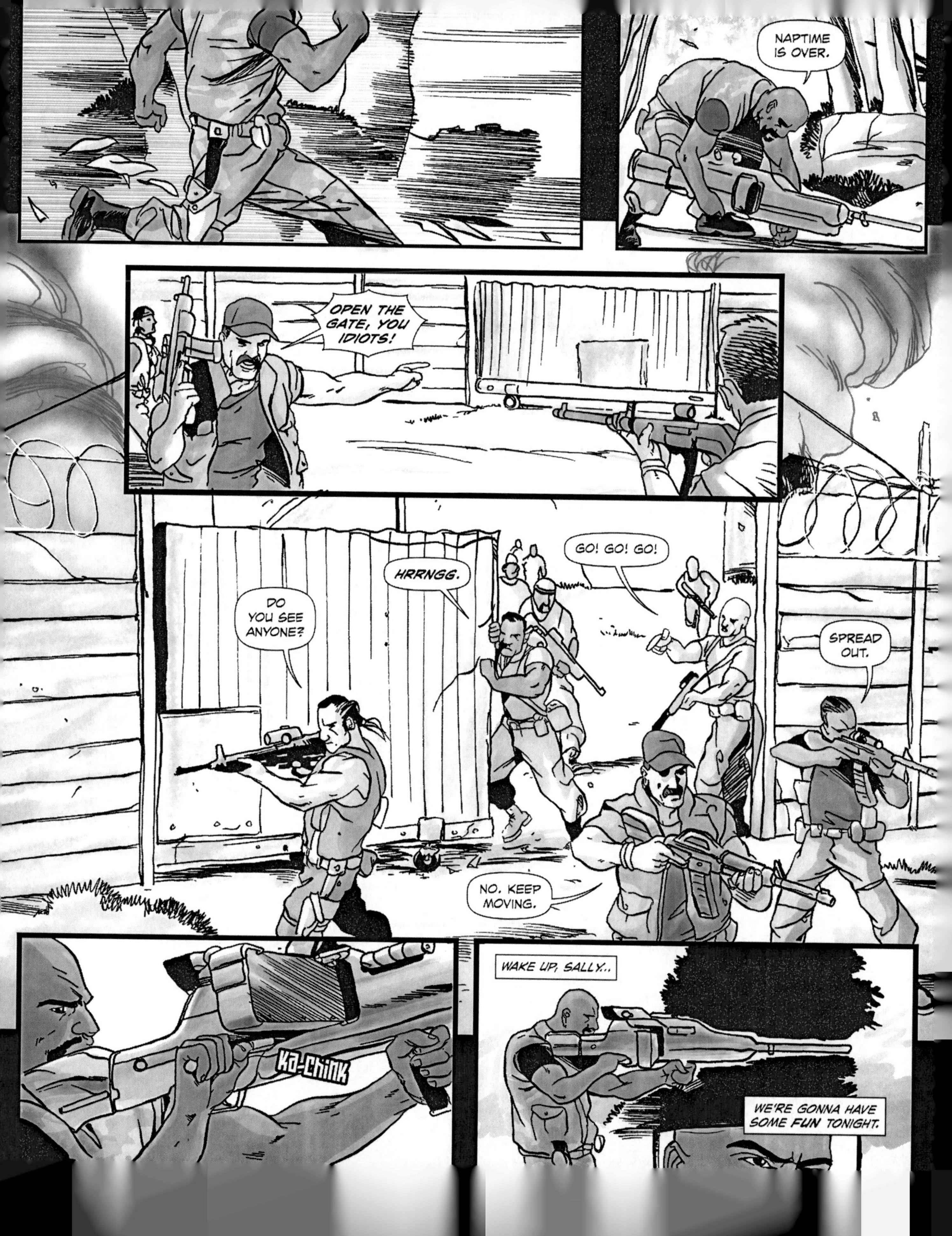
NAPTIME IS OVER.
OPEN THE GATE, YOU IDIOTS!
DO YOU SEE ANYONE?
HRRNGG.
GO! GO! GO!
SPREAD OUT.
NO. KEEP MOVING.
KA-CHINK
WAKE UP, SALLY...
WE'RE GONNA HAVE SOME FUN TONIGHT.

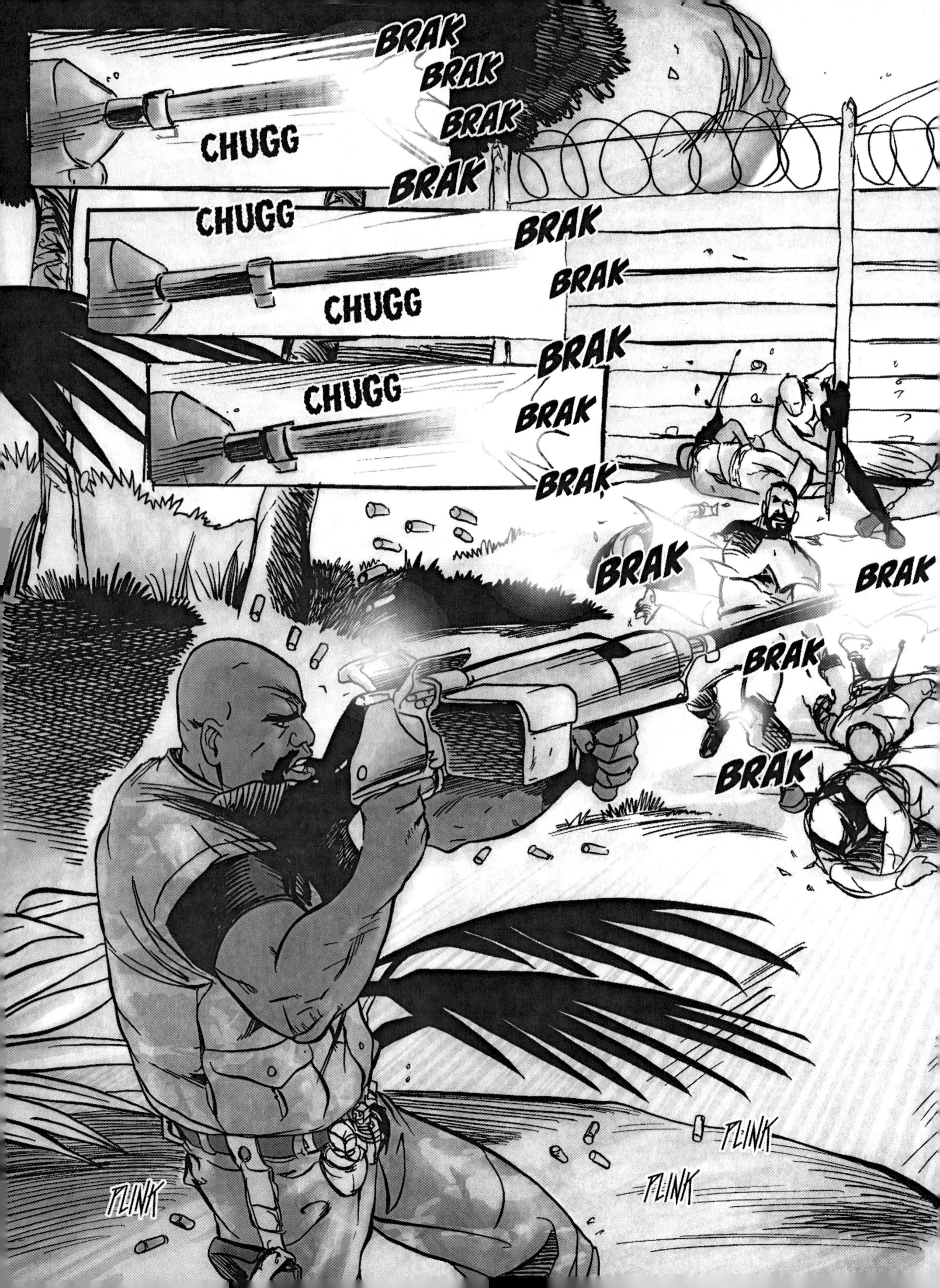
BRAK
BRAK
BRAK
CHUGG
BRAK
CHUGG
BRAK
BRAK
CHUGG
BRAK
CHUGG
BRAK
BRAK
BRAK
BRAK
BRAK
BRAK
PLINK
PLINK
PLINK

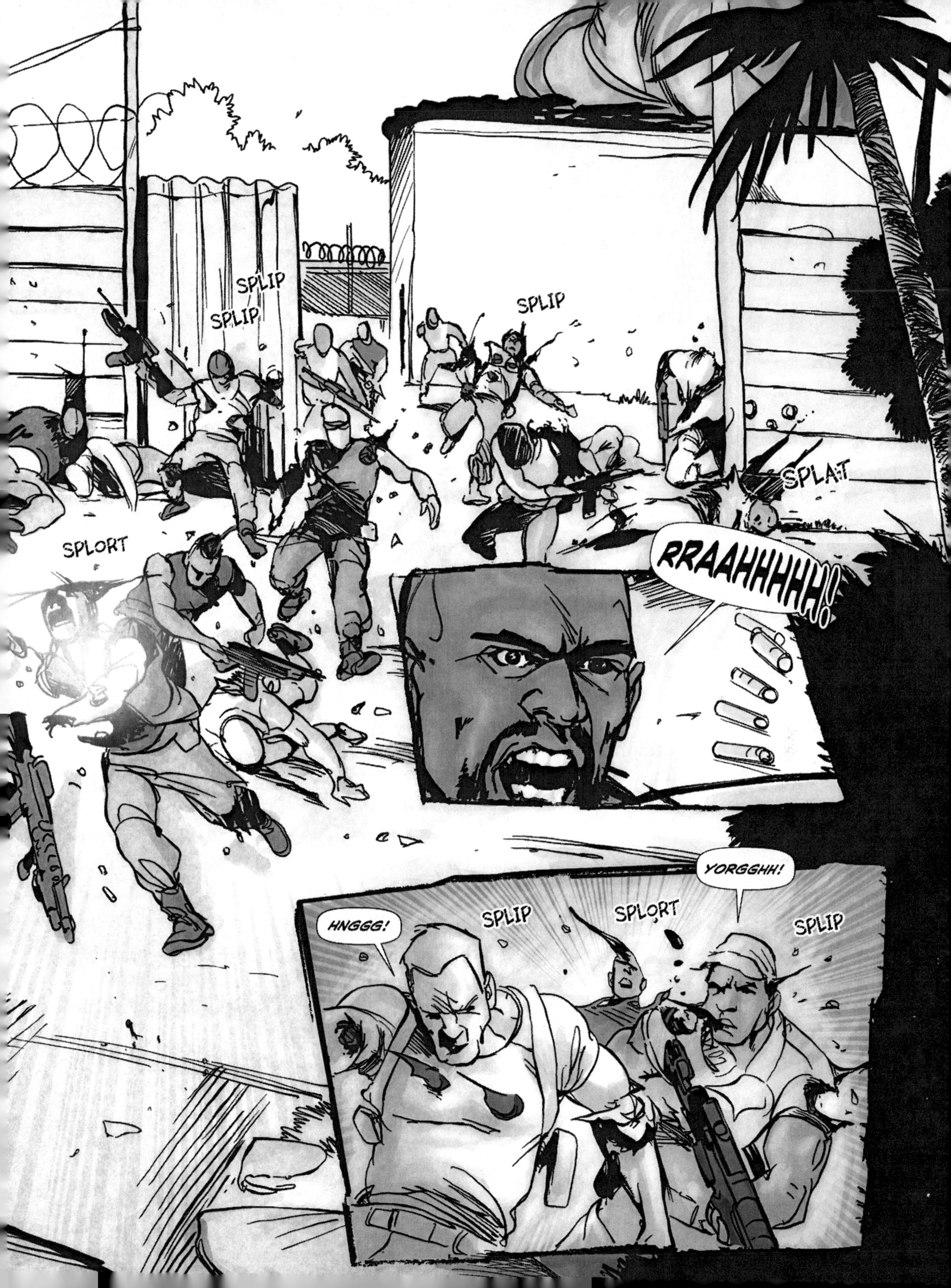
SPLIP
SPLIP
SPLIP
SPLAT
SPLORT
RRAAHHHHH!!
YORGGHH!
HNGGG!
SPLIP
SPLORT
SPLIP

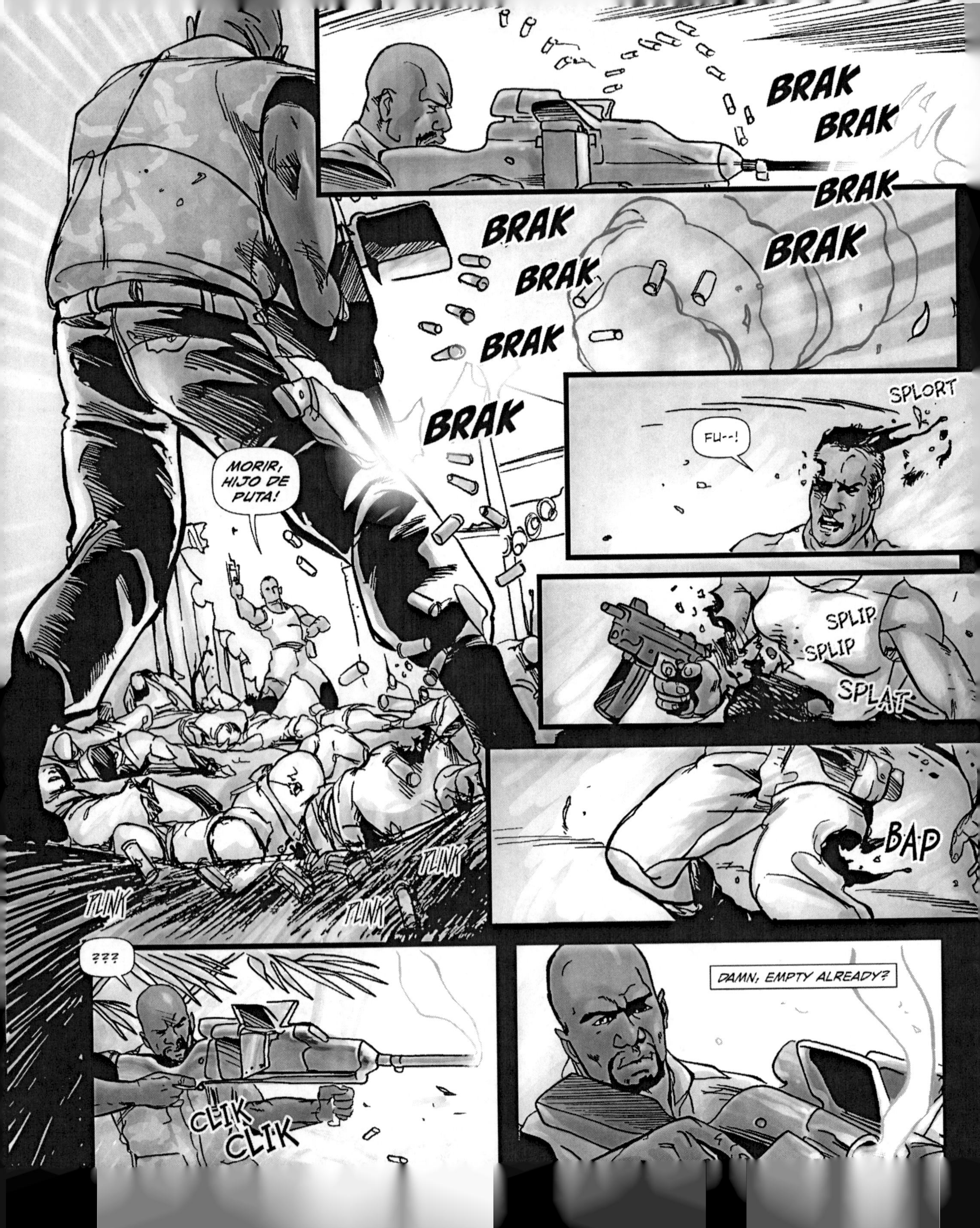
BRAK
BRAK
BRAK
BRAK
BRAK
BRAK
BRAK
BRAK
MORIR, HIJO DE PUTA!
SPLORT
FU--!
SPLIP
SPLIP
SPLAT
TLINK
TLINK
TLINK
BAP
???
CLIK
CLIK
DAMN, EMPTY ALREADY?

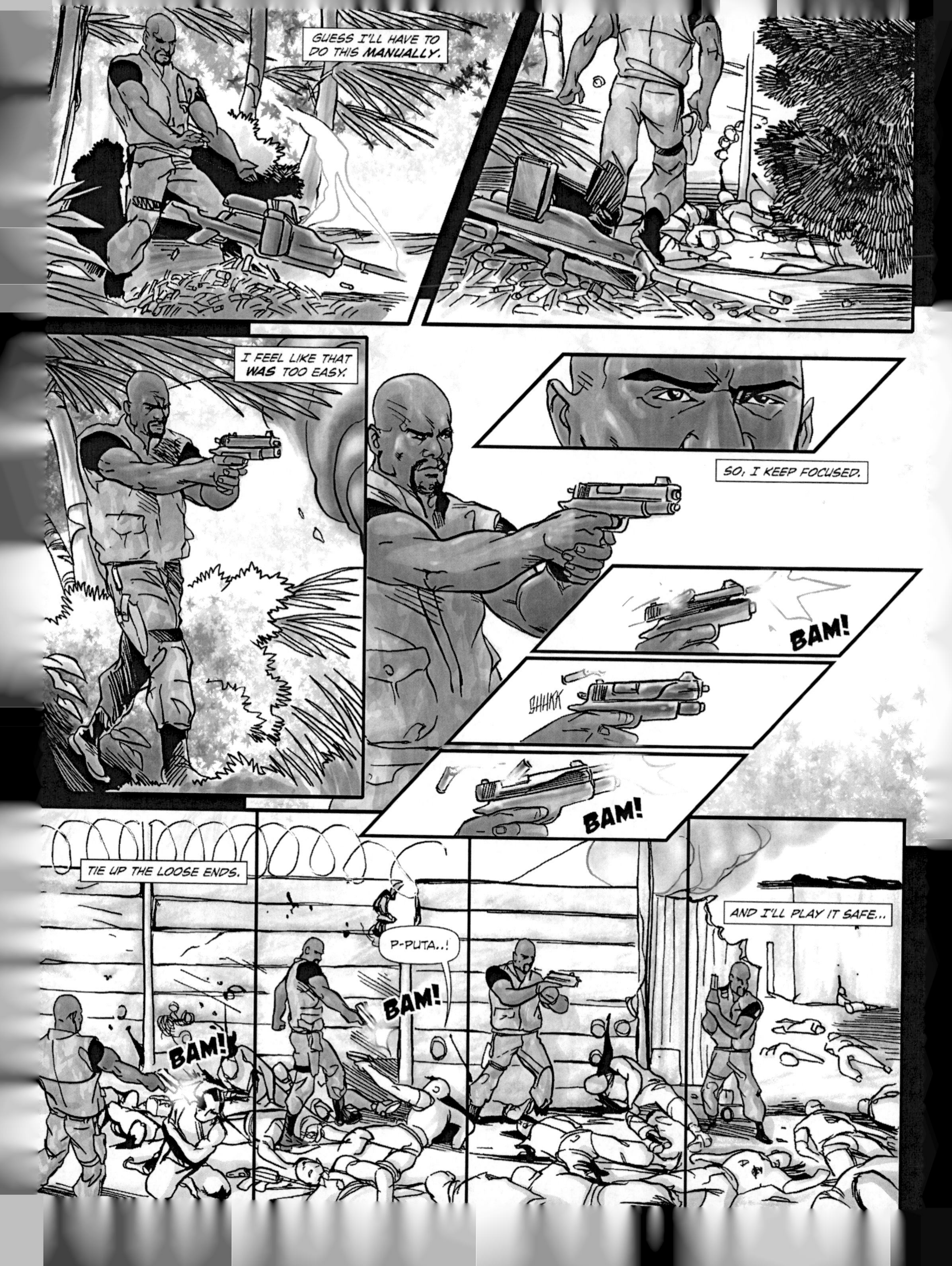
GUESS I'LL HAVE TO DO THIS MANUALLY.
I FEEL LIKE THAT WAS TOO EASY.
SO, I KEEP FOCUSED.
BAM!
SHHKK
BAM!
TIE UP THE LOOSE ENDS.
BAM!
P-PUTA..!
BAM!
AND I'LL PLAY IT SAFE...

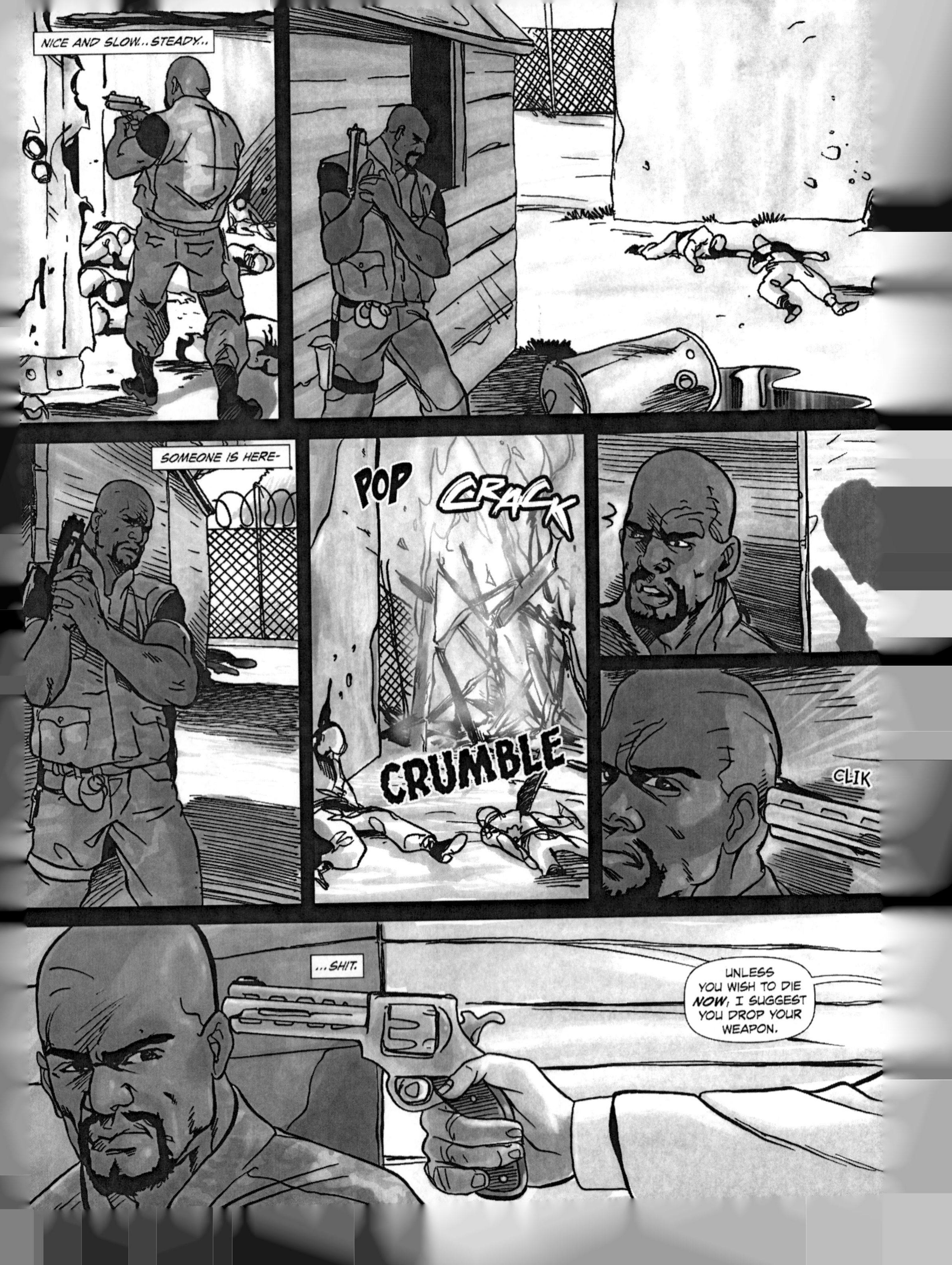
NICE AND SLOW... STEADY...
SOMEONE IS HERE-
POP
CRACK
CRUMBLE
CLIK
...SHIT.
UNLESS YOU WISH TO DIE *NOW*, I SUGGEST YOU DROP YOUR WEAPON.

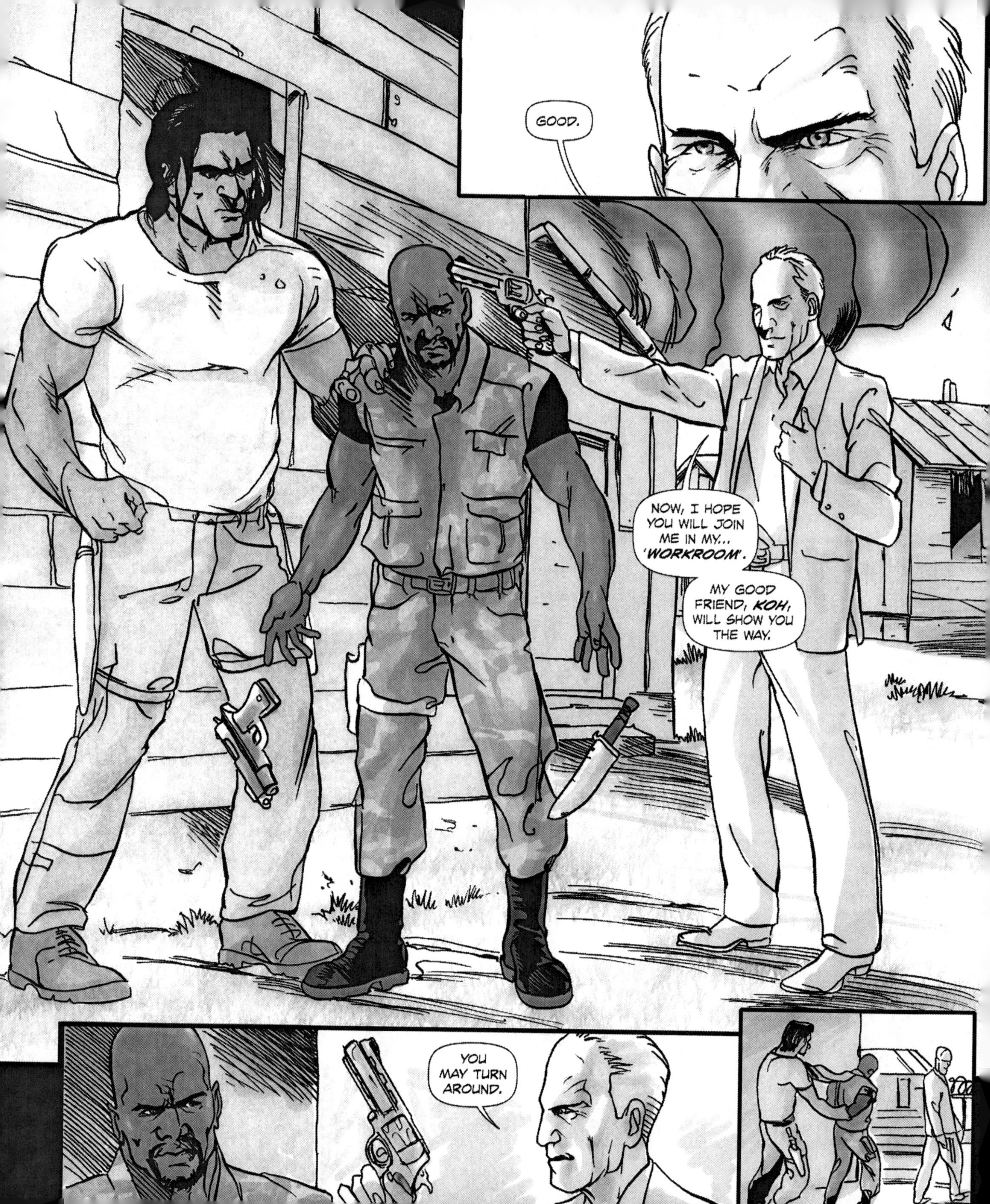
GOOD.
NOW, I HOPE YOU WILL JOIN ME IN MY... 'WORKROOM'.
MY GOOD FRIEND, KOH, WILL SHOW YOU THE WAY.
YOU MAY TURN AROUND.

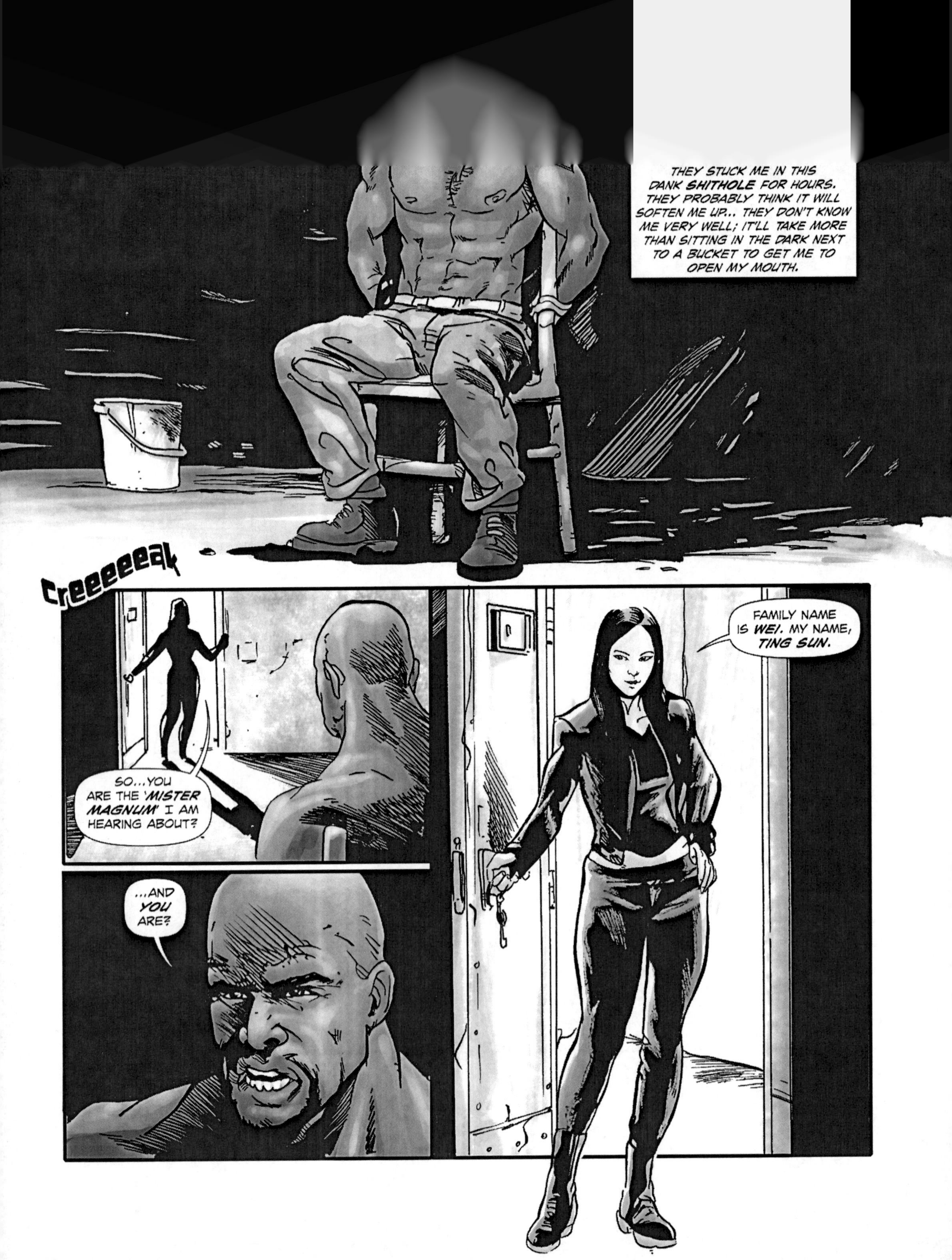
THEY STUCK ME IN THIS DANK SHITHOLE FOR HOURS. THEY PROBABLY THINK IT WILL SOFTEN ME UP... THEY DON'T KNOW ME VERY WELL; IT'LL TAKE MORE THAN SITTING IN THE DARK NEXT TO A BUCKET TO GET ME TO OPEN MY MOUTH.
Creeeeeeak
SO...YOU ARE THE 'MISTER MAGNUM' I AM HEARING ABOUT?
...AND YOU ARE?
FAMILY NAME IS WEI. MY NAME, TING SUN.

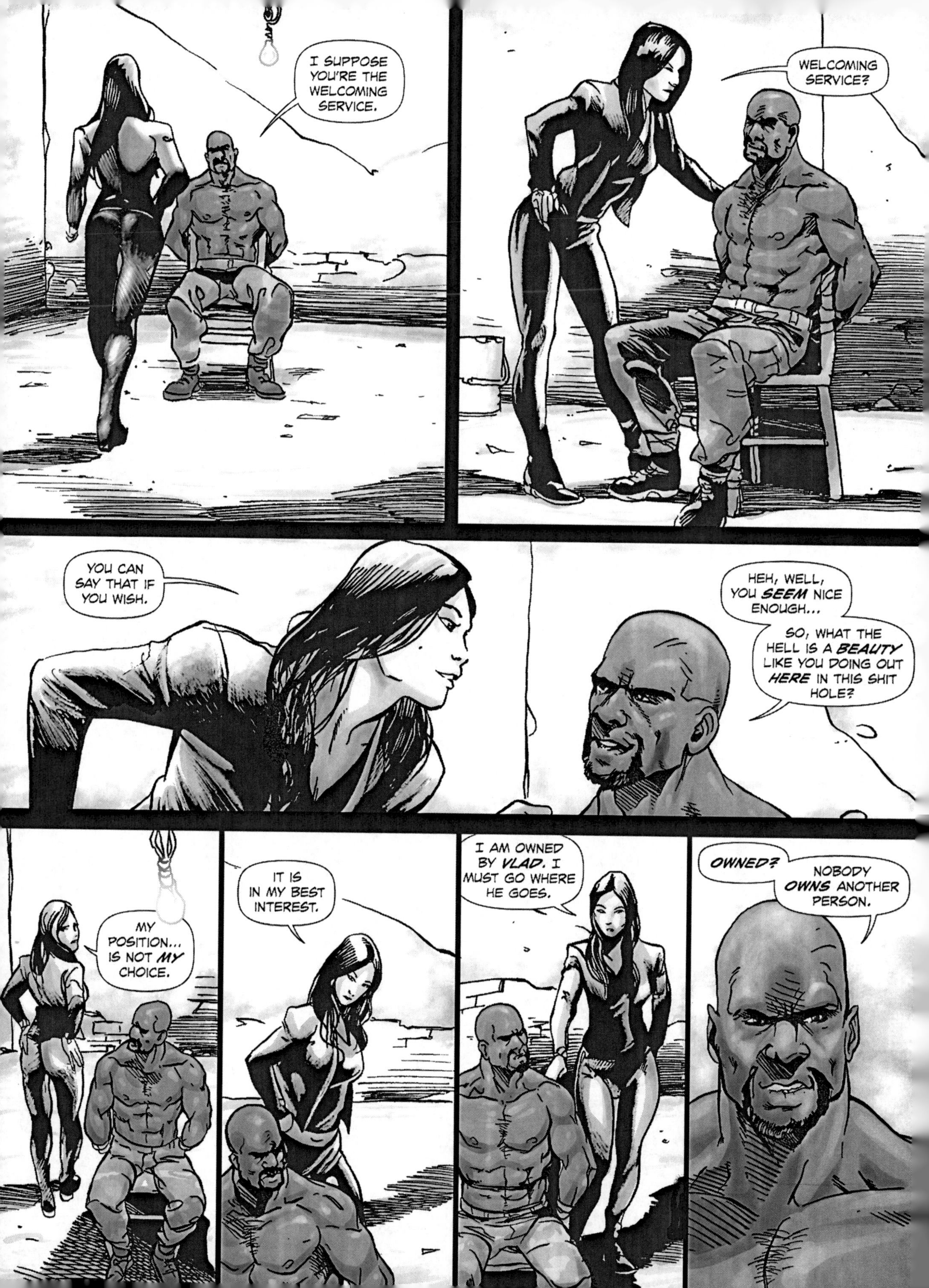
I SUPPOSE YOU'RE THE WELCOMING SERVICE.
WELCOMING SERVICE?
YOU CAN SAY THAT IF YOU WISH.
HEH, WELL, YOU *SEEM* NICE ENOUGH...
SO, WHAT THE HELL IS A *BEAUTY* LIKE YOU DOING OUT *HERE* IN THIS SHIT HOLE?
MY POSITION... IS NOT *MY* CHOICE.
IT IS IN MY BEST INTEREST.
I AM OWNED BY *VLAD*. I MUST GO WHERE HE GOES.
OWNED?
NOBODY *OWNS* ANOTHER PERSON.

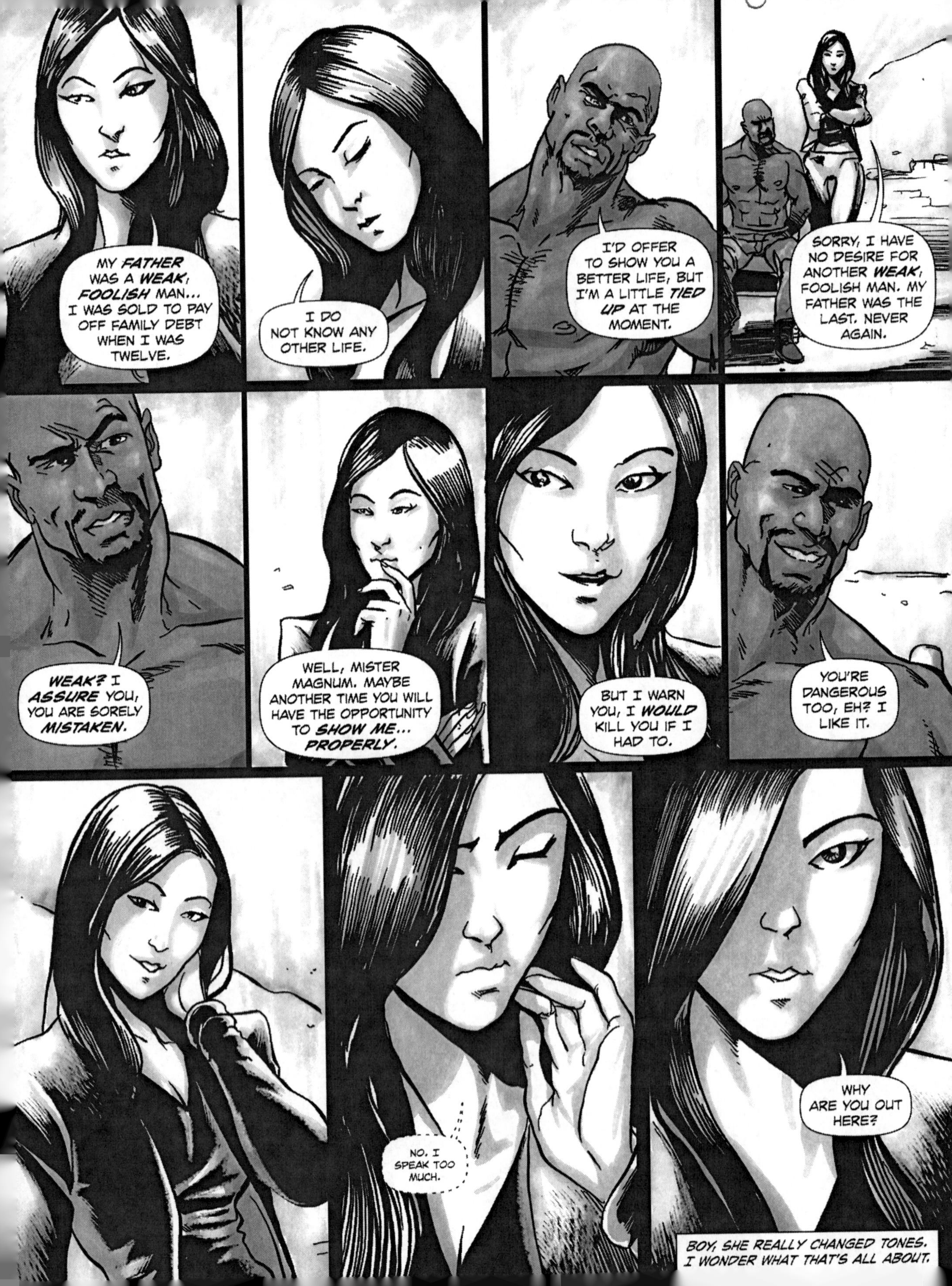
MY FATHER WAS A WEAK, FOOLISH MAN... I WAS SOLD TO PAY OFF FAMILY DEBT WHEN I WAS TWELVE.
I DO NOT KNOW ANY OTHER LIFE.
I'D OFFER TO SHOW YOU A BETTER LIFE, BUT I'M A LITTLE TIED UP AT THE MOMENT.
SORRY, I HAVE NO DESIRE FOR ANOTHER WEAK, FOOLISH MAN. MY FATHER WAS THE LAST. NEVER AGAIN.
WEAK? I ASSURE YOU, YOU ARE SORELY MISTAKEN.
WELL, MISTER MAGNUM. MAYBE ANOTHER TIME YOU WILL HAVE THE OPPORTUNITY TO SHOW ME... PROPERLY.
BUT I WARN YOU, I WOULD KILL YOU IF I HAD TO.
YOU'RE DANGEROUS TOO, EH? I LIKE IT.
NO. I SPEAK TOO MUCH.
WHY ARE YOU OUT HERE?
BOY, SHE REALLY CHANGED TONES. I WONDER WHAT THAT'S ALL ABOUT.

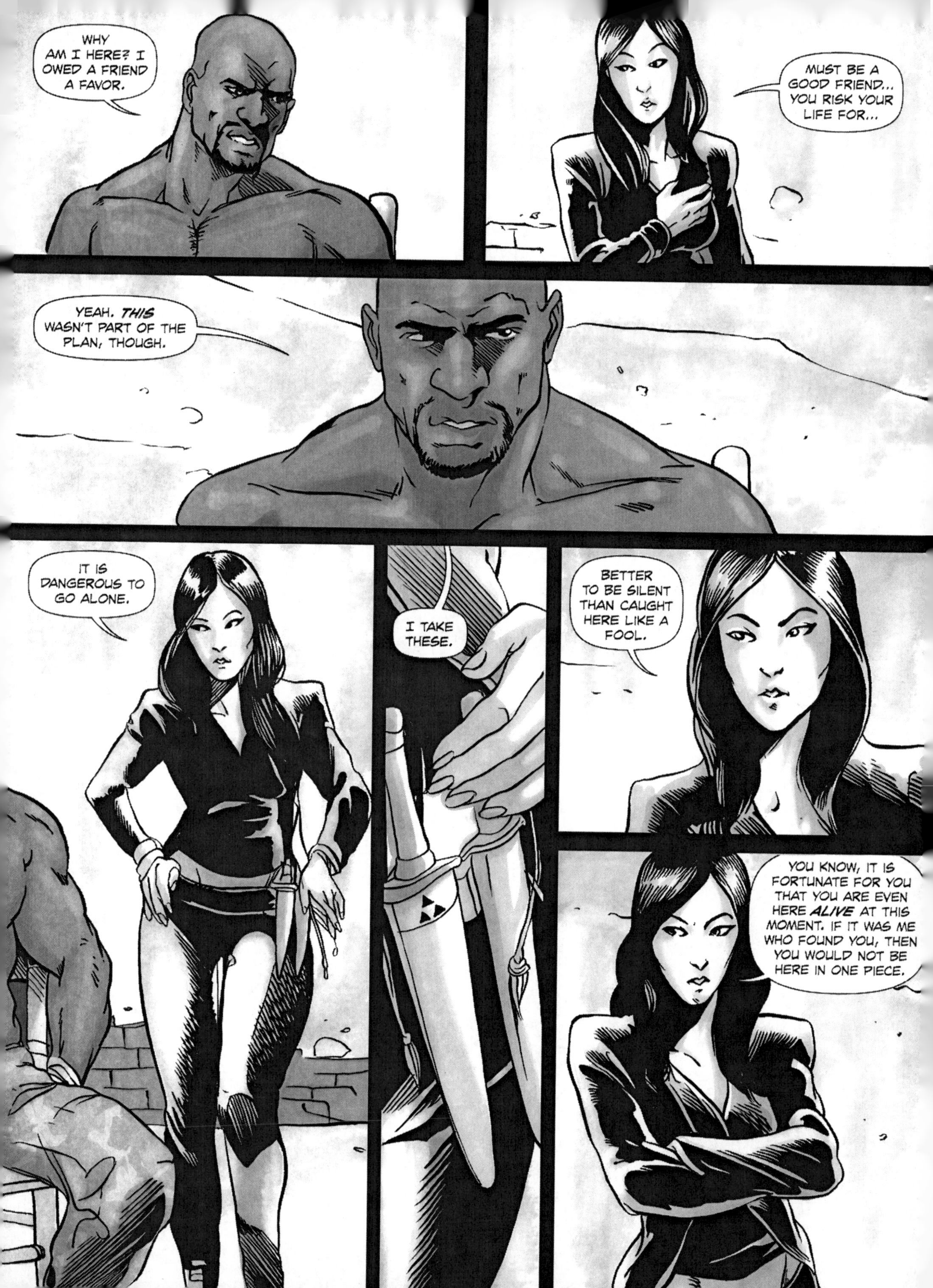
WHY AM I HERE? I OWED A FRIEND A FAVOR.
MUST BE A GOOD FRIEND... YOU RISK YOUR LIFE FOR...
YEAH. THIS WASN'T PART OF THE PLAN, THOUGH.
IT IS DANGEROUS TO GO ALONE.
I TAKE THESE.
BETTER TO BE SILENT THAN CAUGHT HERE LIKE A FOOL.
YOU KNOW, IT IS FORTUNATE FOR YOU THAT YOU ARE EVEN HERE ALIVE AT THIS MOMENT. IF IT WAS ME WHO FOUND YOU, THEN YOU WOULD NOT BE HERE IN ONE PIECE.

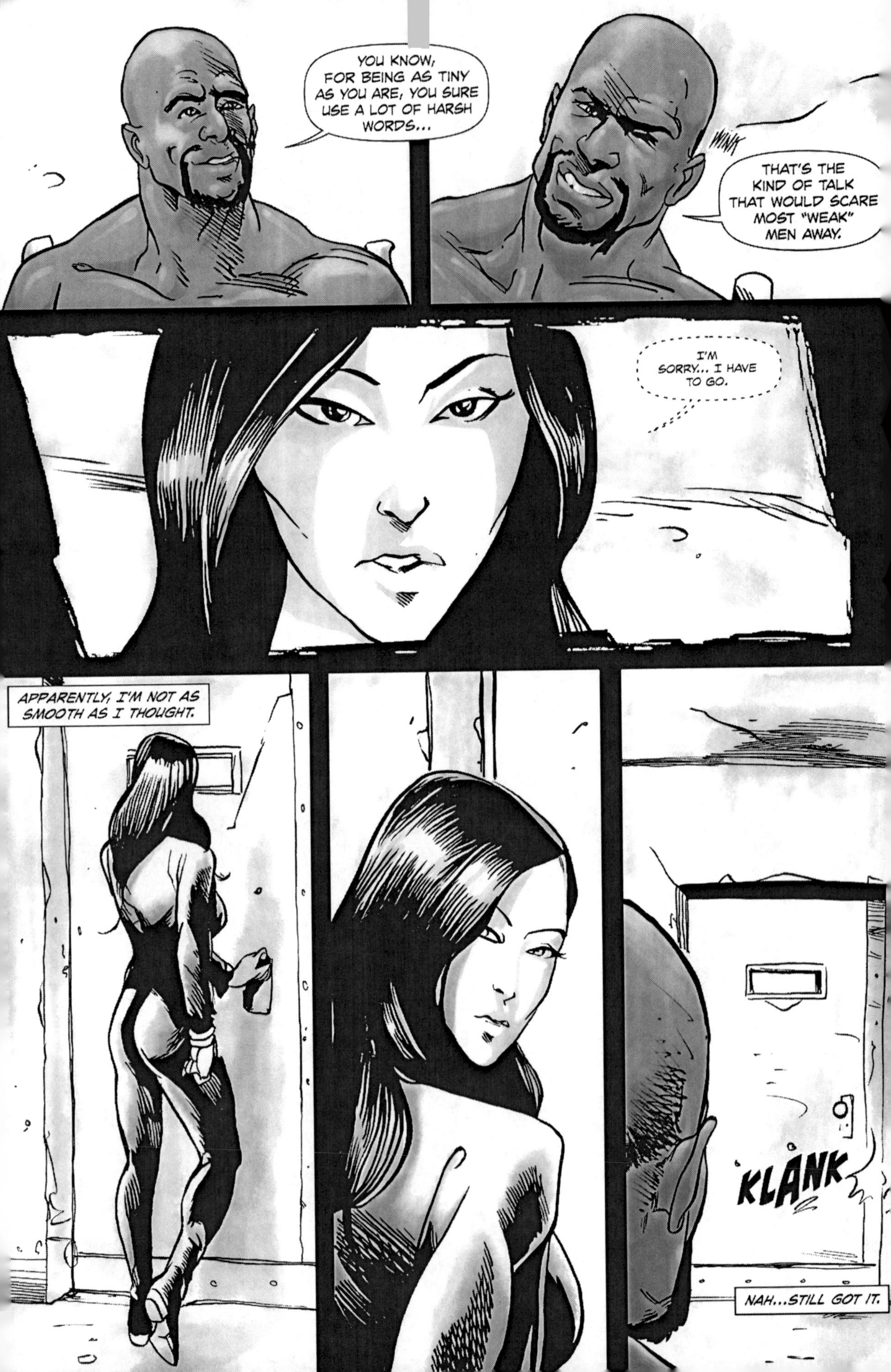
YOU KNOW, FOR BEING AS TINY AS YOU ARE, YOU SURE USE A LOT OF HARSH WORDS...
WINK
THAT'S THE KIND OF TALK THAT WOULD SCARE MOST "WEAK" MEN AWAY.
I'M SORRY... I HAVE TO GO.
APPARENTLY, I'M NOT AS SMOOTH AS I THOUGHT.
KLANK
NAH...STILL GOT IT.

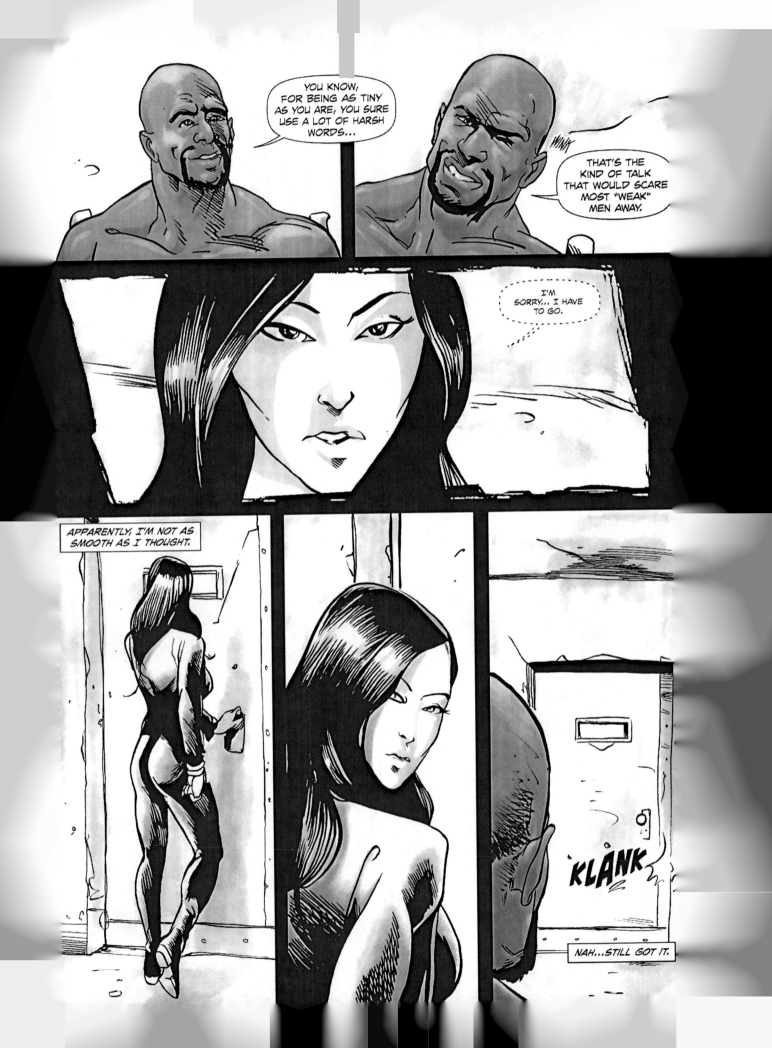

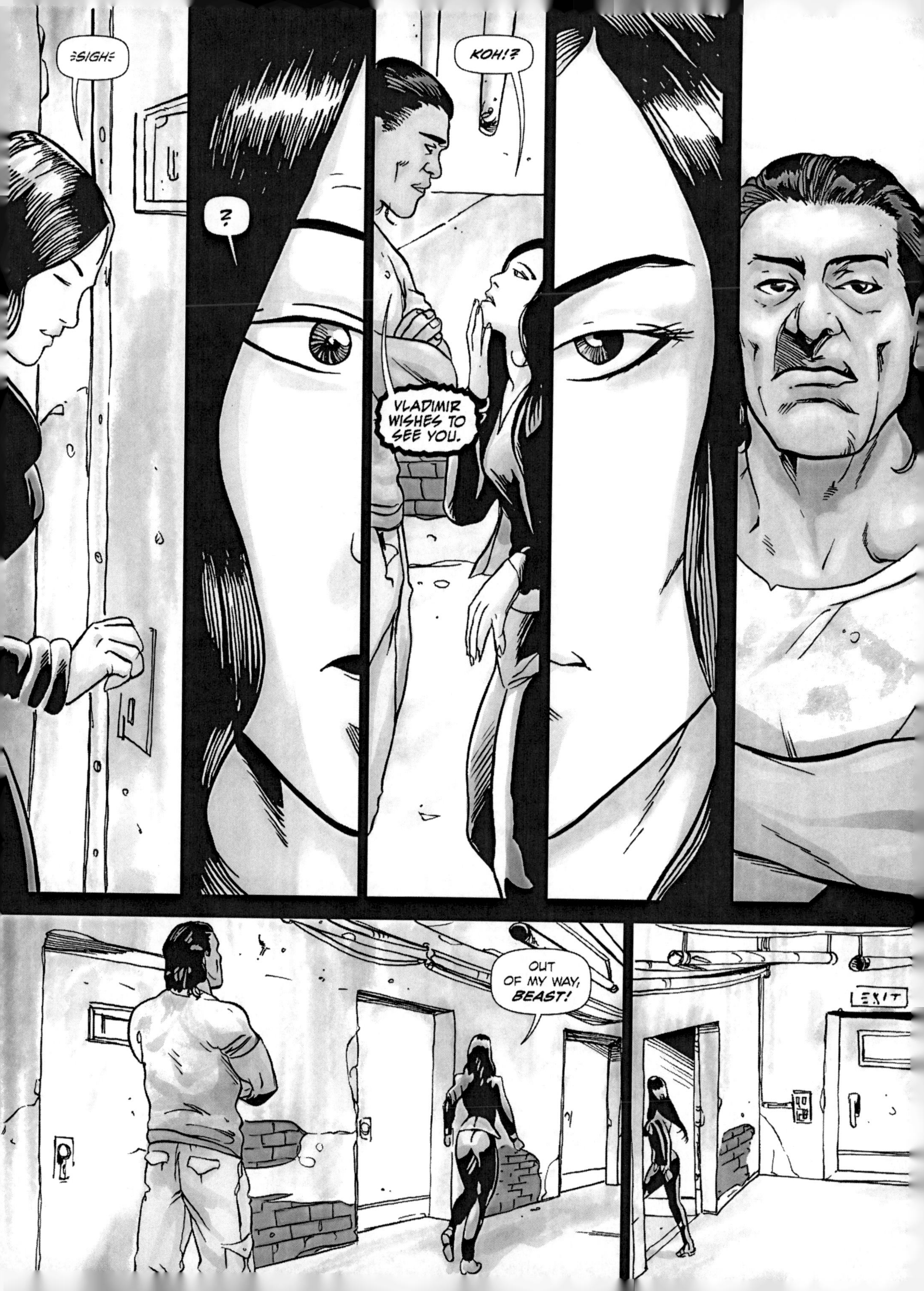

=SIGH=
?
KOH!?
VLADIMIR WISHES TO SEE YOU.
OUT OF MY WAY, BEAST!
EXIT

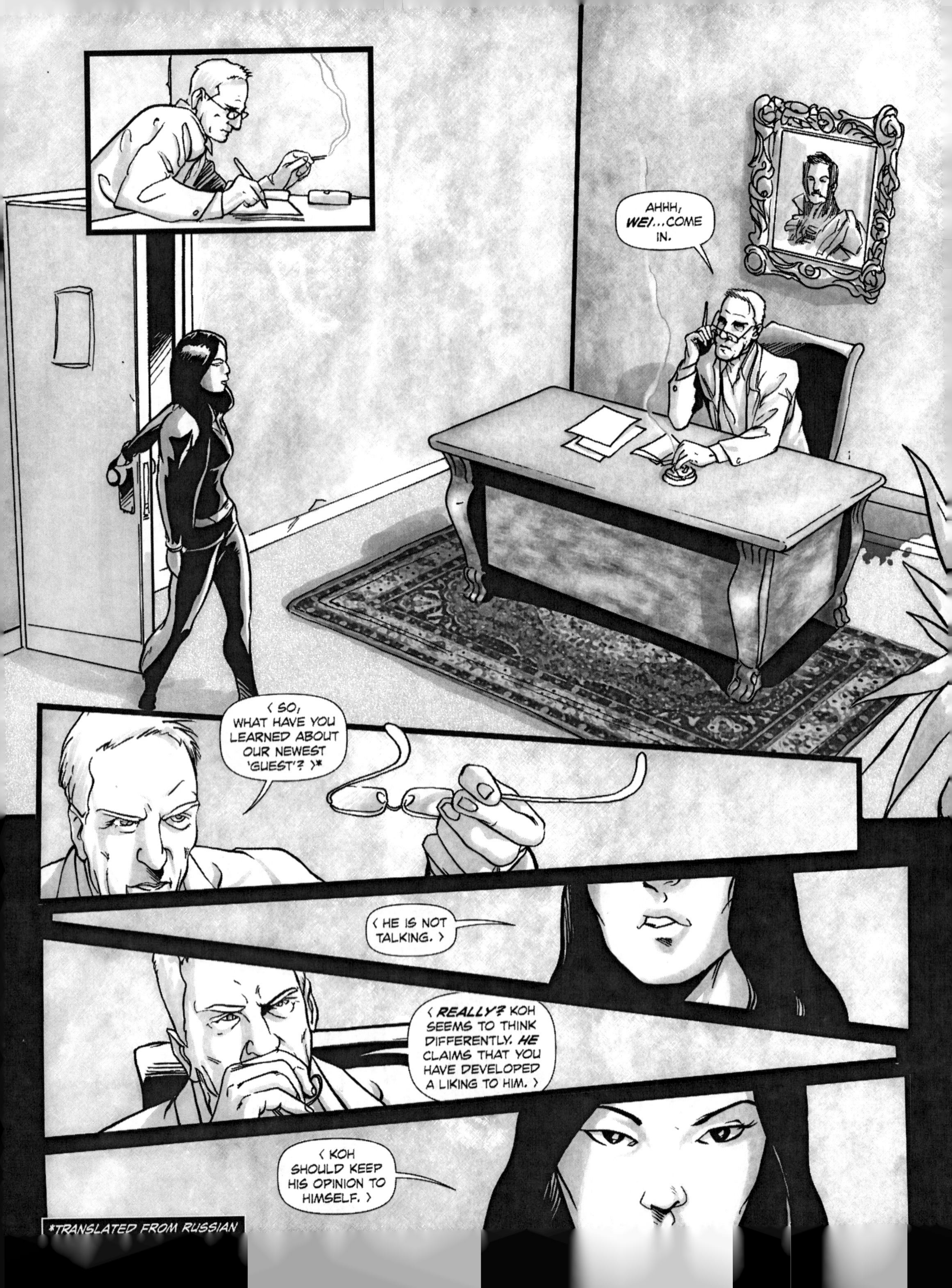
AHHH, WEI...COME IN.
‹ SO, WHAT HAVE YOU LEARNED ABOUT OUR NEWEST 'GUEST'? ›*
‹ HE IS NOT TALKING. ›
‹ REALLY? KOH SEEMS TO THINK DIFFERENTLY. HE CLAIMS THAT YOU HAVE DEVELOPED A LIKING TO HIM. ›
‹ KOH SHOULD KEEP HIS OPINION TO HIMSELF. ›
*TRANSLATED FROM RUSSIAN

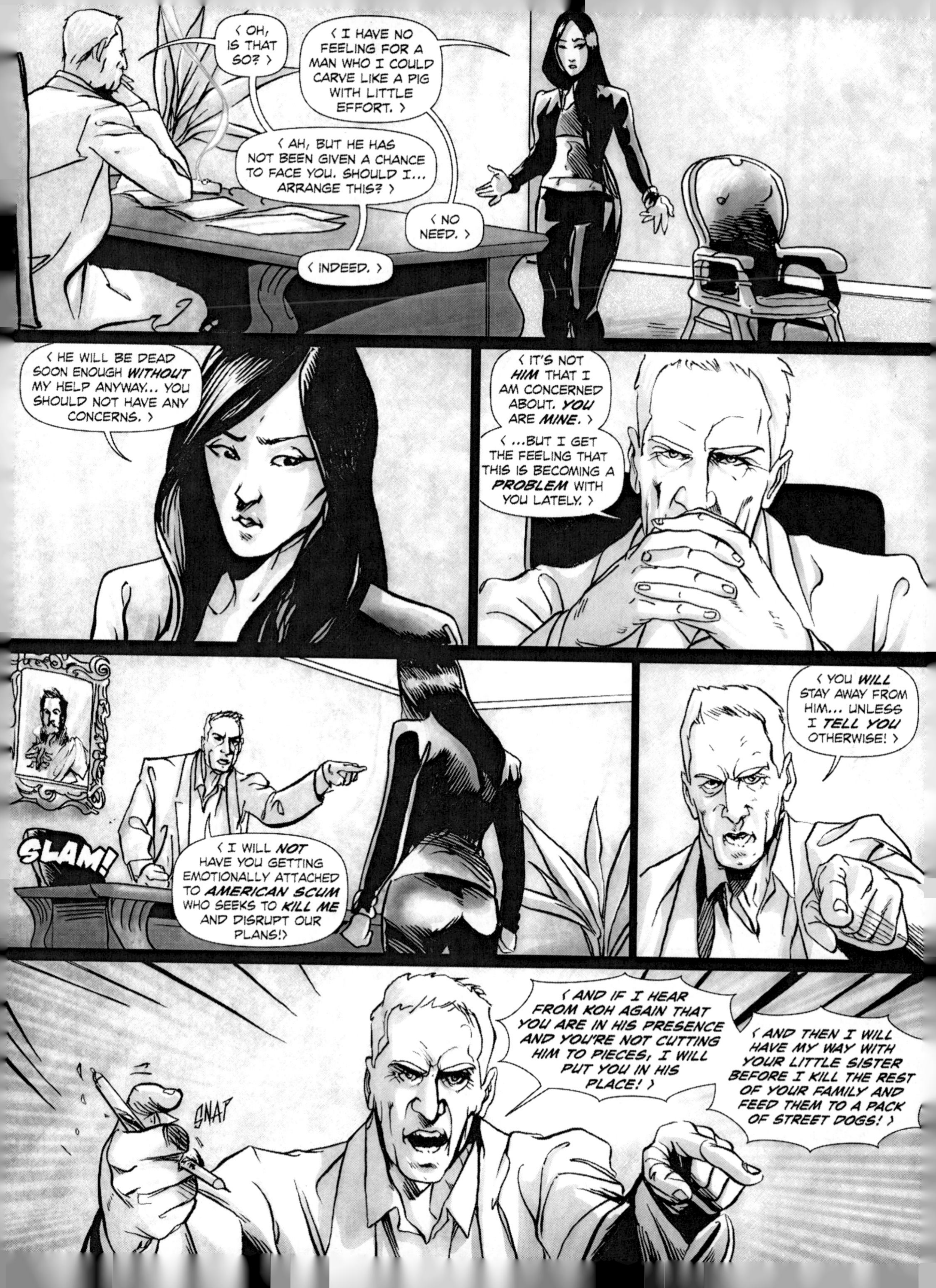

‹ I HAVE NO FEELING FOR A MAN WHO I COULD CARVE LIKE A PIG WITH LITTLE EFFORT. ›
‹ OH, IS THAT SO? ›
‹ AH, BUT HE HAS NOT BEEN GIVEN A CHANCE TO FACE YOU. SHOULD I... ARRANGE THIS? ›
‹ NO NEED. ›
‹ INDEED. ›
‹ HE WILL BE DEAD SOON ENOUGH WITHOUT MY HELP ANYWAY... YOU SHOULD NOT HAVE ANY CONCERNS. ›
‹ IT'S NOT HIM THAT I AM CONCERNED ABOUT. YOU ARE MINE. ›
‹ ...BUT I GET THE FEELING THAT THIS IS BECOMING A PROBLEM WITH YOU LATELY. ›
SLAM!
‹ I WILL NOT HAVE YOU GETTING EMOTIONALLY ATTACHED TO AMERICAN SCUM WHO SEEKS TO KILL ME AND DISRUPT OUR PLANS!›
‹ YOU WILL STAY AWAY FROM HIM... UNLESS I TELL YOU OTHERWISE! ›
SNAP
‹ AND IF I HEAR FROM KOH AGAIN THAT YOU ARE IN HIS PRESENCE AND YOU'RE NOT CUTTING HIM TO PIECES, I WILL PUT YOU IN HIS PLACE! ›
‹ AND THEN I WILL HAVE MY WAY WITH YOUR LITTLE SISTER BEFORE I KILL THE REST OF YOUR FAMILY AND FEED THEM TO A PACK OF STREET DOGS! ›

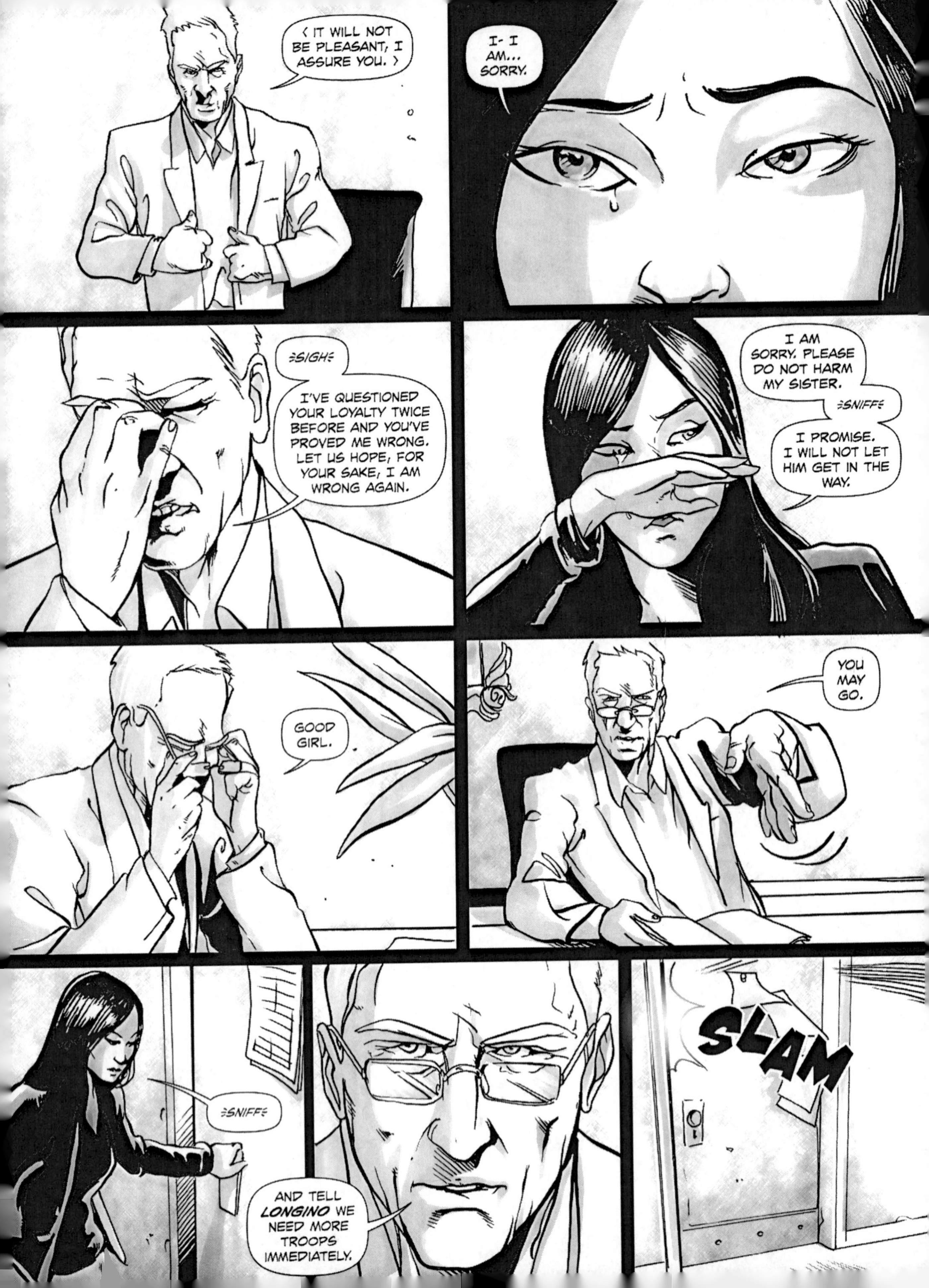
< IT WILL NOT BE PLEASANT, I ASSURE YOU. >
I- I AM... SORRY.
≡SIGH≡
I'VE QUESTIONED YOUR LOYALTY TWICE BEFORE AND YOU'VE PROVED ME WRONG. LET US HOPE, FOR YOUR SAKE, I AM WRONG AGAIN.
I AM SORRY. PLEASE DO NOT HARM MY SISTER.
≡SNIFF≡
I PROMISE. I WILL NOT LET HIM GET IN THE WAY.
GOOD GIRL.
YOU MAY GO.
≡SNIFF≡
AND TELL LONGINO WE NEED MORE TROOPS IMMEDIATELY.
SLAM

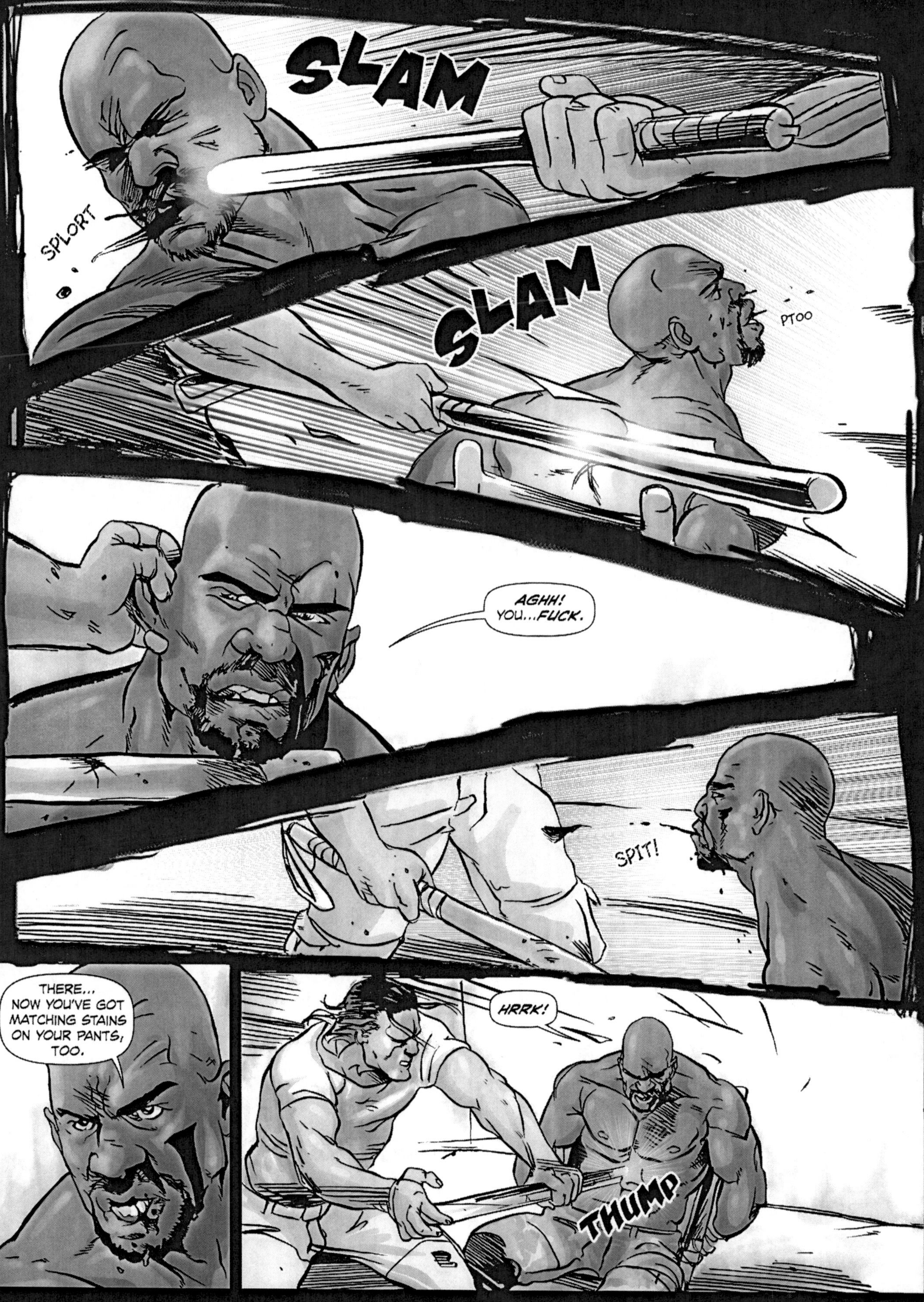
SLAM
SPLORT
SLAM
PTOO
AGHH! YOU...FUCK.
SPIT!
THERE... NOW YOU'VE GOT MATCHING STAINS ON YOUR PANTS, TOO.
HRRK!
THUMP

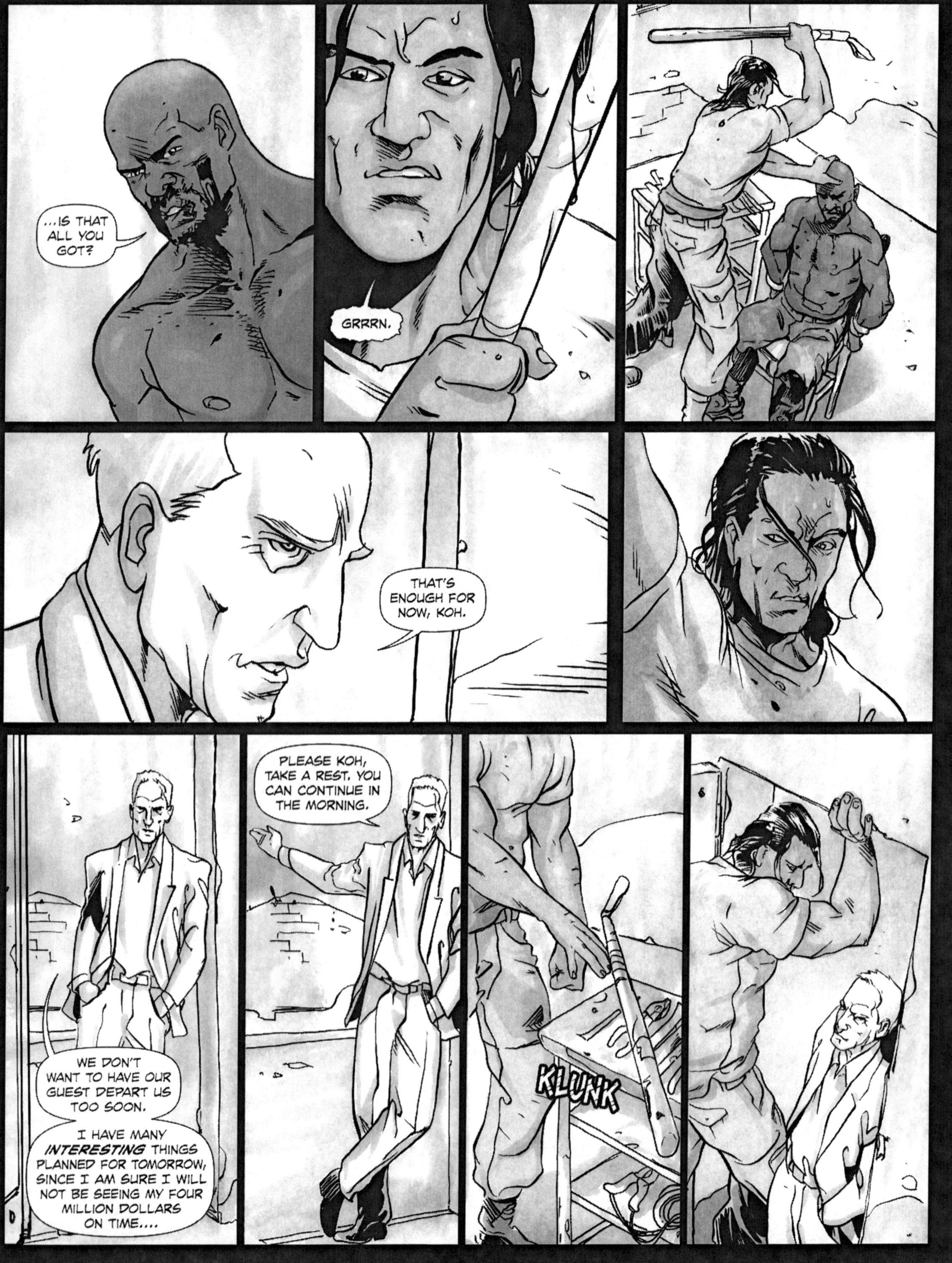
...IS THAT ALL YOU GOT?
GRRRN.
THAT'S ENOUGH FOR NOW, KOH.
WE DON'T WANT TO HAVE OUR GUEST DEPART US TOO SOON.
I HAVE MANY *INTERESTING* THINGS PLANNED FOR TOMORROW, SINCE I AM SURE I WILL NOT BE SEEING MY FOUR MILLION DOLLARS ON TIME....
PLEASE KOH, TAKE A REST. YOU CAN CONTINUE IN THE MORNING.
KLUNK

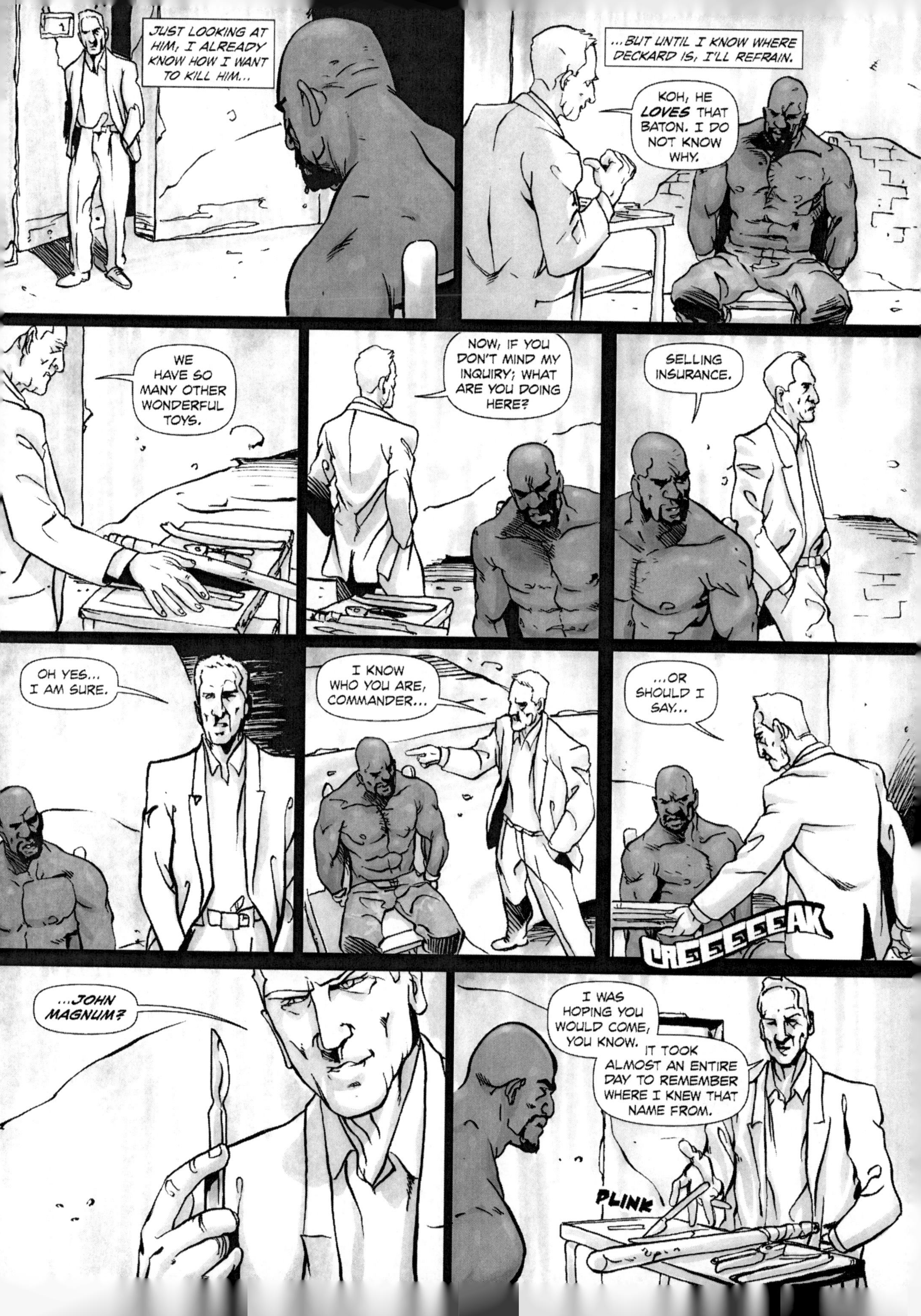
JUST LOOKING AT HIM, I ALREADY KNOW HOW I WANT TO KILL HIM...
...BUT UNTIL I KNOW WHERE DECKARD IS, I'LL REFRAIN.
KOH, HE LOVES THAT BATON. I DO NOT KNOW WHY.
WE HAVE SO MANY OTHER WONDERFUL TOYS.
NOW, IF YOU DON'T MIND MY INQUIRY; WHAT ARE YOU DOING HERE?
SELLING INSURANCE.
OH YES... I AM SURE.
I KNOW WHO YOU ARE, COMMANDER...
...OR SHOULD I SAY...
CREEEEEAK
...JOHN MAGNUM?
I WAS HOPING YOU WOULD COME, YOU KNOW.
IT TOOK ALMOST AN ENTIRE DAY TO REMEMBER WHERE I KNEW THAT NAME FROM.
PLINK

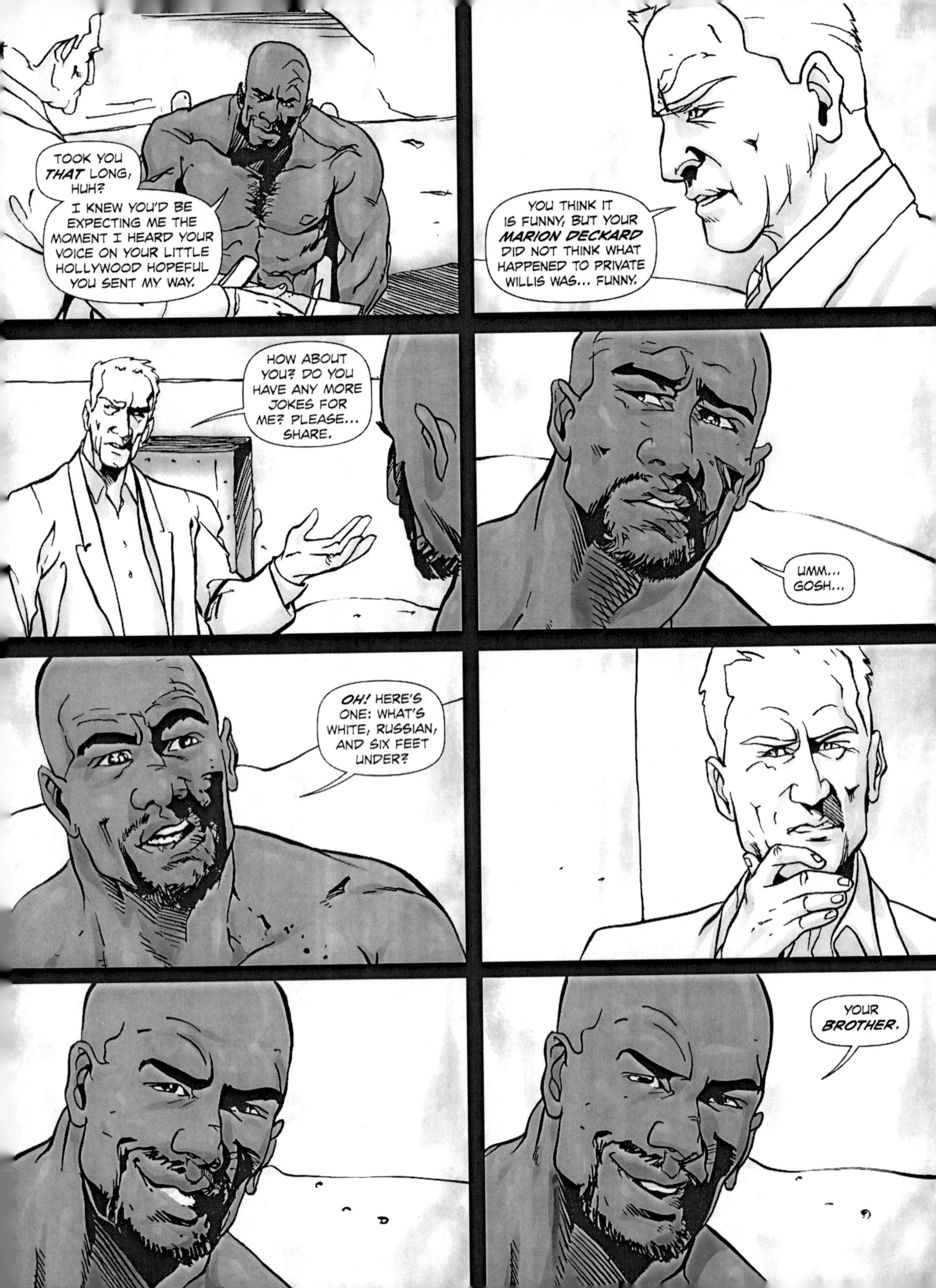
TOOK YOU *THAT* LONG, HUH?
I KNEW YOU'D BE EXPECTING ME THE MOMENT I HEARD YOUR VOICE ON YOUR LITTLE HOLLYWOOD HOPEFUL YOU SENT MY WAY.
YOU THINK IT IS FUNNY, BUT YOUR *MARION DECKARD* DID NOT THINK WHAT HAPPENED TO PRIVATE WILLIS WAS... FUNNY.
HOW ABOUT YOU? DO YOU HAVE ANY MORE JOKES FOR ME? PLEASE... SHARE.
UMM... GOSH...
OH! HERE'S ONE: WHAT'S WHITE, RUSSIAN, AND SIX FEET UNDER?
YOUR *BROTHER*.

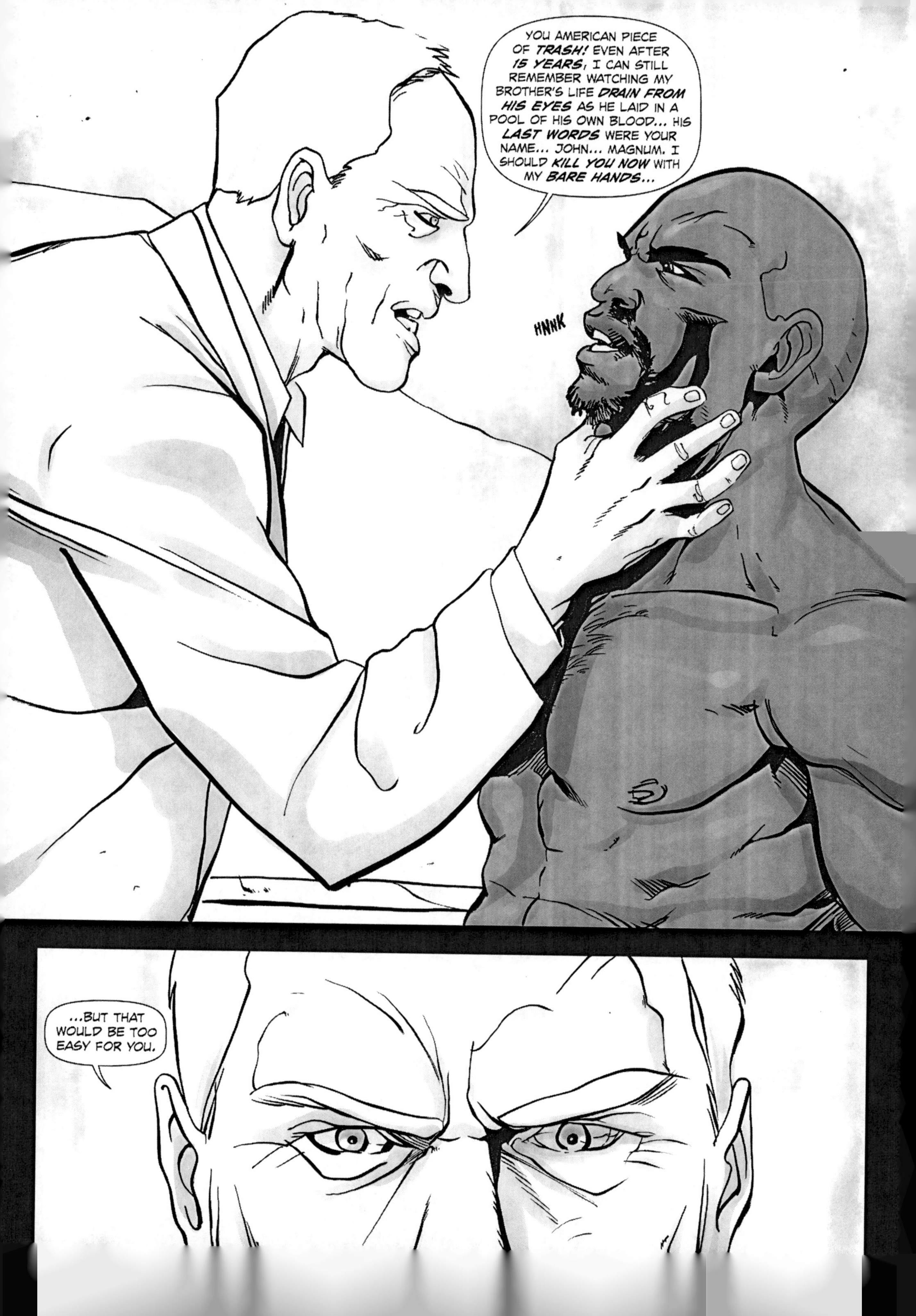
YOU AMERICAN PIECE OF TRASH! EVEN AFTER 15 YEARS, I CAN STILL REMEMBER WATCHING MY BROTHER'S LIFE DRAIN FROM HIS EYES AS HE LAID IN A POOL OF HIS OWN BLOOD... HIS LAST WORDS WERE YOUR NAME... JOHN... MAGNUM. I SHOULD KILL YOU NOW WITH MY BARE HANDS...
HNNK
...BUT THAT WOULD BE TOO EASY FOR YOU.

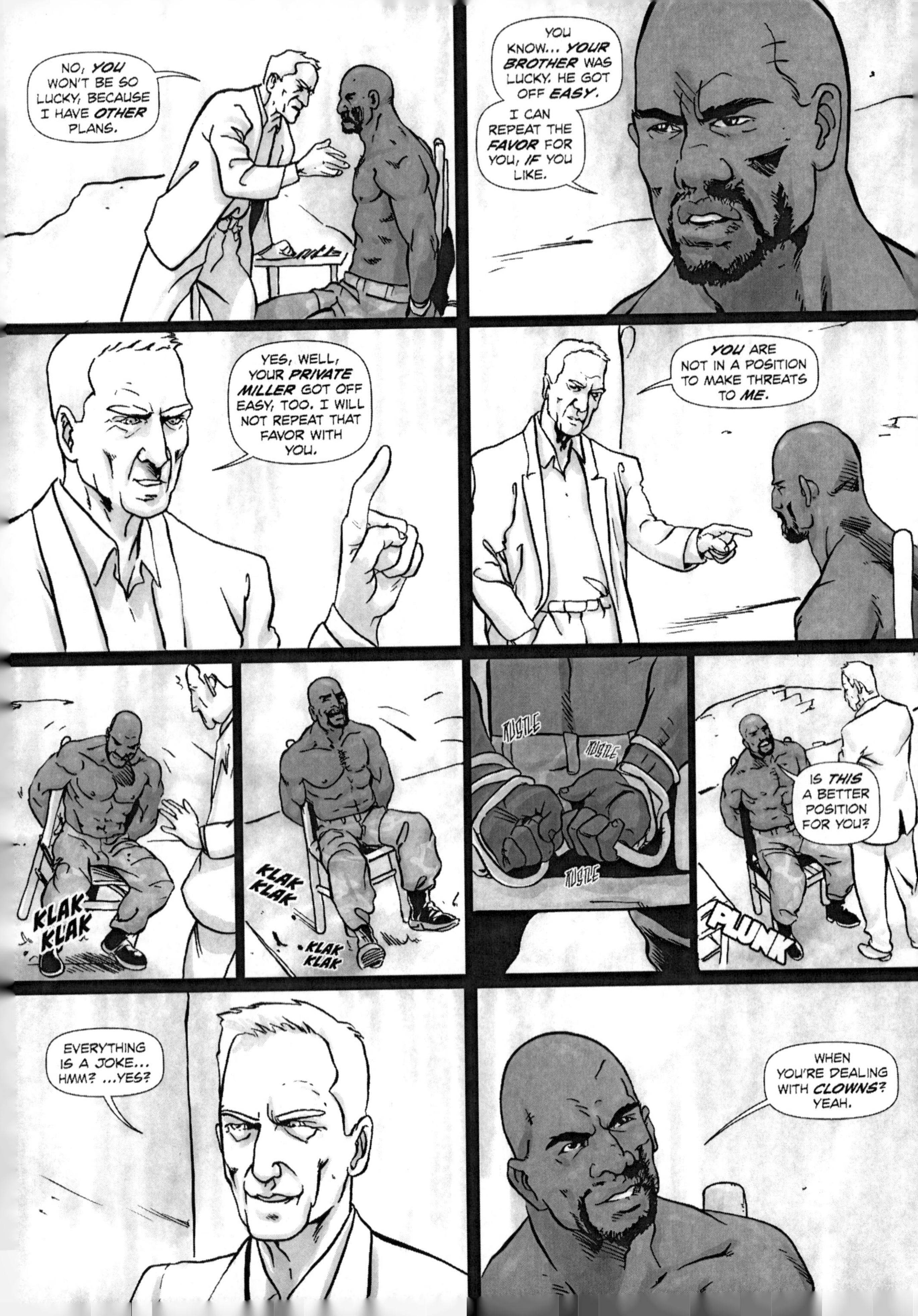
NO, YOU WON'T BE SO LUCKY, BECAUSE I HAVE OTHER PLANS.
YOU KNOW... YOUR BROTHER WAS LUCKY. HE GOT OFF EASY.
I CAN REPEAT THE FAVOR FOR YOU, IF YOU LIKE.
YES, WELL, YOUR PRIVATE MILLER GOT OFF EASY, TOO. I WILL NOT REPEAT THAT FAVOR WITH YOU.
YOU ARE NOT IN A POSITION TO MAKE THREATS TO ME.
KLAK KLAK
KLAK KLAK
KLAK KLAK
IS THIS A BETTER POSITION FOR YOU?
PLUNK
EVERYTHING IS A JOKE... HMM? ...YES?
WHEN YOU'RE DEALING WITH CLOWNS? YEAH.

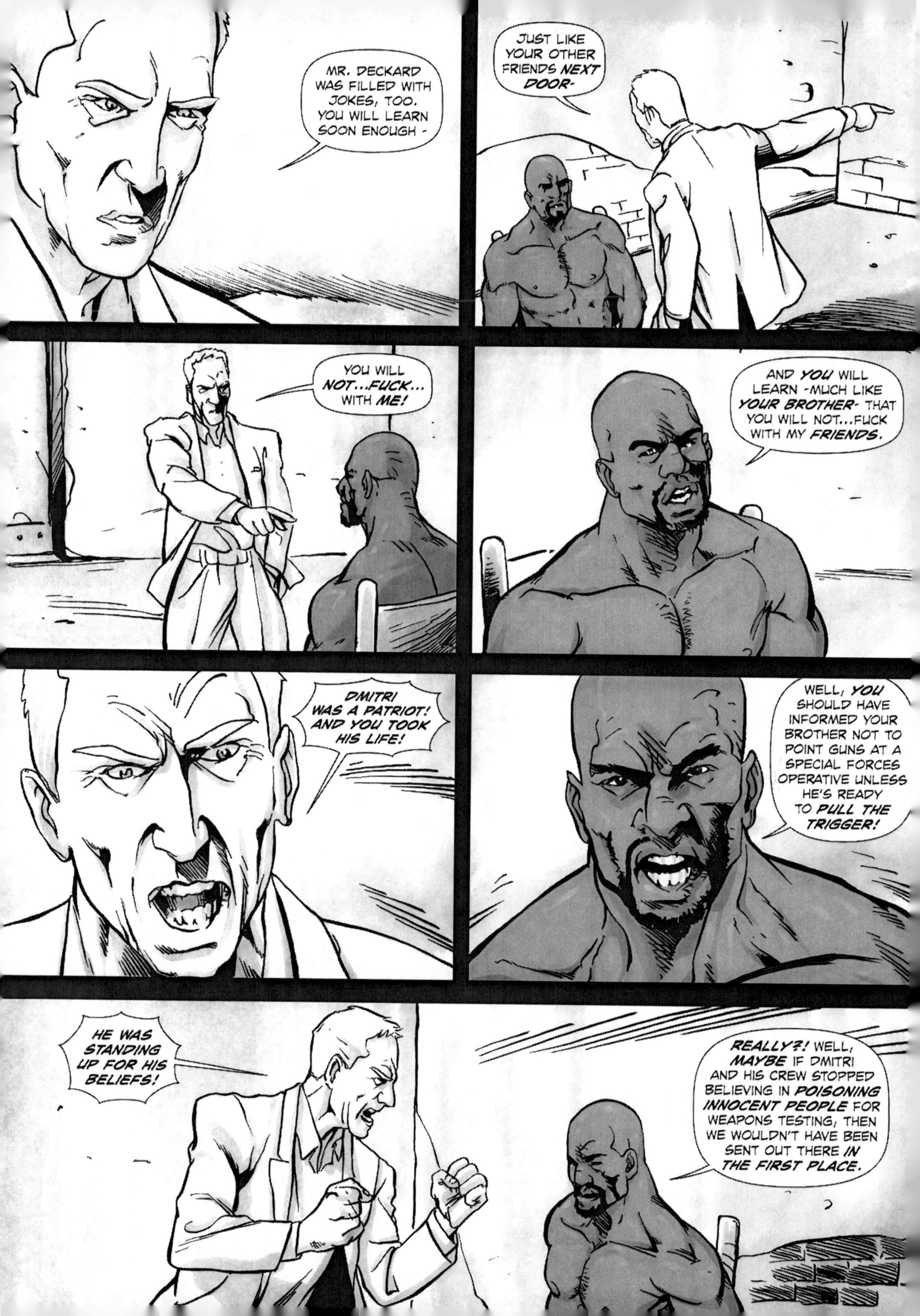
MR. DECKARD WAS FILLED WITH JOKES, TOO. YOU WILL LEARN SOON ENOUGH -
JUST LIKE YOUR OTHER FRIENDS NEXT DOOR-
YOU WILL NOT...FUCK... WITH ME!
AND YOU WILL LEARN -MUCH LIKE YOUR BROTHER- THAT YOU WILL NOT...FUCK WITH MY FRIENDS.
DMITRI WAS A PATRIOT! AND YOU TOOK HIS LIFE!
WELL, YOU SHOULD HAVE INFORMED YOUR BROTHER NOT TO POINT GUNS AT A SPECIAL FORCES OPERATIVE UNLESS HE'S READY TO PULL THE TRIGGER!
HE WAS STANDING UP FOR HIS BELIEFS!
REALLY?! WELL, MAYBE IF DMITRI AND HIS CREW STOPPED BELIEVING IN POISONING INNOCENT PEOPLE FOR WEAPONS TESTING, THEN WE WOULDN'T HAVE BEEN SENT OUT THERE IN THE FIRST PLACE.

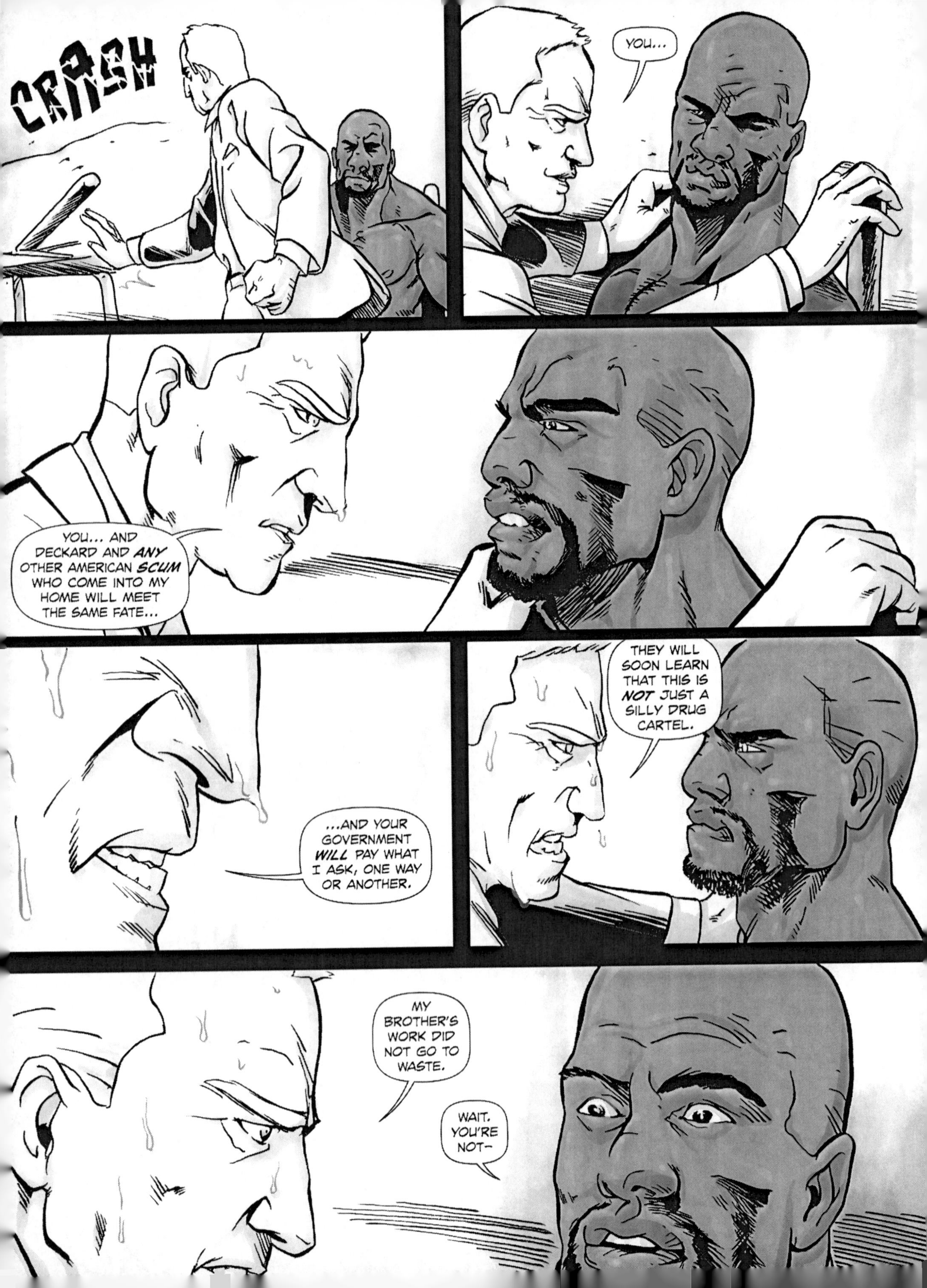
CRASH
YOU...
YOU... AND DECKARD AND ANY OTHER AMERICAN SCUM WHO COME INTO MY HOME WILL MEET THE SAME FATE...
...AND YOUR GOVERNMENT WILL PAY WHAT I ASK, ONE WAY OR ANOTHER.
THEY WILL SOON LEARN THAT THIS IS NOT JUST A SILLY DRUG CARTEL.
MY BROTHER'S WORK DID NOT GO TO WASTE.
WAIT. YOU'RE NOT-

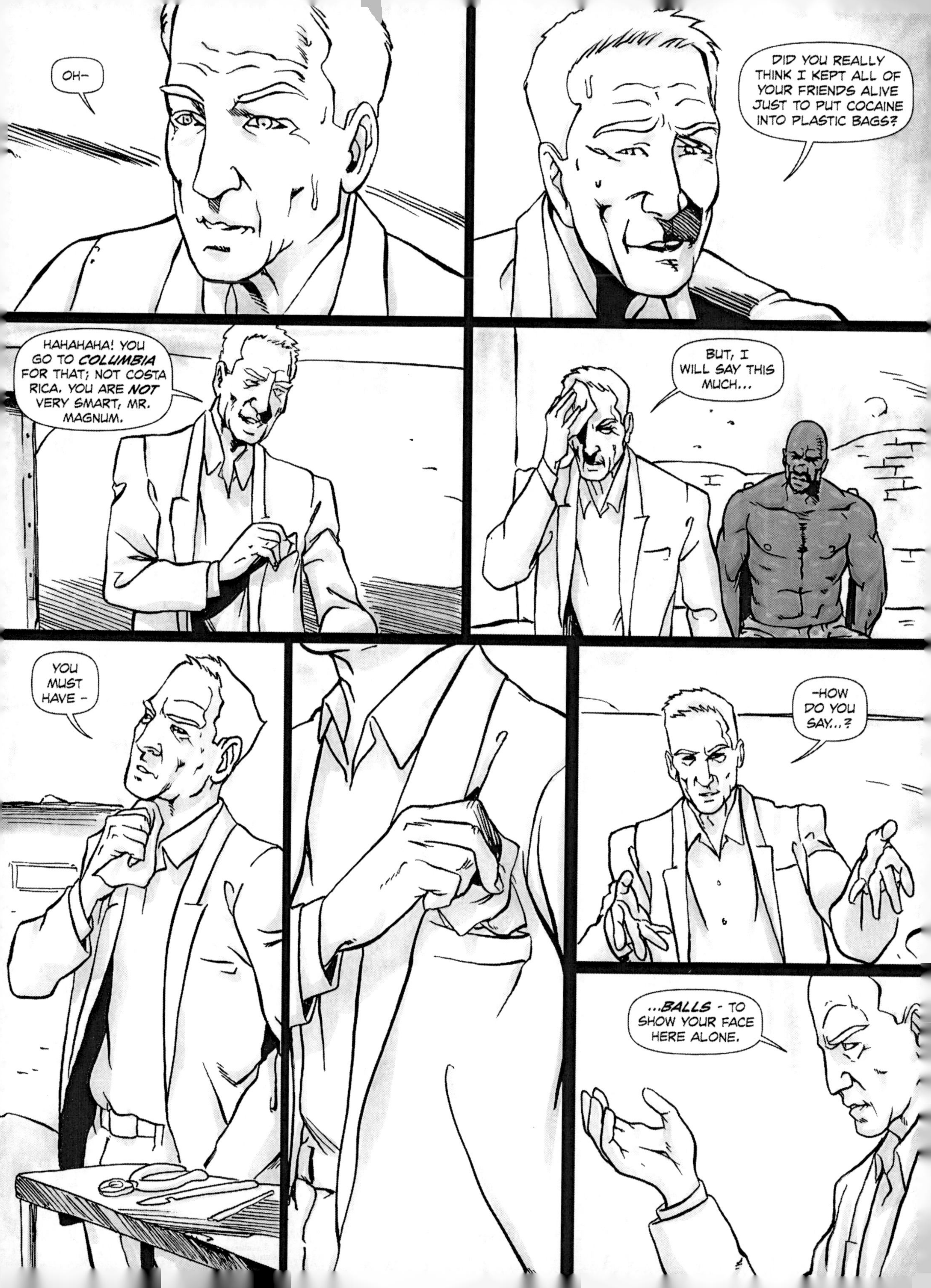
OH-
DID YOU REALLY THINK I KEPT ALL OF YOUR FRIENDS ALIVE JUST TO PUT COCAINE INTO PLASTIC BAGS?
HAHAHAHA! YOU GO TO COLUMBIA FOR THAT; NOT COSTA RICA. YOU ARE NOT VERY SMART, MR. MAGNUM.
BUT, I WILL SAY THIS MUCH...
YOU MUST HAVE -
-HOW DO YOU SAY...?
...BALLS - TO SHOW YOUR FACE HERE ALONE.

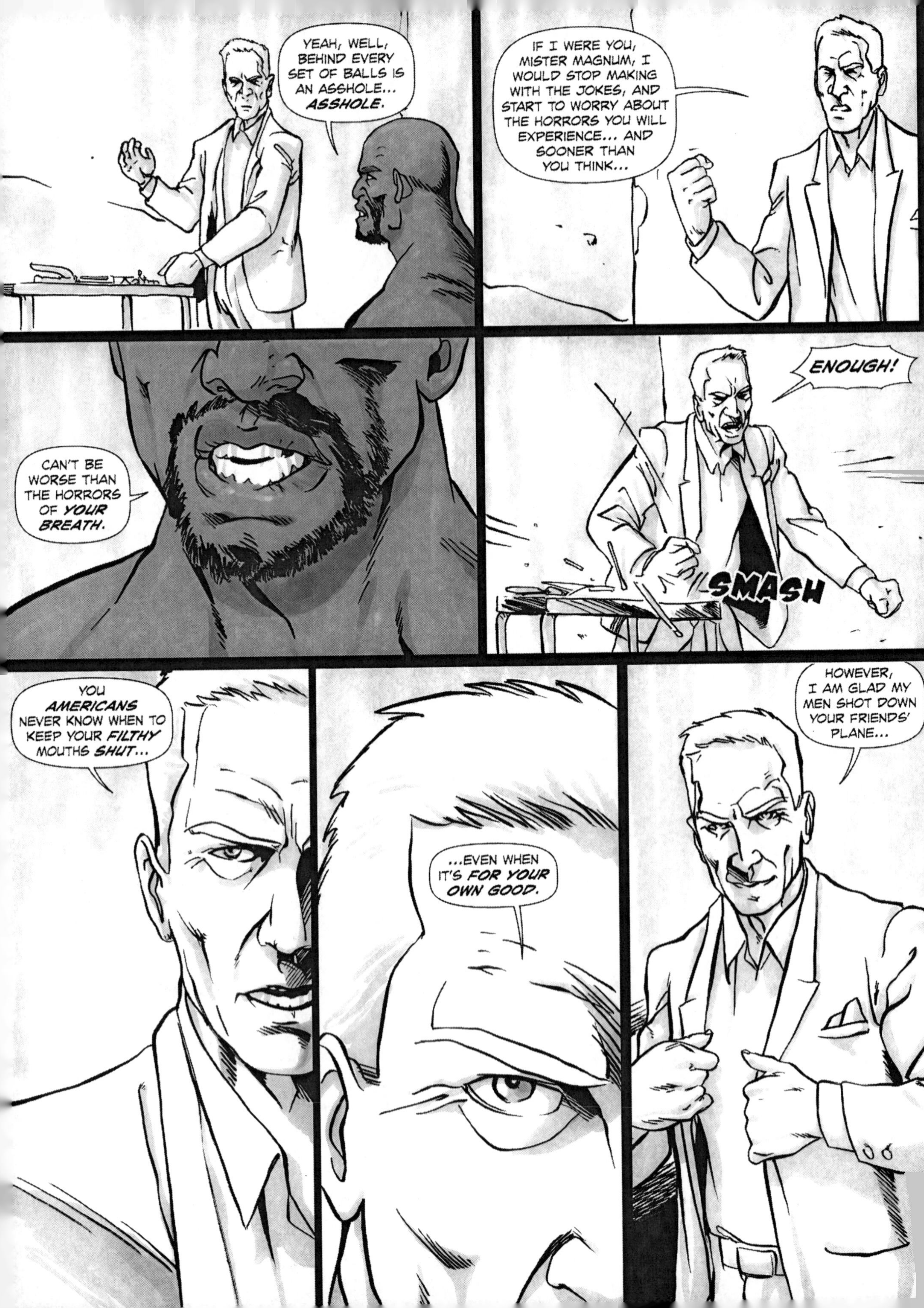
YEAH, WELL, BEHIND EVERY SET OF BALLS IS AN ASSHOLE... ***ASSHOLE***.
IF I WERE YOU, MISTER MAGNUM, I WOULD STOP MAKING WITH THE JOKES, AND START TO WORRY ABOUT THE HORRORS YOU WILL EXPERIENCE... AND SOONER THAN YOU THINK...
CAN'T BE WORSE THAN THE HORRORS OF ***YOUR BREATH***.
ENOUGH!
SMASH
YOU ***AMERICANS*** NEVER KNOW WHEN TO KEEP YOUR ***FILTHY*** MOUTHS ***SHUT***...
...EVEN WHEN IT'S ***FOR YOUR OWN GOOD***.
HOWEVER, I AM GLAD MY MEN SHOT DOWN YOUR FRIENDS' PLANE...

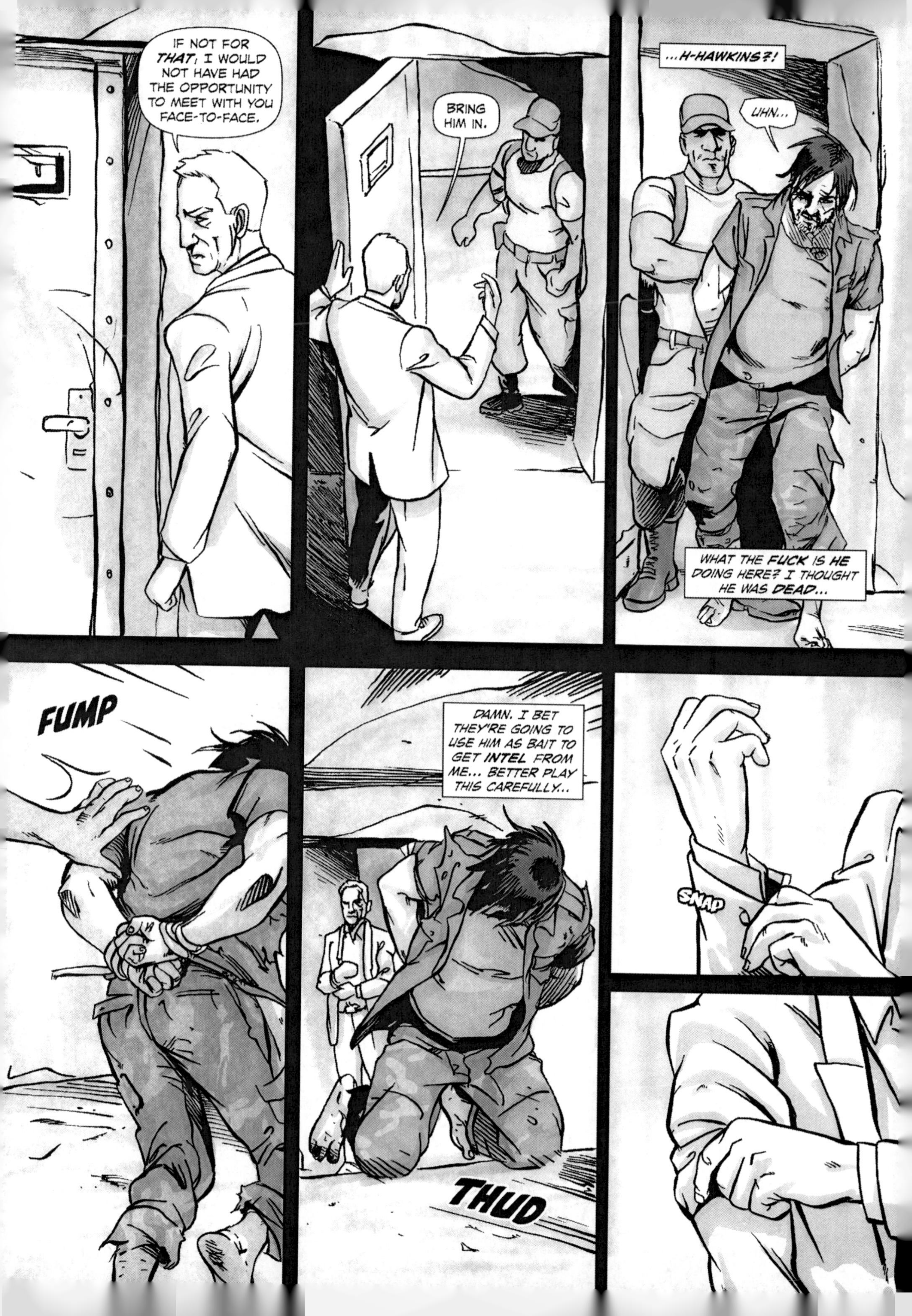
IF NOT FOR THAT, I WOULD NOT HAVE HAD THE OPPORTUNITY TO MEET WITH YOU FACE-TO-FACE.
BRING HIM IN.
...H-HAWKINS?!
UHN...
WHAT THE FUCK IS HE DOING HERE? I THOUGHT HE WAS DEAD...
FUMP
DAMN. I BET THEY'RE GOING TO USE HIM AS BAIT TO GET INTEL FROM ME... BETTER PLAY THIS CAREFULLY...
THUD
SNAP

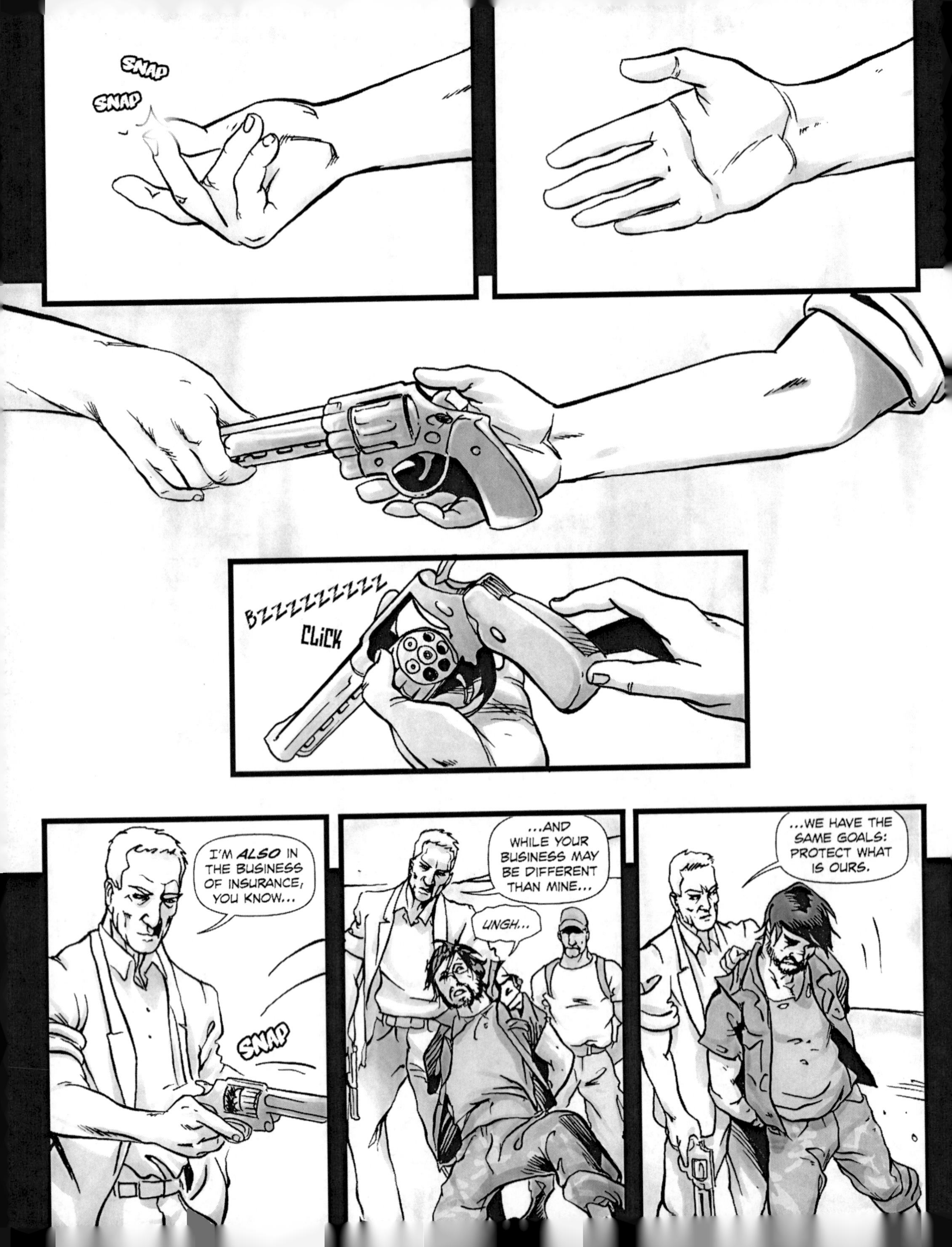
SNAP
SNAP
BZZZZZZZZZZ
CLICK
I'M *ALSO* IN THE BUSINESS OF INSURANCE, YOU KNOW...
SNAP
...AND WHILE YOUR BUSINESS MAY BE DIFFERENT THAN MINE...
UNGH...
...WE HAVE THE SAME GOALS: PROTECT WHAT IS OURS.

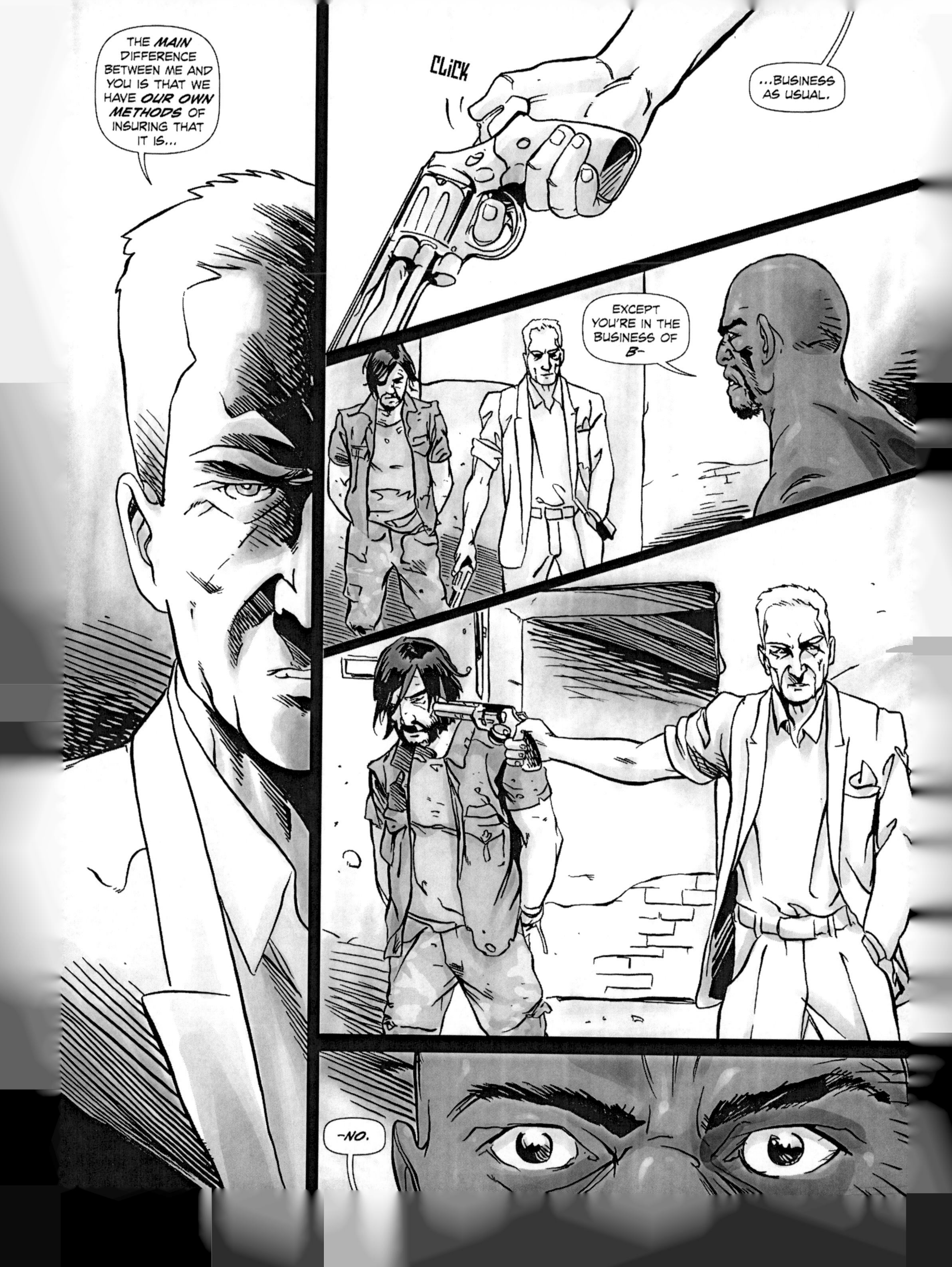
THE MAIN DIFFERENCE BETWEEN ME AND YOU IS THAT WE HAVE OUR OWN METHODS OF INSURING THAT IT IS...
CLICK
...BUSINESS AS USUAL.
EXCEPT YOU'RE IN THE BUSINESS OF B-
-NO.

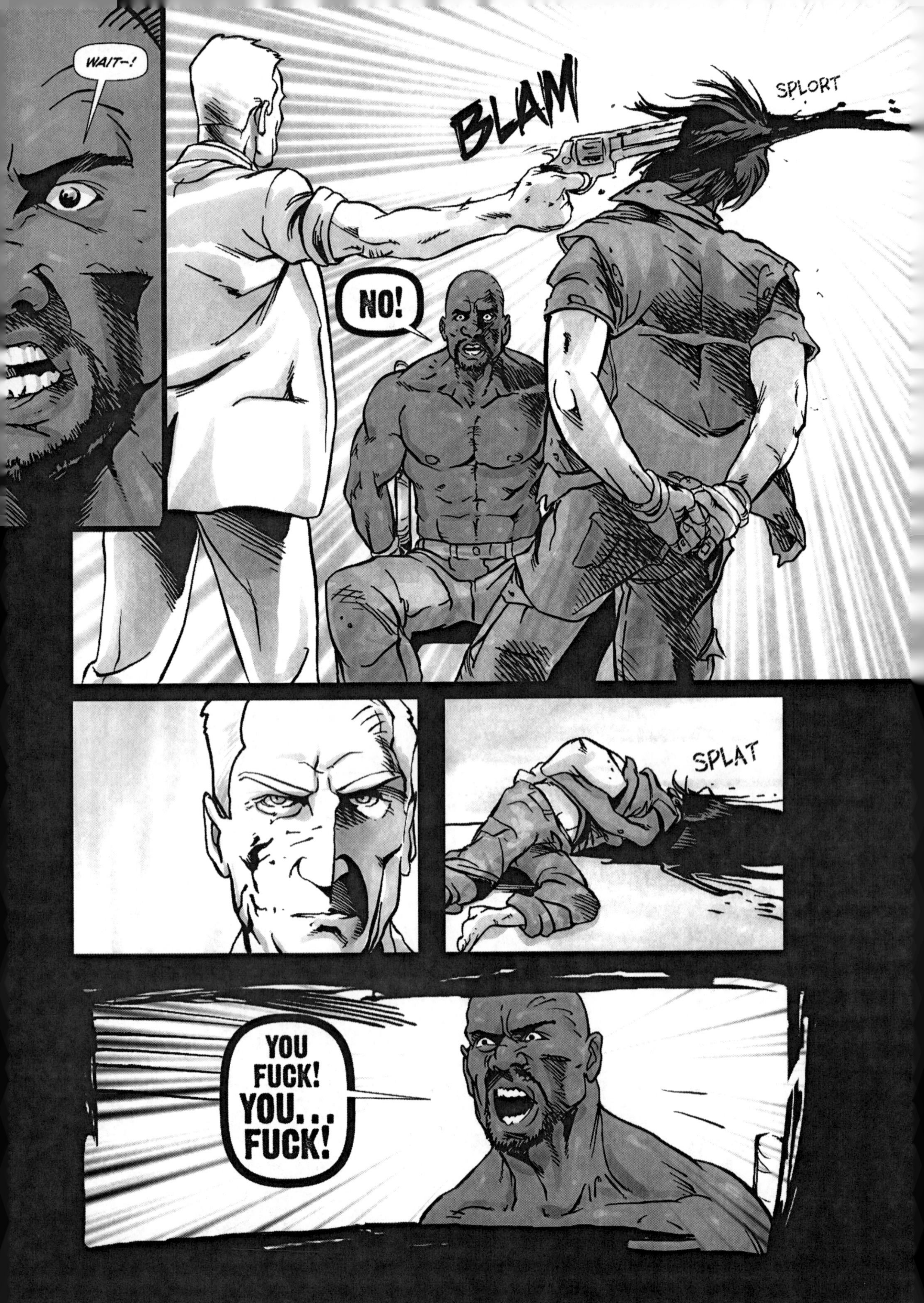
WAIT-!
BLAM
SPLORT
NO!
SPLAT
YOU FUCK! YOU... FUCK!

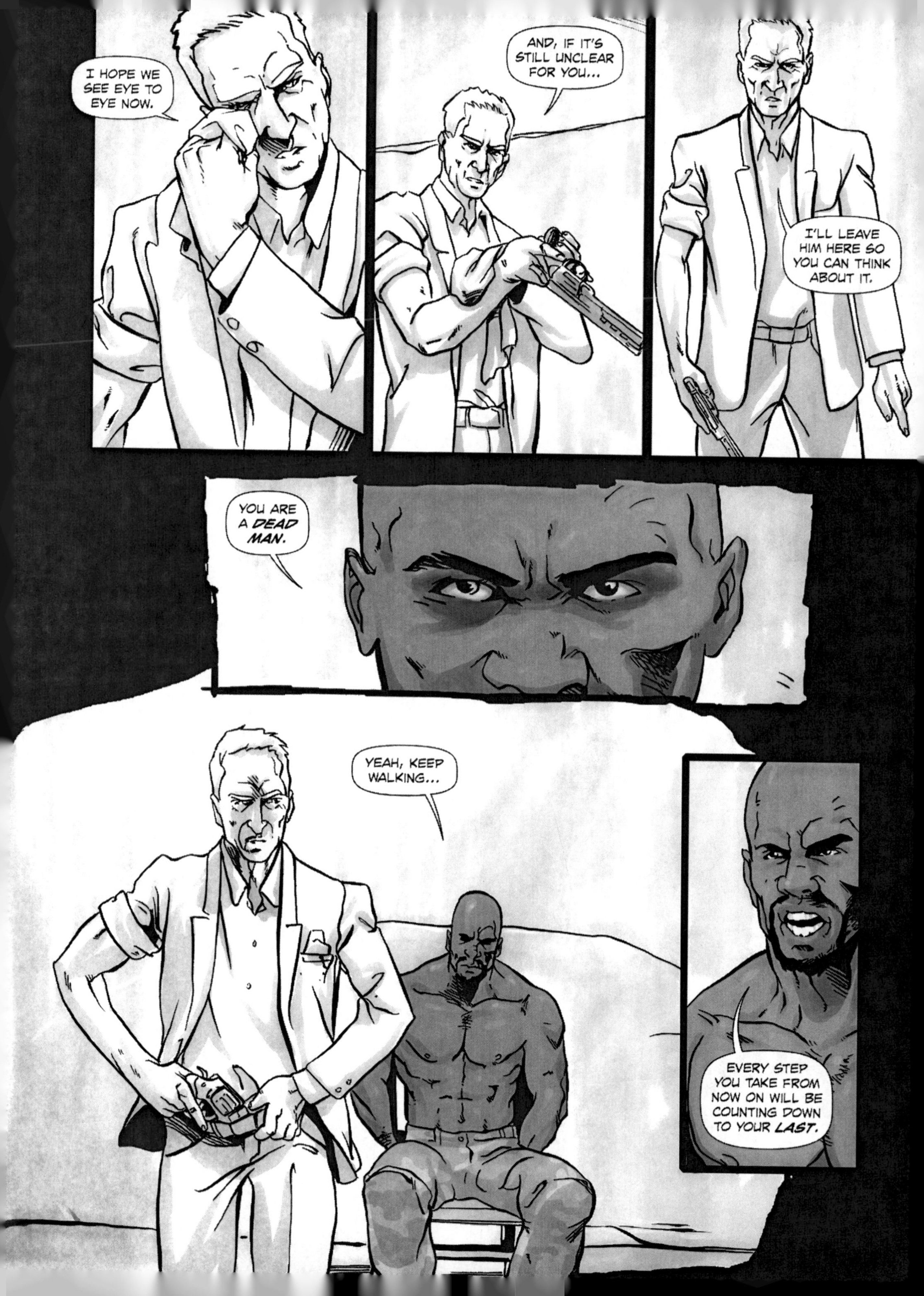
I HOPE WE SEE EYE TO EYE NOW.
AND, IF IT'S STILL UNCLEAR FOR YOU...
I'LL LEAVE HIM HERE SO YOU CAN THINK ABOUT IT.
YOU ARE A *DEAD MAN*.
YEAH, KEEP WALKING...
EVERY STEP YOU TAKE FROM NOW ON WILL BE COUNTING DOWN TO YOUR *LAST*.

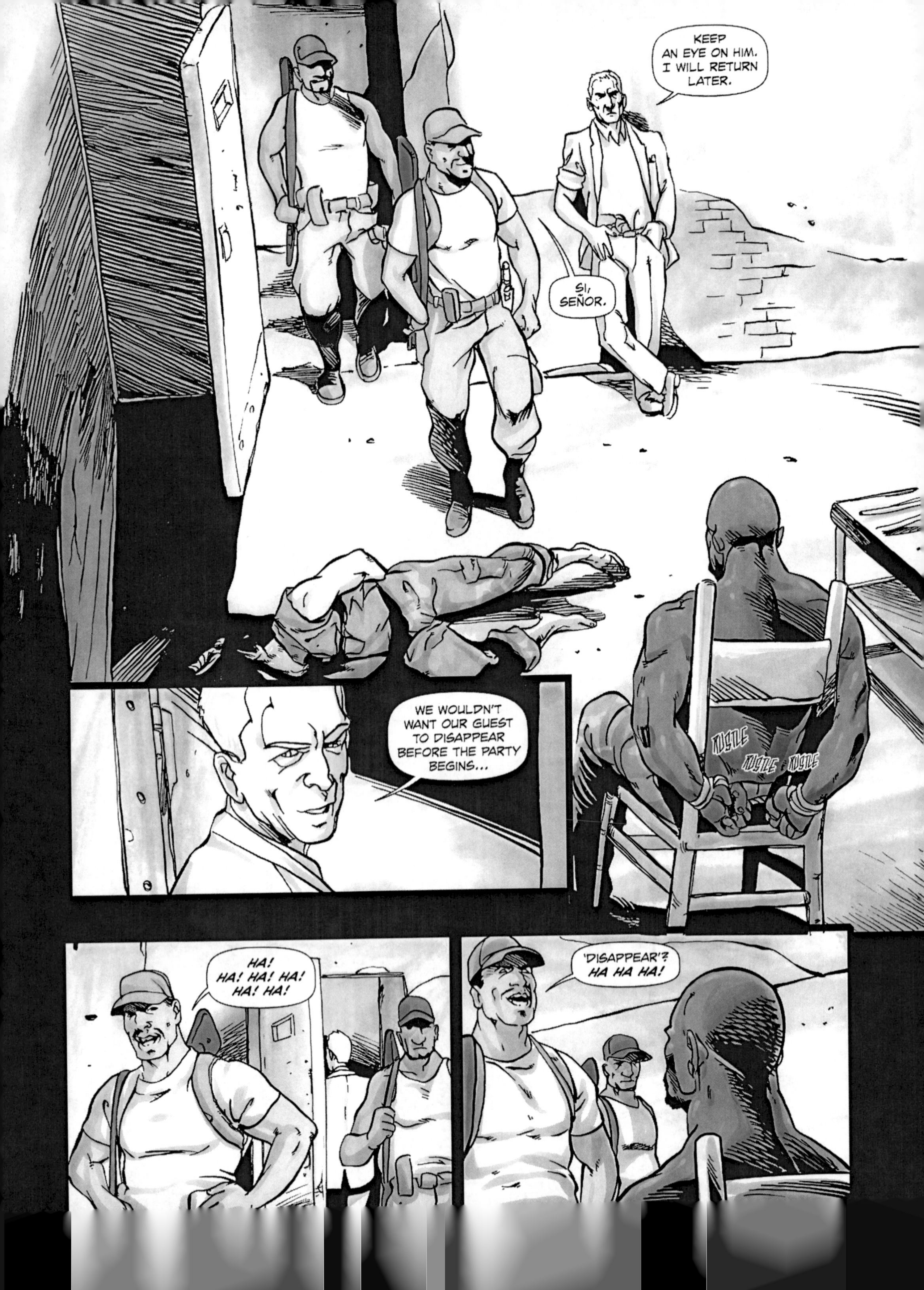
KEEP AN EYE ON HIM. I WILL RETURN LATER.
SI, SEÑOR.
WE WOULDN'T WANT OUR GUEST TO DISAPPEAR BEFORE THE PARTY BEGINS...
RUSTLE
RUSTLE
RUSTLE
HA! HA! HA! HA! HA! HA!
'DISAPPEAR'? HA HA HA!

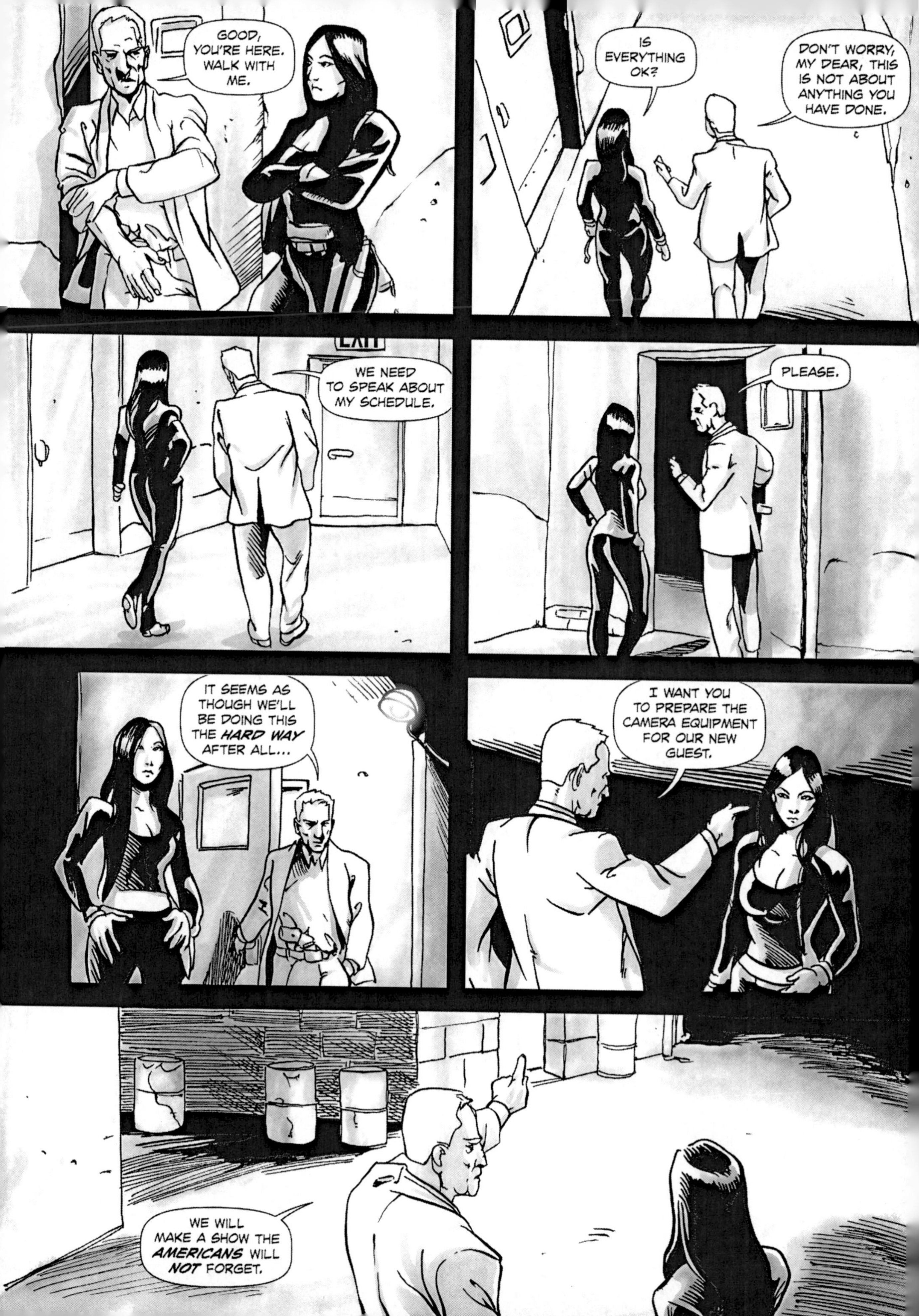
GOOD, YOU'RE HERE. WALK WITH ME.
IS EVERYTHING OK?
DON'T WORRY, MY DEAR, THIS IS NOT ABOUT ANYTHING YOU HAVE DONE.
EXIT
WE NEED TO SPEAK ABOUT MY SCHEDULE.
PLEASE.
IT SEEMS AS THOUGH WE'LL BE DOING THIS THE *HARD WAY* AFTER ALL...
I WANT YOU TO PREPARE THE CAMERA EQUIPMENT FOR OUR NEW GUEST.
WE WILL MAKE A SHOW THE *AMERICANS* WILL *NOT* FORGET.

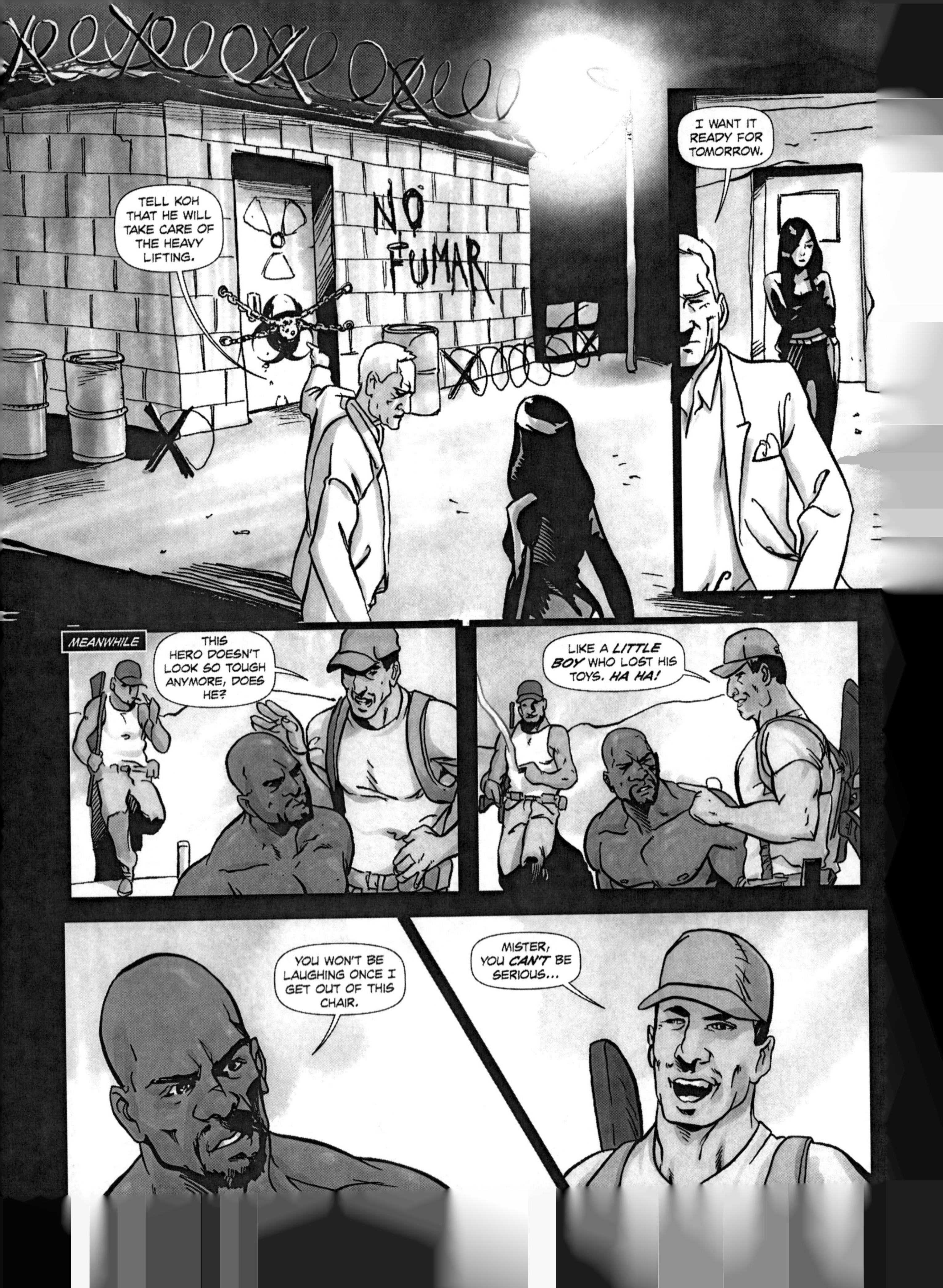
NO FUMAR
TELL KOH THAT HE WILL TAKE CARE OF THE HEAVY LIFTING.
I WANT IT READY FOR TOMORROW.
MEANWHILE
THIS HERO DOESN'T LOOK SO TOUGH ANYMORE, DOES HE?
LIKE A *LITTLE BOY* WHO LOST HIS TOYS. *HA HA!*
YOU WON'T BE LAUGHING ONCE I GET OUT OF THIS CHAIR.
MISTER, YOU *CAN'T* BE SERIOUS...

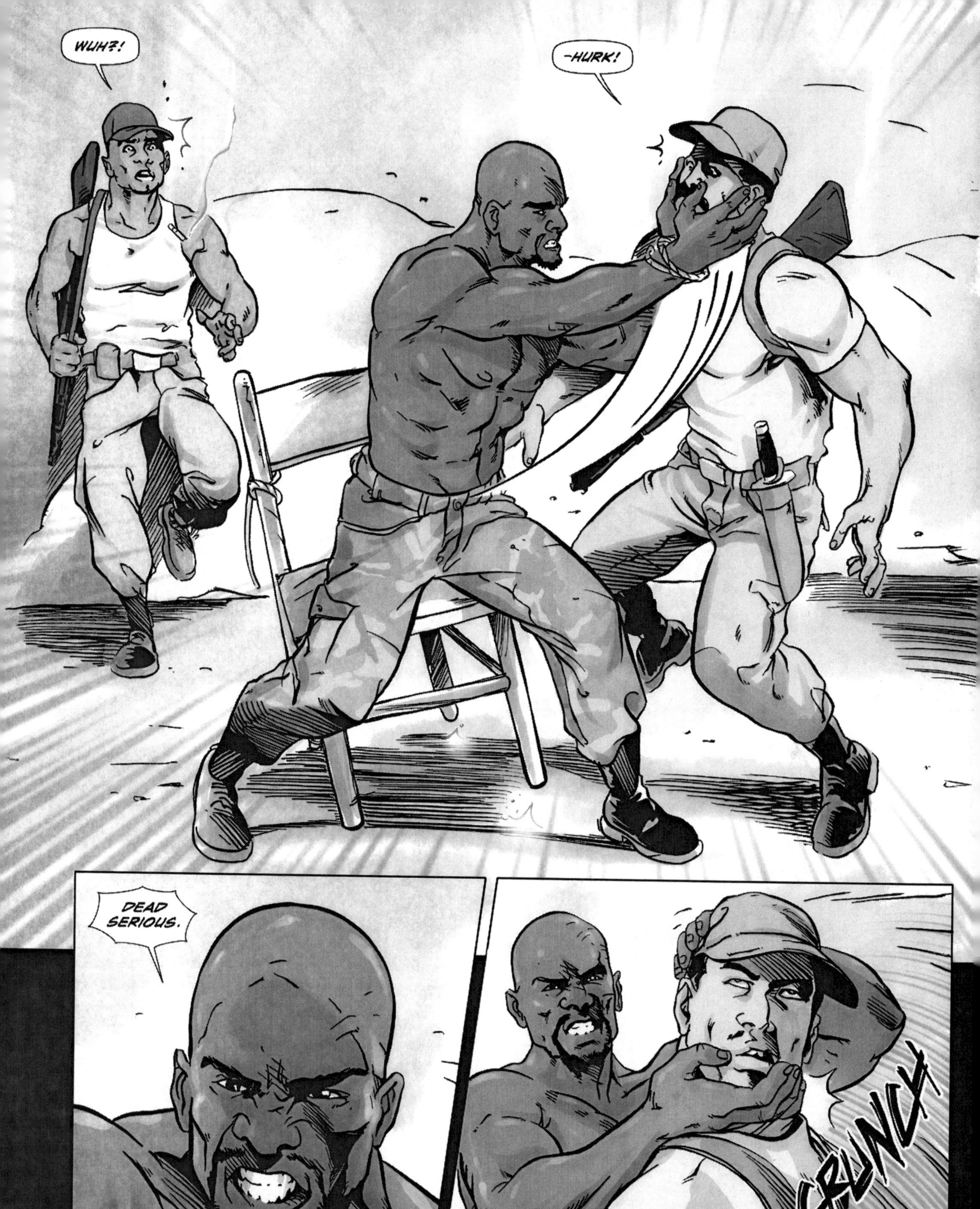
WUH?!
-HURK!
DEAD SERIOUS.
CRUNCH

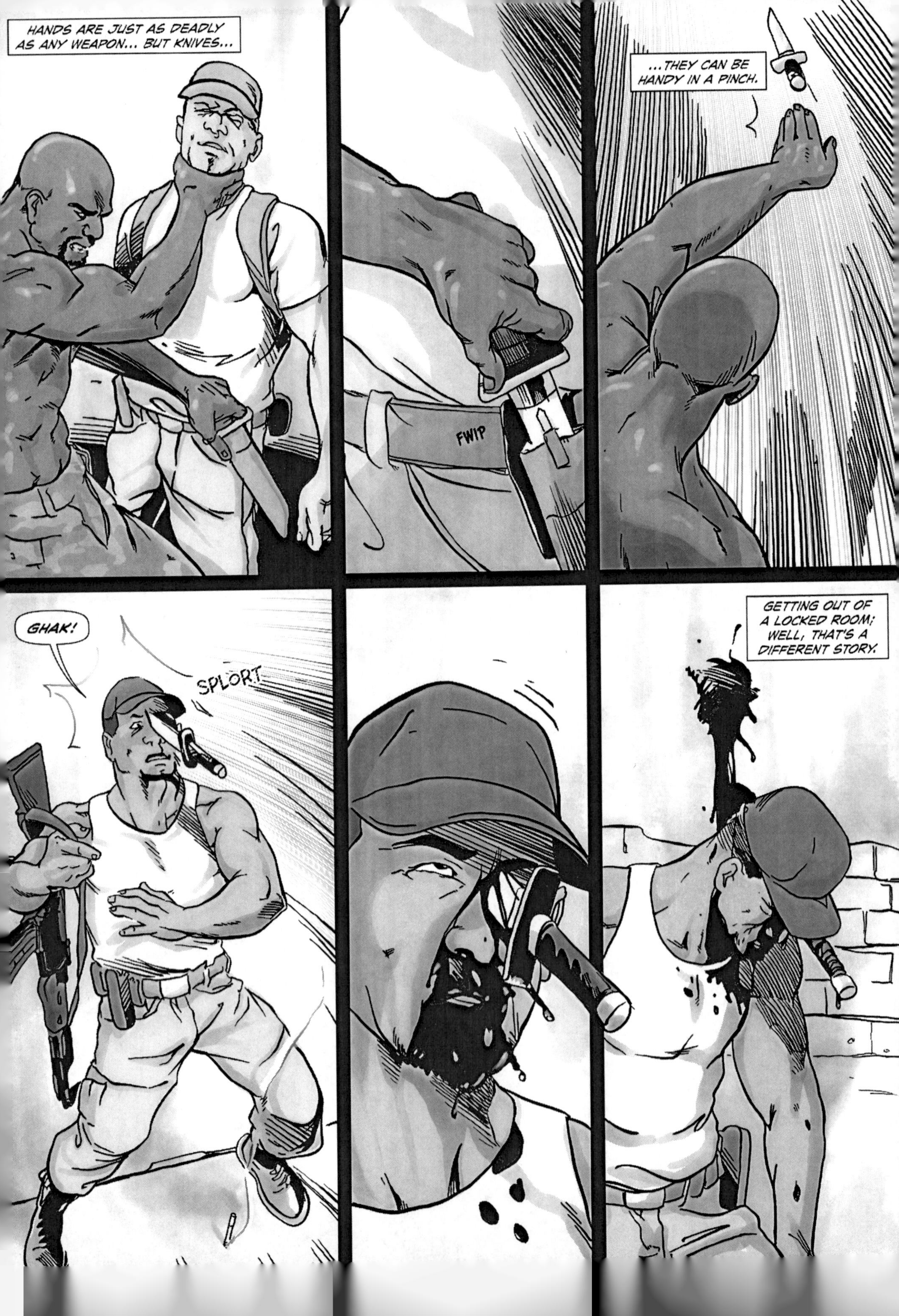
HANDS ARE JUST AS DEADLY AS ANY WEAPON... BUT KNIVES...
FWIP
...THEY CAN BE HANDY IN A PINCH.
GHAK!
SPLORT
GETTING OUT OF A LOCKED ROOM; WELL, THAT'S A DIFFERENT STORY.

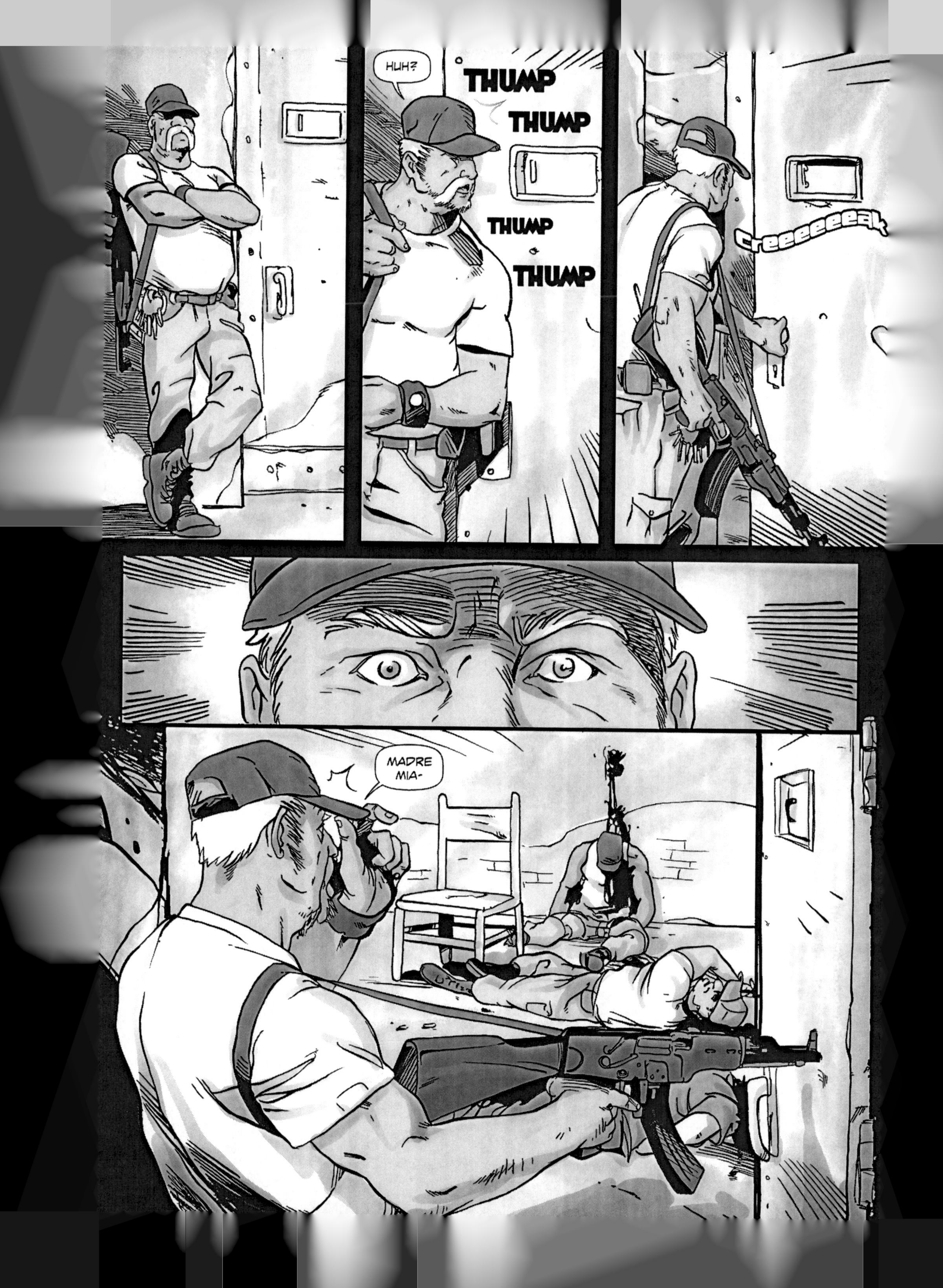
HUH?
THUMP
THUMP
THUMP
THUMP
creeeeeeak
MADRE MIA-

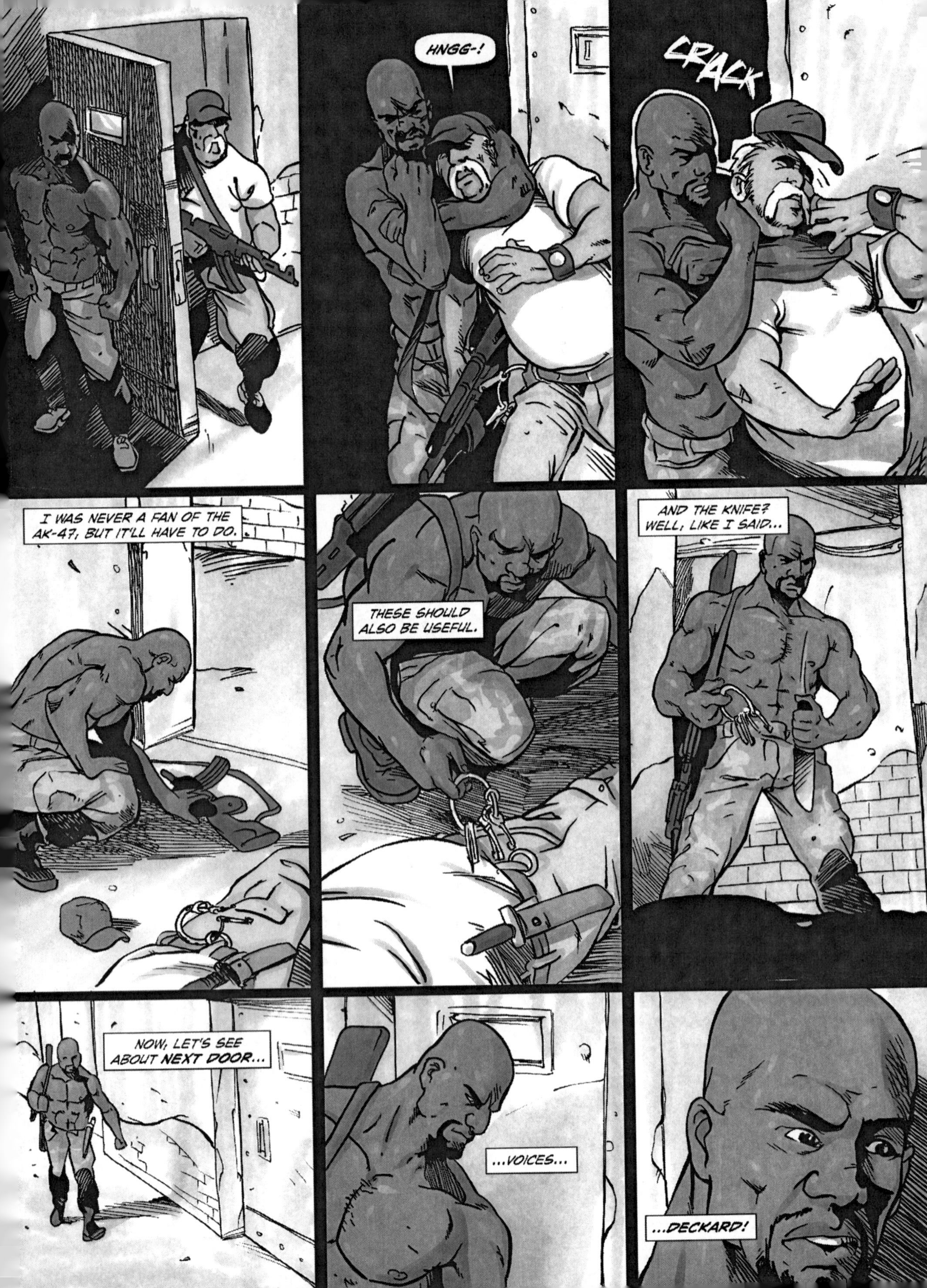
HNGG-!
CRACK
I WAS NEVER A FAN OF THE AK-47, BUT IT'LL HAVE TO DO.
THESE SHOULD ALSO BE USEFUL.
AND THE KNIFE? WELL, LIKE I SAID...
NOW, LET'S SEE ABOUT NEXT DOOR...
...VOICES...
...DECKARD!

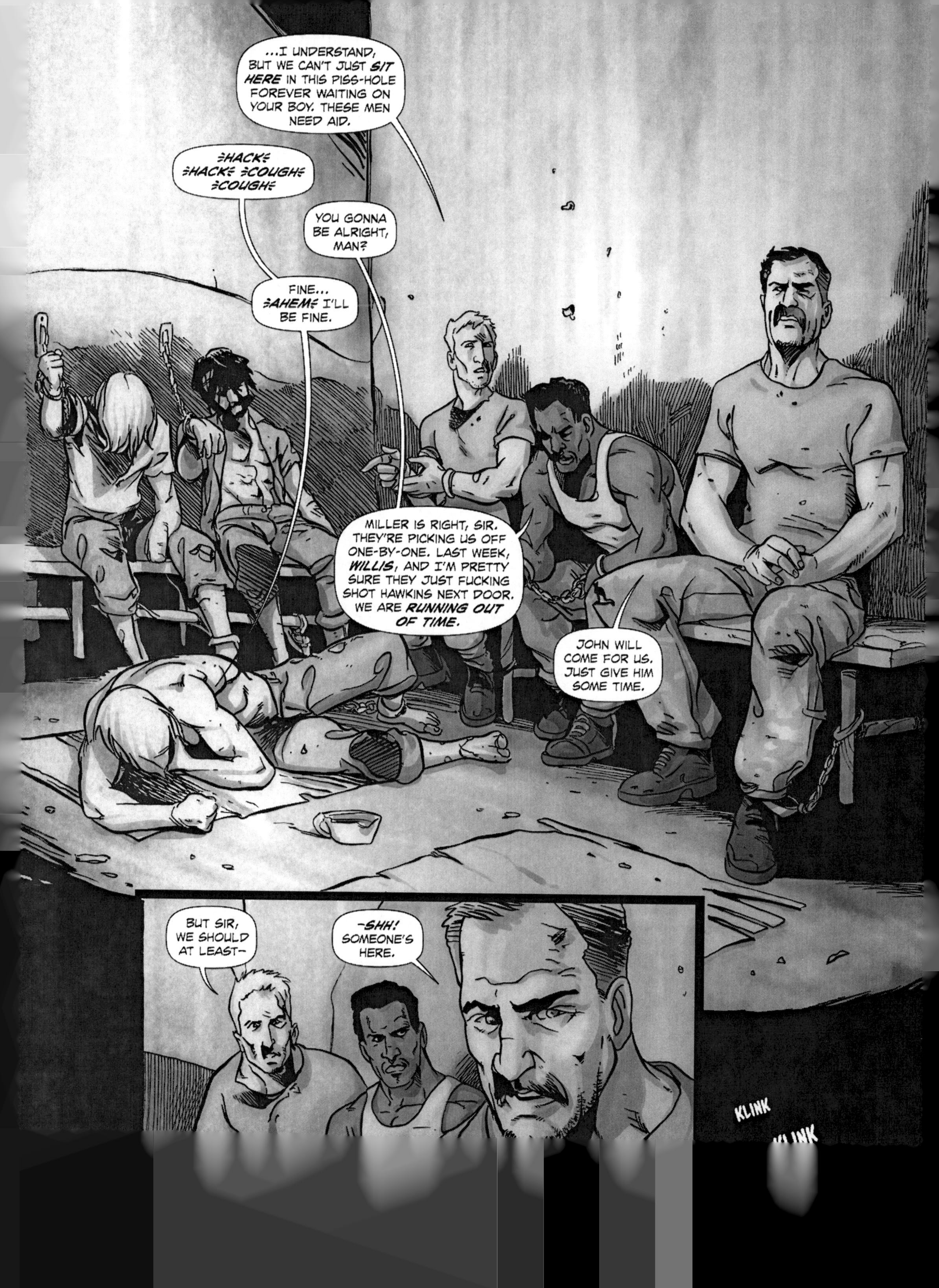
...I UNDERSTAND, BUT WE CAN'T JUST SIT HERE IN THIS PISS-HOLE FOREVER WAITING ON YOUR BOY. THESE MEN NEED AID.
HACK HACK COUGH COUGH
YOU GONNA BE ALRIGHT, MAN?
FINE... AHEM I'LL BE FINE.
MILLER IS RIGHT, SIR. THEY'RE PICKING US OFF ONE-BY-ONE. LAST WEEK, WILLIS, AND I'M PRETTY SURE THEY JUST FUCKING SHOT HAWKINS NEXT DOOR. WE ARE RUNNING OUT OF TIME.
JOHN WILL COME FOR US. JUST GIVE HIM SOME TIME.
BUT SIR, WE SHOULD AT LEAST-
-SHH! SOMEONE'S HERE.
KLINK
KLINK

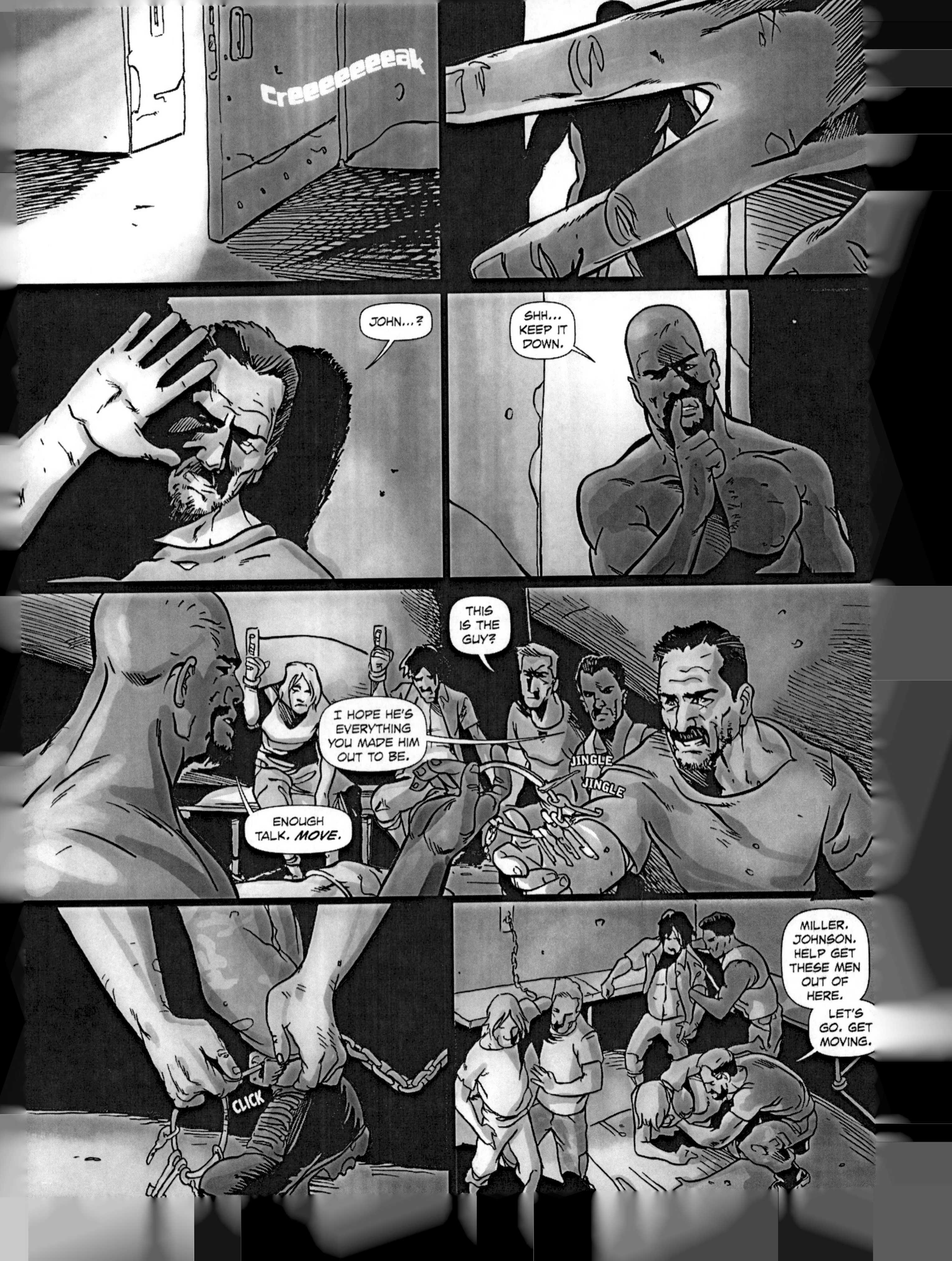
Creeeeeeeak
JOHN...?
SHH... KEEP IT DOWN.
THIS IS THE GUY?
I HOPE HE'S EVERYTHING YOU MADE HIM OUT TO BE.
JINGLE
JINGLE
ENOUGH TALK. MOVE.
CLICK
MILLER. JOHNSON. HELP GET THESE MEN OUT OF HERE.
LET'S GO. GET MOVING.

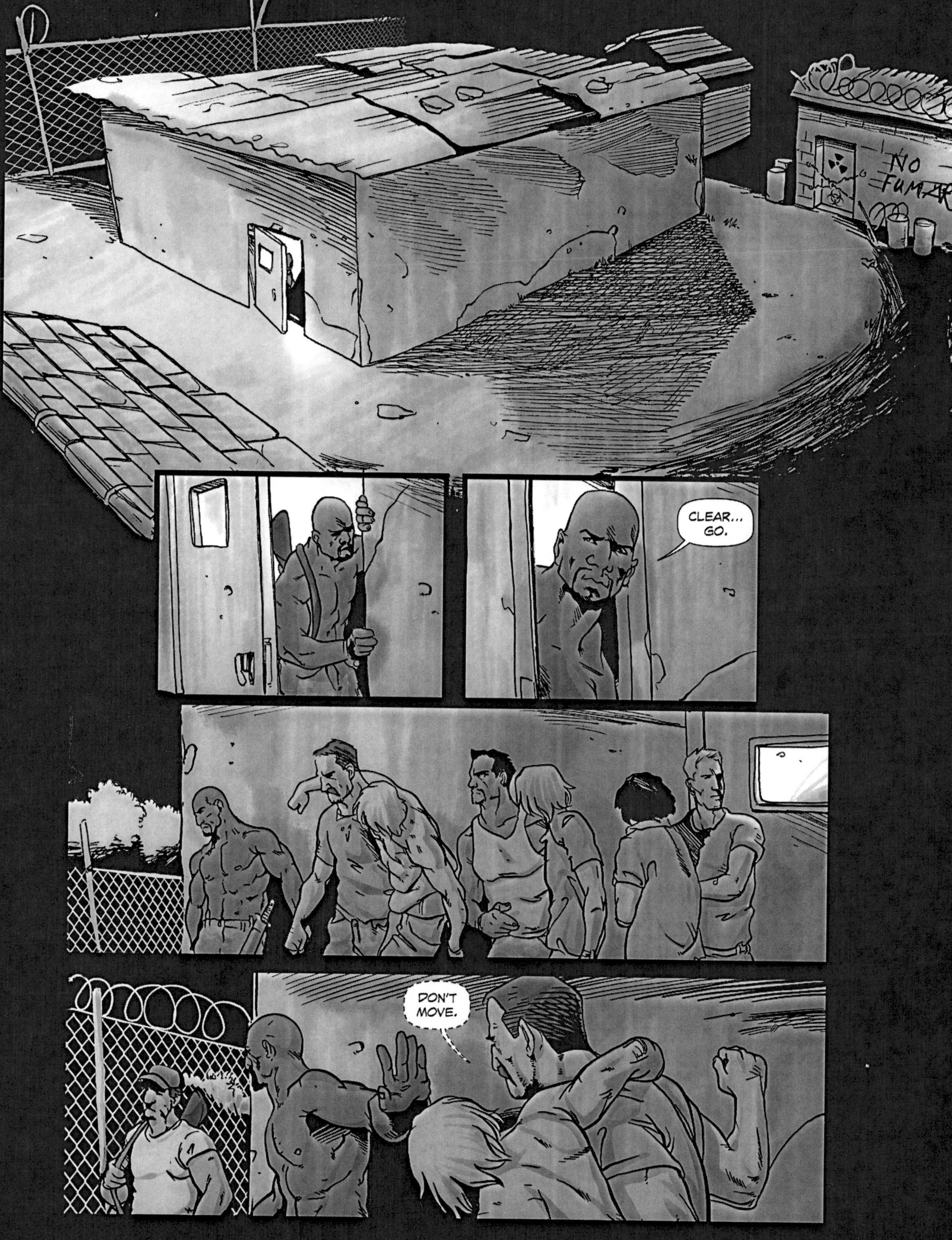
NO FUMAR
CLEAR... GO.
DON'T MOVE.

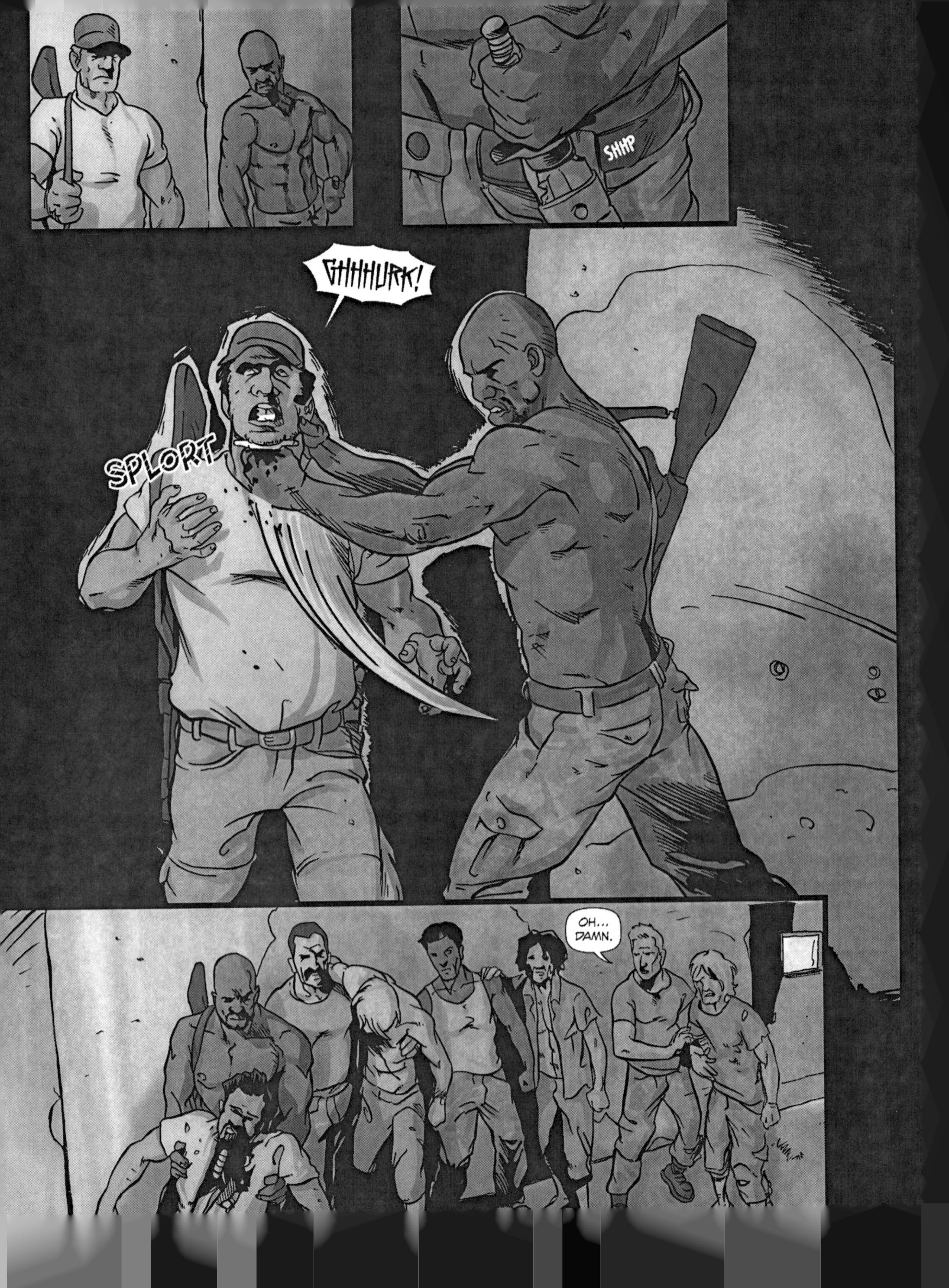
SHHP
GHHHURK!
SPLORT
OH... DAMN.

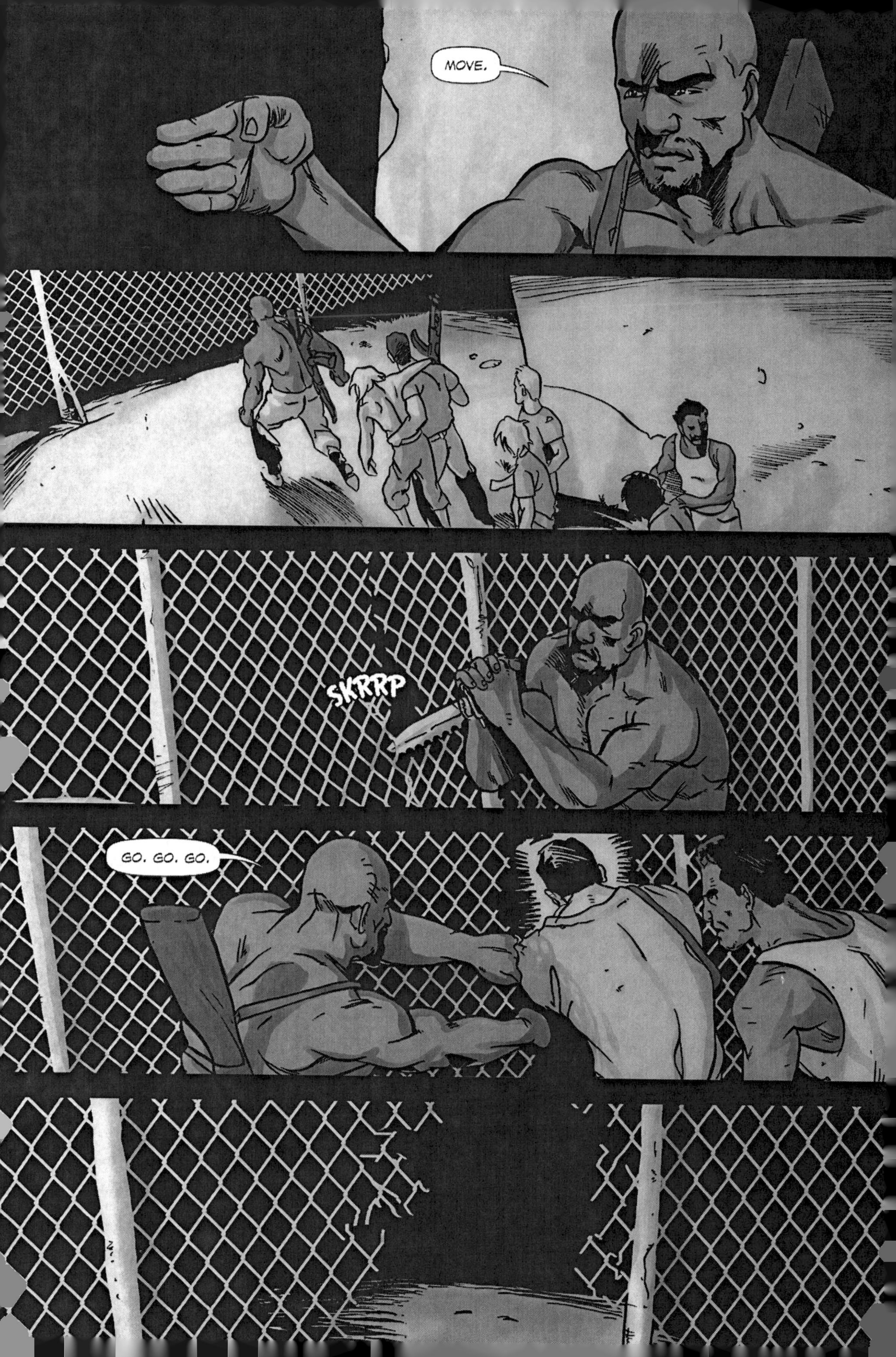
MOVE.
SKRRP
GO. GO. GO.

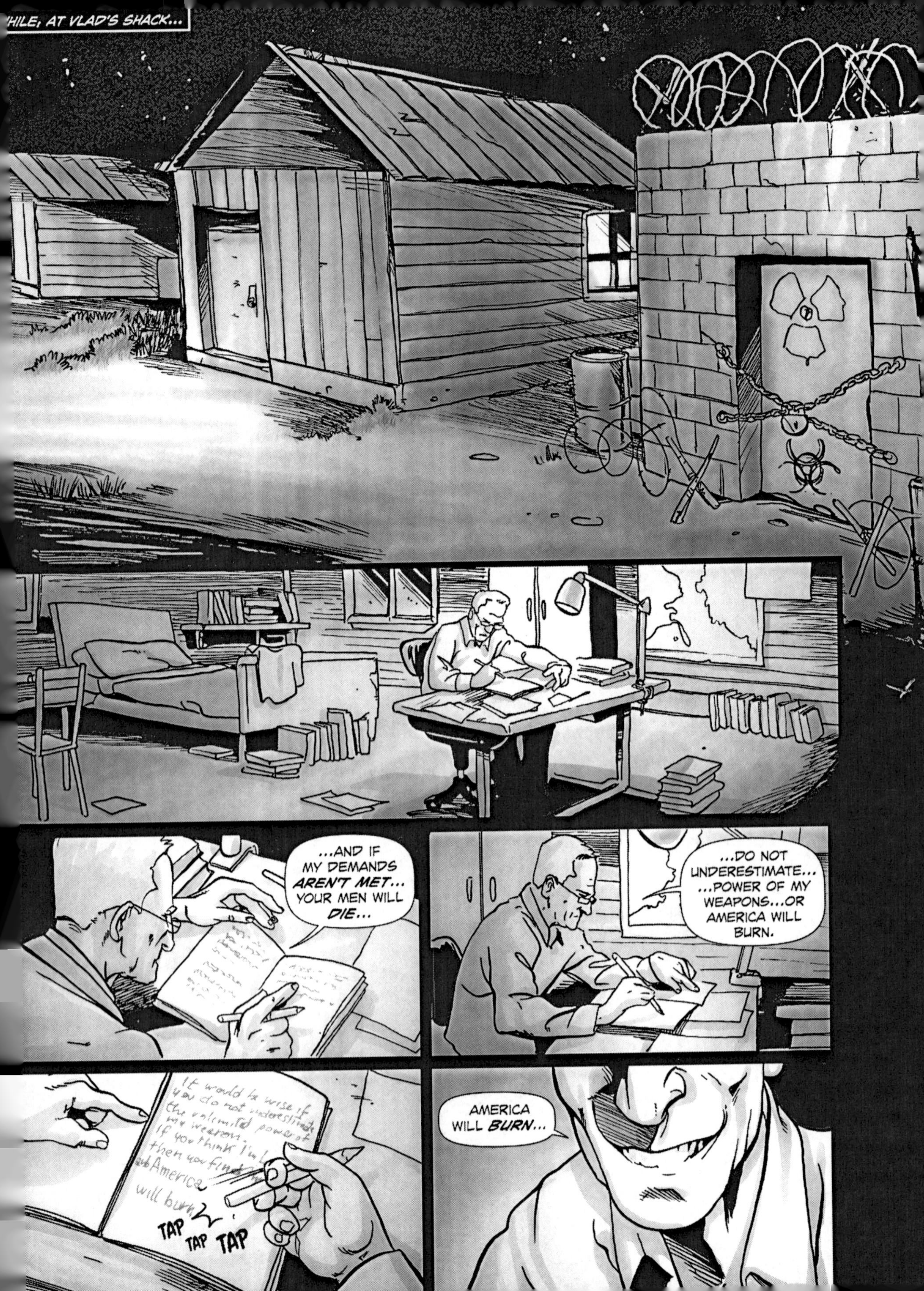
HILE, AT VLAD'S SHACK...
...AND IF MY DEMANDS AREN'T MET... YOUR MEN WILL DIE...
...DO NOT UNDERESTIMATE... ...POWER OF MY WEAPONS...OR AMERICA WILL BURN.
It would be wise if you do not underestimate the unlimited power of my weapon.
If you think I'm
then you find
America will burn
TAP TAP TAP
AMERICA WILL BURN...

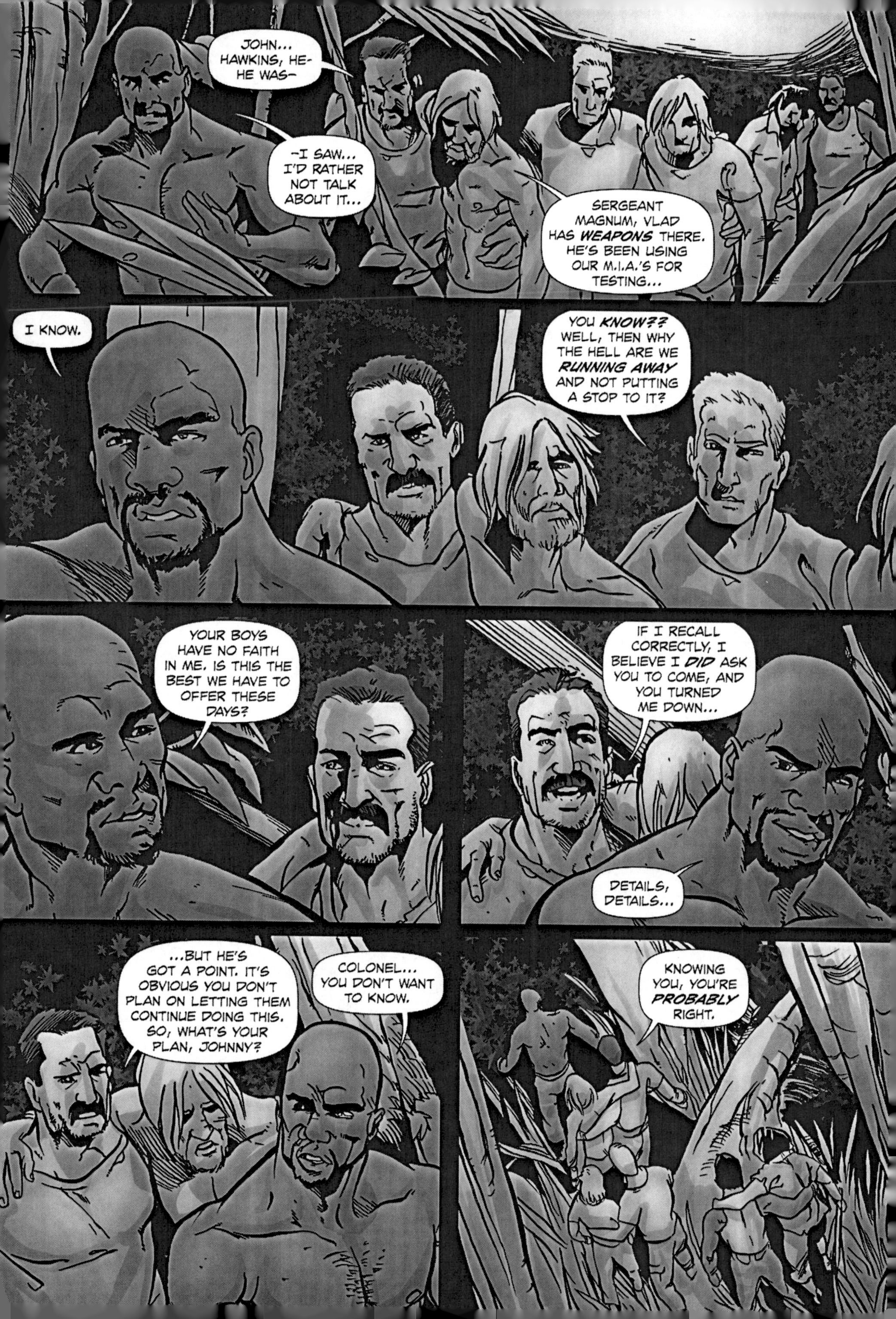
JOHN... HAWKINS, HE- HE WAS-
-I SAW... I'D RATHER NOT TALK ABOUT IT...
SERGEANT MAGNUM, VLAD HAS WEAPONS THERE. HE'S BEEN USING OUR M.I.A.'S FOR TESTING...
I KNOW.
YOU KNOW?? WELL, THEN WHY THE HELL ARE WE RUNNING AWAY AND NOT PUTTING A STOP TO IT?
YOUR BOYS HAVE NO FAITH IN ME. IS THIS THE BEST WE HAVE TO OFFER THESE DAYS?
IF I RECALL CORRECTLY, I BELIEVE I DID ASK YOU TO COME, AND YOU TURNED ME DOWN...
DETAILS, DETAILS...
...BUT HE'S GOT A POINT. IT'S OBVIOUS YOU DON'T PLAN ON LETTING THEM CONTINUE DOING THIS. SO, WHAT'S YOUR PLAN, JOHNNY?
COLONEL... YOU DON'T WANT TO KNOW.
KNOWING YOU, YOU'RE PROBABLY RIGHT.

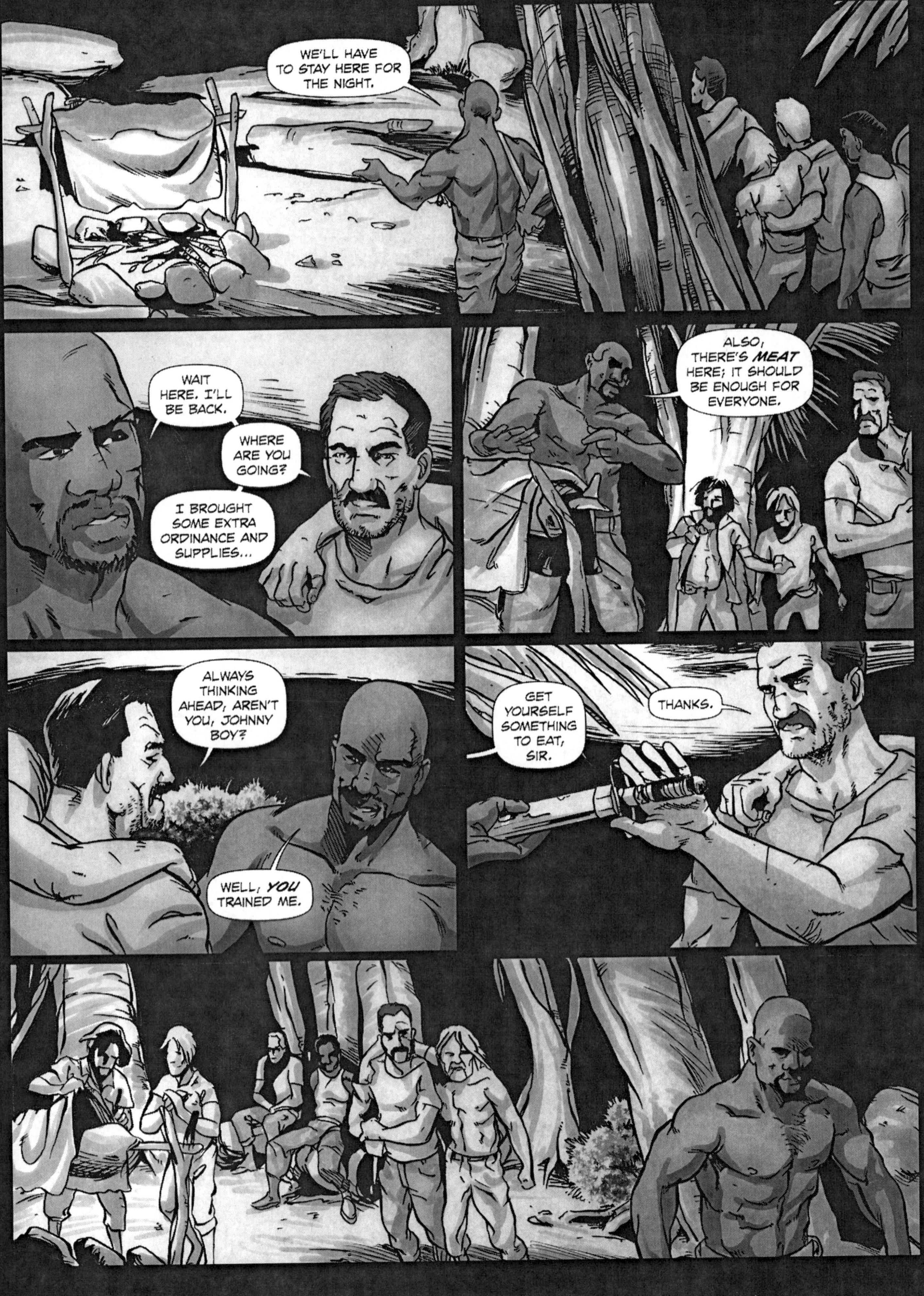
WE'LL HAVE TO STAY HERE FOR THE NIGHT.
WAIT HERE. I'LL BE BACK.
WHERE ARE YOU GOING?
I BROUGHT SOME EXTRA ORDINANCE AND SUPPLIES...
ALSO, THERE'S MEAT HERE; IT SHOULD BE ENOUGH FOR EVERYONE.
ALWAYS THINKING AHEAD, AREN'T YOU, JOHNNY BOY?
WELL, YOU TRAINED ME.
GET YOURSELF SOMETHING TO EAT, SIR.
THANKS.

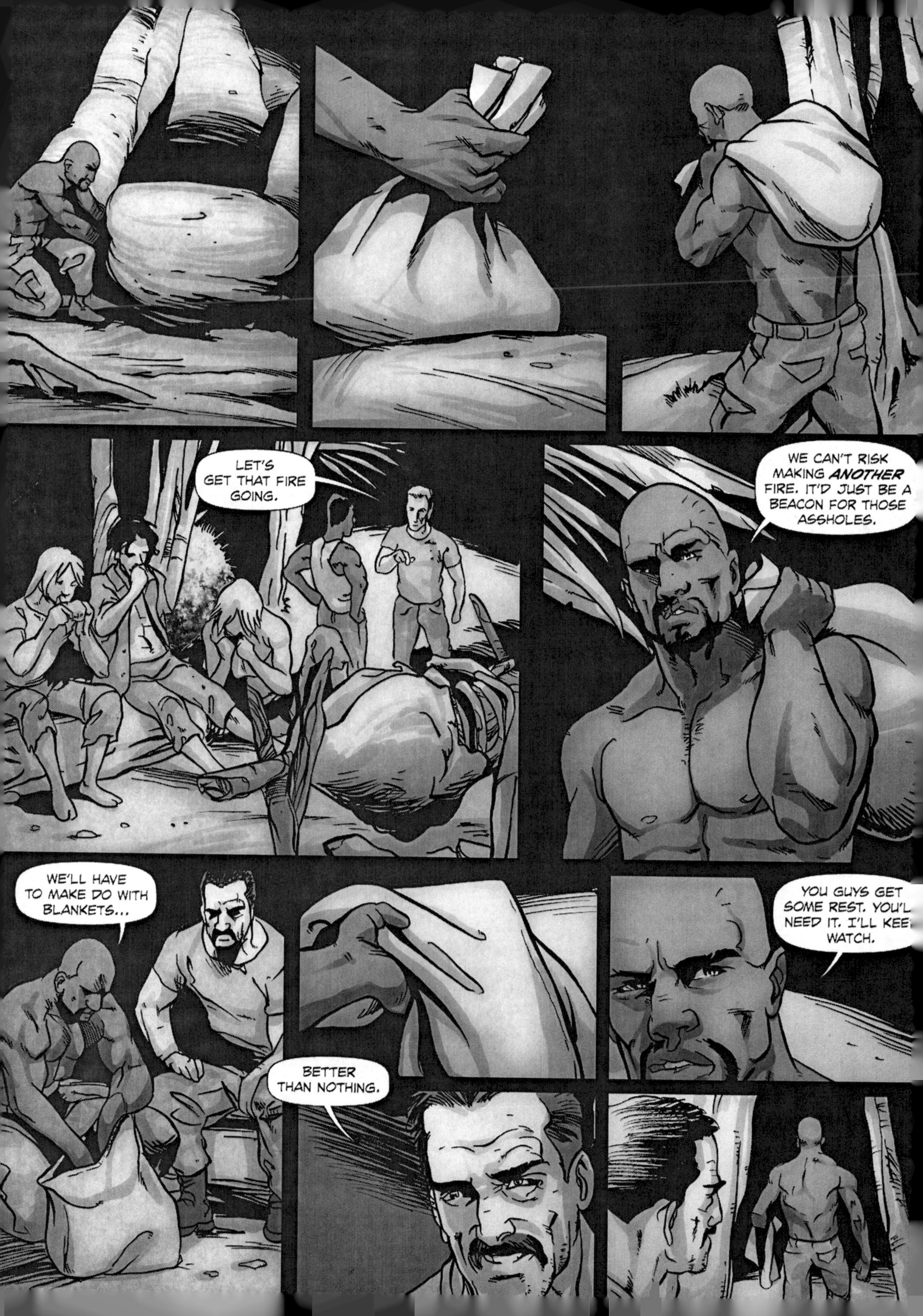

LET'S GET THAT FIRE GOING.
WE CAN'T RISK MAKING **ANOTHER** FIRE. IT'D JUST BE A BEACON FOR THOSE ASSHOLES.
WE'LL HAVE TO MAKE DO WITH BLANKETS...
YOU GUYS GET SOME REST. YOU'L NEED IT. I'LL KEE WATCH.
BETTER THAN NOTHING.

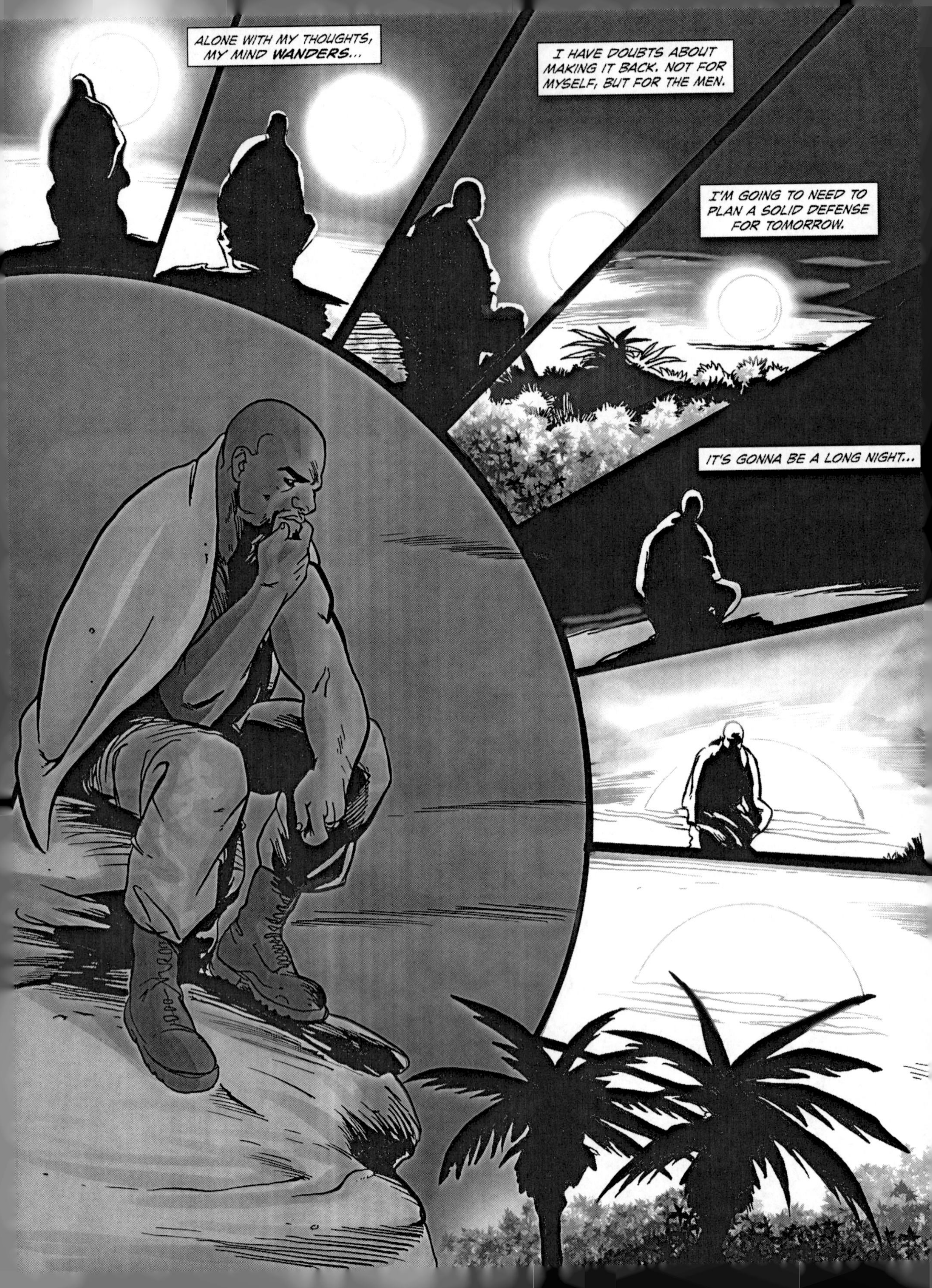
ALONE WITH MY THOUGHTS, MY MIND WANDERS...
I HAVE DOUBTS ABOUT MAKING IT BACK. NOT FOR MYSELF, BUT FOR THE MEN.
I'M GOING TO NEED TO PLAN A SOLID DEFENSE FOR TOMORROW.
IT'S GONNA BE A LONG NIGHT...

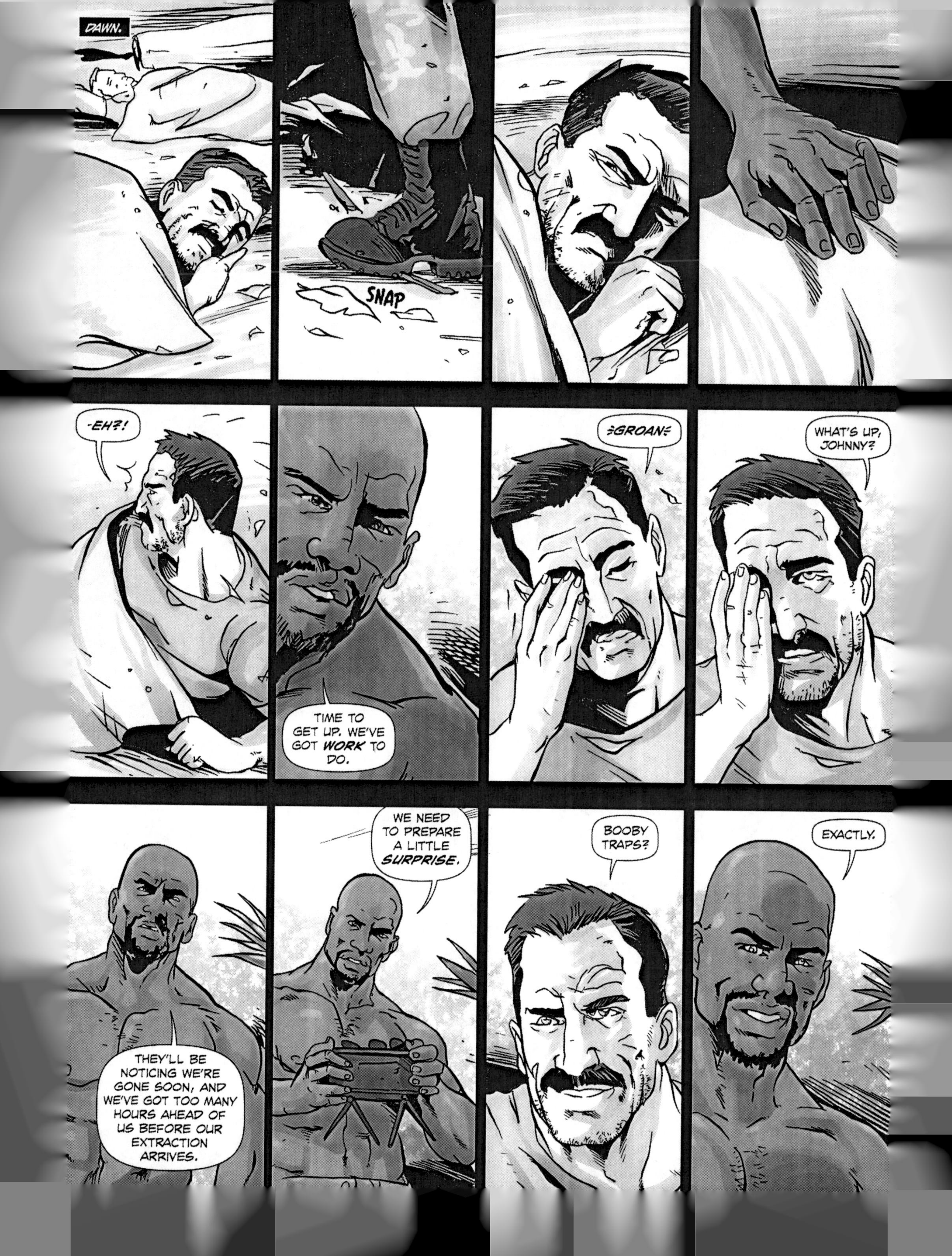
DAWN.
SNAP
-EH?!
TIME TO GET UP. WE'VE GOT WORK TO DO.
GROAN
WHAT'S UP, JOHNNY?
THEY'LL BE NOTICING WE'RE GONE SOON, AND WE'VE GOT TOO MANY HOURS AHEAD OF US BEFORE OUR EXTRACTION ARRIVES.
WE NEED TO PREPARE A LITTLE SURPRISE.
BOOBY TRAPS?
EXACTLY.

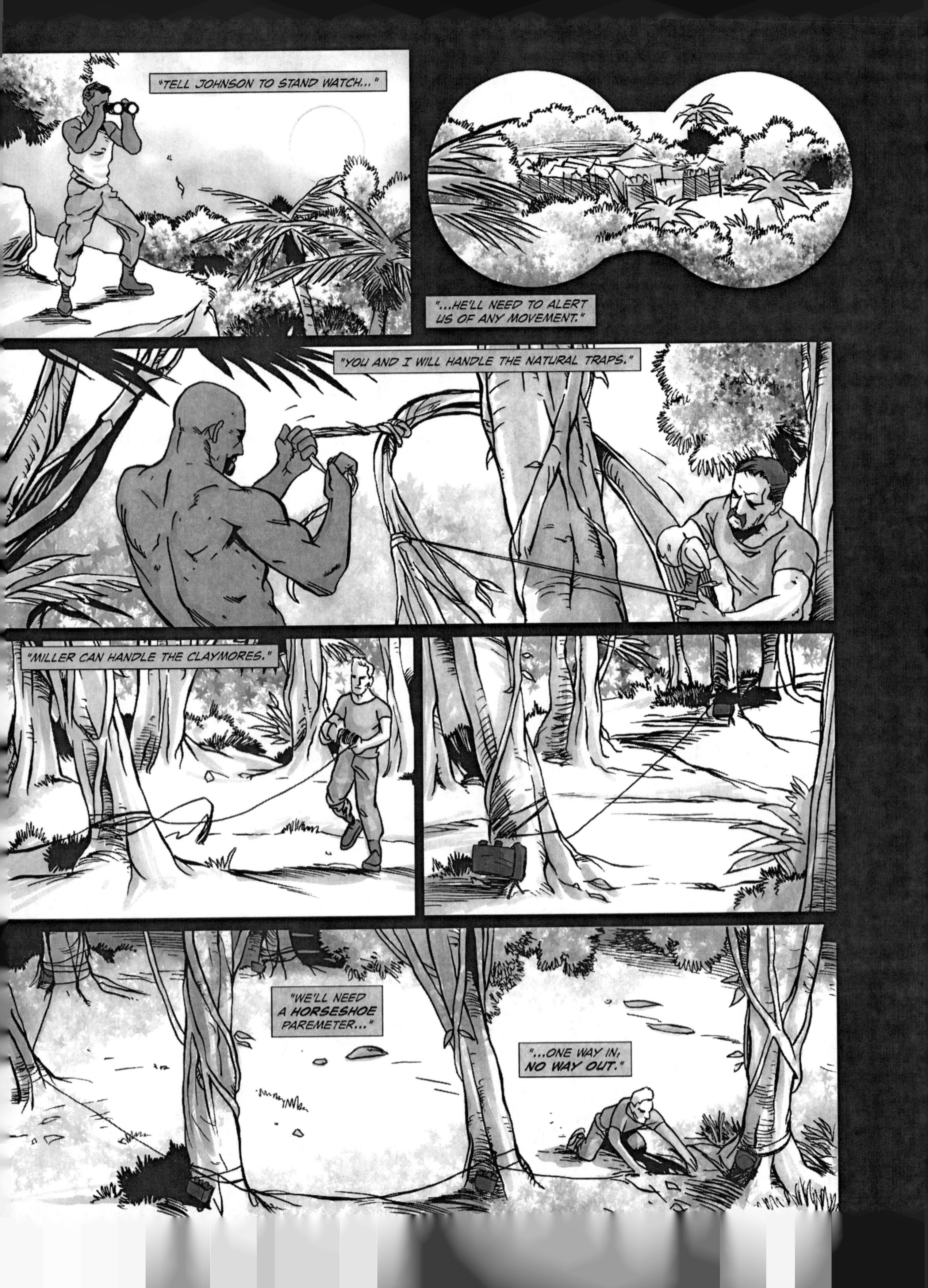
"TELL JOHNSON TO STAND WATCH..."
"...HE'LL NEED TO ALERT US OF ANY MOVEMENT."
"YOU AND I WILL HANDLE THE NATURAL TRAPS."
"MILLER CAN HANDLE THE CLAYMORES."
"WE'LL NEED A HORSESHOE PAREMETER..."
"...ONE WAY IN, NO WAY OUT."

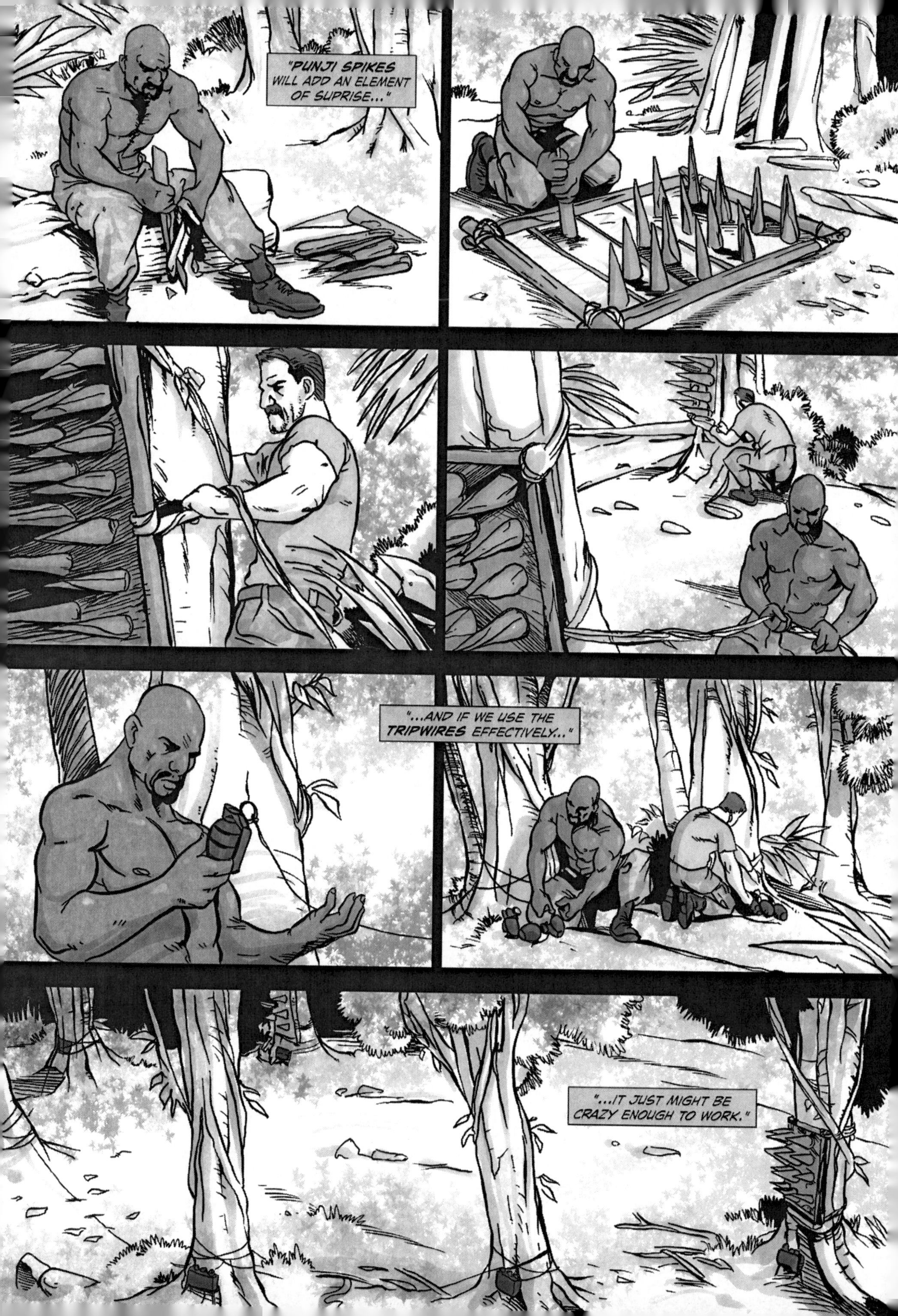
"PUNJI SPIKES WILL ADD AN ELEMENT OF SUPRISE..."
"...AND IF WE USE THE TRIPWIRES EFFECTIVELY..."
"...IT JUST MIGHT BE CRAZY ENOUGH TO WORK."

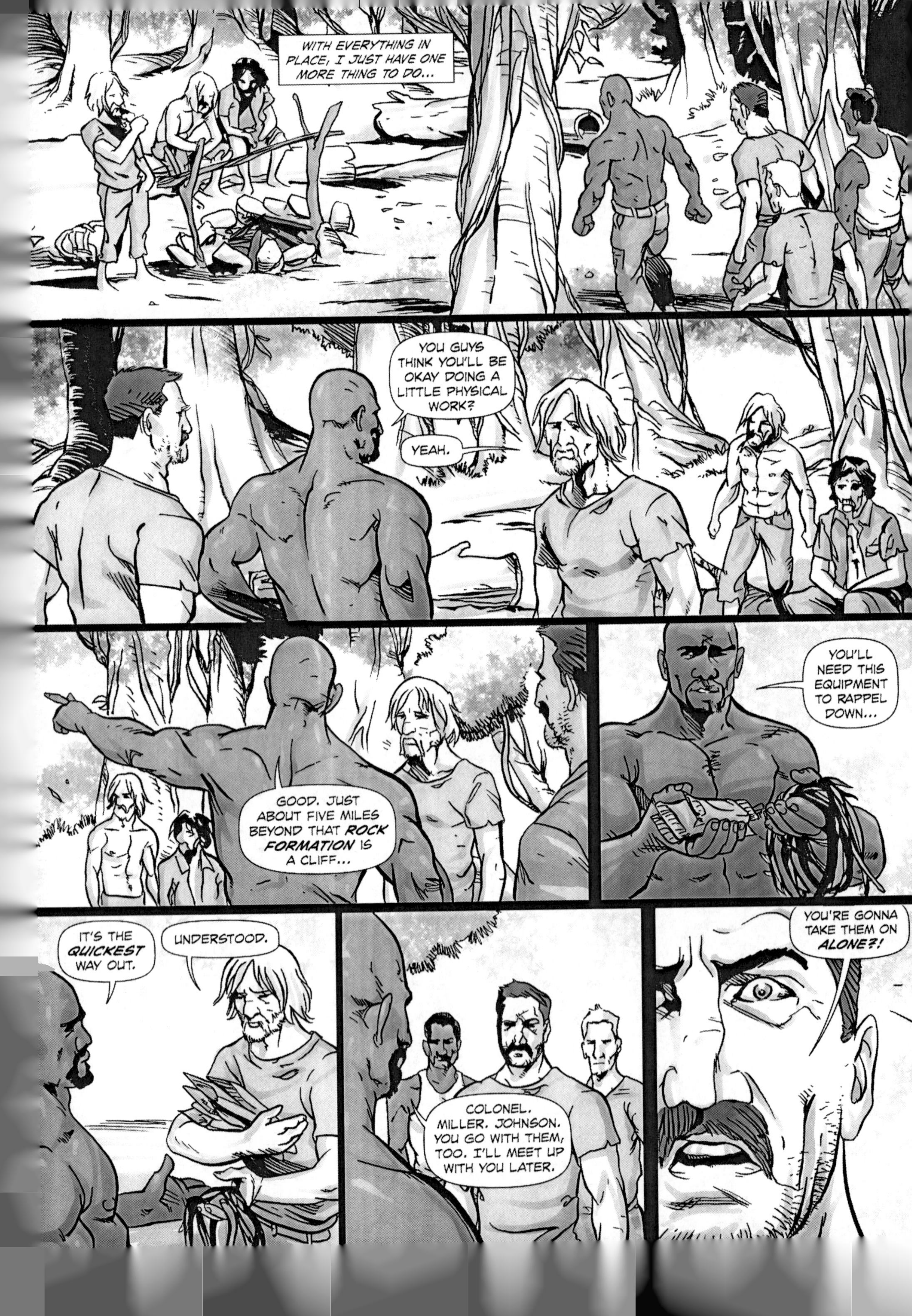
WITH EVERYTHING IN PLACE, I JUST HAVE ONE MORE THING TO DO...
YOU GUYS THINK YOU'LL BE OKAY DOING A LITTLE PHYSICAL WORK?
YEAH.
GOOD. JUST ABOUT FIVE MILES BEYOND THAT ROCK FORMATION IS A CLIFF...
YOU'LL NEED THIS EQUIPMENT TO RAPPEL DOWN...
IT'S THE QUICKEST WAY OUT.
UNDERSTOOD.
COLONEL. MILLER. JOHNSON. YOU GO WITH THEM, TOO. I'LL MEET UP WITH YOU LATER.
YOU'RE GONNA TAKE THEM ON ALONE?!

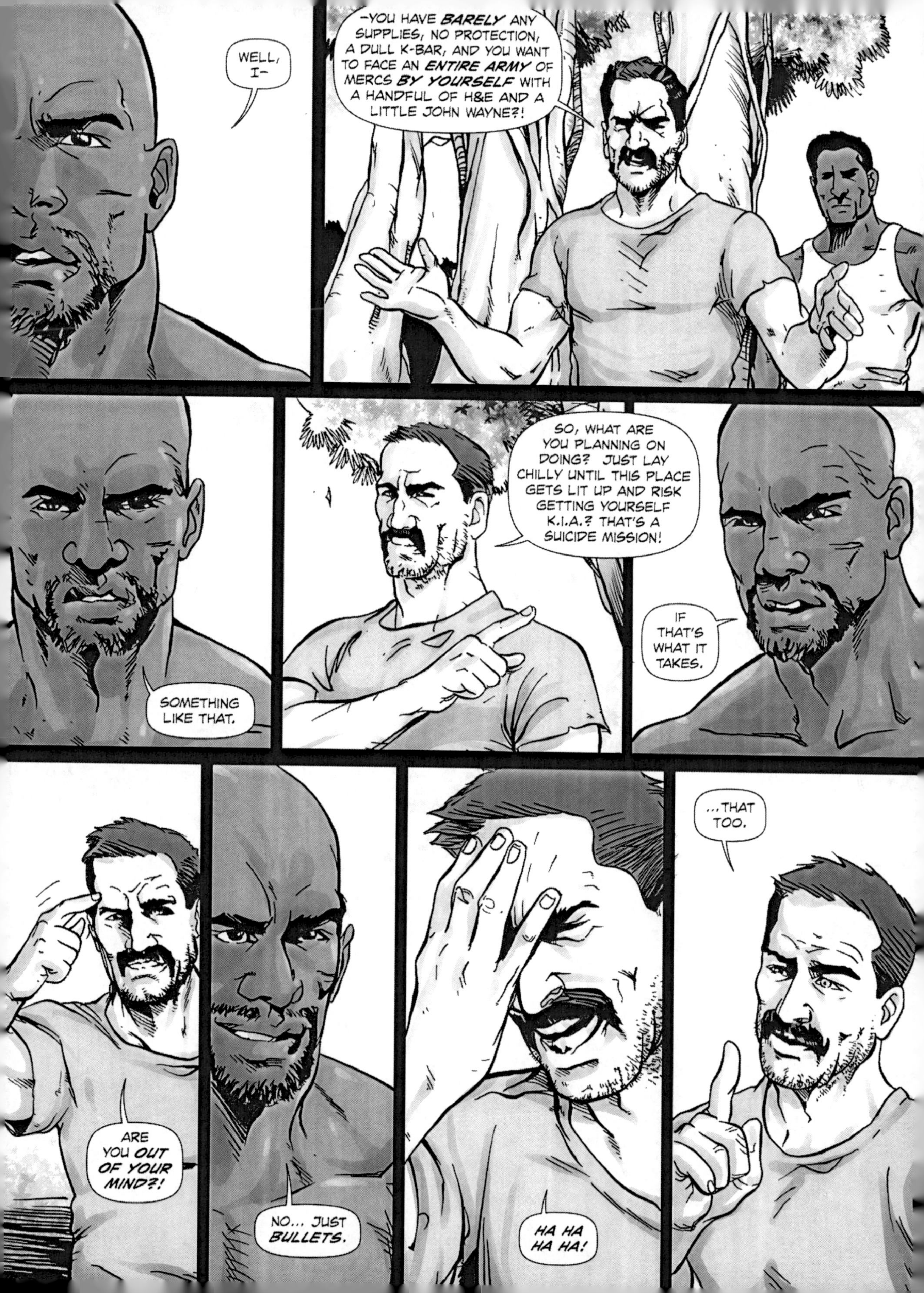
WELL, I–
–YOU HAVE BARELY ANY SUPPLIES, NO PROTECTION, A DULL K-BAR, AND YOU WANT TO FACE AN ENTIRE ARMY OF MERCS BY YOURSELF WITH A HANDFUL OF H&E AND A LITTLE JOHN WAYNE?!
SO, WHAT ARE YOU PLANNING ON DOING? JUST LAY CHILLY UNTIL THIS PLACE GETS LIT UP AND RISK GETTING YOURSELF K.I.A.? THAT'S A SUICIDE MISSION!
SOMETHING LIKE THAT.
IF THAT'S WHAT IT TAKES.
ARE YOU OUT OF YOUR MIND?!
NO... JUST BULLETS.
HA HA HA HA!
...THAT TOO.

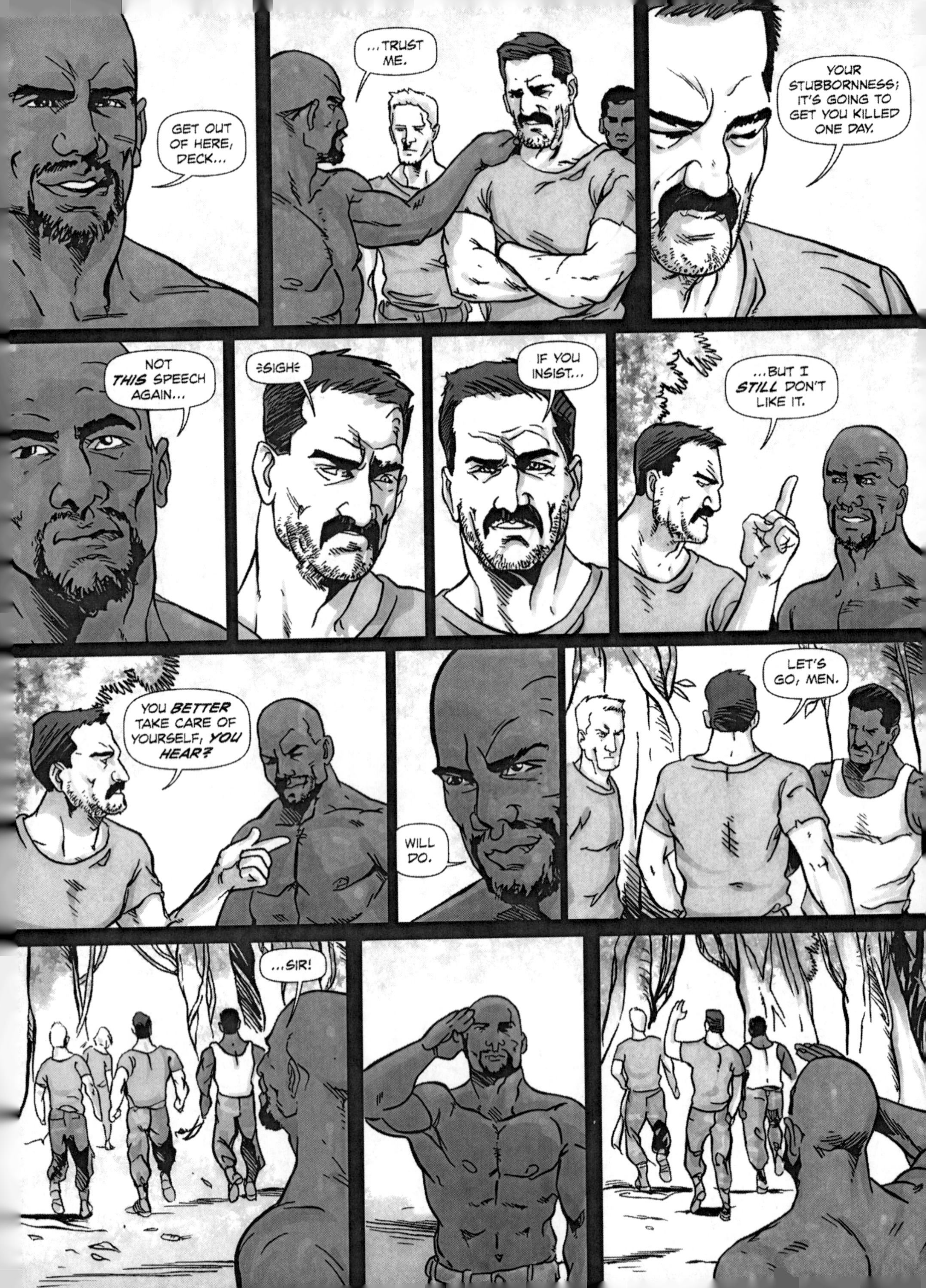
GET OUT OF HERE, DECK...
...TRUST ME.
YOUR STUBBORNNESS; IT'S GOING TO GET YOU KILLED ONE DAY.
NOT THIS SPEECH AGAIN...
SIGH
IF YOU INSIST...
...BUT I STILL DON'T LIKE IT.
YOU BETTER TAKE CARE OF YOURSELF, YOU HEAR?
WILL DO.
LET'S GO, MEN.
...SIR!

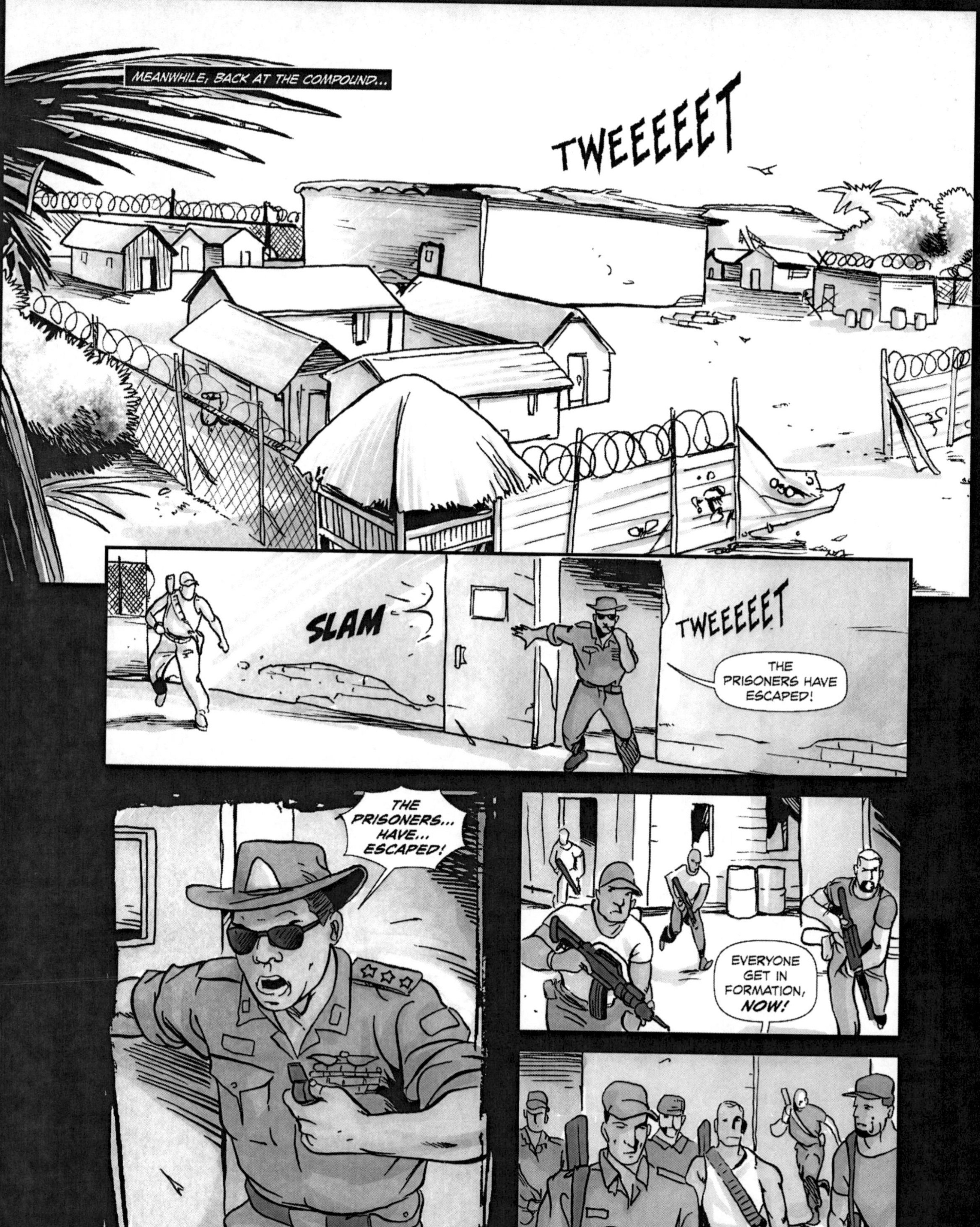
MEANWHILE, BACK AT THE COMPOUND...
TWEEEEET
SLAM
TWEEEEET
THE PRISONERS HAVE ESCAPED!
THE PRISONERS... HAVE... ESCAPED!
EVERYONE GET IN FORMATION, NOW!

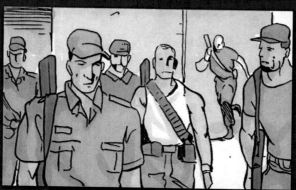

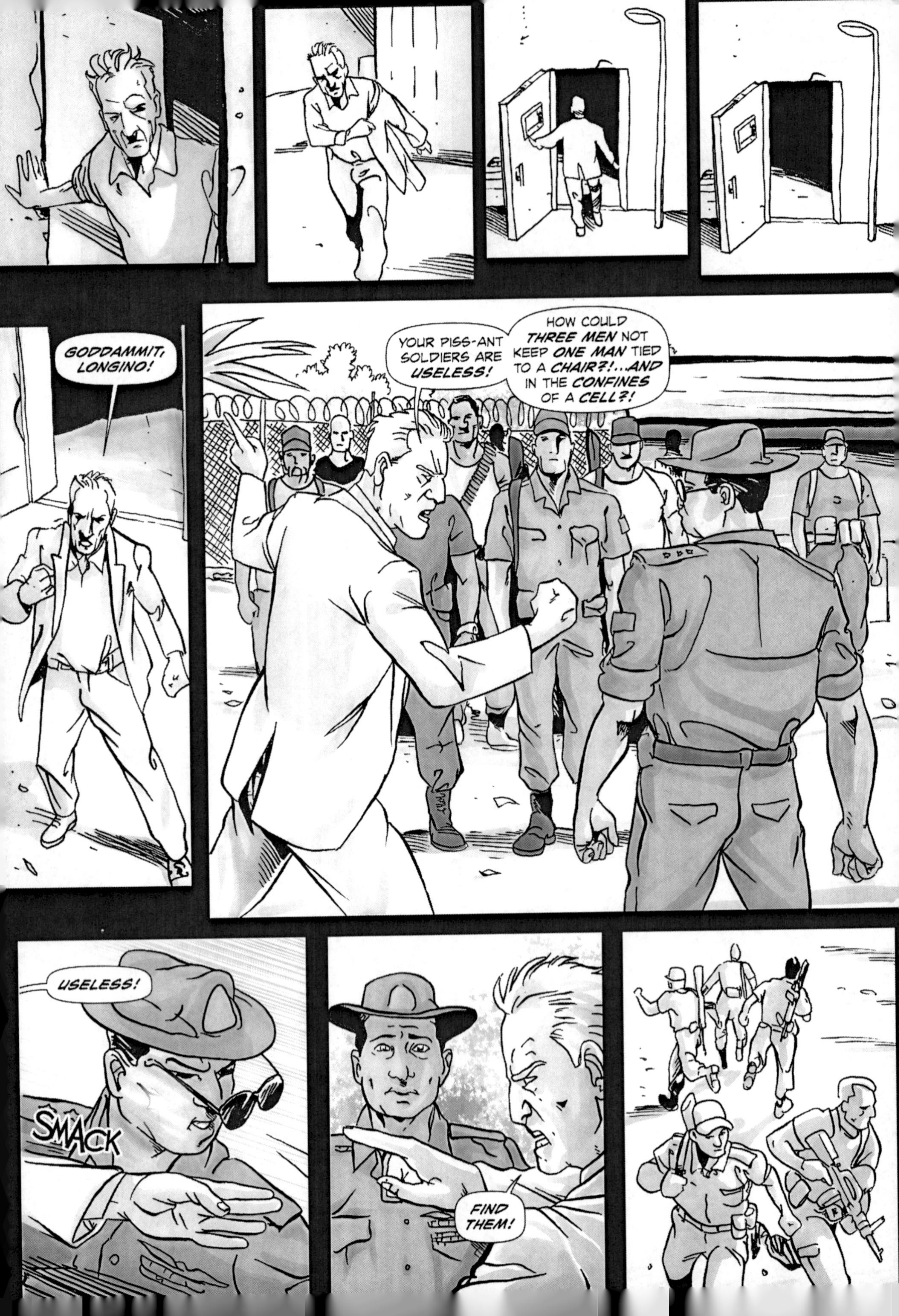
GODDAMMIT, LONGINO!
YOUR PISS-ANT SOLDIERS ARE USELESS!
HOW COULD THREE MEN NOT KEEP ONE MAN TIED TO A CHAIR?!...AND IN THE CONFINES OF A CELL?!
USELESS!
SMACK
FIND THEM!

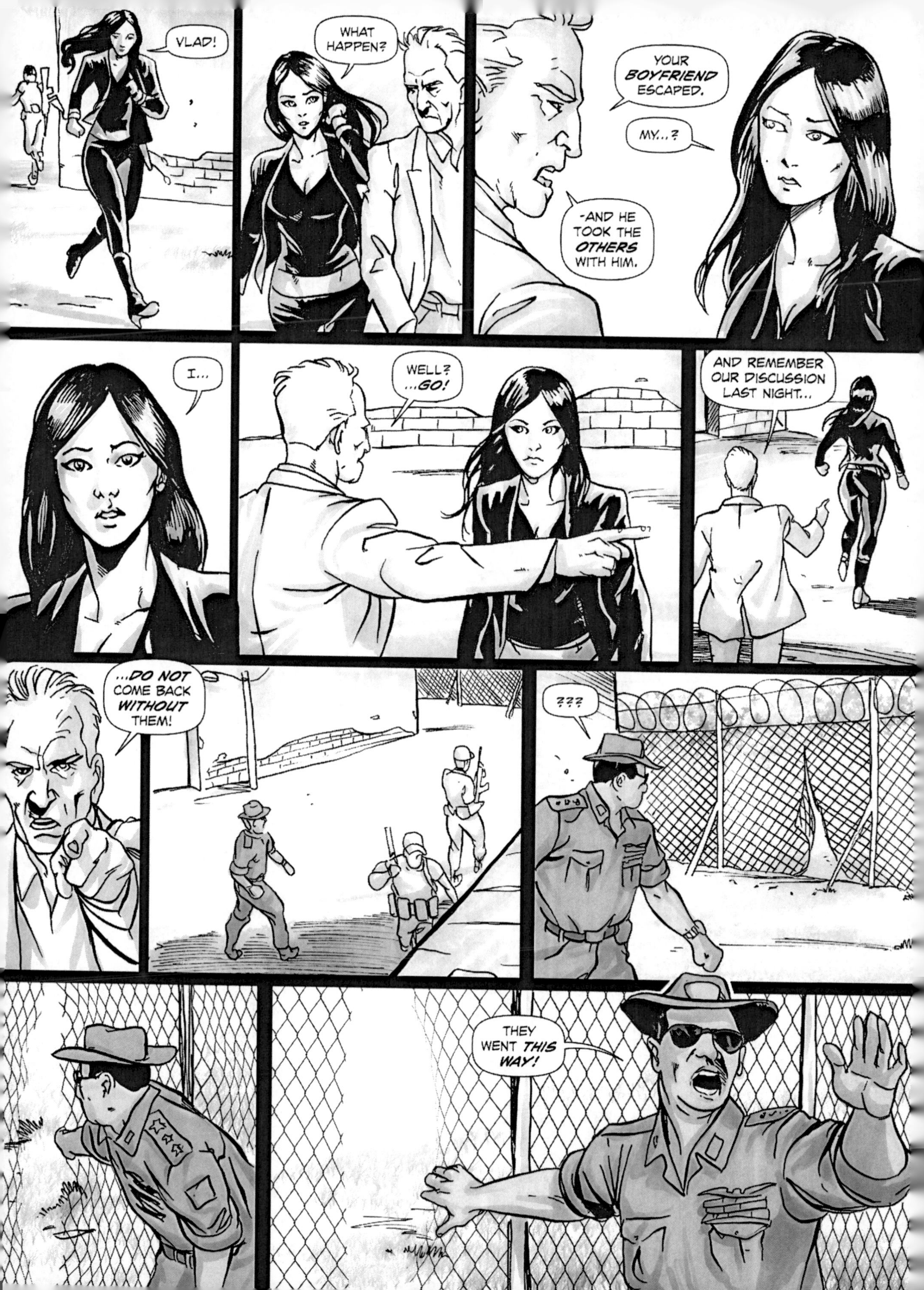
VLAD!
WHAT HAPPEN?
YOUR BOYFRIEND ESCAPED.
MY...?
-AND HE TOOK THE OTHERS WITH HIM.
I...
WELL? ...GO!
AND REMEMBER OUR DISCUSSION LAST NIGHT...
...DO NOT COME BACK WITHOUT THEM!
???
THEY WENT THIS WAY!

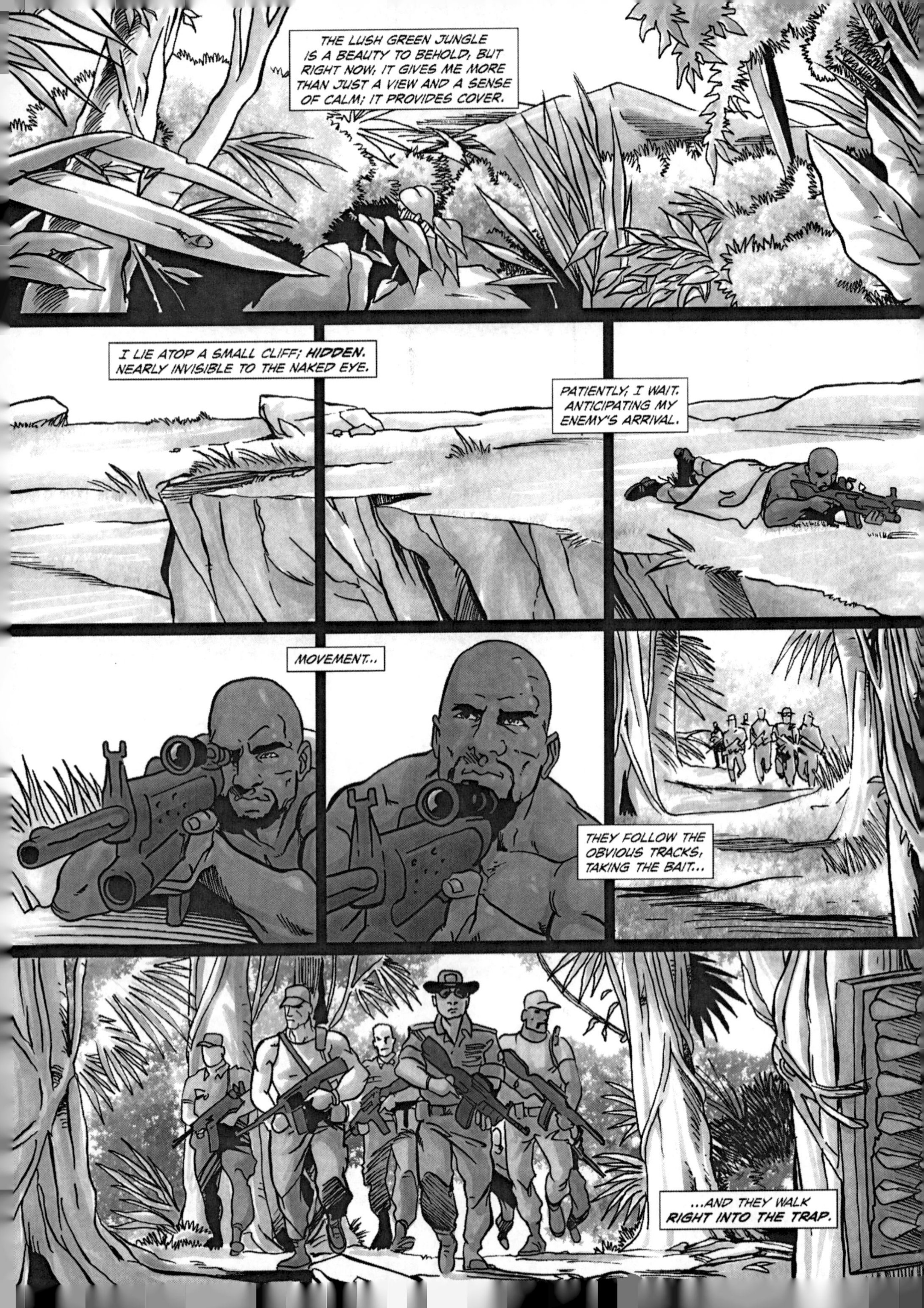
THE LUSH GREEN JUNGLE IS A BEAUTY TO BEHOLD, BUT RIGHT NOW, IT GIVES ME MORE THAN JUST A VIEW AND A SENSE OF CALM; IT PROVIDES COVER.
I LIE ATOP A SMALL CLIFF; HIDDEN. NEARLY INVISIBLE TO THE NAKED EYE.
PATIENTLY, I WAIT. ANTICIPATING MY ENEMY'S ARRIVAL.
MOVEMENT...
THEY FOLLOW THE OBVIOUS TRACKS, TAKING THE BAIT...
...AND THEY WALK RIGHT INTO THE TRAP.

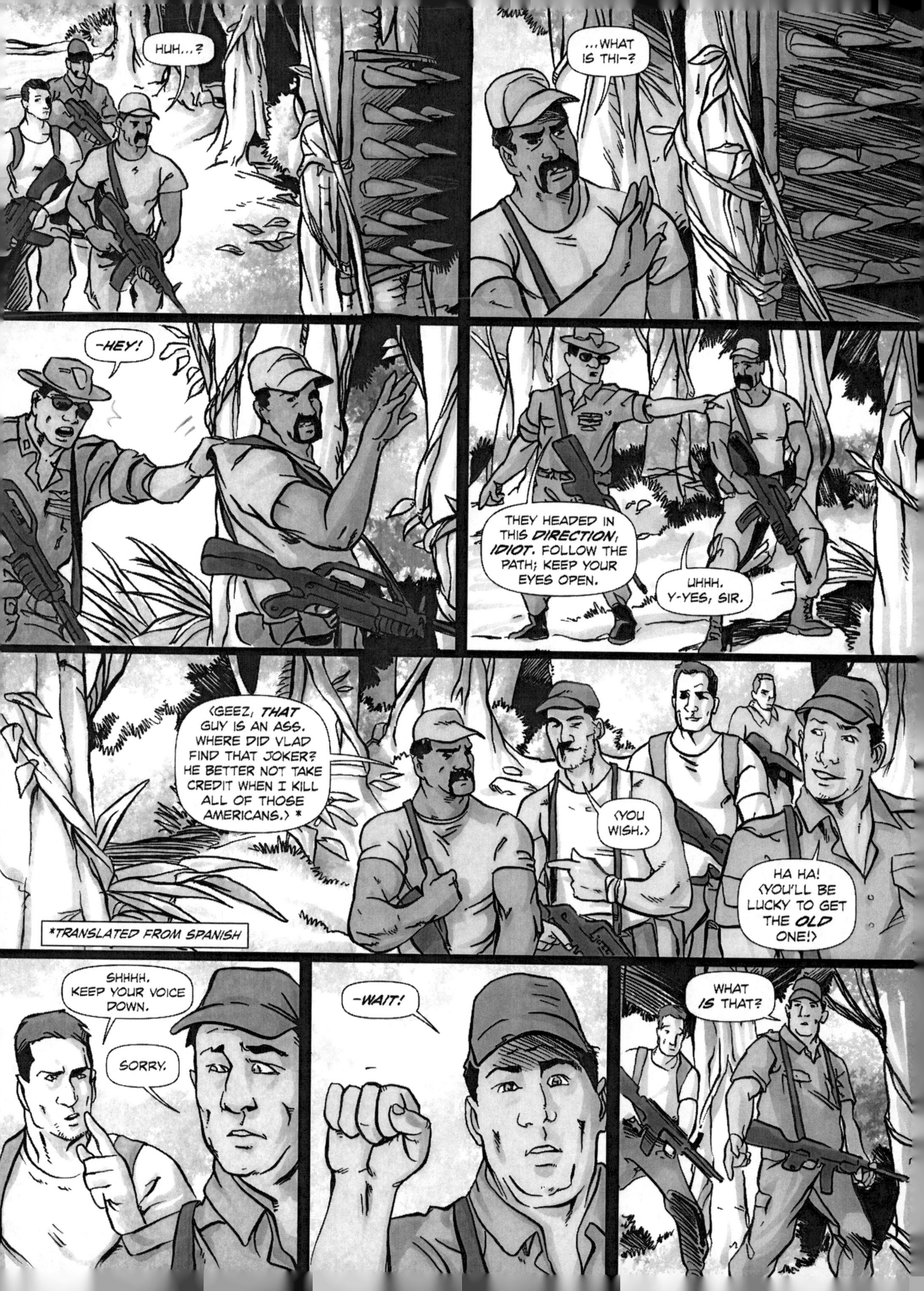
HUH...?
...WHAT IS THI—?
—HEY!
THEY HEADED IN THIS DIRECTION, IDIOT. FOLLOW THE PATH; KEEP YOUR EYES OPEN.
UHHH. Y-YES, SIR.
‹GEEZ, THAT GUY IS AN ASS. WHERE DID VLAD FIND THAT JOKER? HE BETTER NOT TAKE CREDIT WHEN I KILL ALL OF THOSE AMERICANS.› *
‹YOU WISH.›
HA HA! ‹YOU'LL BE LUCKY TO GET THE OLD ONE!›
*TRANSLATED FROM SPANISH
SHHHH. KEEP YOUR VOICE DOWN.
SORRY.
—WAIT!
WHAT IS THAT?

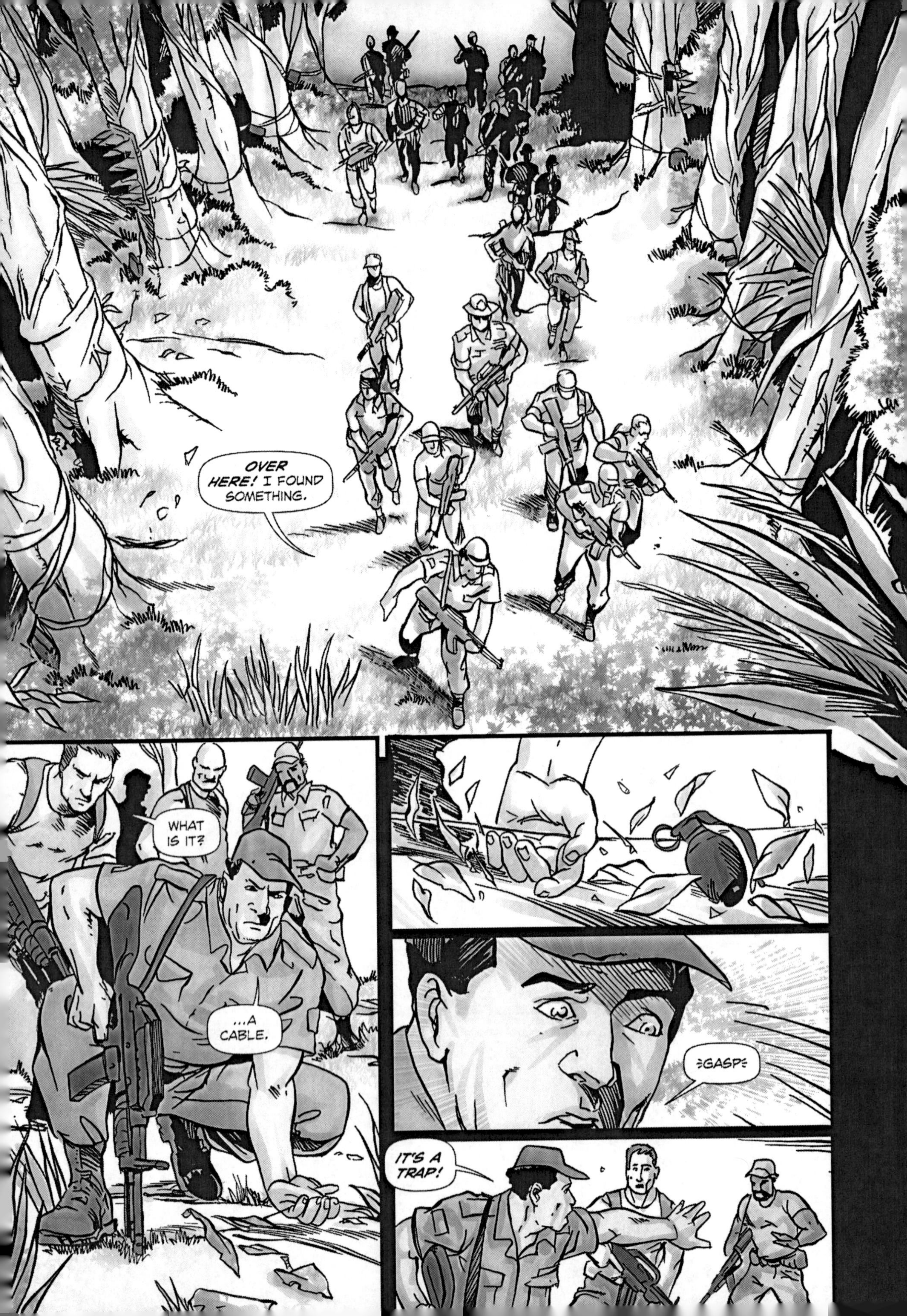
OVER HERE! I FOUND SOMETHING.
WHAT IS IT?
...A CABLE.
GASP
IT'S A TRAP!

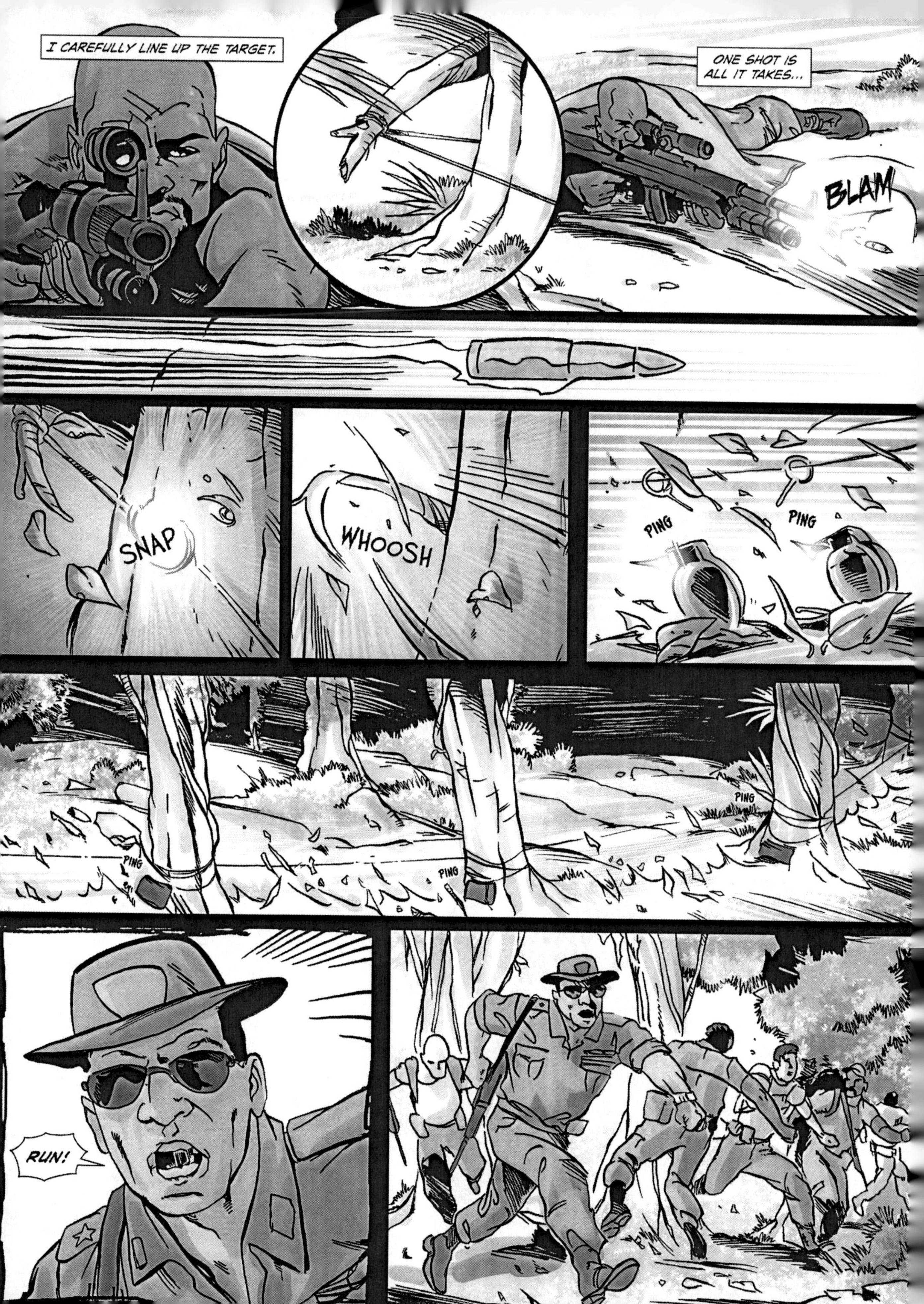
I CAREFULLY LINE UP THE TARGET.
ONE SHOT IS ALL IT TAKES...
BLAM
SNAP
WHOOSH
PING
PING
PING
PING
PING
RUN!

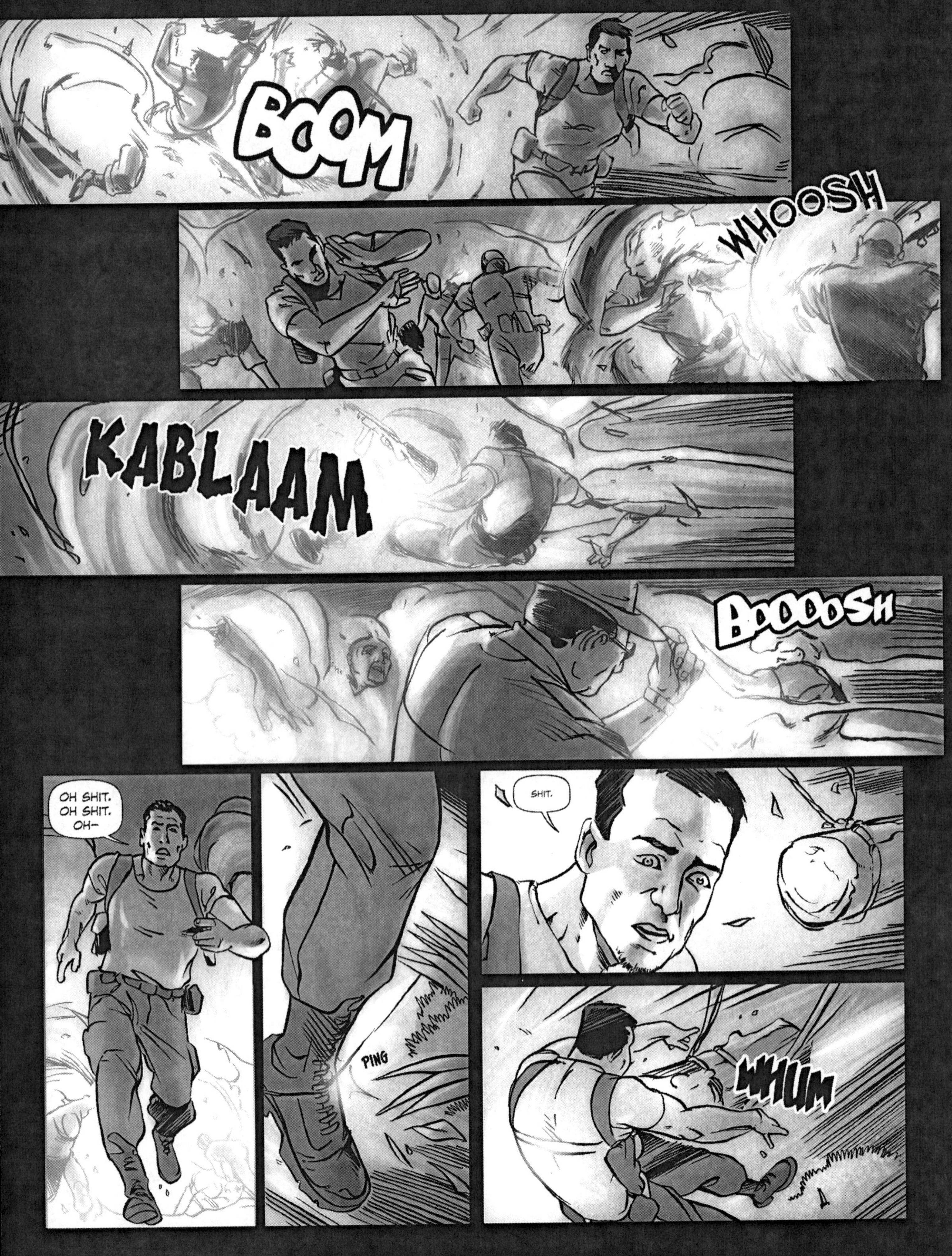
BOOM
WHOOSH
KABLAAM
BOOOOOSH
OH SHIT. OH SHIT. OH–
PING
SHIT.
WHUM

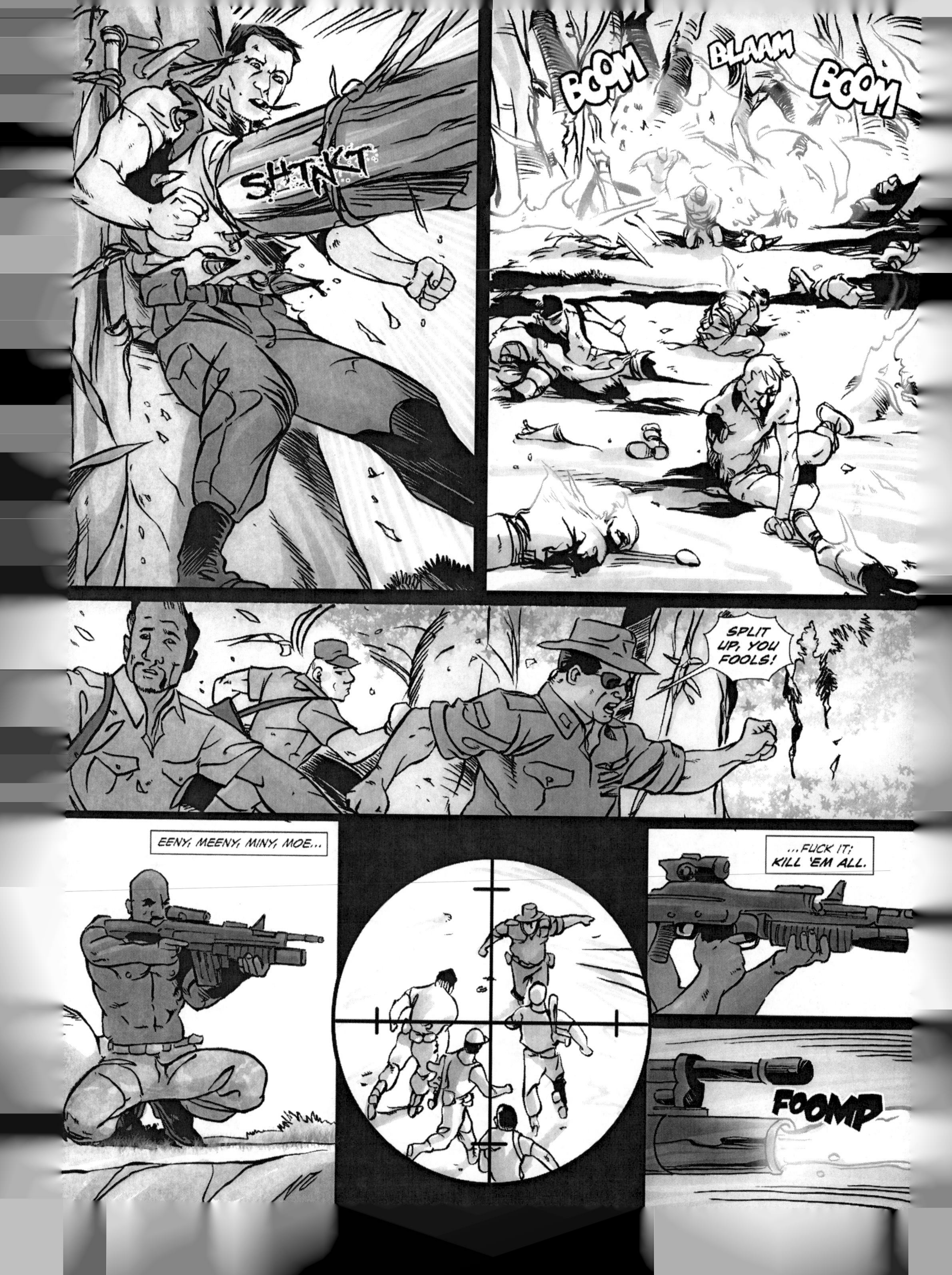
SHTNKT
BOOM
BLAAM
BOOM
SPLIT UP, YOU FOOLS!
EENY, MEENY, MINY, MOE...
...FUCK IT; KILL 'EM ALL.
FOOMP

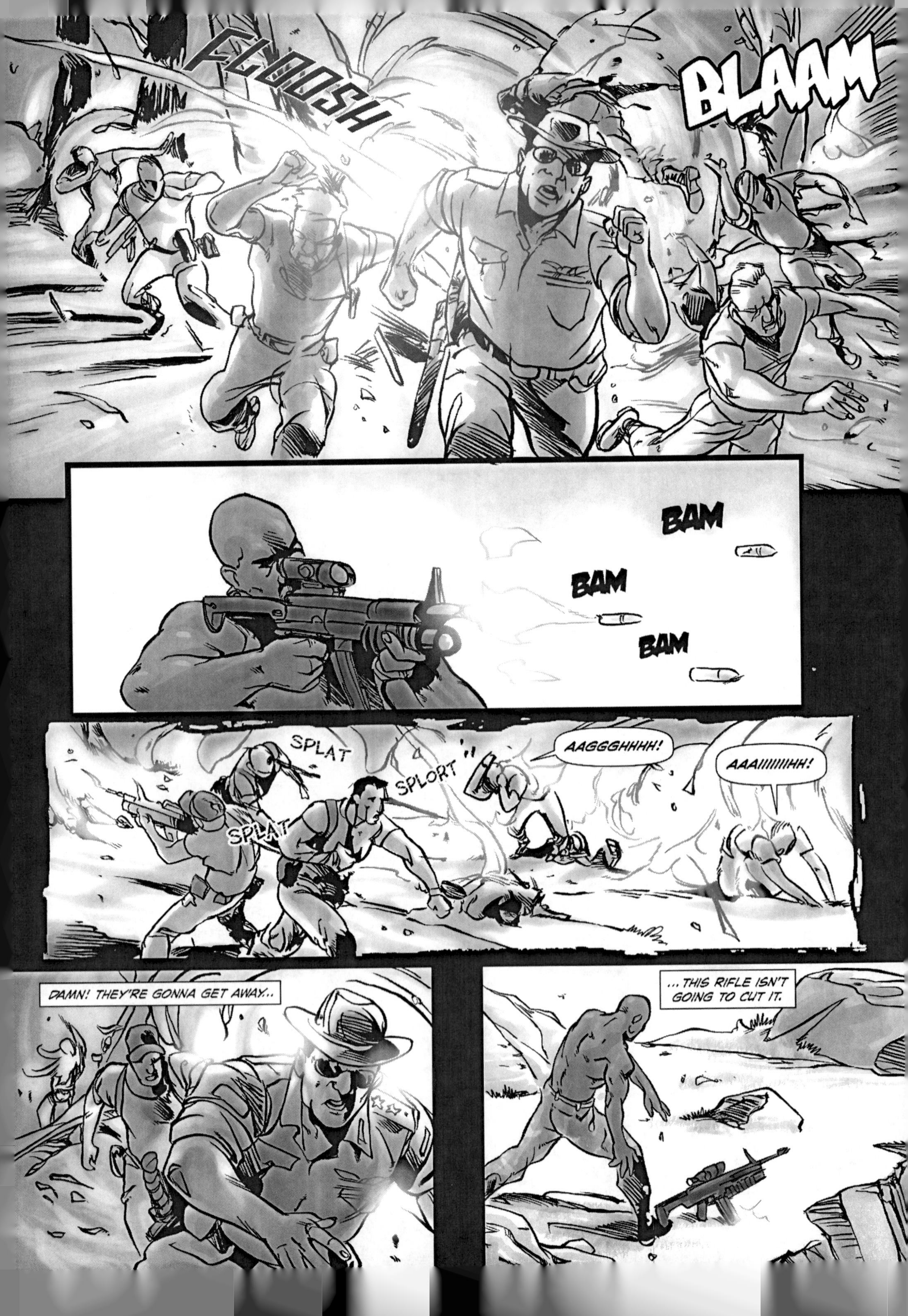
FLOOSH
BLAAM
BAM
BAM
BAM
SPLAT
SPLORT
SPLAT
AAGGGHHHH!
AAAIIIIIIIHH!
DAMN! THEY'RE GONNA GET AWAY...
...THIS RIFLE ISN'T GOING TO CUT IT.

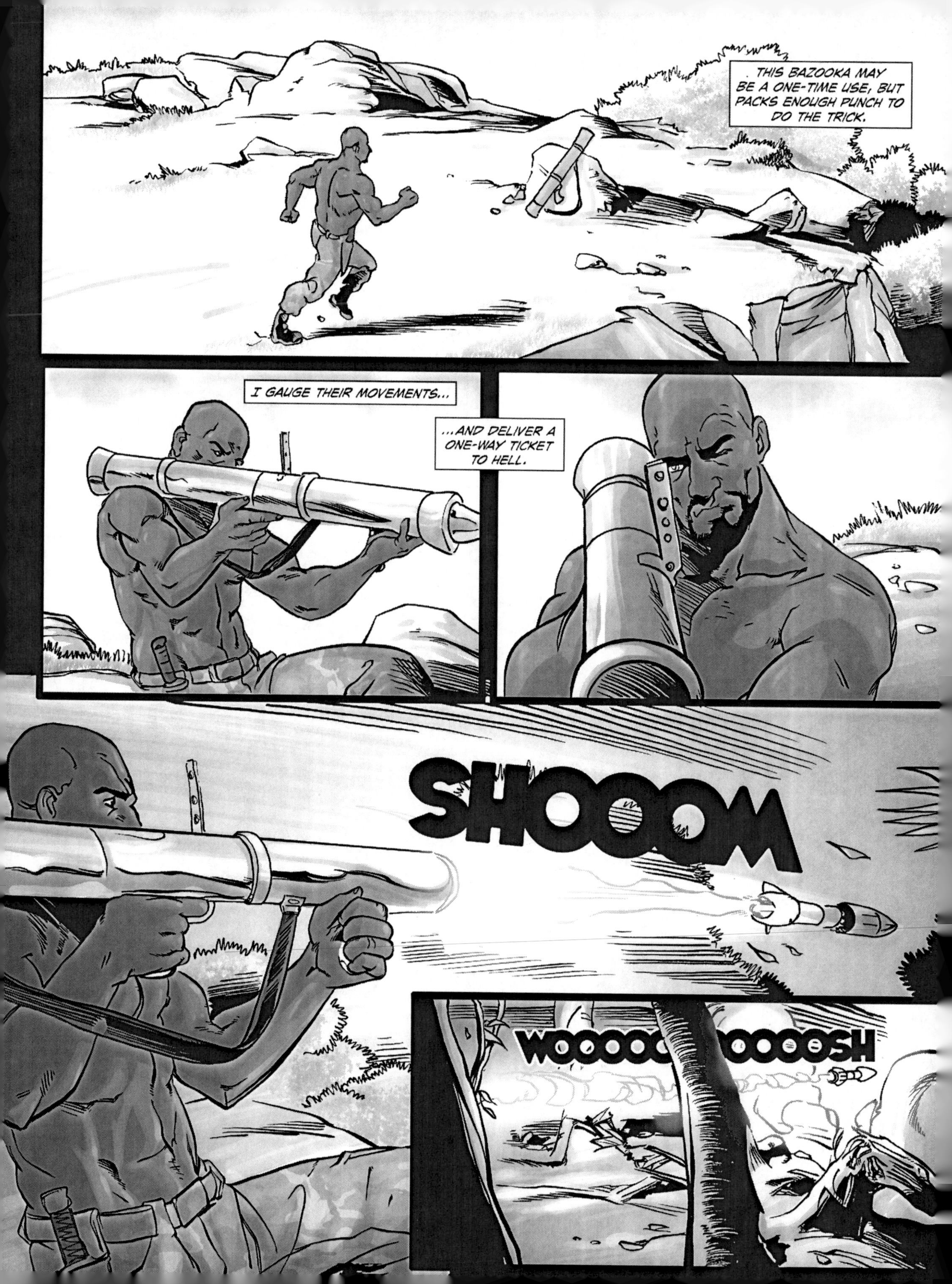
THIS BAZOOKA MAY BE A ONE-TIME USE, BUT PACKS ENOUGH PUNCH TO DO THE TRICK.
I GAUGE THEIR MOVEMENTS...
...AND DELIVER A ONE-WAY TICKET TO HELL.
SHOOOM
WOOOOO OOOOOSH

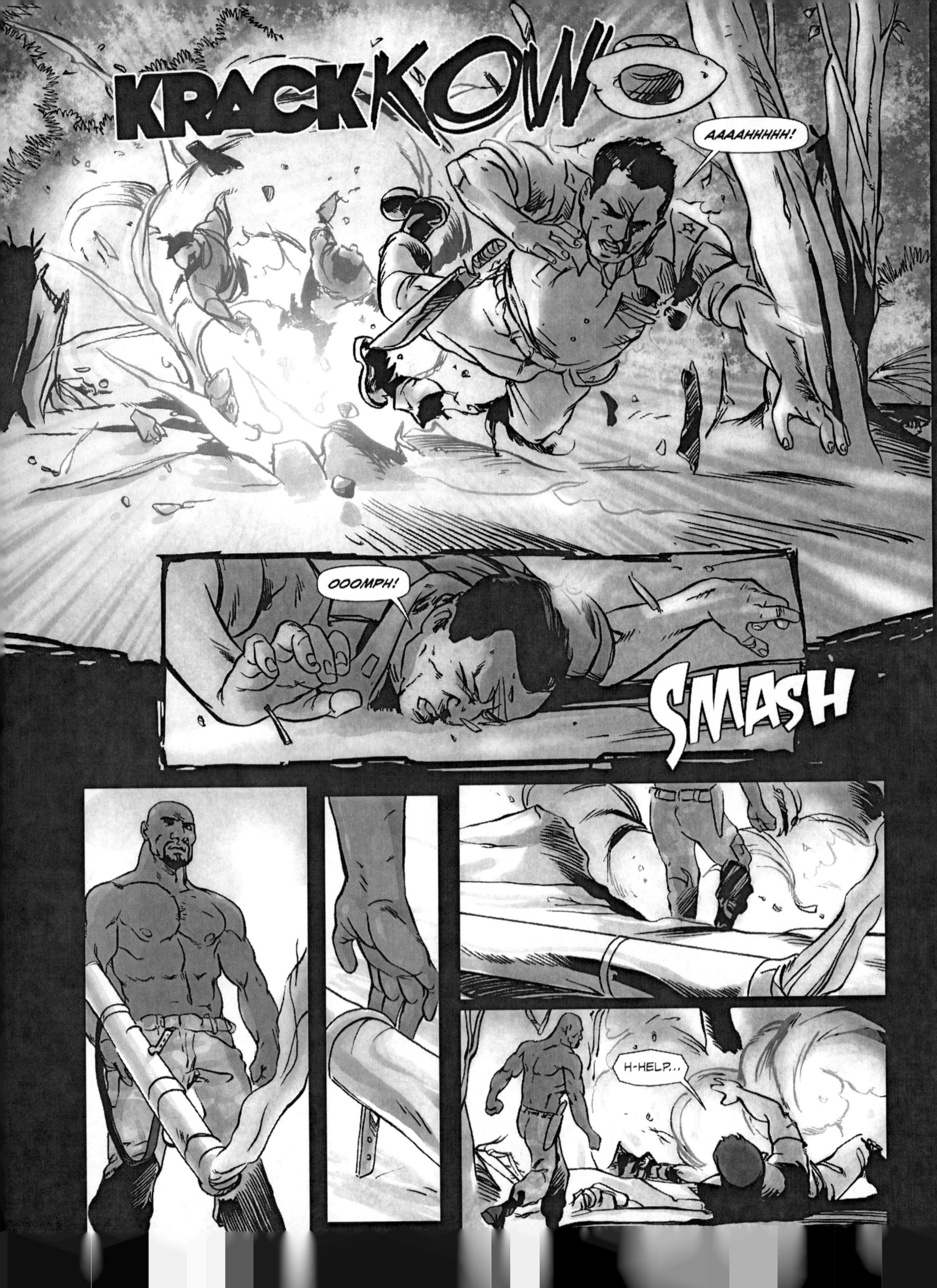
KRACKKOW
AAAAHHHHH!
OOOMPH!
SMASH
H-HELP...

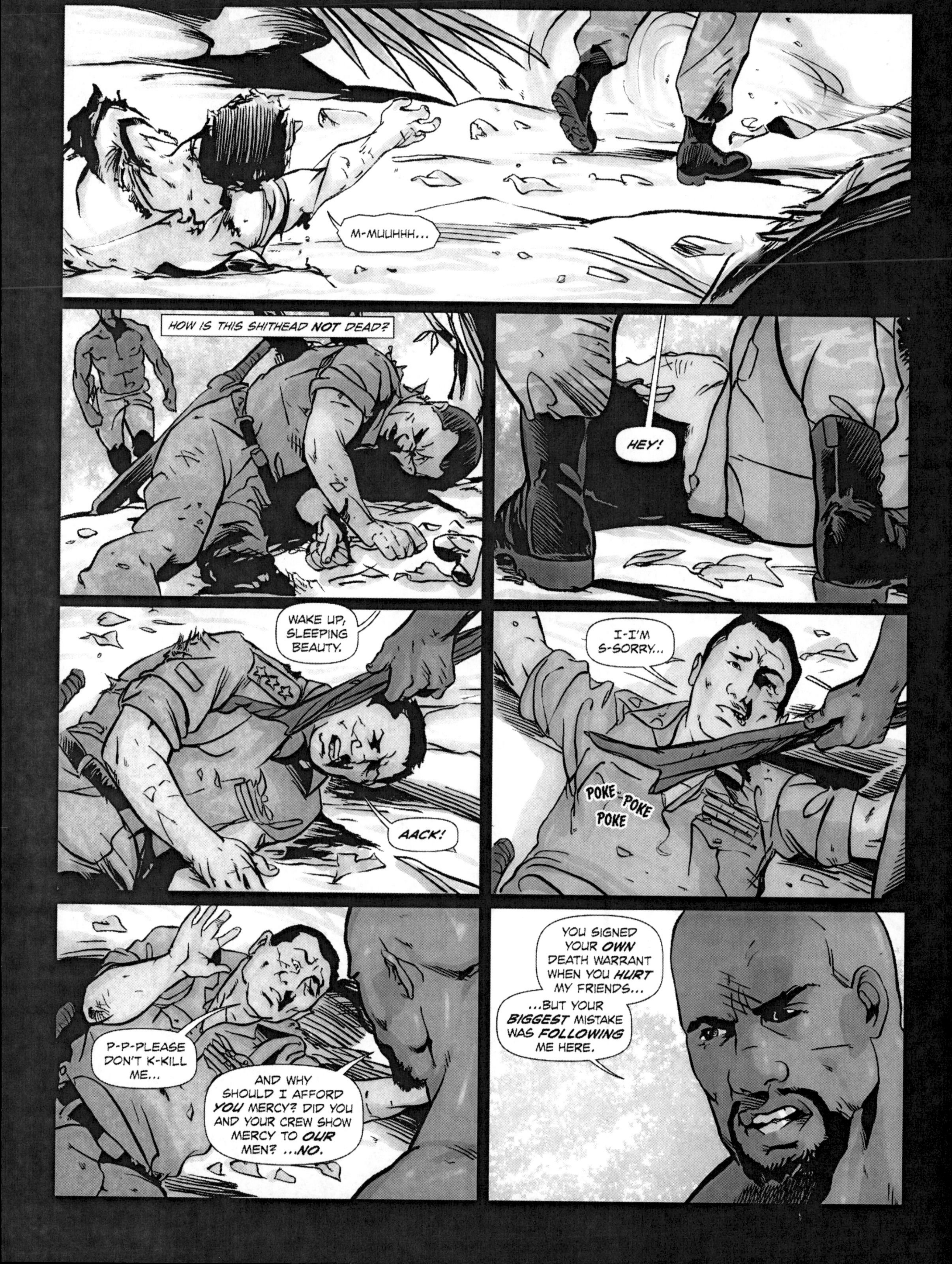
M-MUUHHH...
HOW IS THIS SHITHEAD NOT DEAD?
HEY!
WAKE UP, SLEEPING BEAUTY.
AACK!
I-I'M S-SORRY...
POKE POKE POKE
P-P-PLEASE DON'T K-KILL ME...
AND WHY SHOULD I AFFORD YOU MERCY? DID YOU AND YOUR CREW SHOW MERCY TO OUR MEN? ...NO.
YOU SIGNED YOUR OWN DEATH WARRANT WHEN YOU HURT MY FRIENDS...
...BUT YOUR BIGGEST MISTAKE WAS FOLLOWING ME HERE.

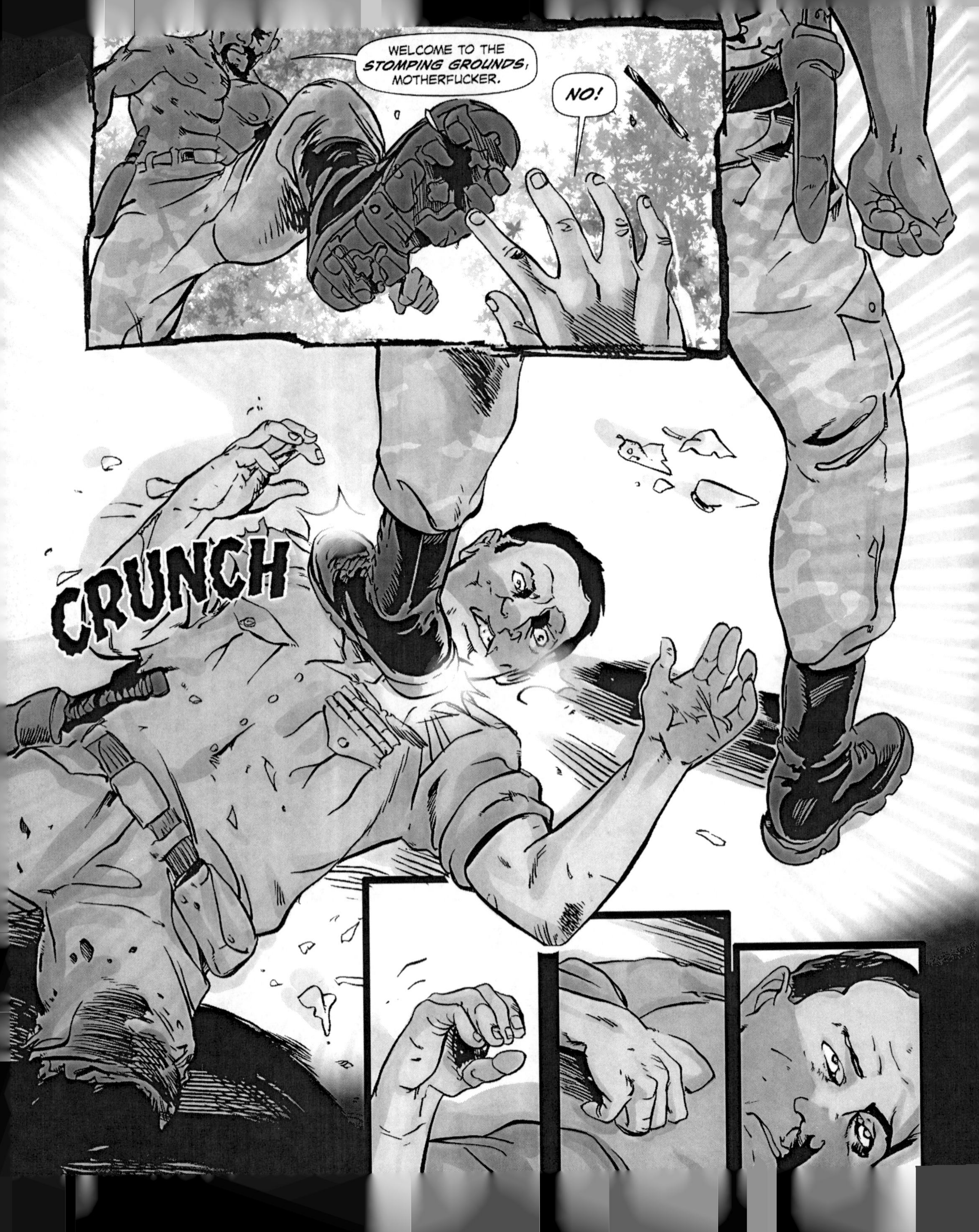

WELCOME TO THE STOMPING GROUNDS, MOTHERFUCKER.
NO!
CRUNCH

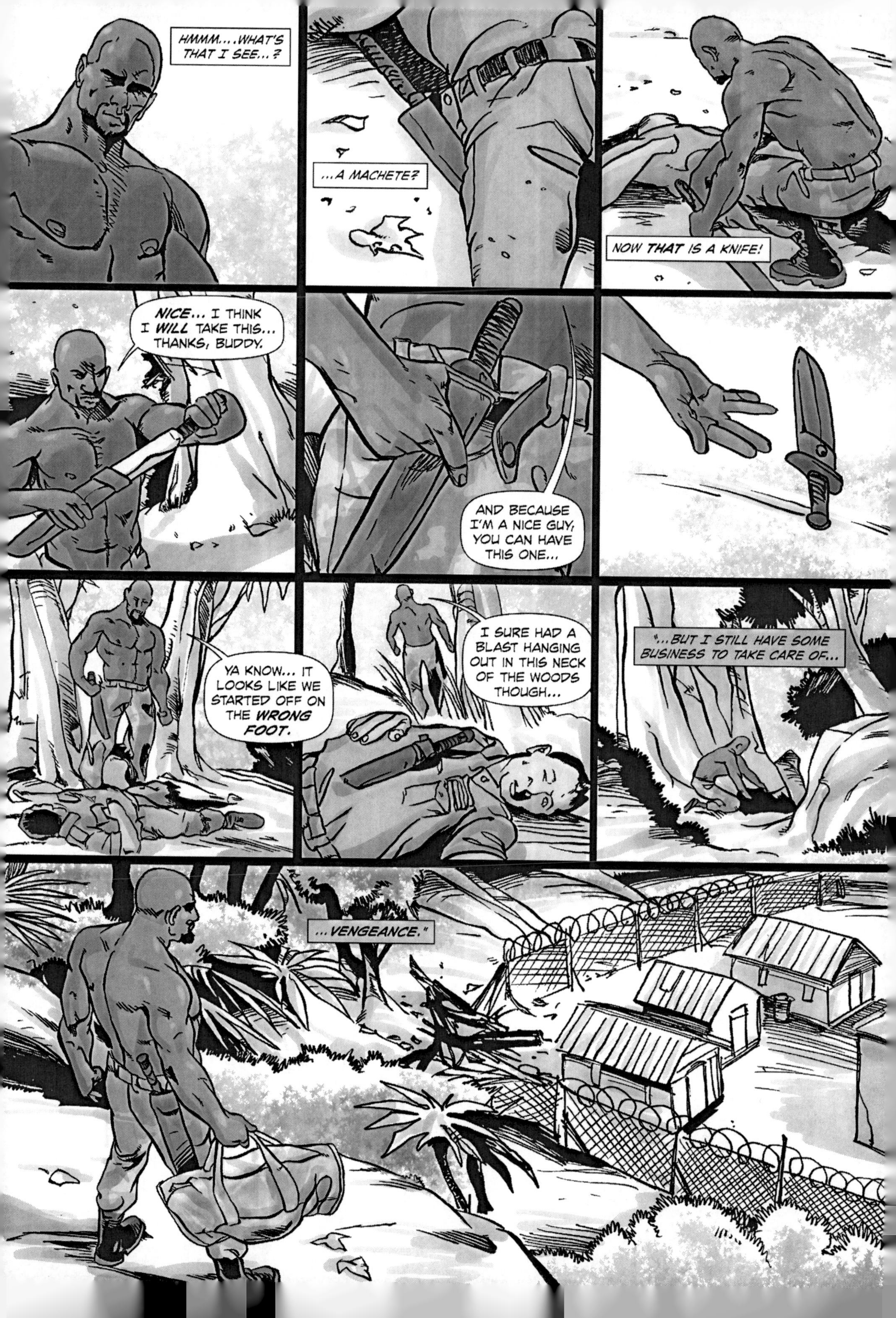

HMMM....WHAT'S THAT I SEE...?
...A MACHETE?
NOW THAT IS A KNIFE!
NICE... I THINK I WILL TAKE THIS... THANKS, BUDDY.
AND BECAUSE I'M A NICE GUY, YOU CAN HAVE THIS ONE...
YA KNOW... IT LOOKS LIKE WE STARTED OFF ON THE WRONG FOOT.
I SURE HAD A BLAST HANGING OUT IN THIS NECK OF THE WOODS THOUGH...
"...BUT I STILL HAVE SOME BUSINESS TO TAKE CARE OF...
...VENGEANCE."

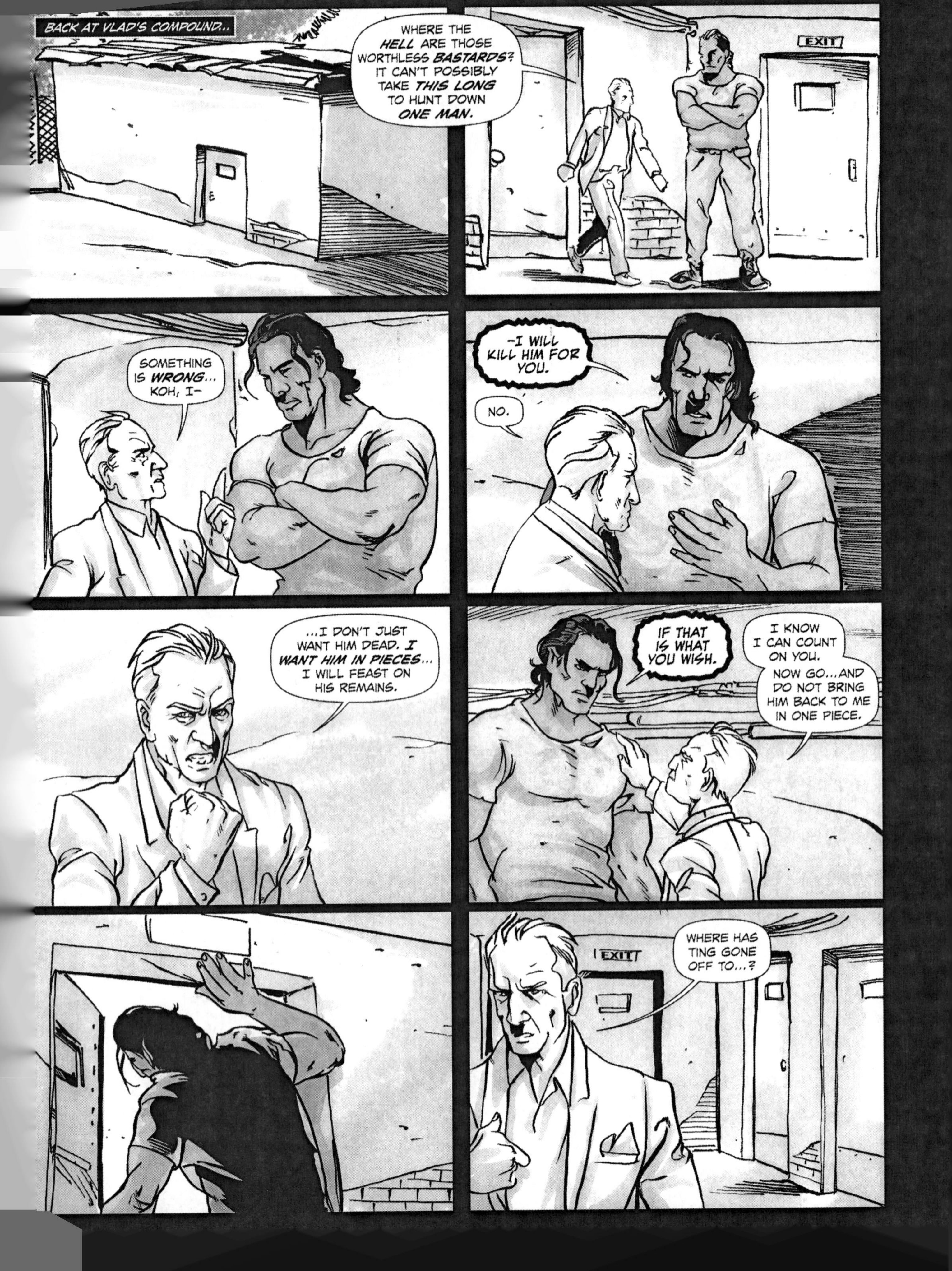
BACK AT VLAD'S COMPOUND...
WHERE THE HELL ARE THOSE WORTHLESS BASTARDS? IT CAN'T POSSIBLY TAKE THIS LONG TO HUNT DOWN ONE MAN.
EXIT
SOMETHING IS WRONG... KOH; I-
-I WILL KILL HIM FOR YOU.
NO.
...I DON'T JUST WANT HIM DEAD. I WANT HIM IN PIECES... I WILL FEAST ON HIS REMAINS.
IF THAT IS WHAT YOU WISH.
I KNOW I CAN COUNT ON YOU.
NOW GO...AND DO NOT BRING HIM BACK TO ME IN ONE PIECE.
EXIT
WHERE HAS TING GONE OFF TO...?

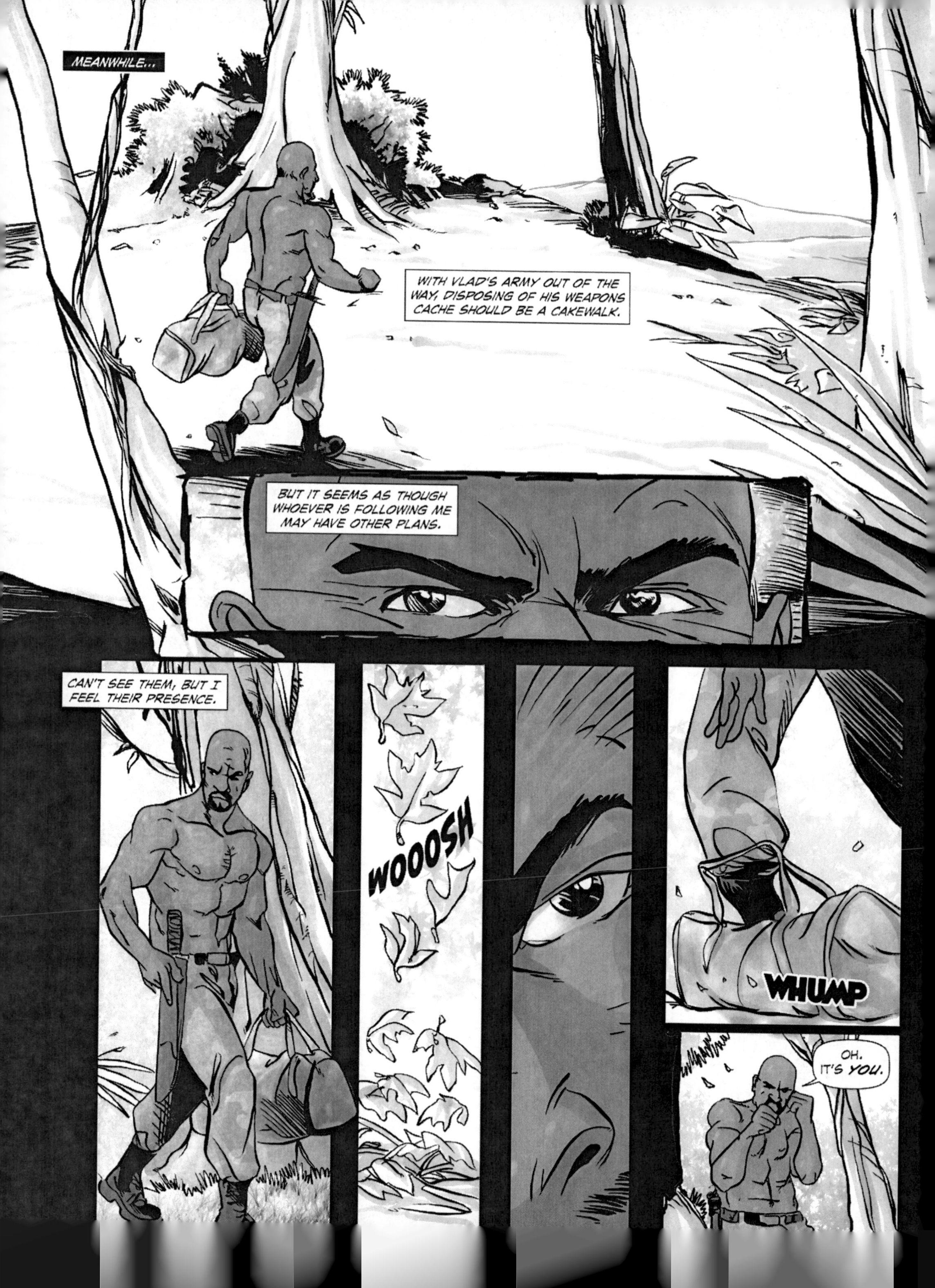
MEANWHILE...
WITH VLAD'S ARMY OUT OF THE WAY, DISPOSING OF HIS WEAPONS CACHE SHOULD BE A CAKEWALK.
BUT IT SEEMS AS THOUGH WHOEVER IS FOLLOWING ME MAY HAVE OTHER PLANS.
CAN'T SEE THEM, BUT I FEEL THEIR PRESENCE.
WOOOSH
WHUMP
OH. IT'S YOU.

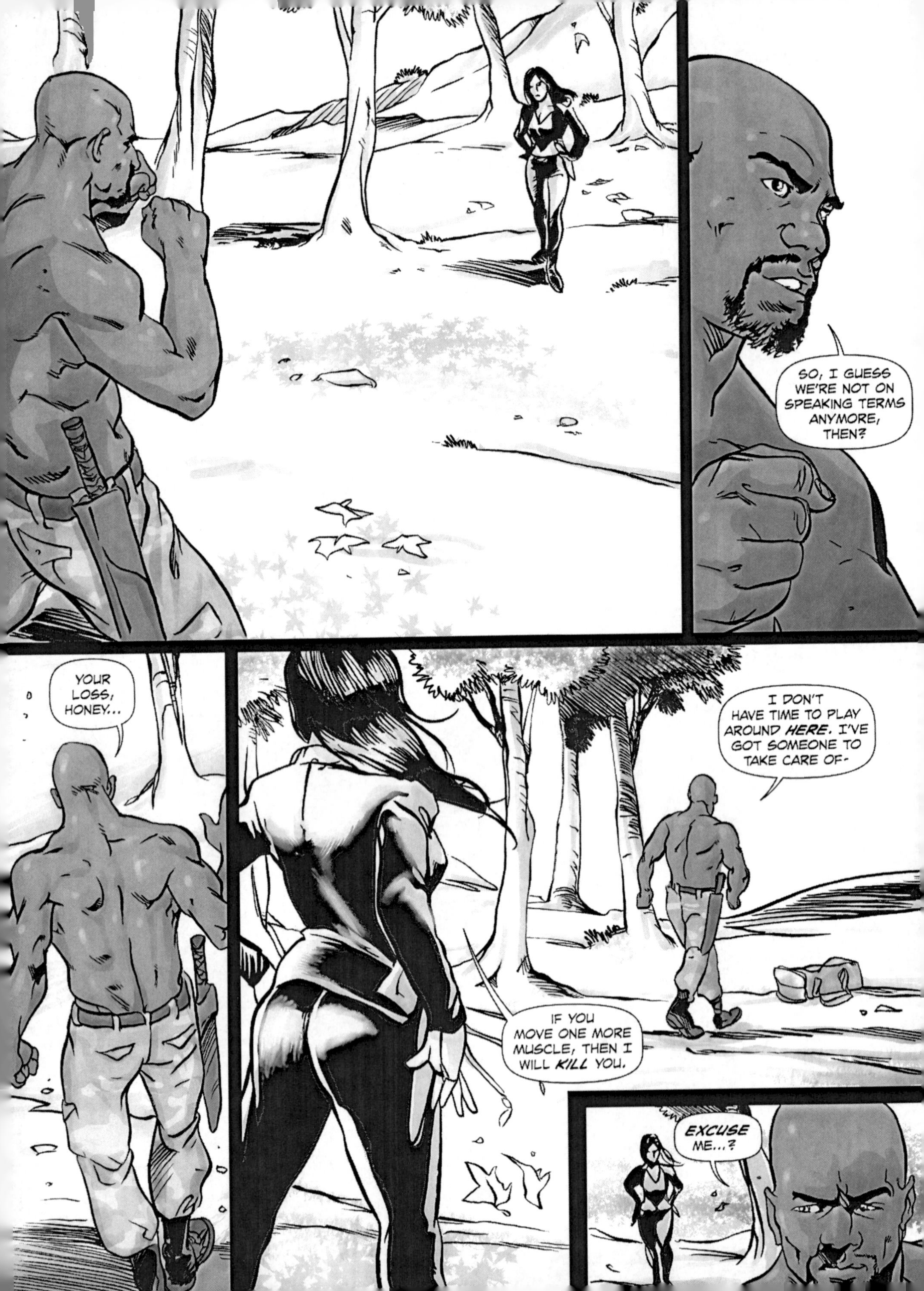
SO, I GUESS WE'RE NOT ON SPEAKING TERMS ANYMORE, THEN?
YOUR LOSS, HONEY...
I DON'T HAVE TIME TO PLAY AROUND HERE. I'VE GOT SOMEONE TO TAKE CARE OF-
IF YOU MOVE ONE MORE MUSCLE, THEN I WILL KILL YOU.
EXCUSE ME...?

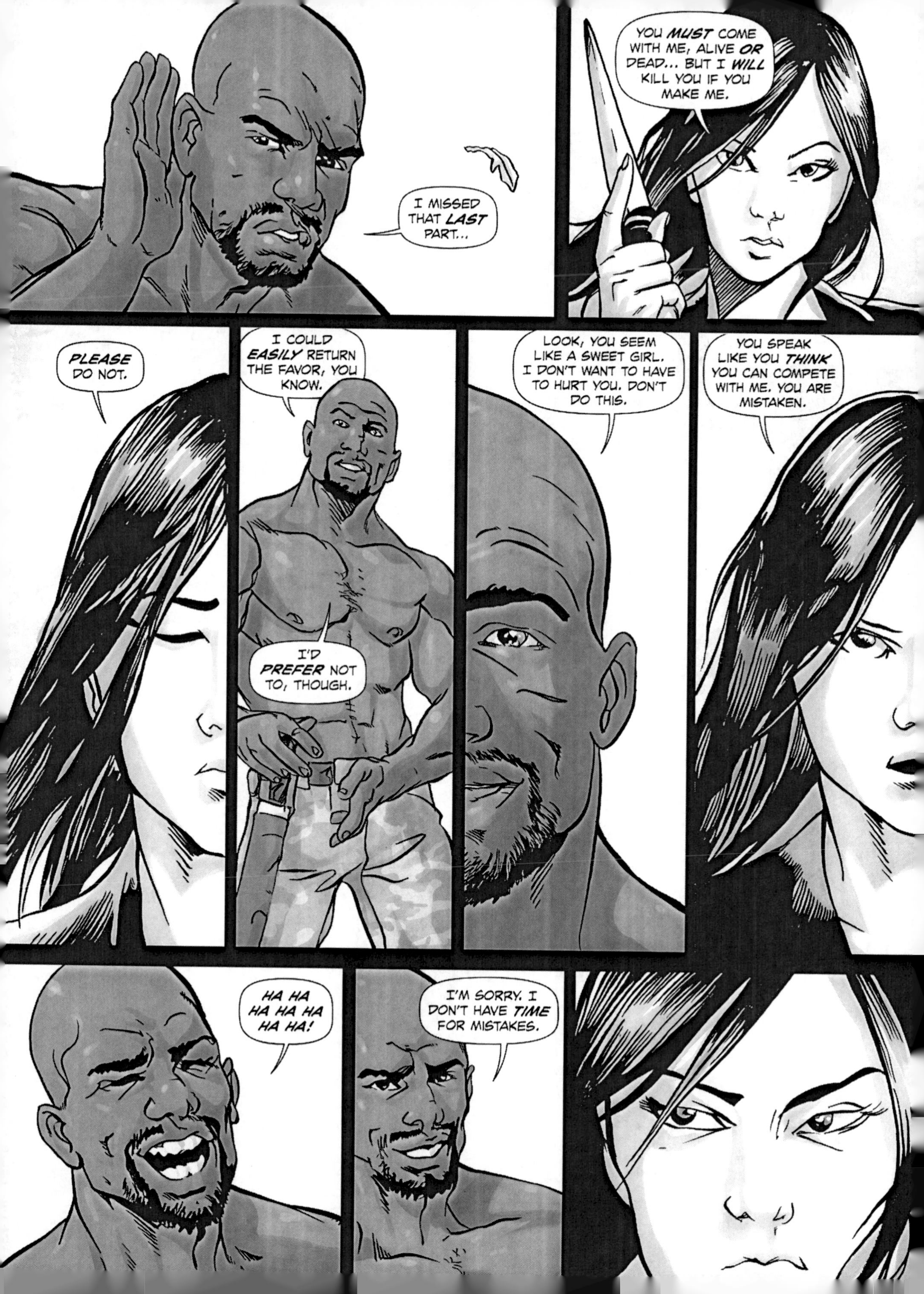
I MISSED THAT LAST PART...
YOU MUST COME WITH ME, ALIVE OR DEAD... BUT I WILL KILL YOU IF YOU MAKE ME.
PLEASE DO NOT.
I COULD EASILY RETURN THE FAVOR, YOU KNOW.
I'D PREFER NOT TO, THOUGH.
LOOK, YOU SEEM LIKE A SWEET GIRL. I DON'T WANT TO HAVE TO HURT YOU. DON'T DO THIS.
YOU SPEAK LIKE YOU THINK YOU CAN COMPETE WITH ME. YOU ARE MISTAKEN.
HA HA HA HA HA HA HA!
I'M SORRY. I DON'T HAVE TIME FOR MISTAKES.

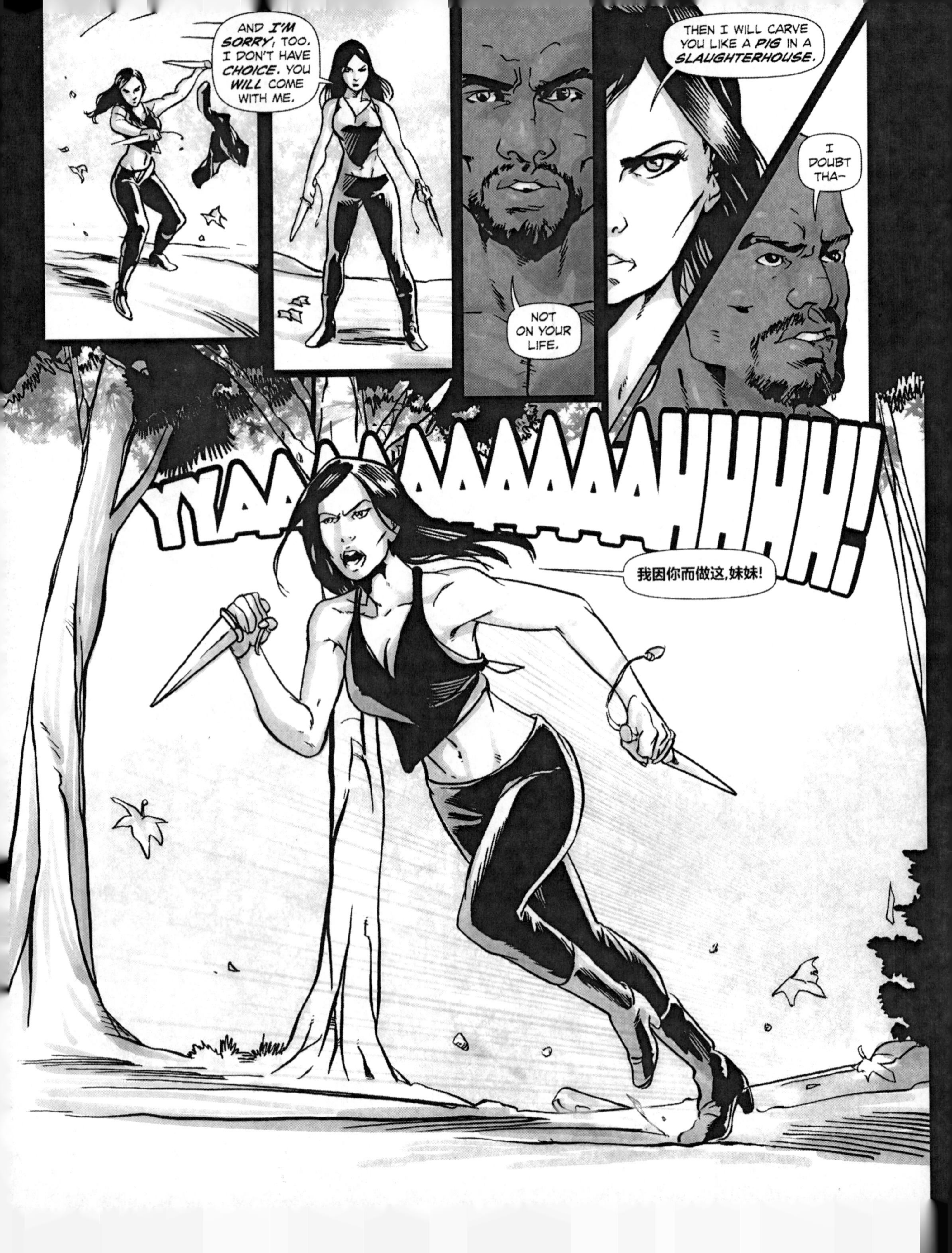
AND I'M SORRY, TOO. I DON'T HAVE CHOICE. YOU WILL COME WITH ME.
NOT ON YOUR LIFE.
THEN I WILL CARVE YOU LIKE A PIG IN A SLAUGHTERHOUSE.
I DOUBT THA–
YYAAAAAAAAAAAHHHHH!
我因你而做这,妹妹!

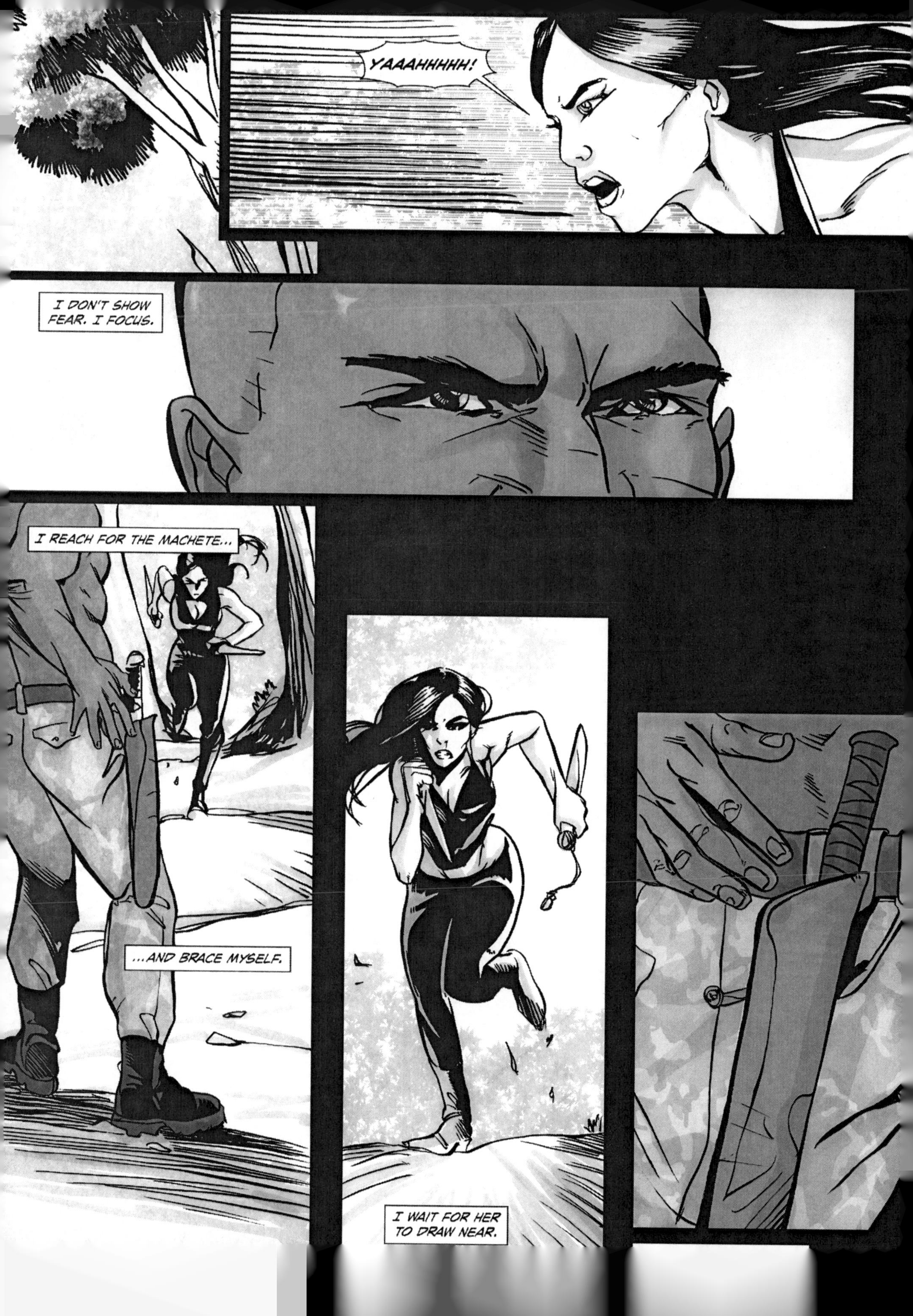
YAAAHHHHH!
I DON'T SHOW FEAR. I FOCUS.
I REACH FOR THE MACHETE...
...AND BRACE MYSELF.
I WAIT FOR HER TO DRAW NEAR.

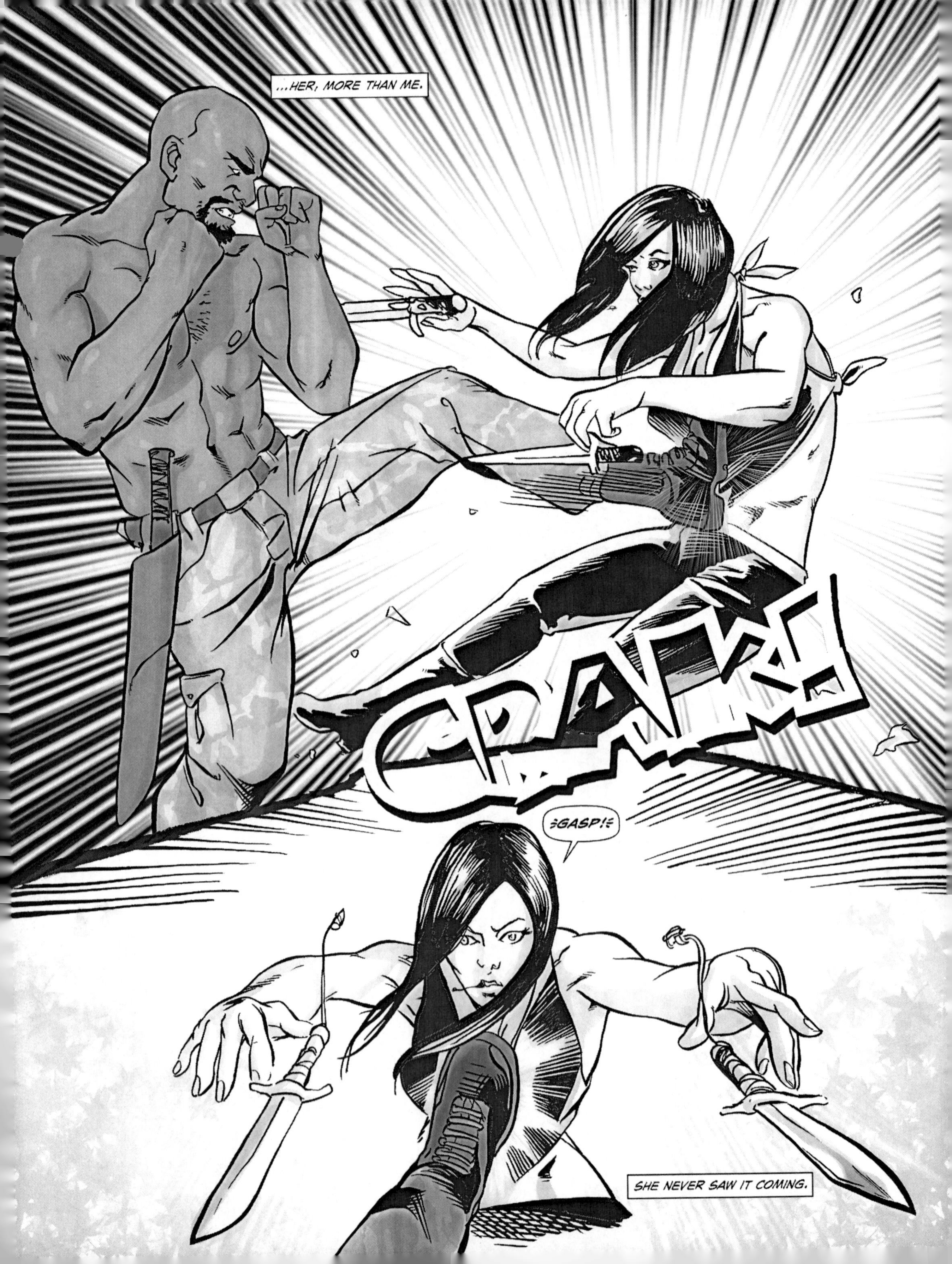
...HER, MORE THAN ME.
CRACK!
GASP!
SHE NEVER SAW IT COMING.

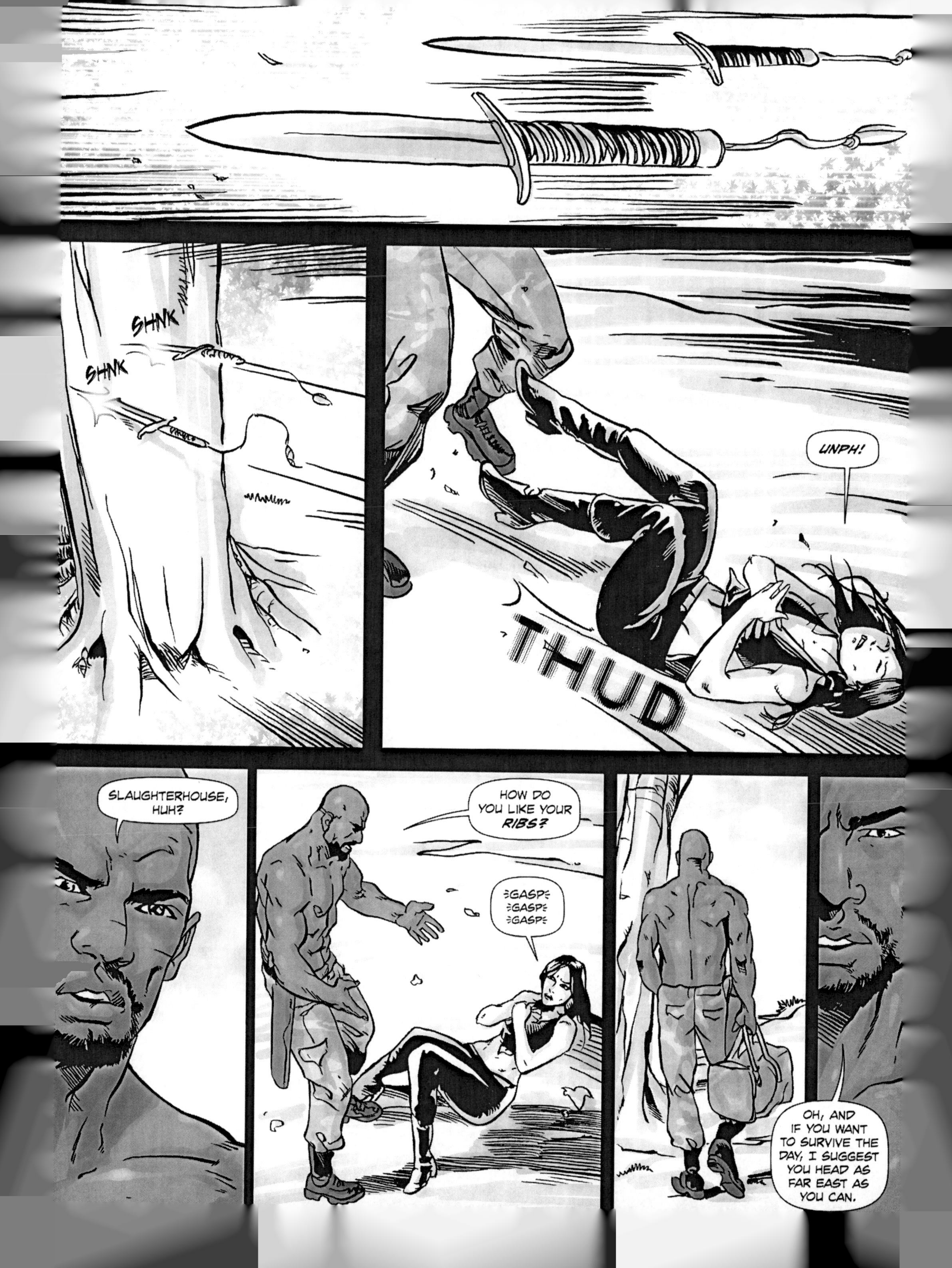
SHNK
SHNK
UNPH!
THUD
SLAUGHTERHOUSE, HUH?
HOW DO YOU LIKE YOUR *RIBS?*
GASP GASP GASP
OH, AND IF YOU WANT TO SURVIVE THE DAY, I SUGGEST YOU HEAD AS FAR EAST AS YOU CAN.

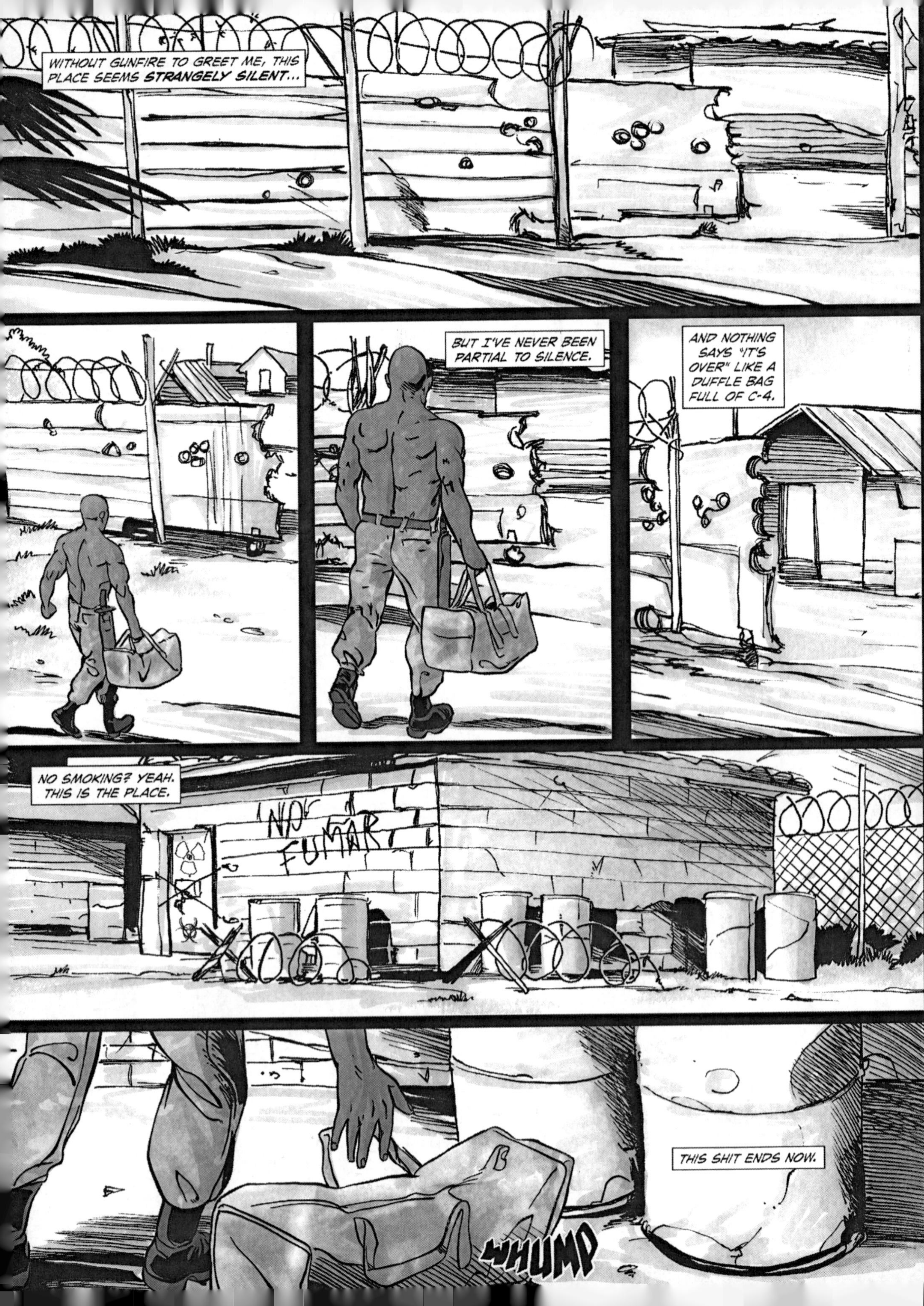
WITHOUT GUNFIRE TO GREET ME, THIS PLACE SEEMS STRANGELY SILENT...
BUT I'VE NEVER BEEN PARTIAL TO SILENCE.
AND NOTHING SAYS "IT'S OVER" LIKE A DUFFLE BAG FULL OF C-4.
NO SMOKING? YEAH. THIS IS THE PLACE.
NO FUMAR
THIS SHIT ENDS NOW.
WHUMP

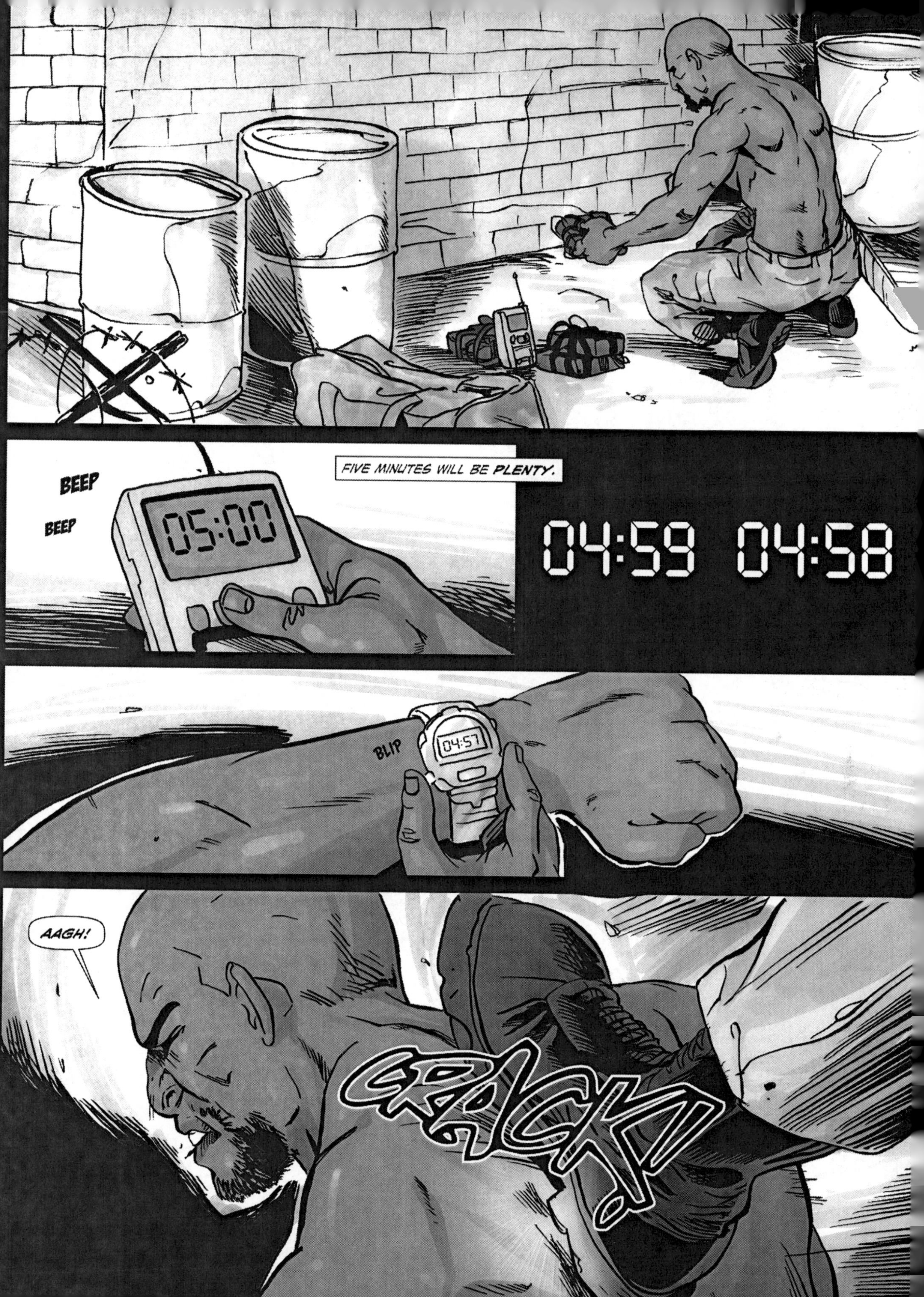

BEEP
BEEP
05:00
FIVE MINUTES WILL BE PLENTY.
04:59 04:58
BLIP
04:57
AAGH!
CRACK!

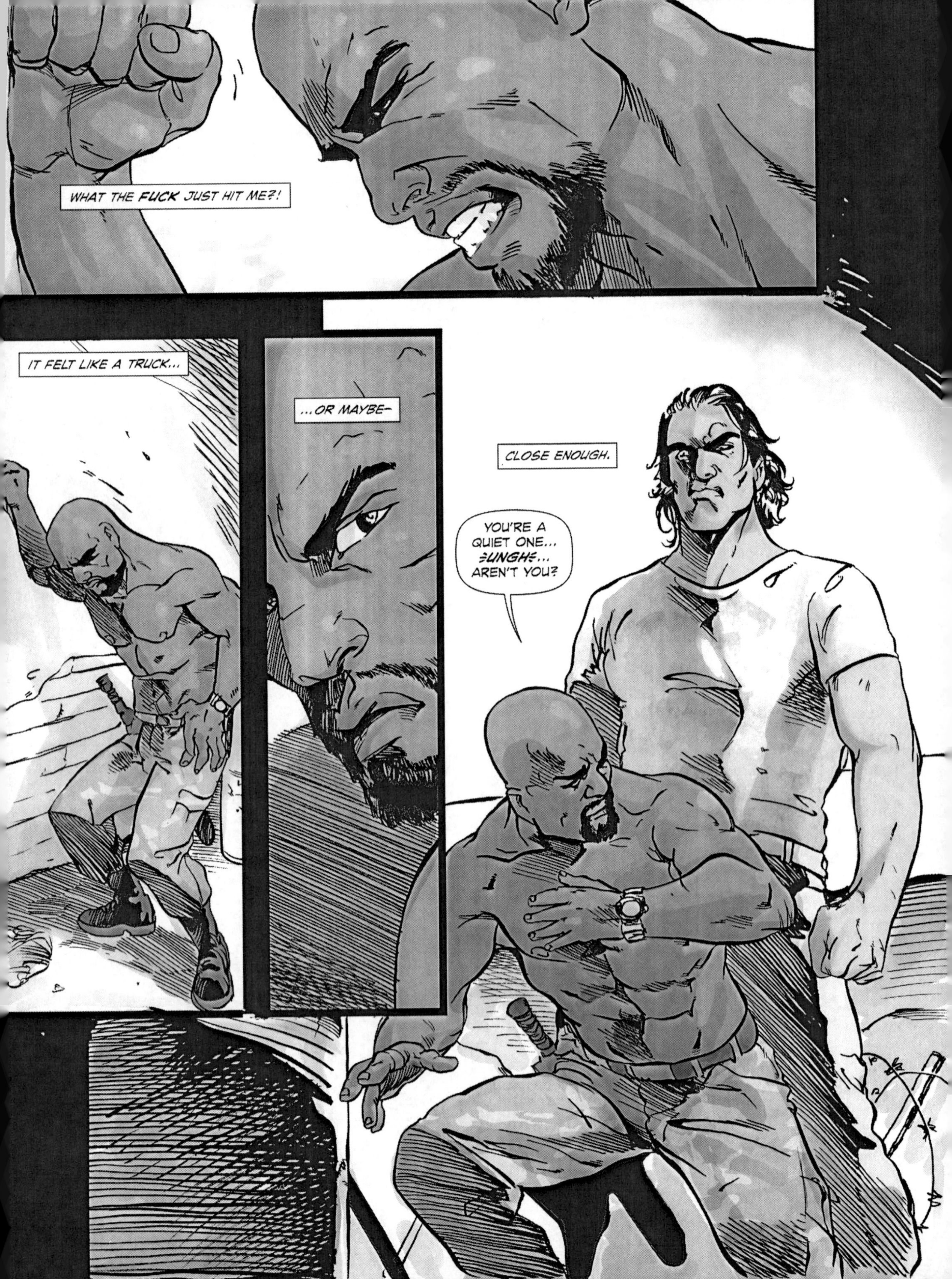
WHAT THE FUCK JUST HIT ME?!
IT FELT LIKE A TRUCK...
...OR MAYBE-
CLOSE ENOUGH.
YOU'RE A QUIET ONE... =UNGH=... AREN'T YOU?

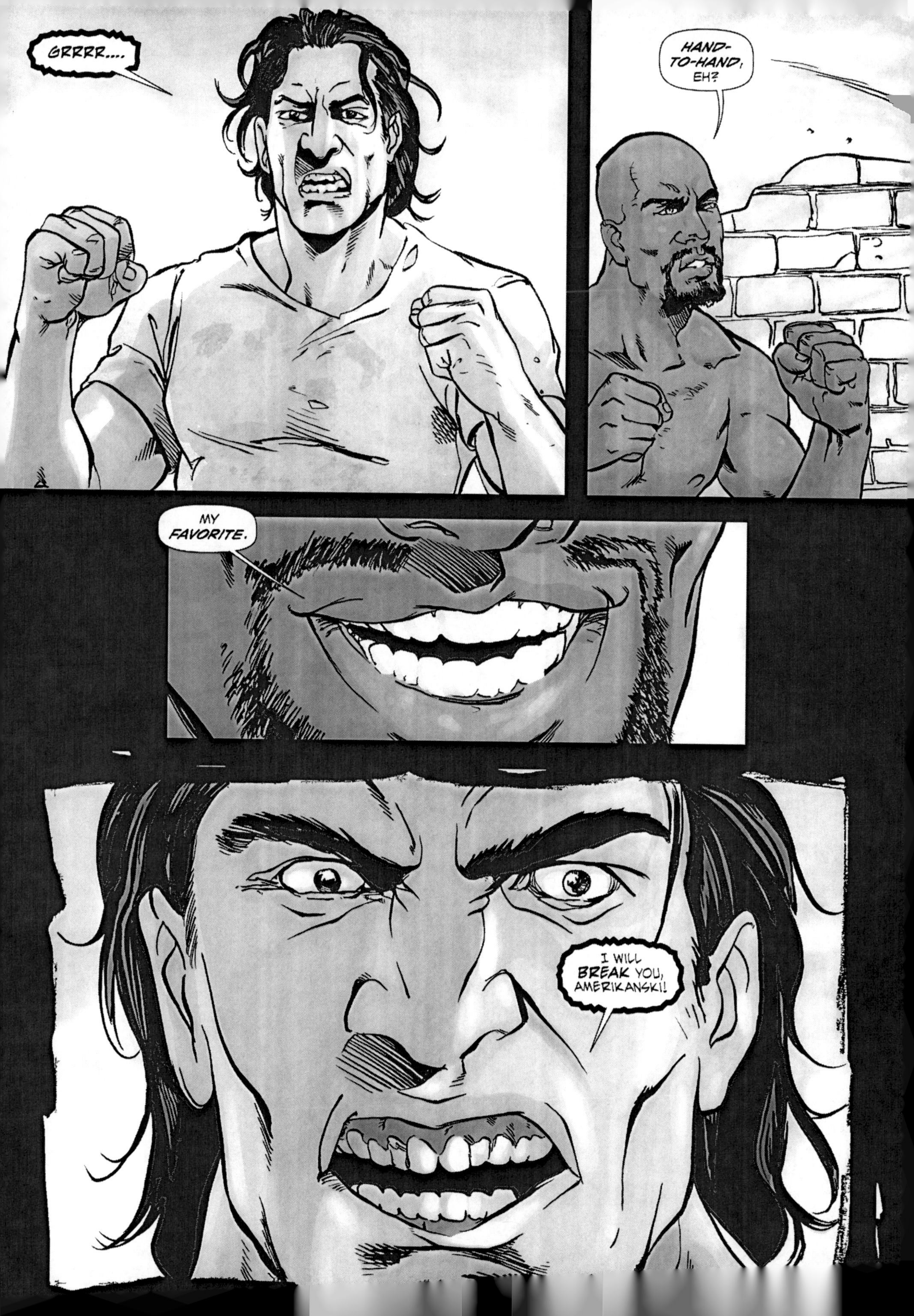
GRRRR....
HAND-TO-HAND, EH?
MY FAVORITE.
I WILL BREAK YOU, AMERIKANSKI!

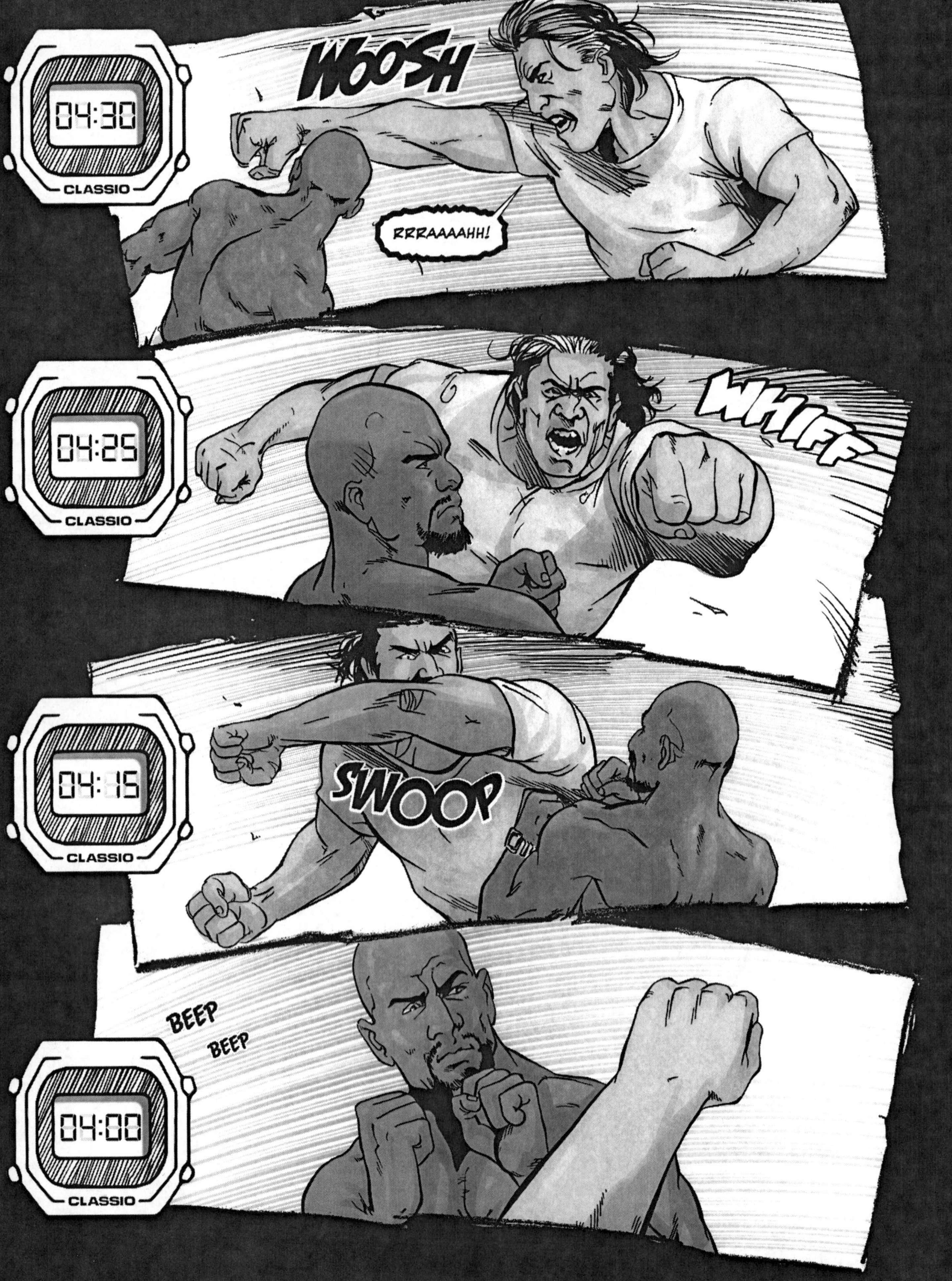
CLASSIO
04:30
WOOSH
RRRAAAAHH!
CLASSIO
04:25
WHIFF
CLASSIO
04:15
SWOOP
BEEP
BEEP
CLASSIO
04:00

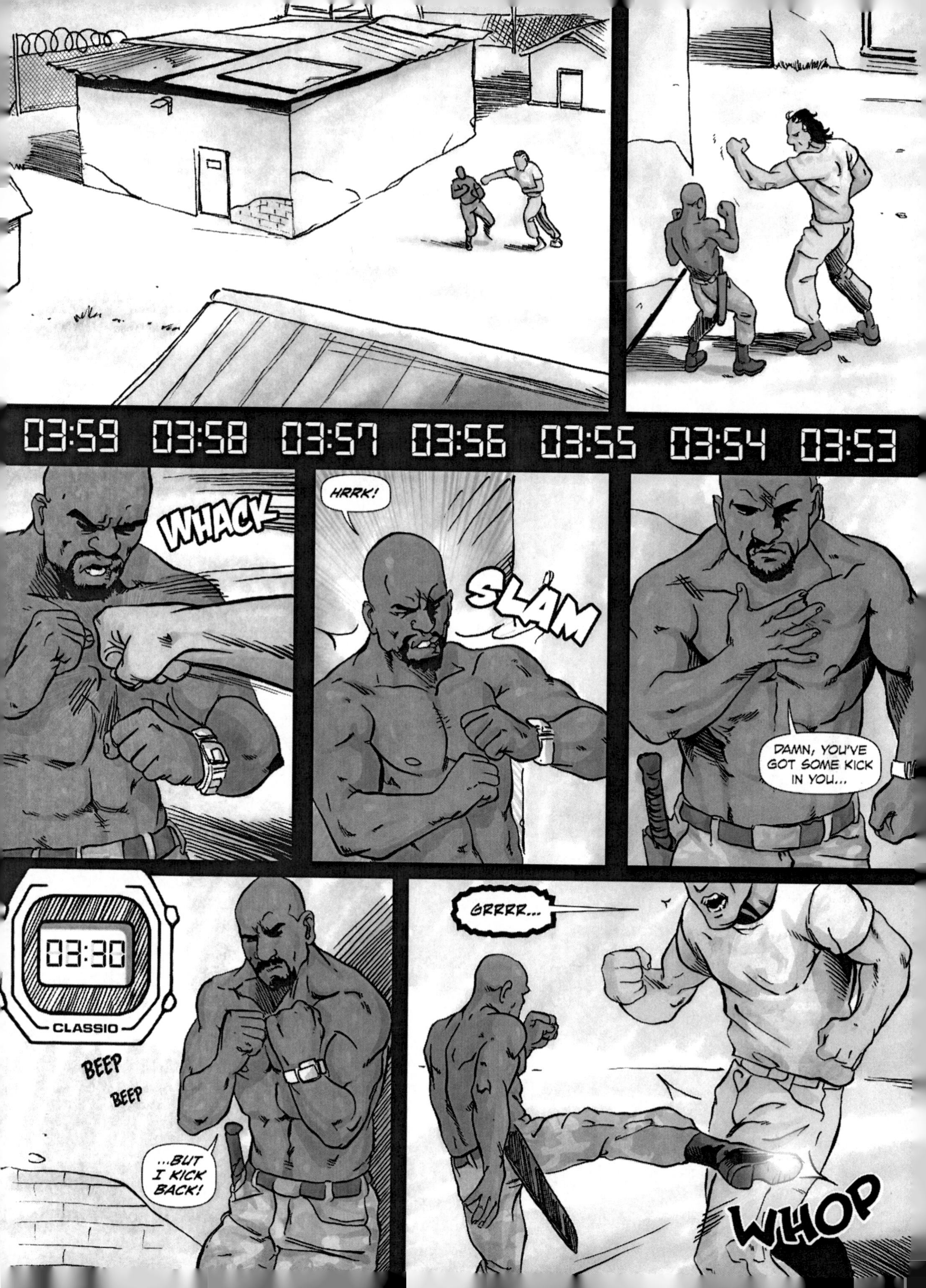
03:59 03:58 03:57 03:56 03:55 03:54 03:53
WHACK
HRRK!
SLAM
DAMN, YOU'VE GOT SOME KICK IN YOU...
03:30
CLASSIO
BEEP
BEEP
...BUT I KICK BACK!
GRRRR...
WHOP

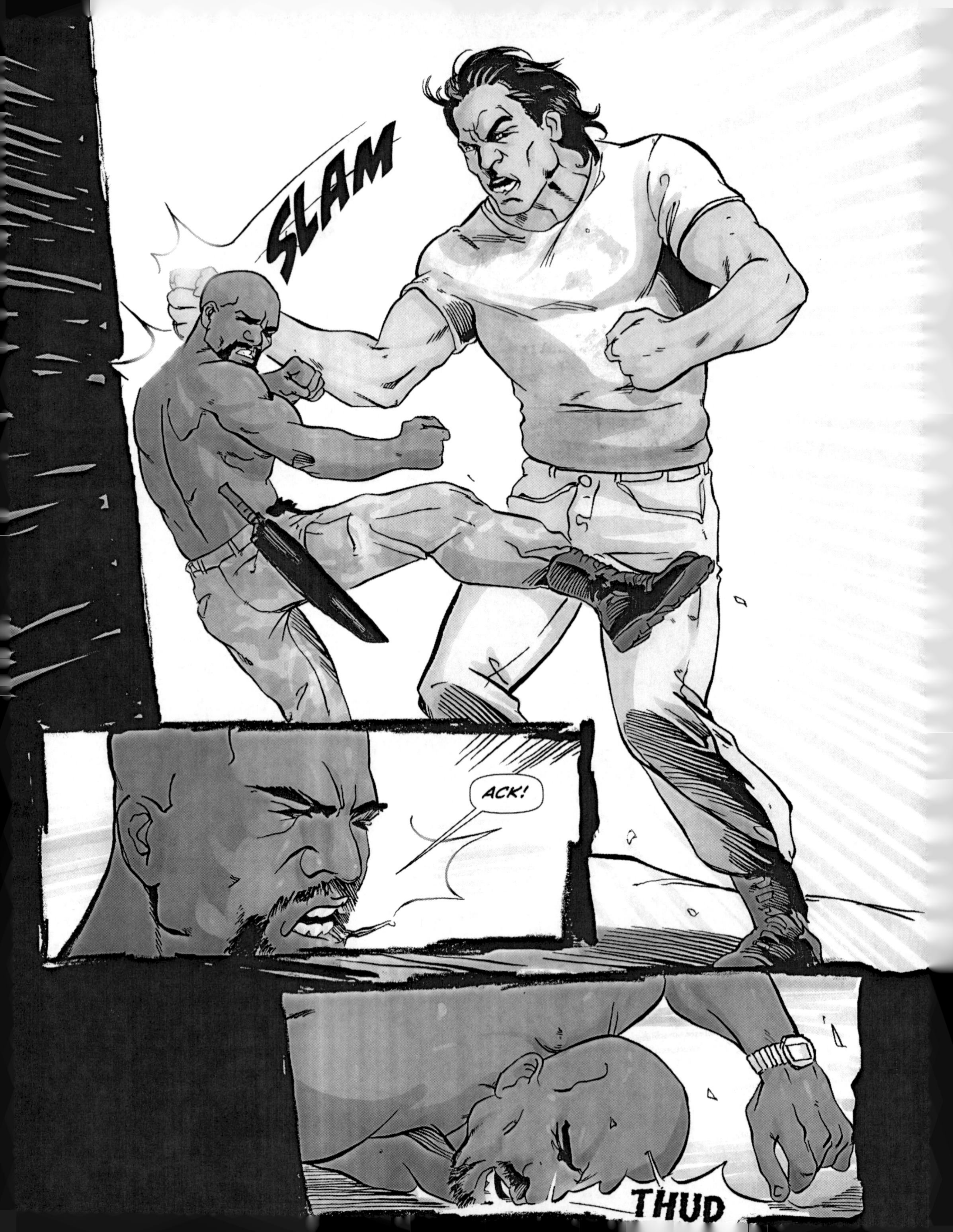
SLAM
ACK!
THUD

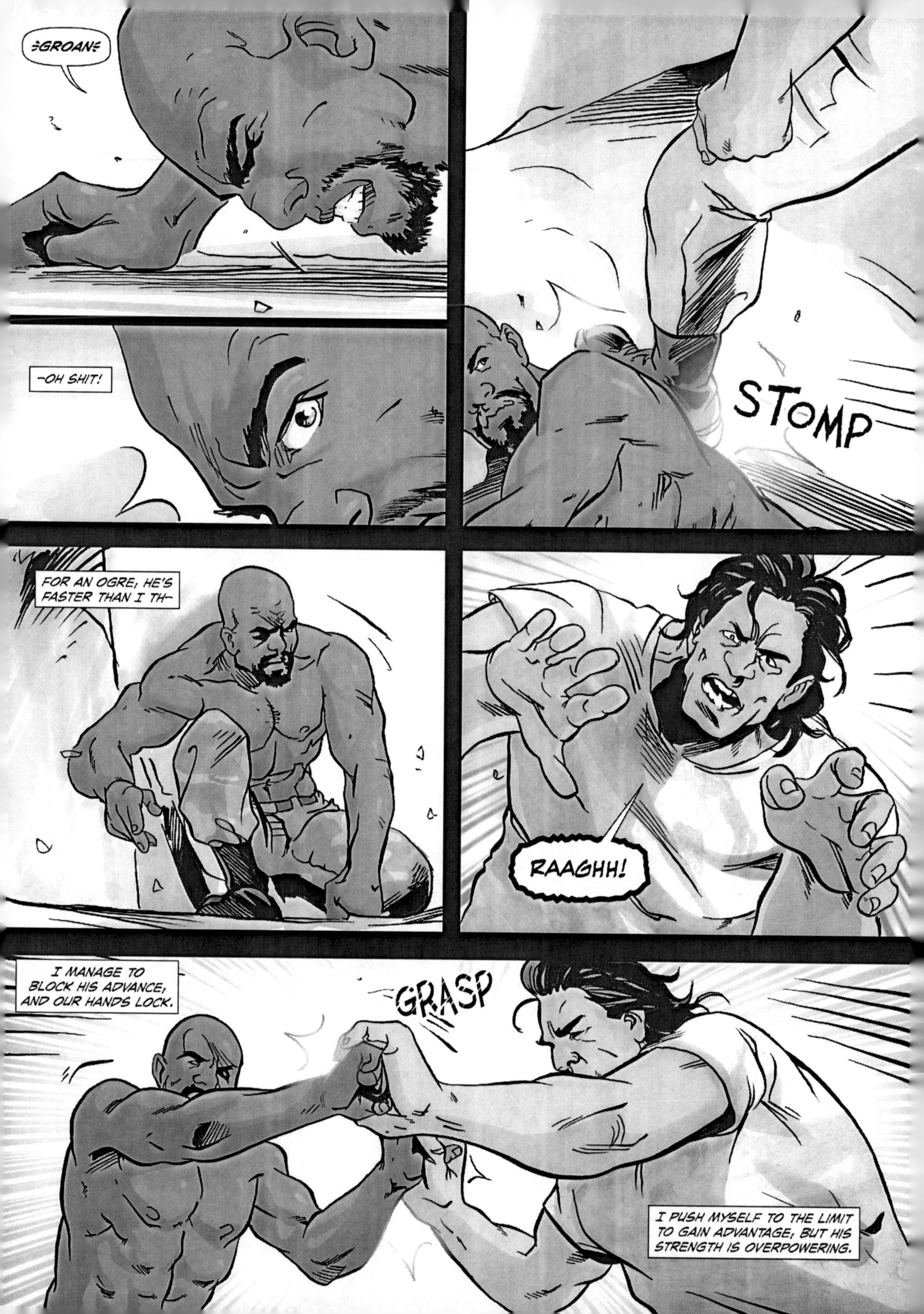

GROAN
STOMP
–OH SHIT!
FOR AN OGRE, HE'S FASTER THAN I TH–
RAAGHH!
I MANAGE TO BLOCK HIS ADVANCE, AND OUR HANDS LOCK.
GRASP
I PUSH MYSELF TO THE LIMIT TO GAIN ADVANTAGE, BUT HIS STRENGTH IS OVERPOWERING.

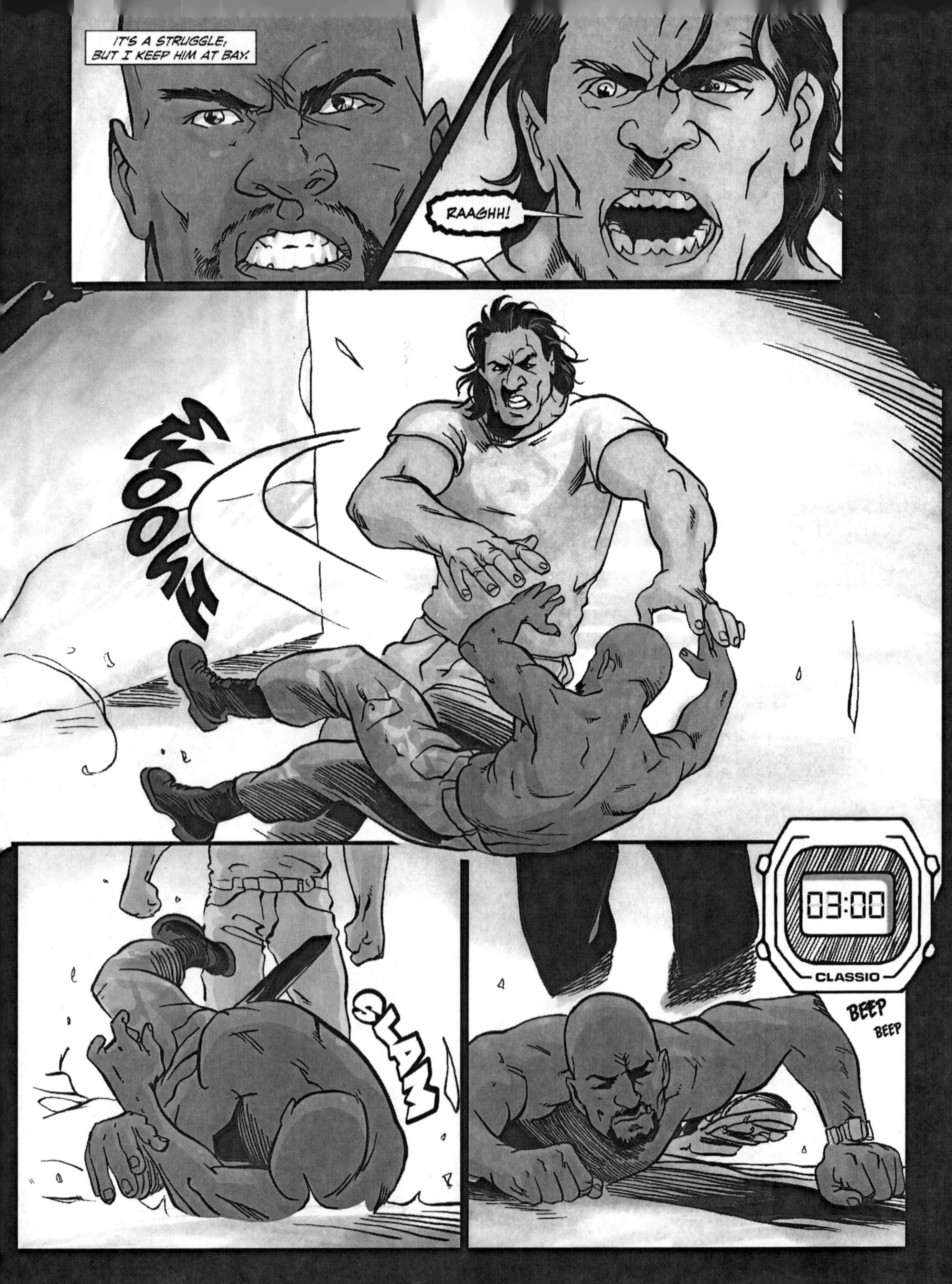

IT'S A STRUGGLE, BUT I KEEP HIM AT BAY.
RAAGHH!
SWOOSH
SLAM
03:00
CLASSIO
BEEP
BEEP

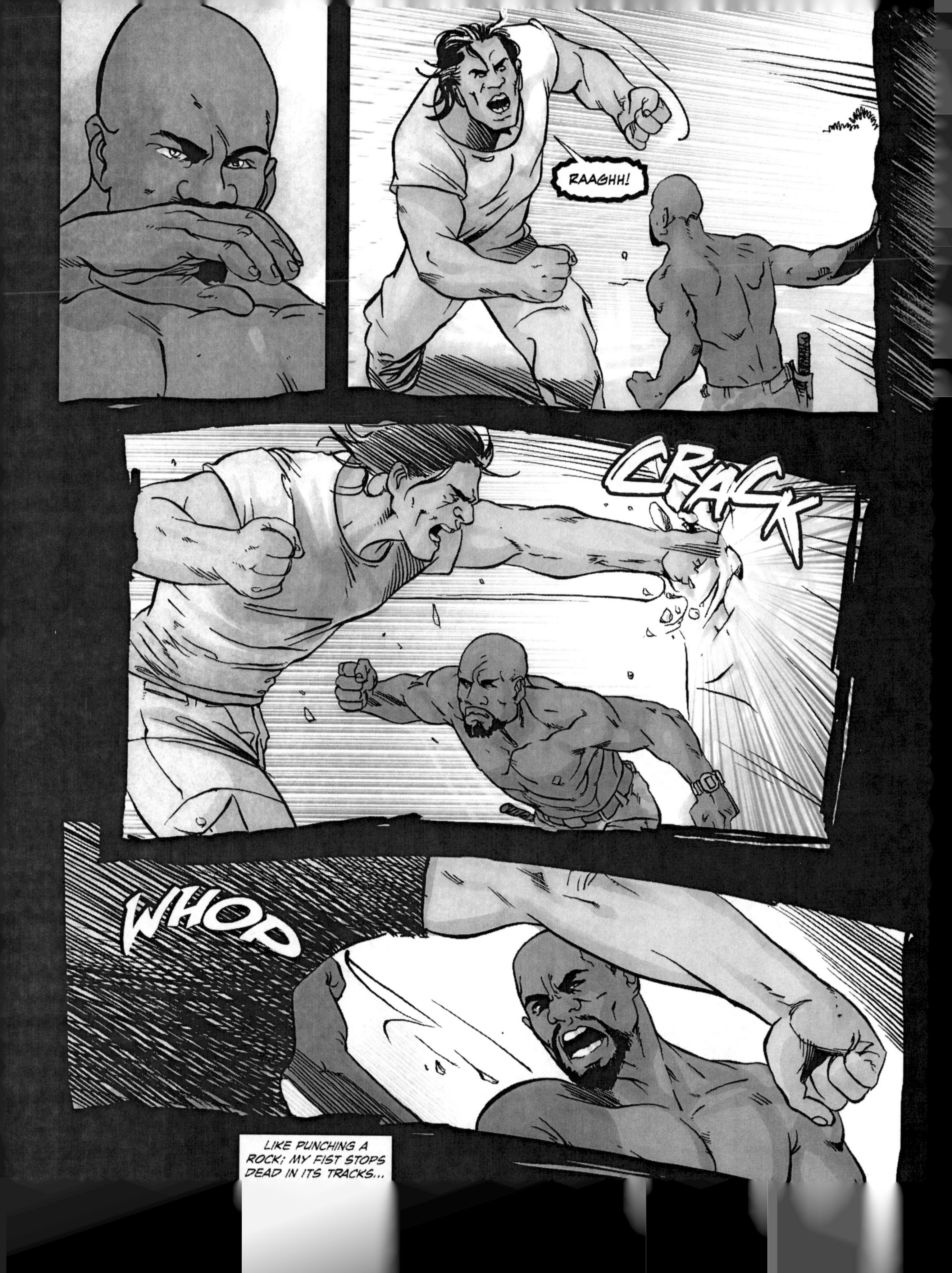
RAAGHH!
CRACK
WHOP
LIKE PUNCHING A ROCK; MY FIST STOPS DEAD IN ITS TRACKS...

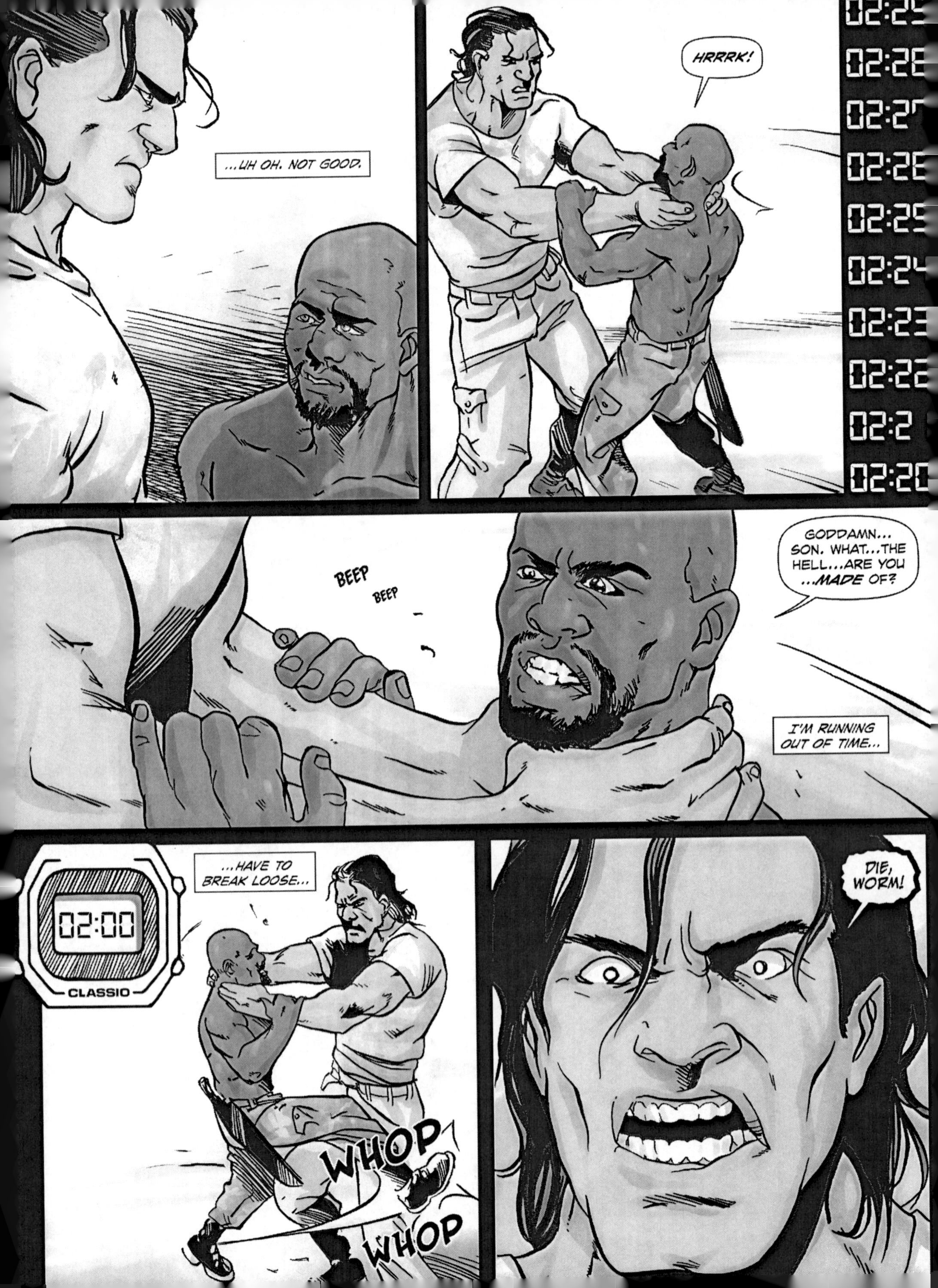
...UH OH. NOT GOOD.
HRRRK!
02:25
02:26
02:27
02:26
02:25
02:24
02:23
02:22
02:2
02:20
BEEP
BEEP
GODDAMN... SON. WHAT...THE HELL...ARE YOU ...MADE OF?
I'M RUNNING OUT OF TIME...
02:00
CLASSIO
...HAVE TO BREAK LOOSE...
WHOP
WHOP
DIE, WORM!

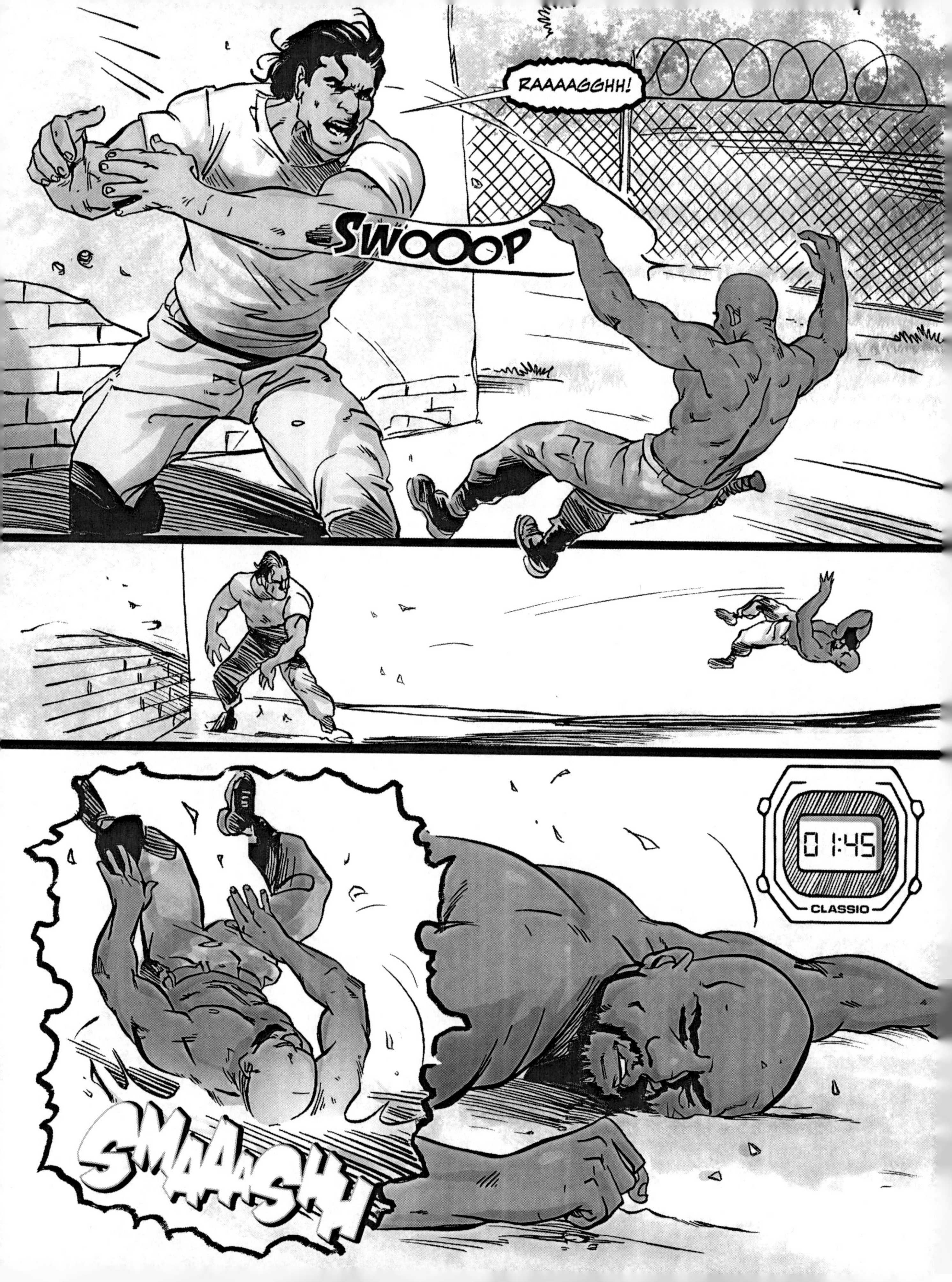
RAAAAGGHH!
SWOOOP
SMAAASH
01:45
CLASSIO

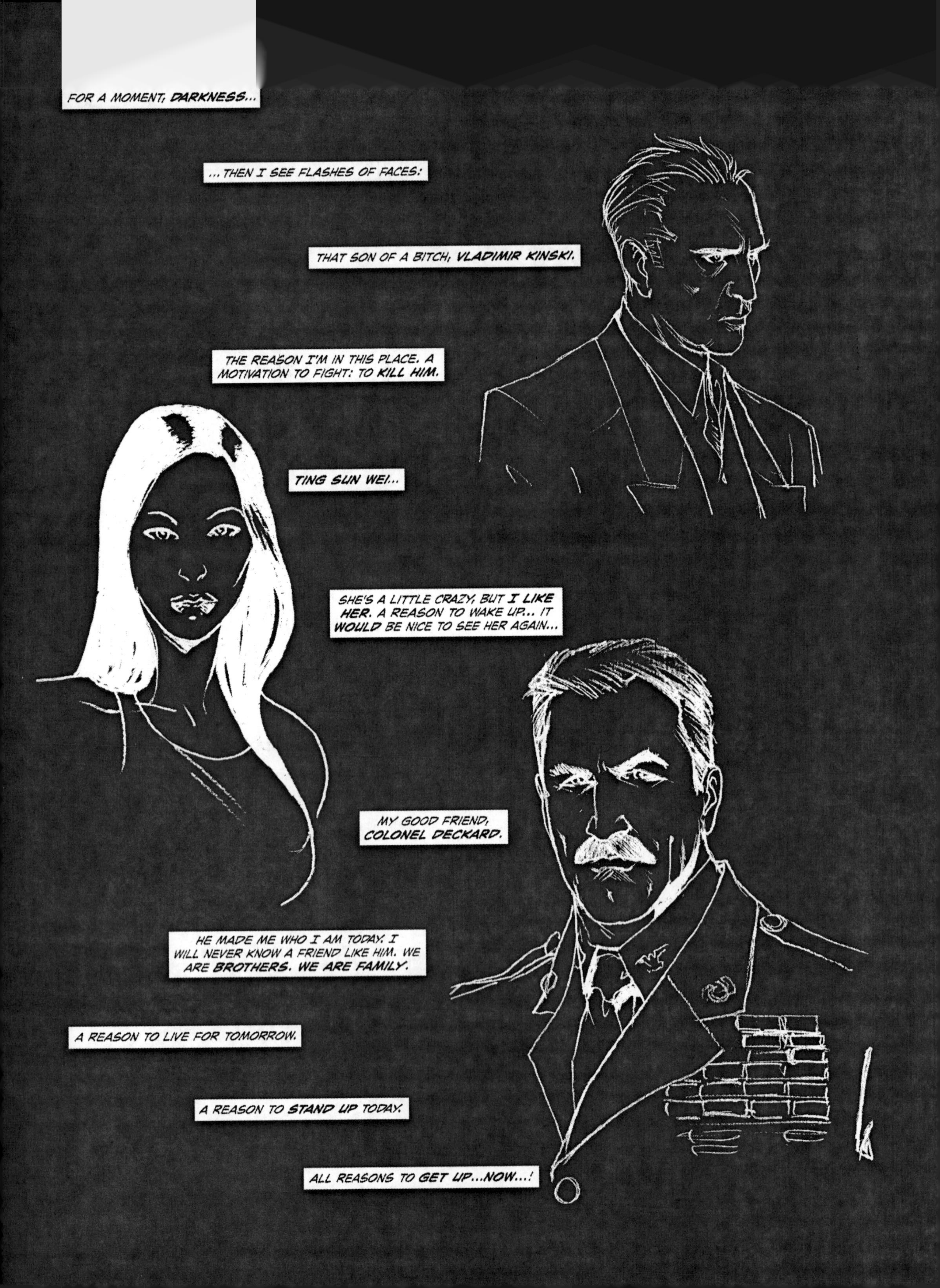
FOR A MOMENT, DARKNESS...
...THEN I SEE FLASHES OF FACES:
THAT SON OF A BITCH, VLADIMIR KINSKI.
THE REASON I'M IN THIS PLACE. A MOTIVATION TO FIGHT: TO KILL HIM.
TING SUN WEI...
SHE'S A LITTLE CRAZY, BUT I LIKE HER. A REASON TO WAKE UP... IT WOULD BE NICE TO SEE HER AGAIN...
MY GOOD FRIEND, COLONEL DECKARD.
HE MADE ME WHO I AM TODAY. I WILL NEVER KNOW A FRIEND LIKE HIM. WE ARE BROTHERS. WE ARE FAMILY.
A REASON TO LIVE FOR TOMORROW.
A REASON TO STAND UP TODAY.
ALL REASONS TO GET UP...NOW...!

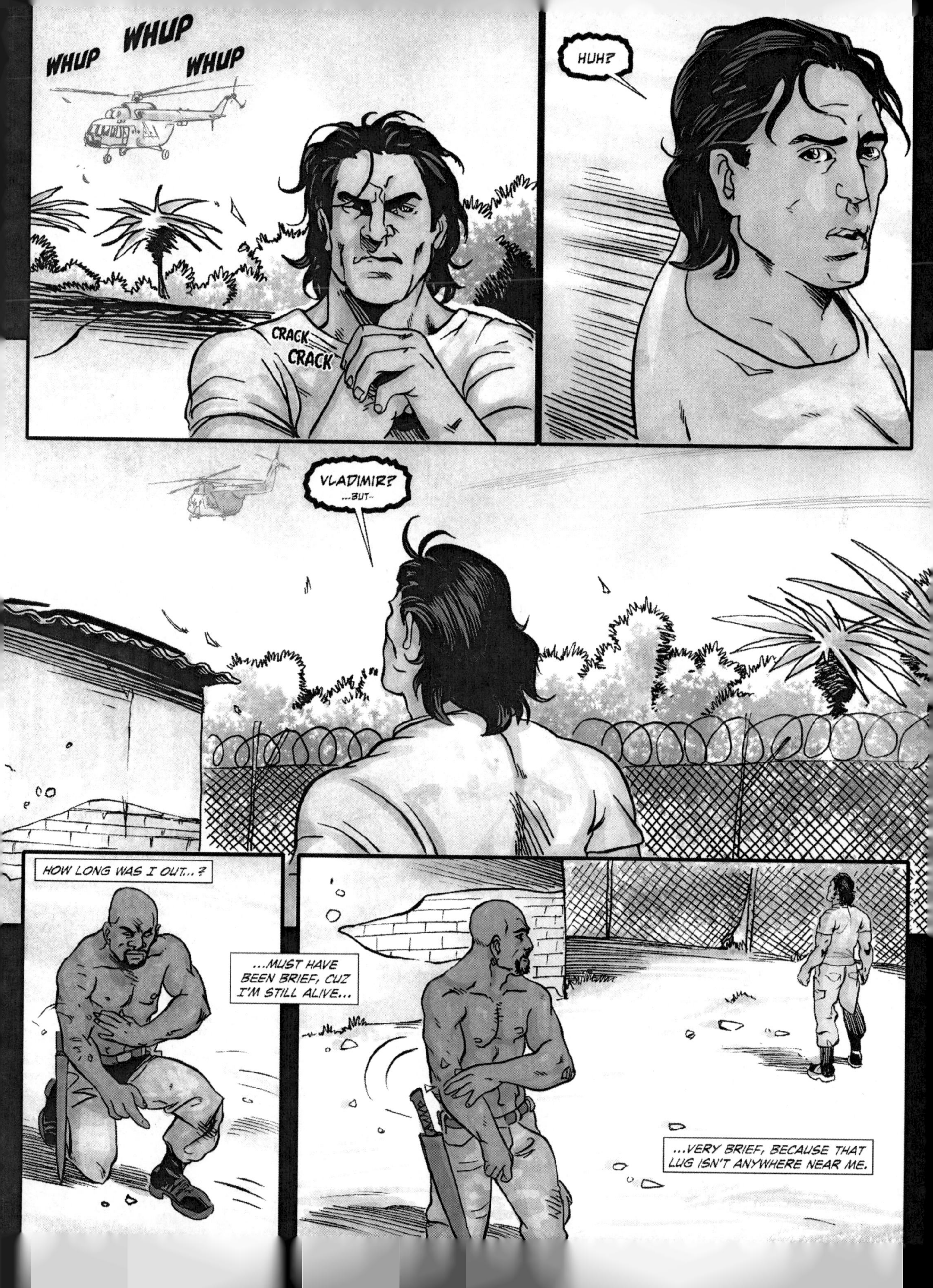

WHUP WHUP WHUP
CRACK CRACK
HUH?
VLADIMIR? ...BUT--
HOW LONG WAS I OUT...?
...MUST HAVE BEEN BRIEF, CUZ I'M STILL ALIVE...
...VERY BRIEF, BECAUSE THAT LUG ISN'T ANYWHERE NEAR ME.

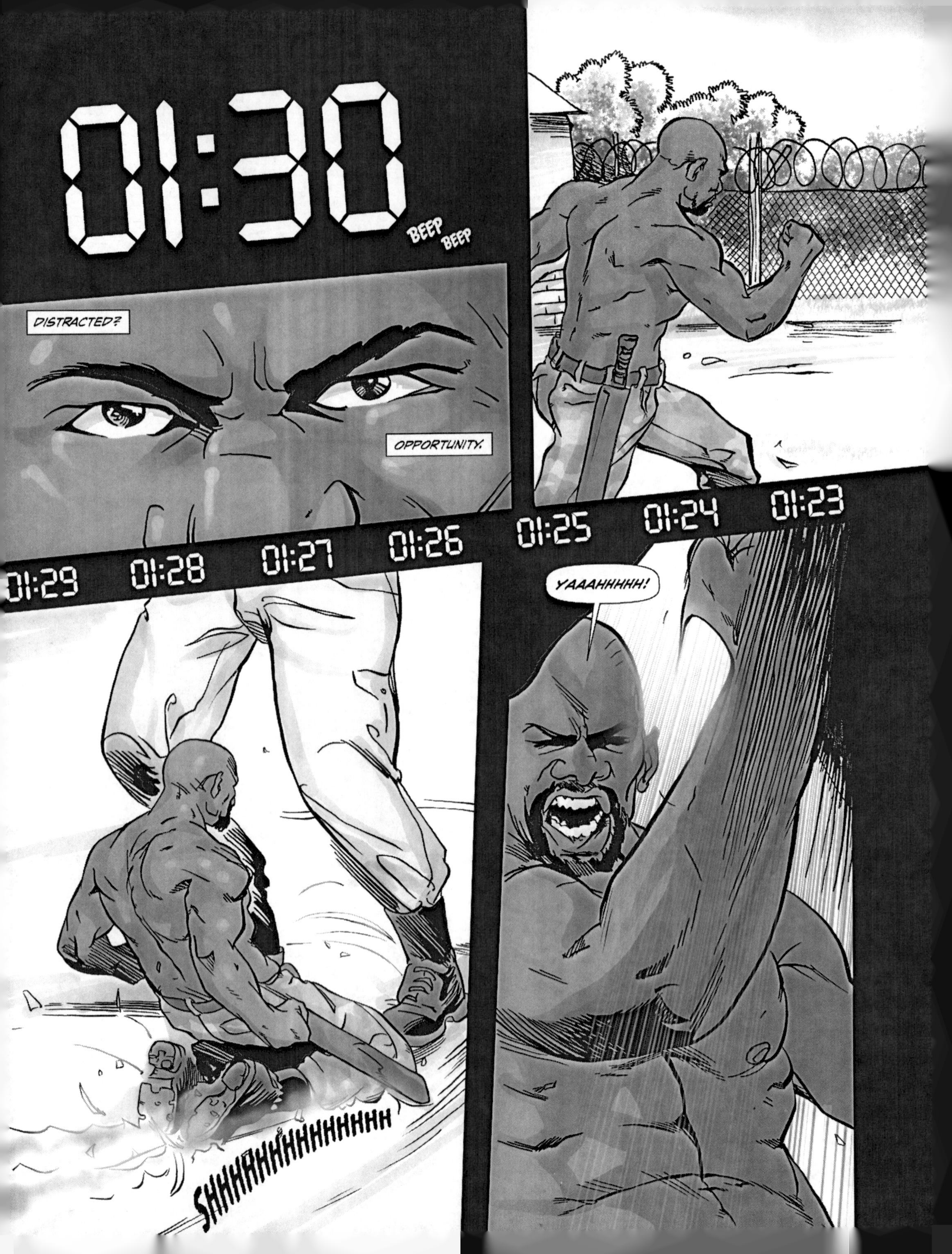
01:30
BEEP BEEP
DISTRACTED?
OPPORTUNITY.
01:29
01:28
01:27
01:26
01:25
01:24
01:23
SHHHHHHHHHHHHHH
YAAAHHHHH!

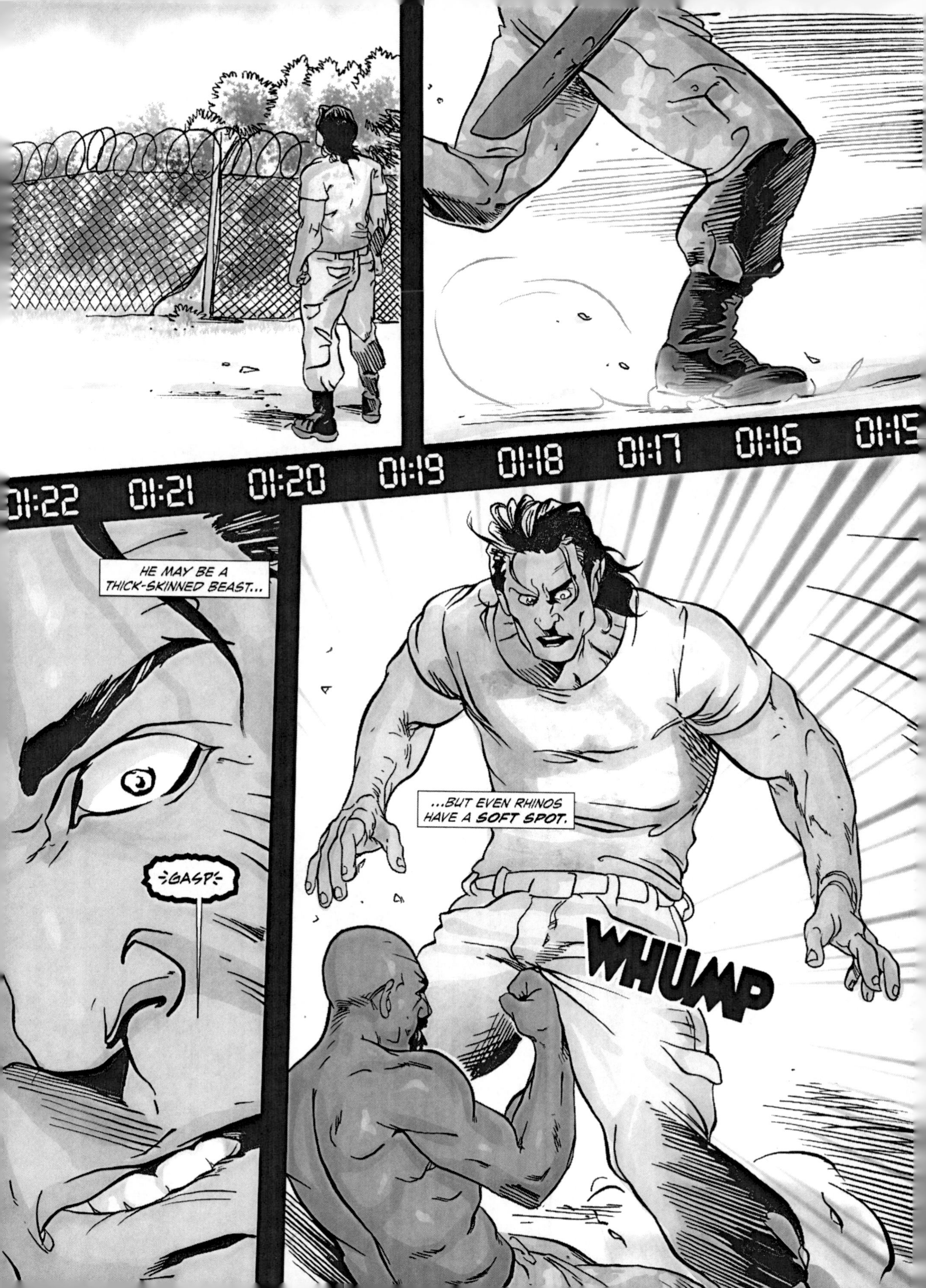
01:22
01:21
01:20
01:19
01:18
01:17
01:16
01:15
HE MAY BE A THICK-SKINNED BEAST...
-GASP-
...BUT EVEN RHINOS HAVE A SOFT SPOT.
WHUMP

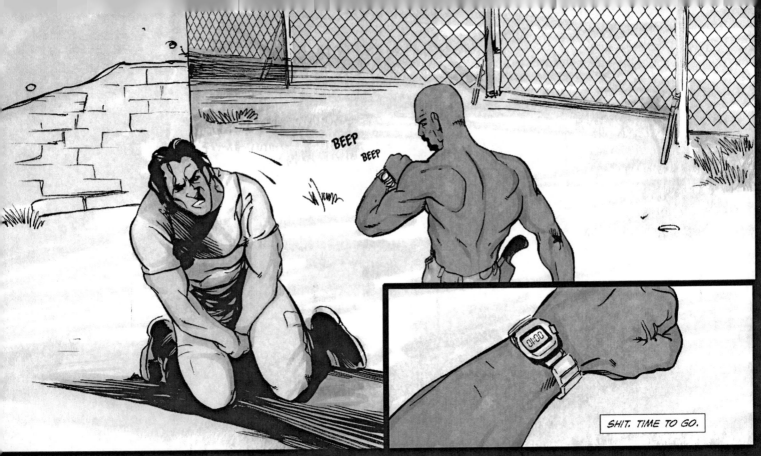

BEEP
BEEP

SHIT. TIME TO GO.

00:59 00:58 00:57 00:56 00:55

...BUT I'VE GOTTA BLOW THIS JOINT.

IT'S BEEN A *BALL*...

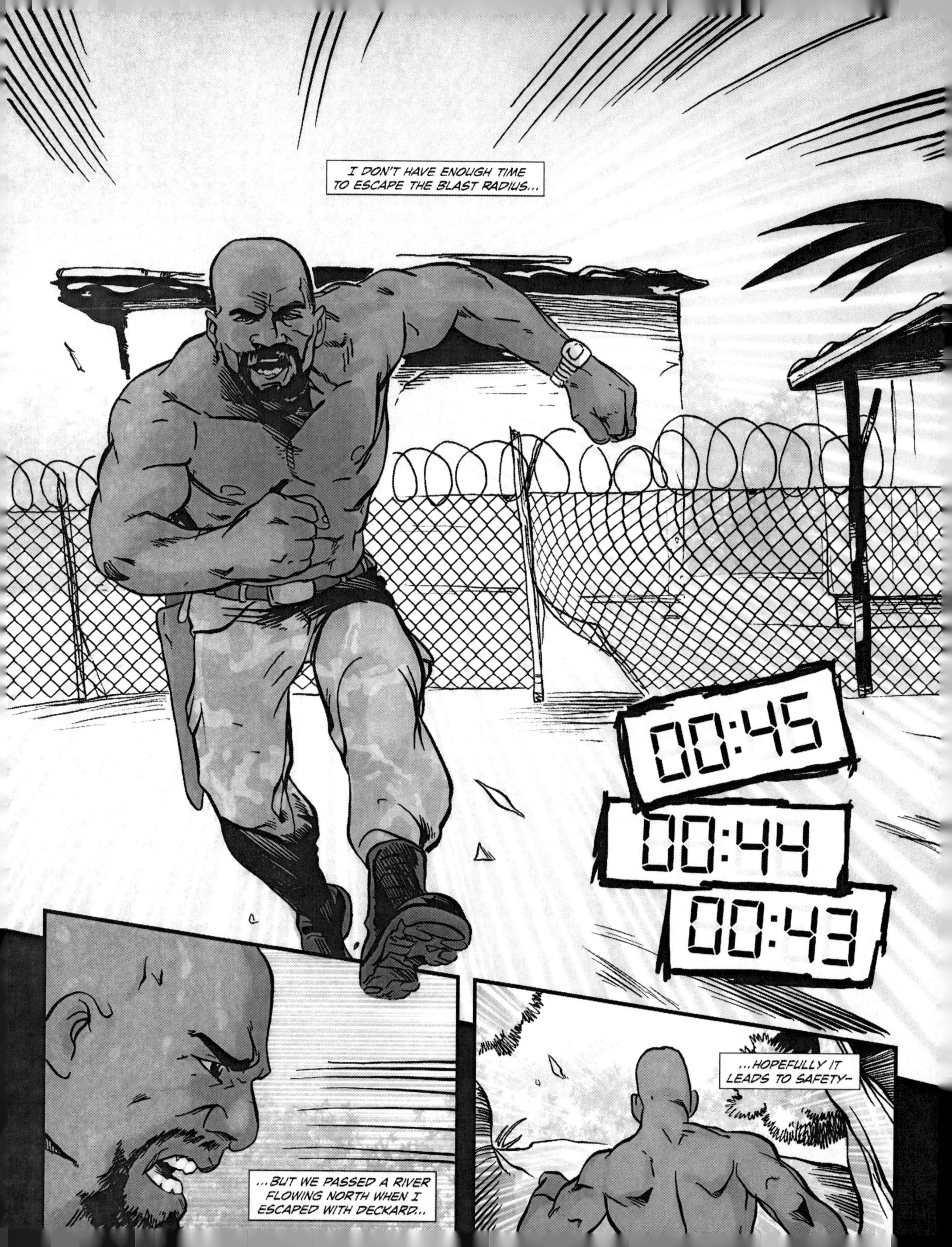
I DON'T HAVE ENOUGH TIME TO ESCAPE THE BLAST RADIUS...
00:45
00:44
00:43
...BUT WE PASSED A RIVER FLOWING NORTH WHEN I ESCAPED WITH DECKARD...
...HOPEFULLY IT LEADS TO SAFETY-

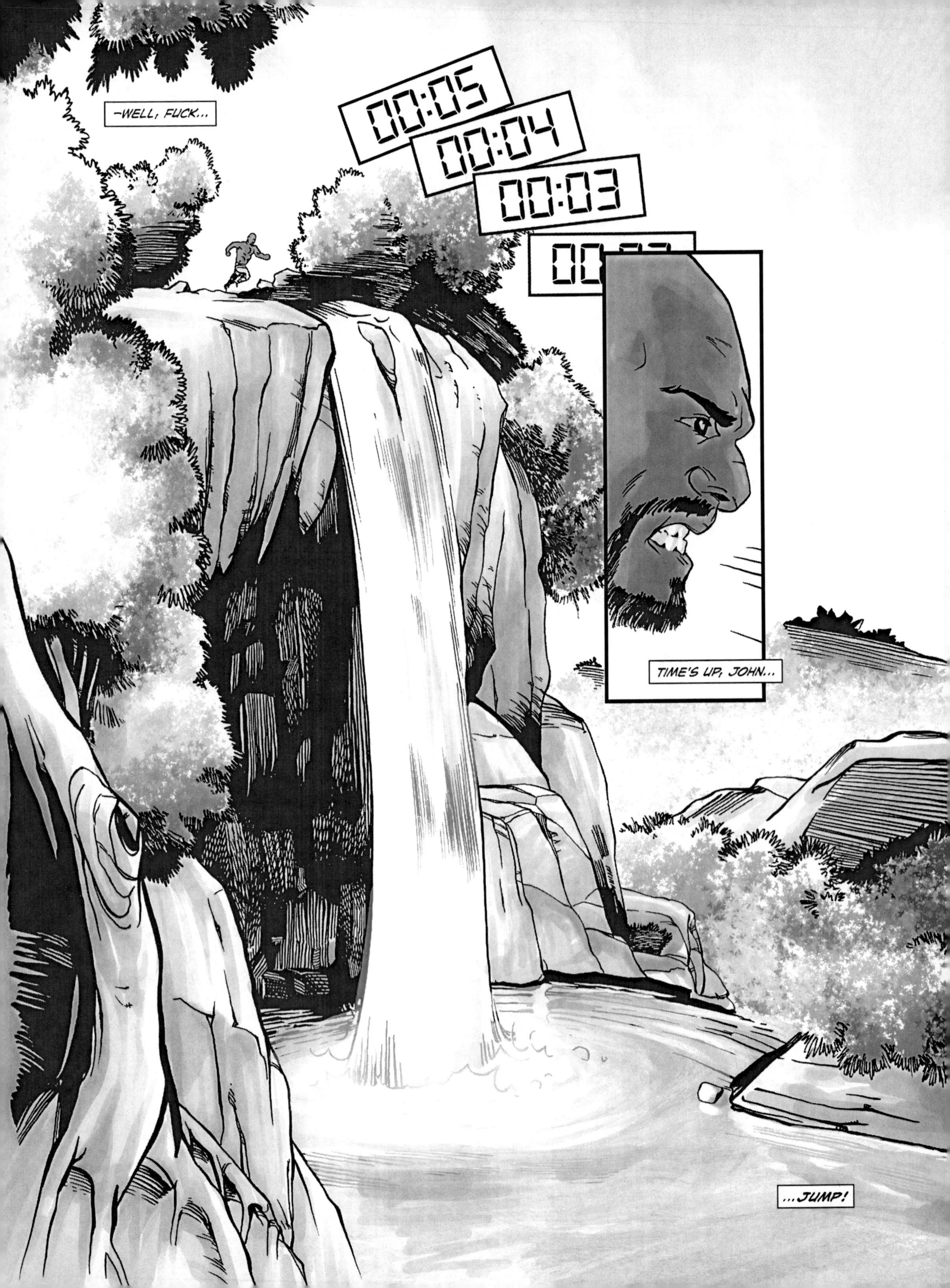
-WELL, FUCK...
00:05
00:04
00:03
TIME'S UP, JOHN...
...JUMP!

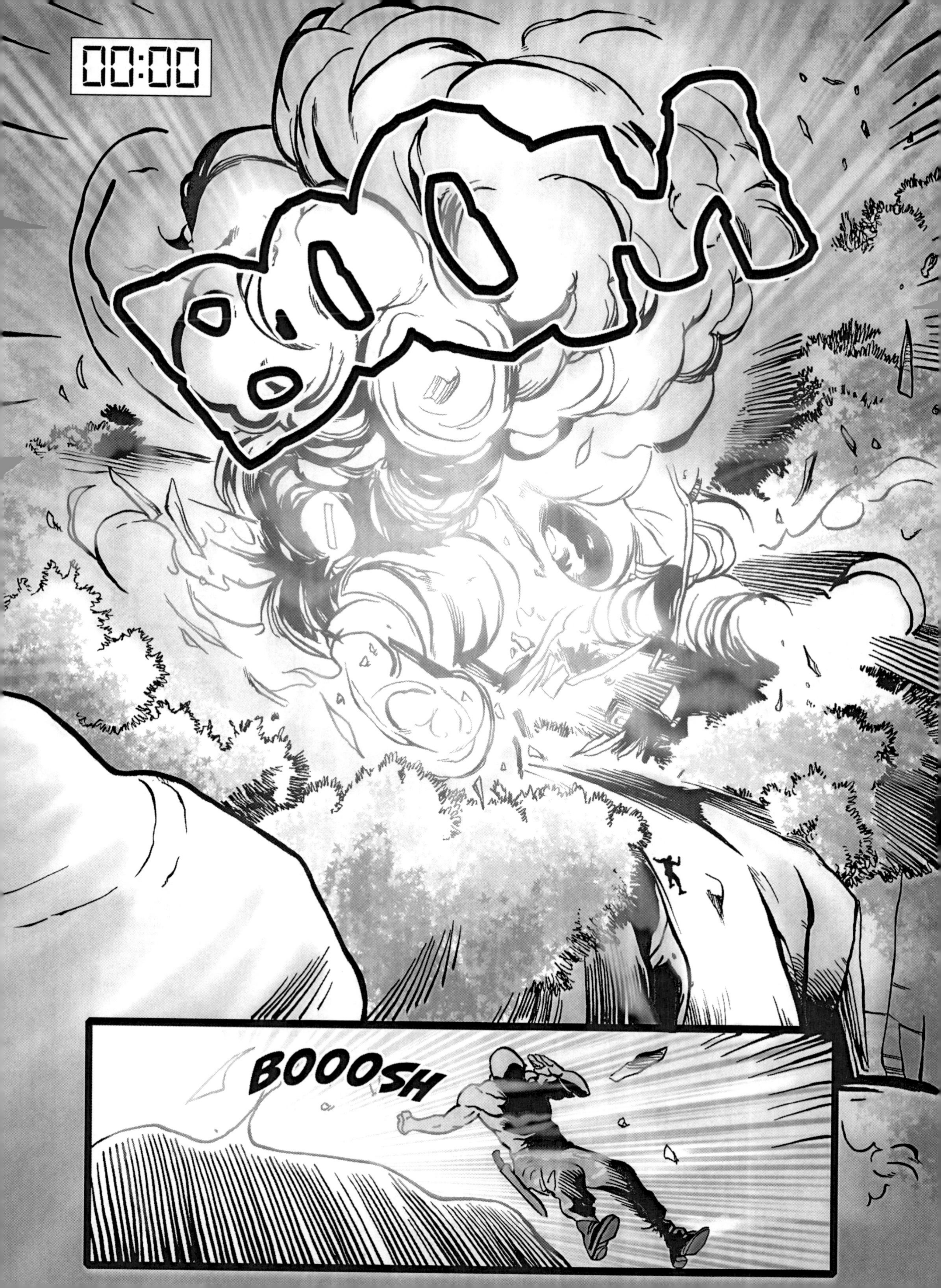
00:00
BOOM
BOOOSH

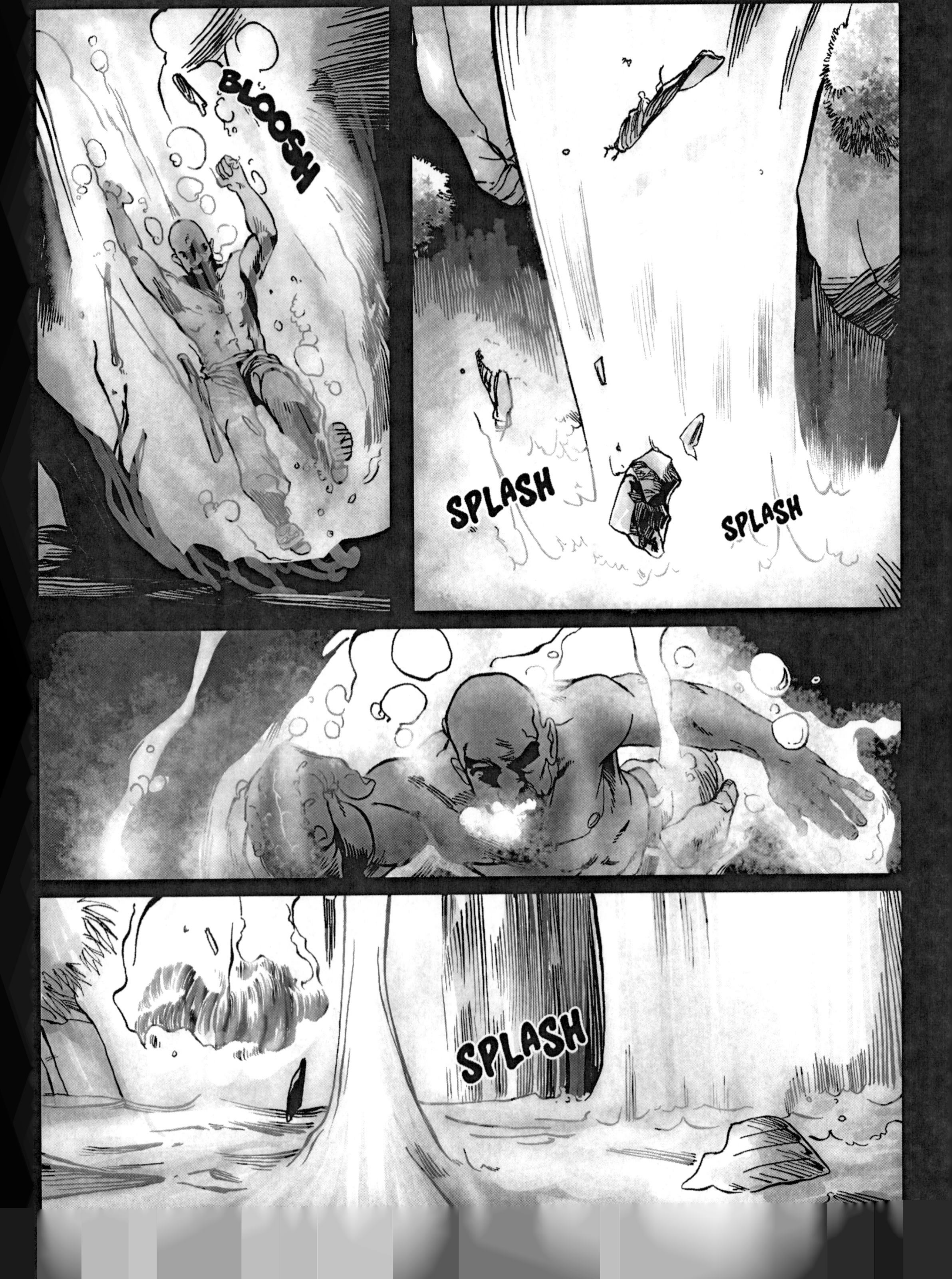
BLOOSH
SPLASH
SPLASH
SPLASH

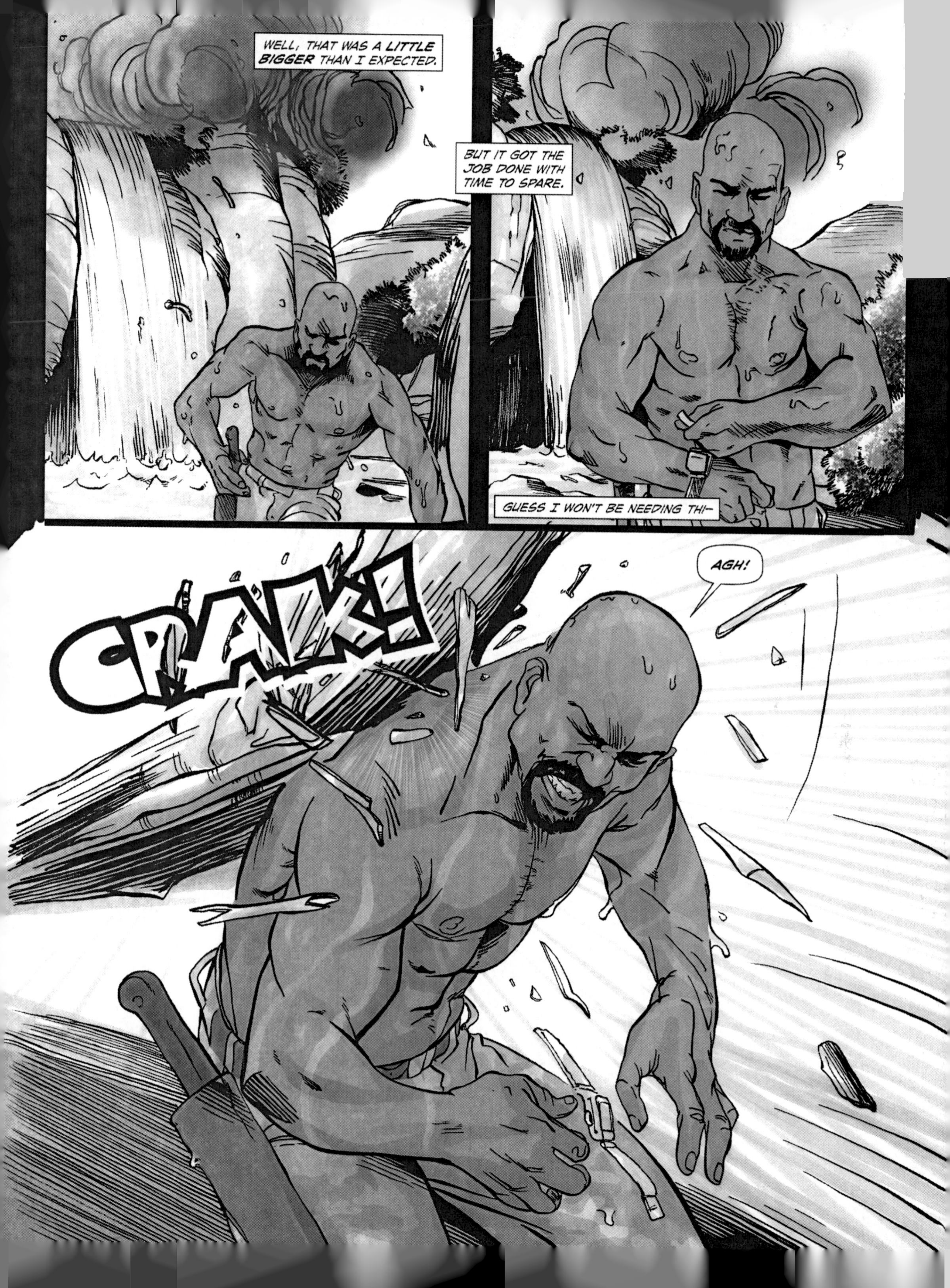
WELL, THAT WAS A LITTLE BIGGER THAN I EXPECTED.
BUT IT GOT THE JOB DONE WITH TIME TO SPARE.
GUESS I WON'T BE NEEDING THI—
CRAAAK!
AGH!

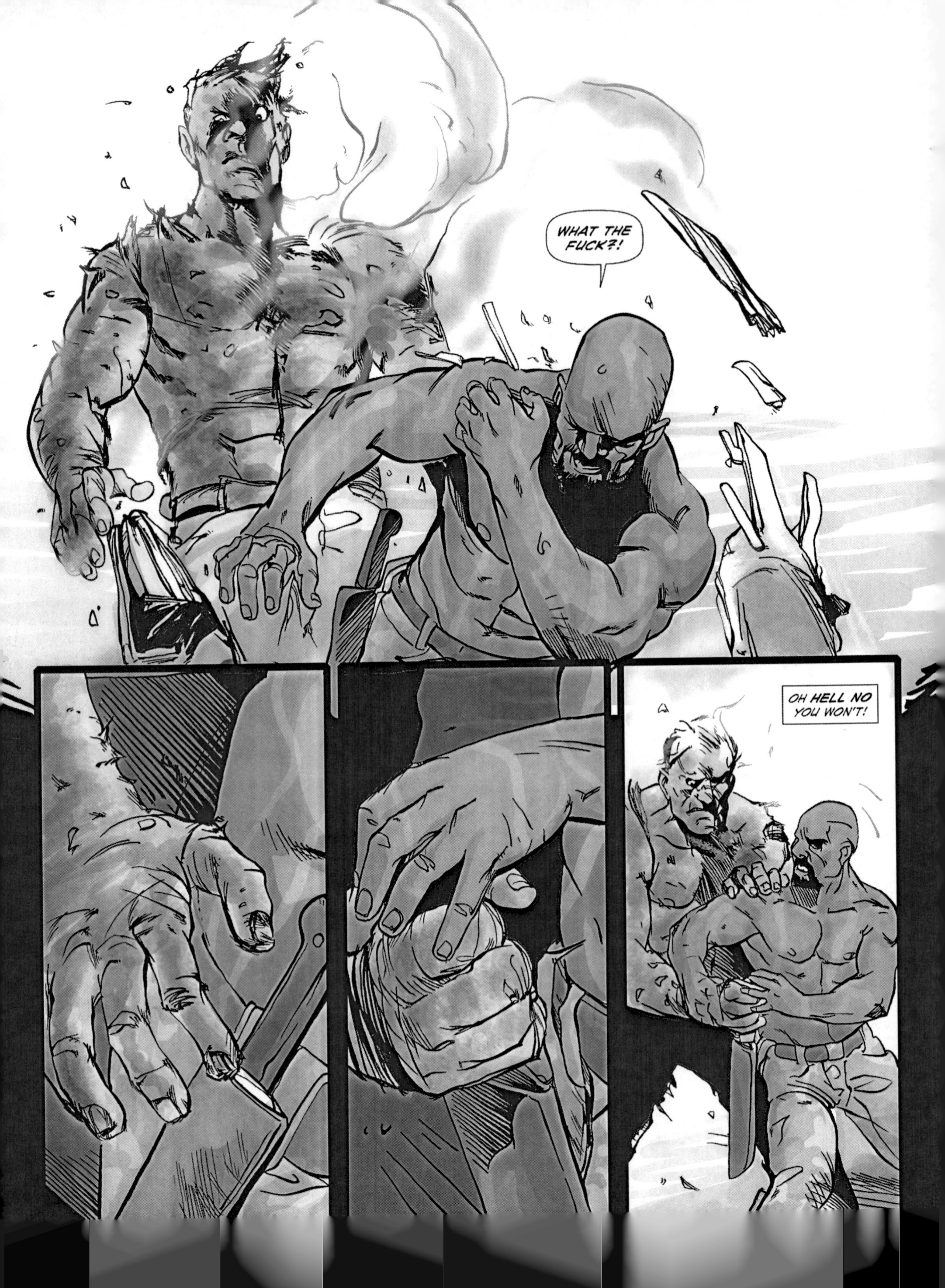
WHAT THE FUCK?!
OH HELL NO YOU WON'T!

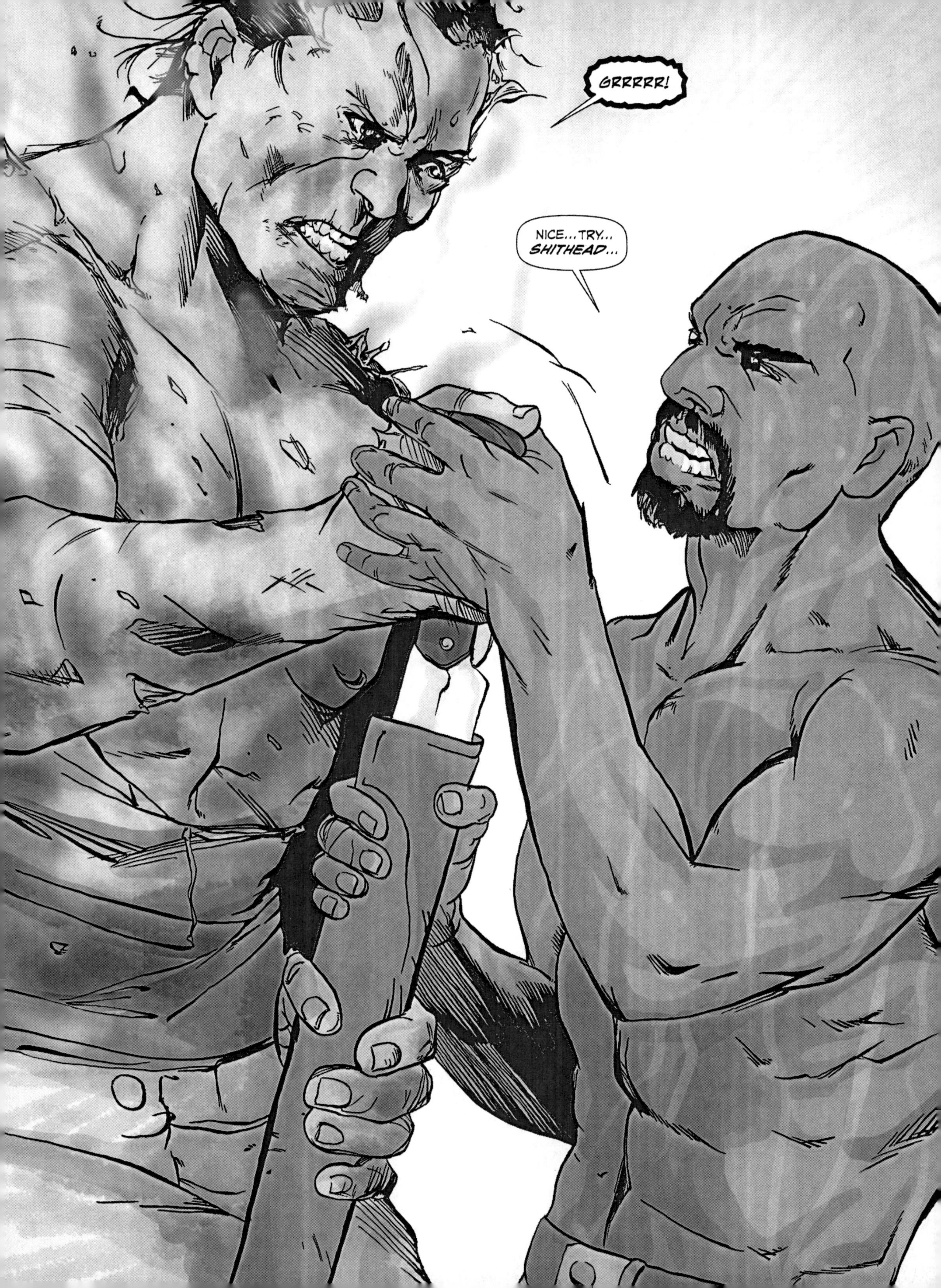
GRRRRR!
NICE...TRY... SHITHEAD...

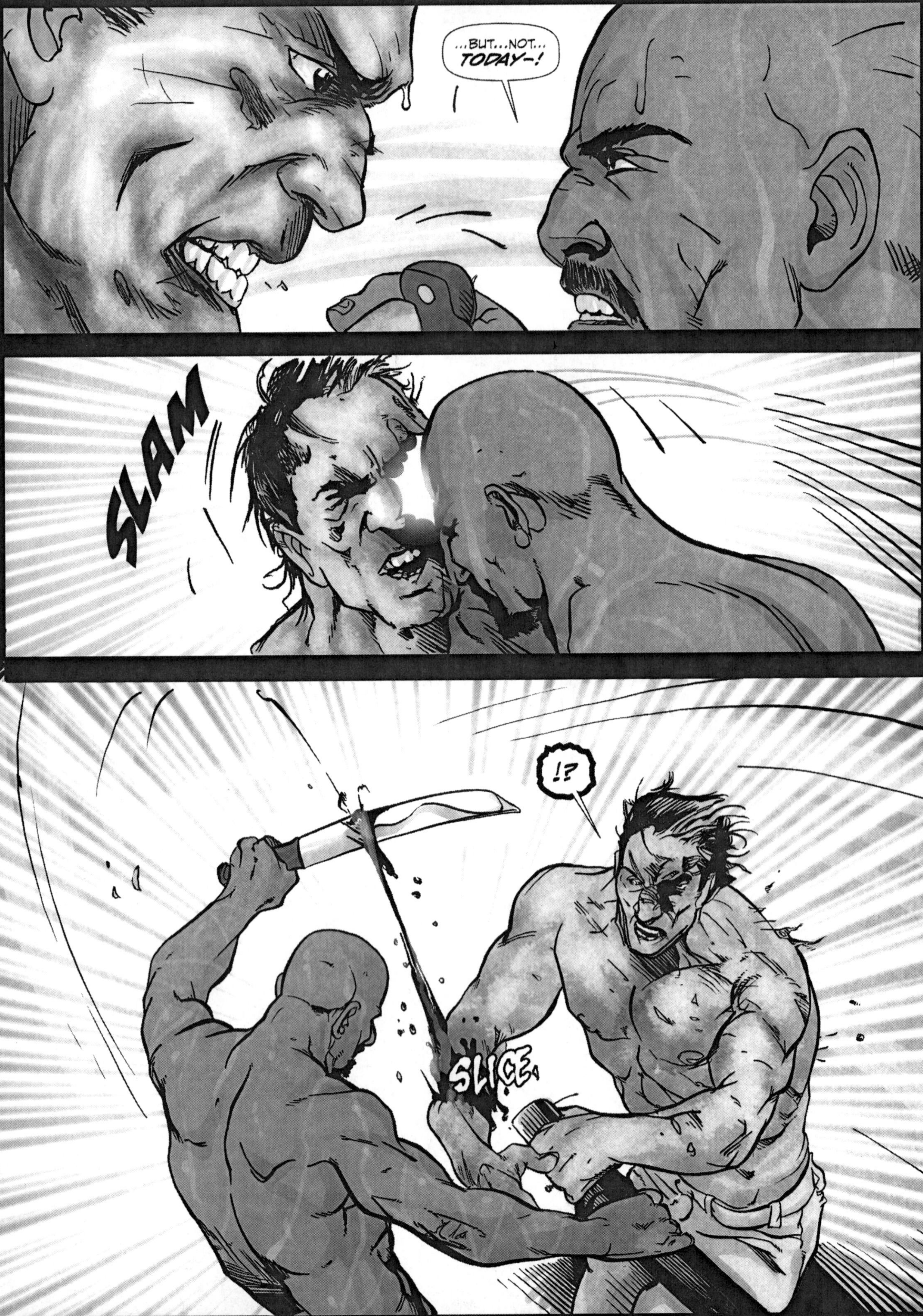
...BUT...NOT...
TODAY–!
SLAM
!?
SLICE

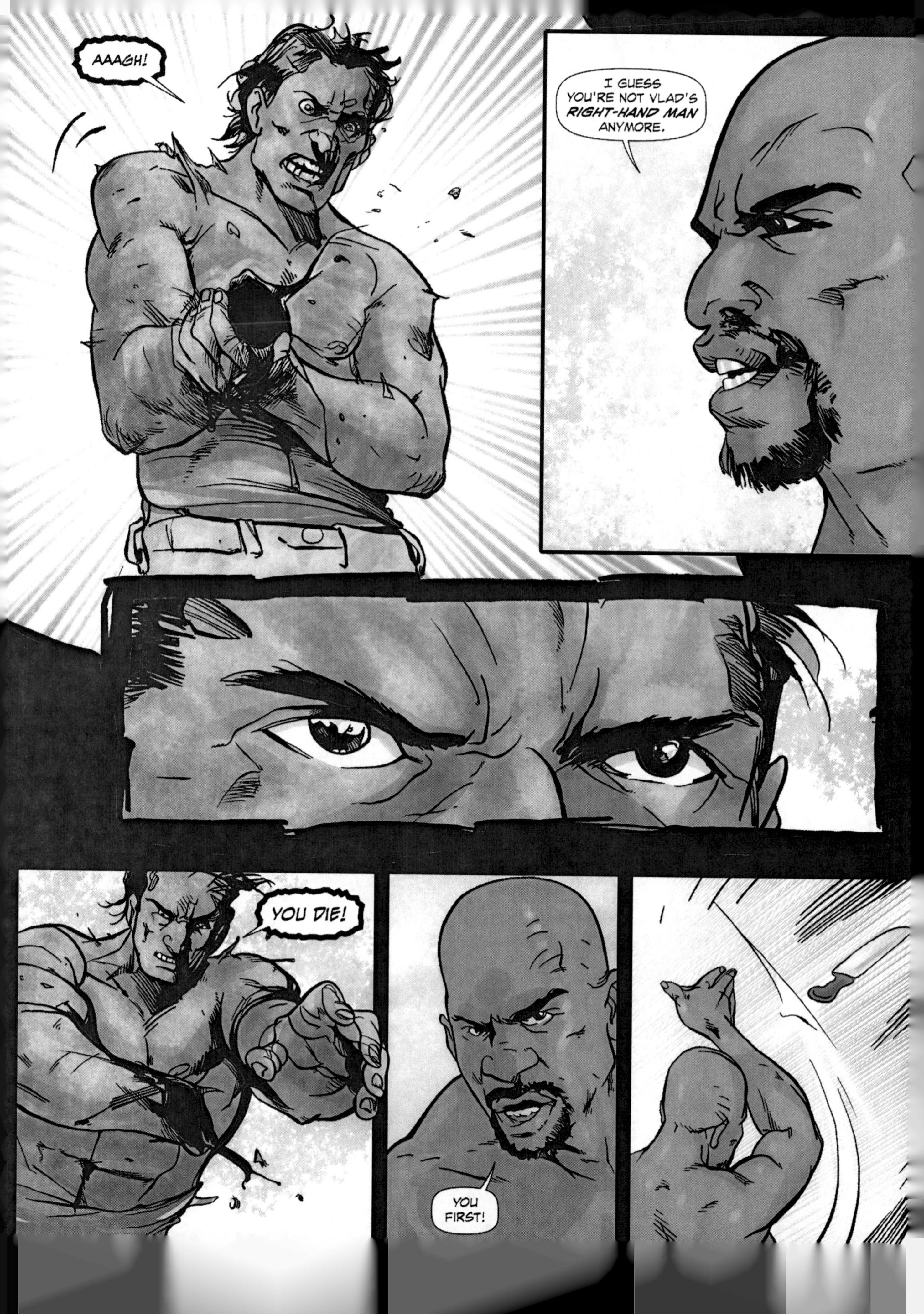
AAAGH!
I GUESS YOU'RE NOT VLAD'S RIGHT-HAND MAN ANYMORE.
YOU DIE!
YOU FIRST!

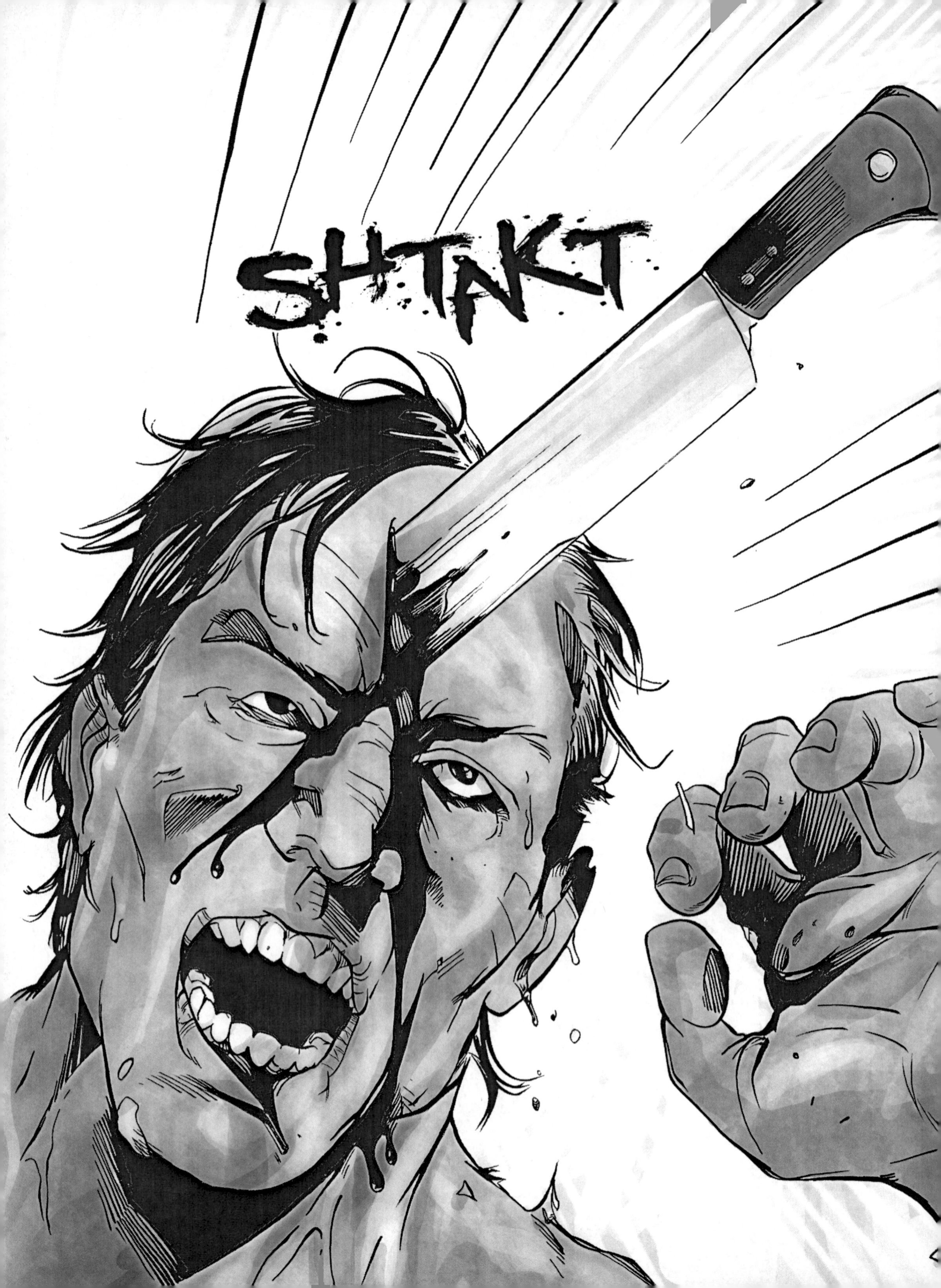
SHTAKT

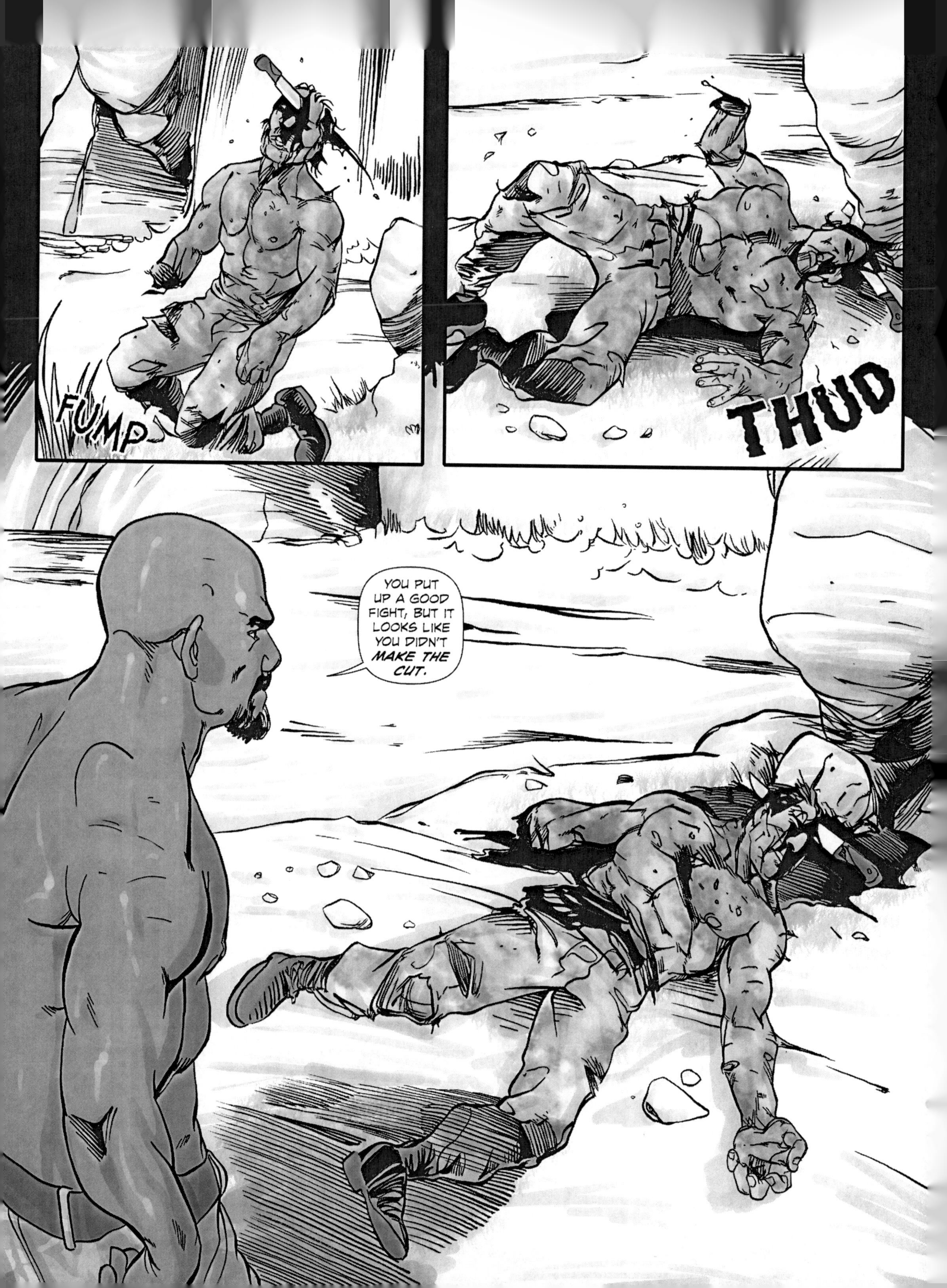
FUMP
THUD
YOU PUT UP A GOOD FIGHT, BUT IT LOOKS LIKE YOU DIDN'T *MAKE THE CUT*.

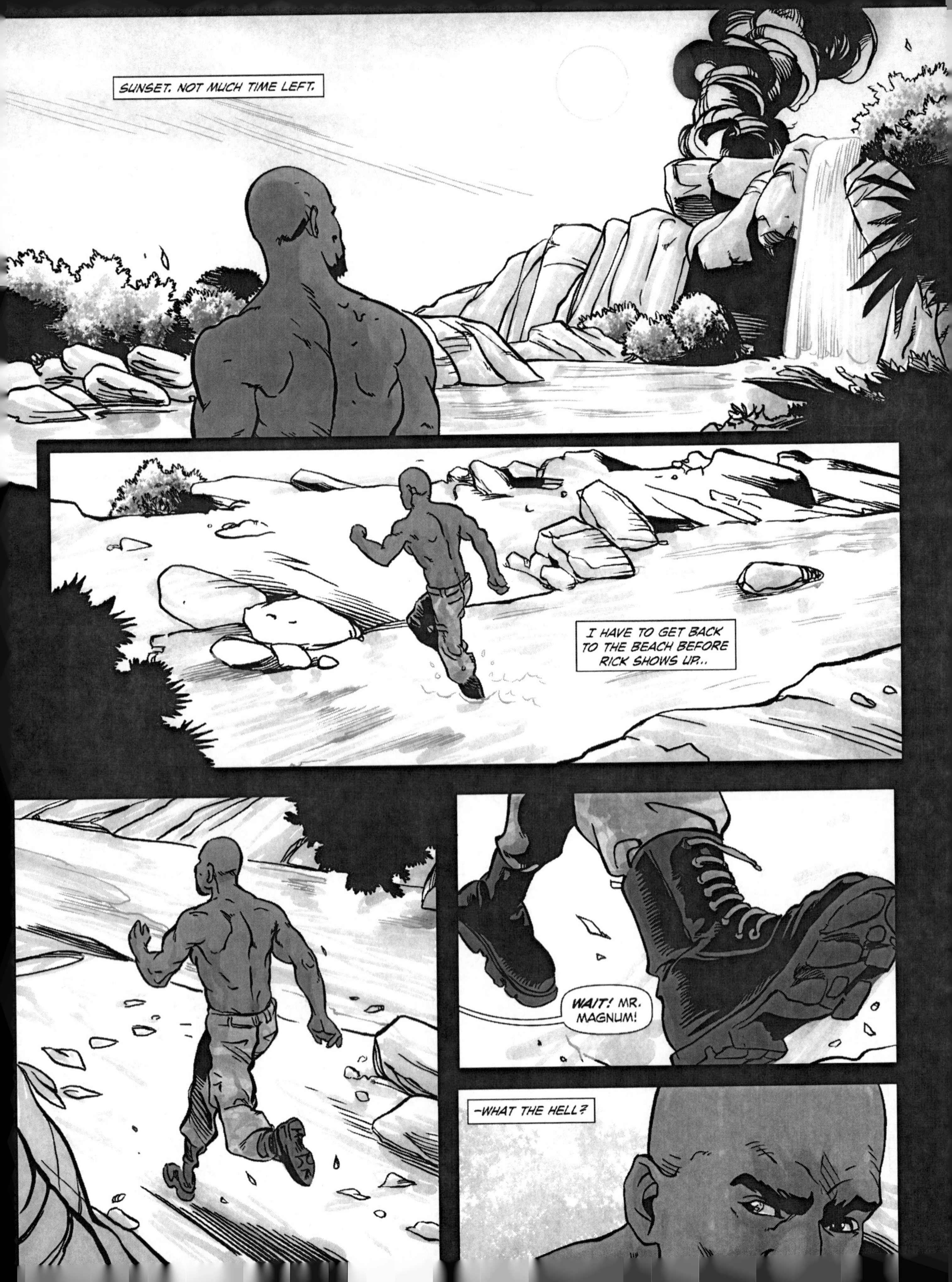
SUNSET. NOT MUCH TIME LEFT.
I HAVE TO GET BACK TO THE BEACH BEFORE RICK SHOWS UP..
WAIT! MR. MAGNUM!
–WHAT THE HELL?

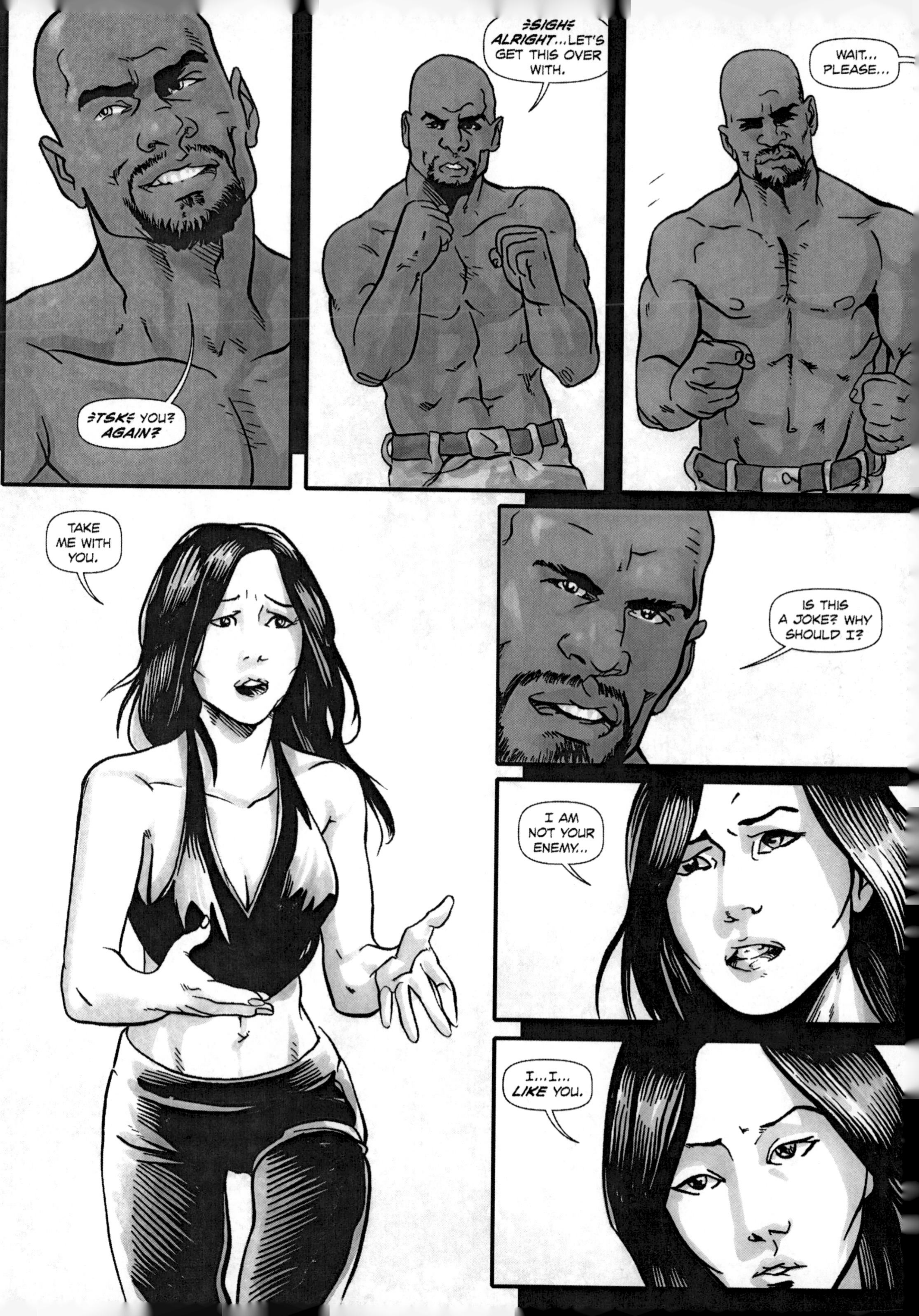

≠TSK≠ YOU? AGAIN?
≠SIGH≠ ALRIGHT... LET'S GET THIS OVER WITH.
WAIT... PLEASE...
TAKE ME WITH YOU.
IS THIS A JOKE? WHY SHOULD I?
I AM NOT YOUR ENEMY...
I... I... LIKE YOU.

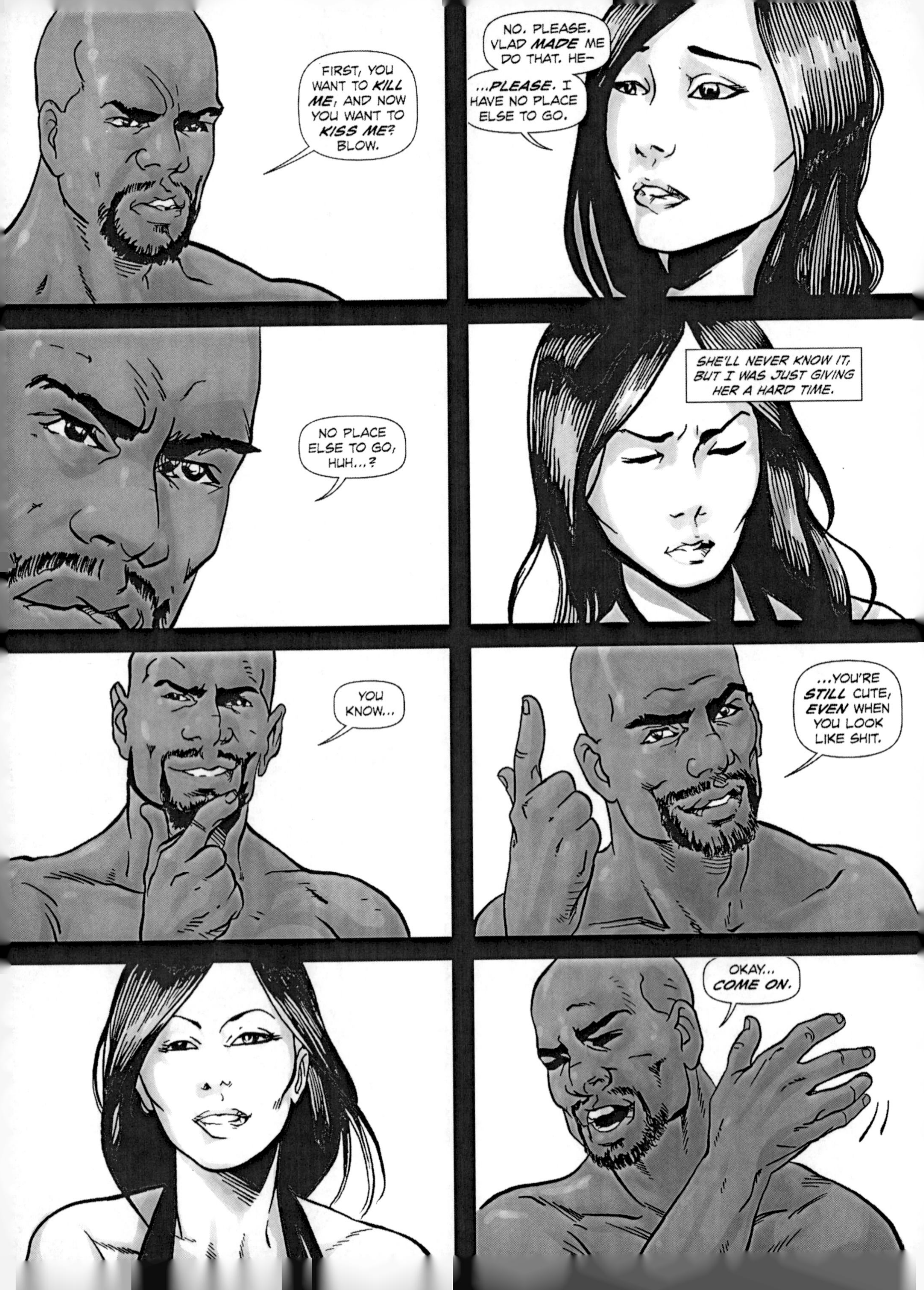
FIRST, YOU WANT TO KILL ME, AND NOW YOU WANT TO KISS ME? BLOW.
NO. PLEASE. VLAD MADE ME DO THAT. HE–
...PLEASE. I HAVE NO PLACE ELSE TO GO.
NO PLACE ELSE TO GO, HUH...?
SHE'LL NEVER KNOW IT, BUT I WAS JUST GIVING HER A HARD TIME.
YOU KNOW...
...YOU'RE STILL CUTE, EVEN WHEN YOU LOOK LIKE SHIT.
OKAY... COME ON.

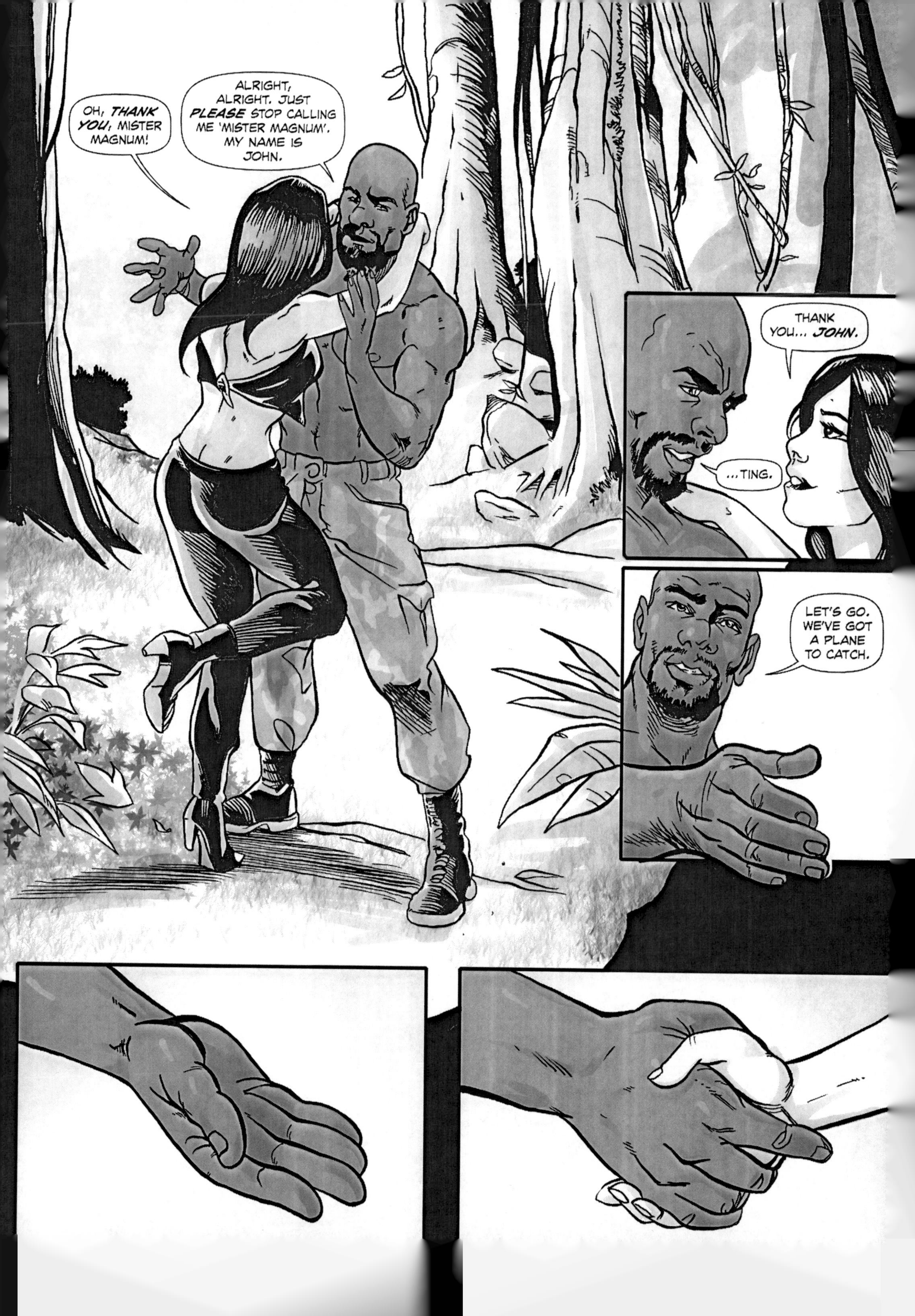
OH, THANK YOU, MISTER MAGNUM!
ALRIGHT, ALRIGHT. JUST PLEASE STOP CALLING ME 'MISTER MAGNUM'. MY NAME IS JOHN.
THANK YOU... JOHN.
...TING.
LET'S GO. WE'VE GOT A PLANE TO CATCH.

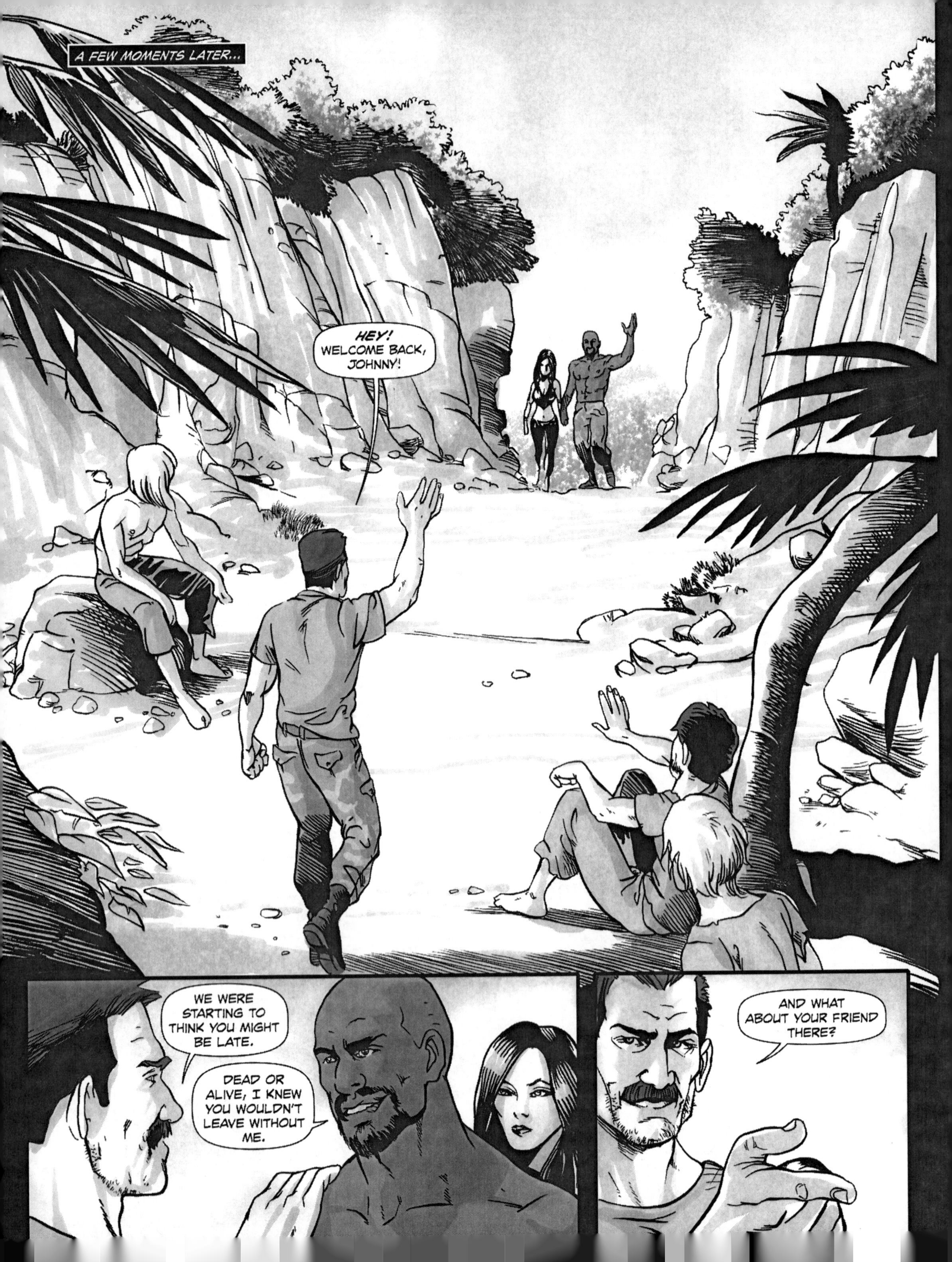

A FEW MOMENTS LATER...
HEY! WELCOME BACK, JOHNNY!
WE WERE STARTING TO THINK YOU MIGHT BE LATE.
DEAD OR ALIVE, I KNEW YOU WOULDN'T LEAVE WITHOUT ME.
AND WHAT ABOUT YOUR FRIEND THERE?

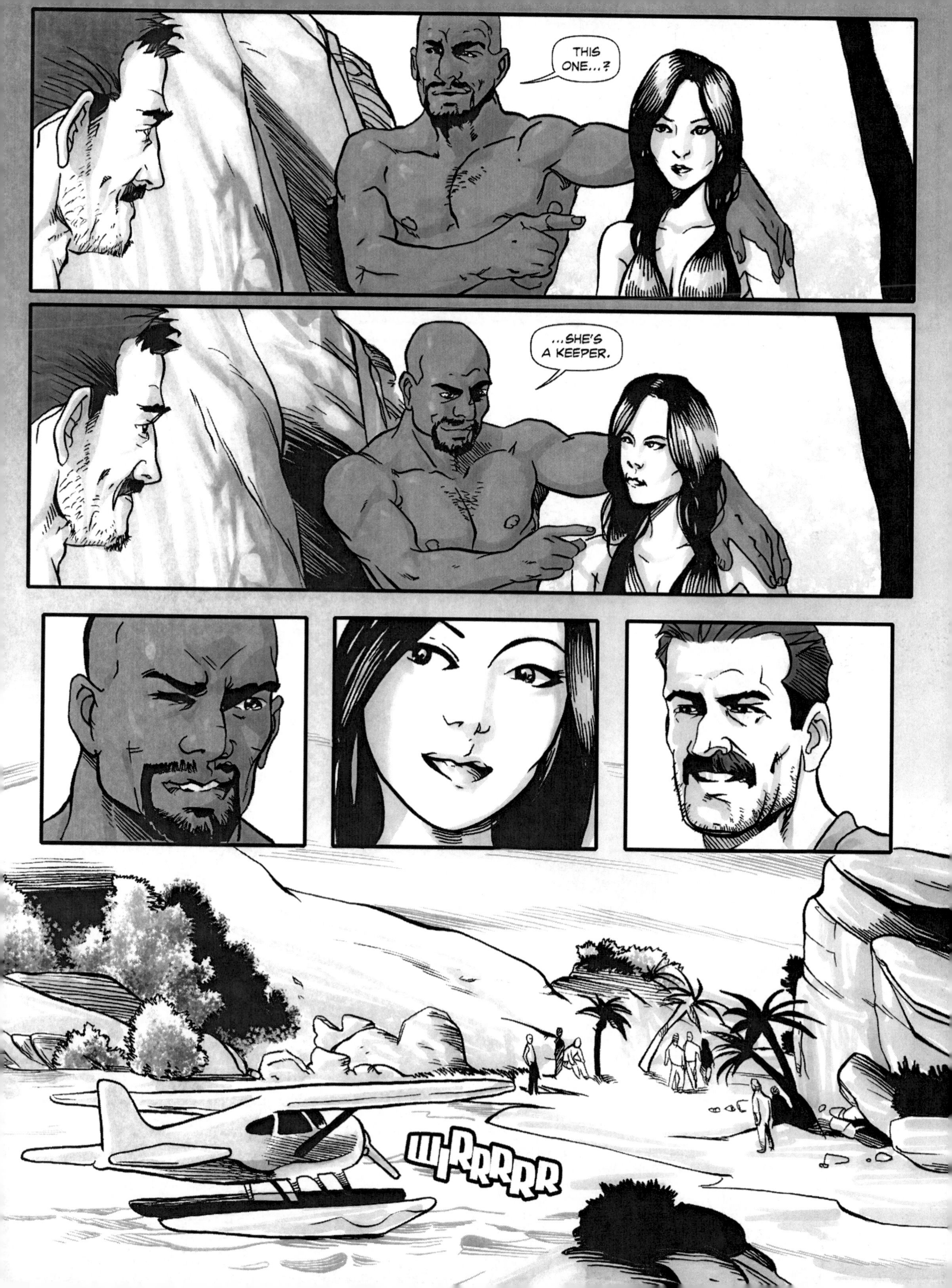
THIS ONE...?
...SHE'S A KEEPER.
WIRRRRRR

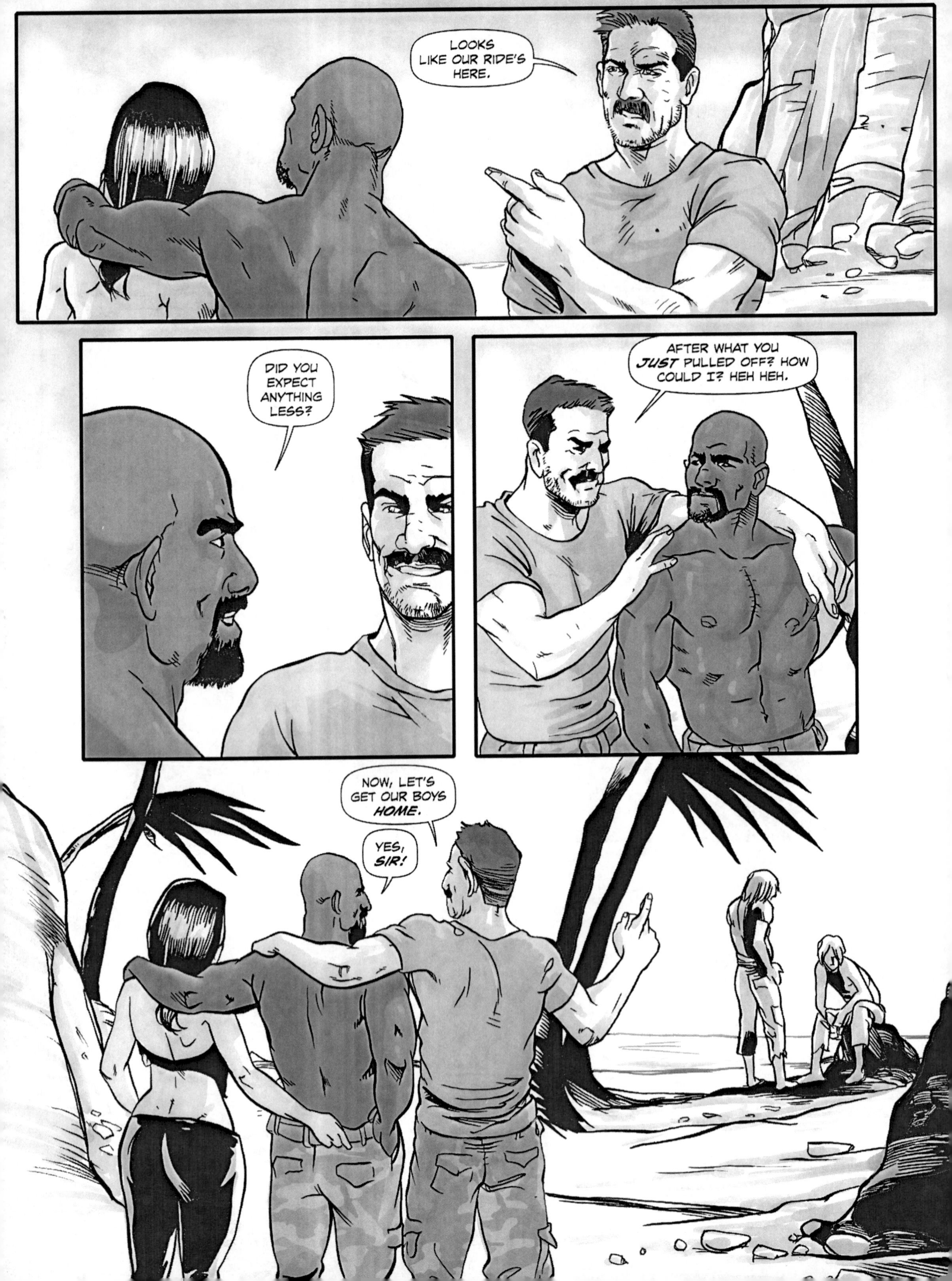

LOOKS LIKE OUR RIDE'S HERE.
DID YOU EXPECT ANYTHING LESS?
AFTER WHAT YOU *JUST* PULLED OFF? HOW COULD I? HEH HEH.
NOW, LET'S GET OUR BOYS *HOME*.
YES, *SIR!*

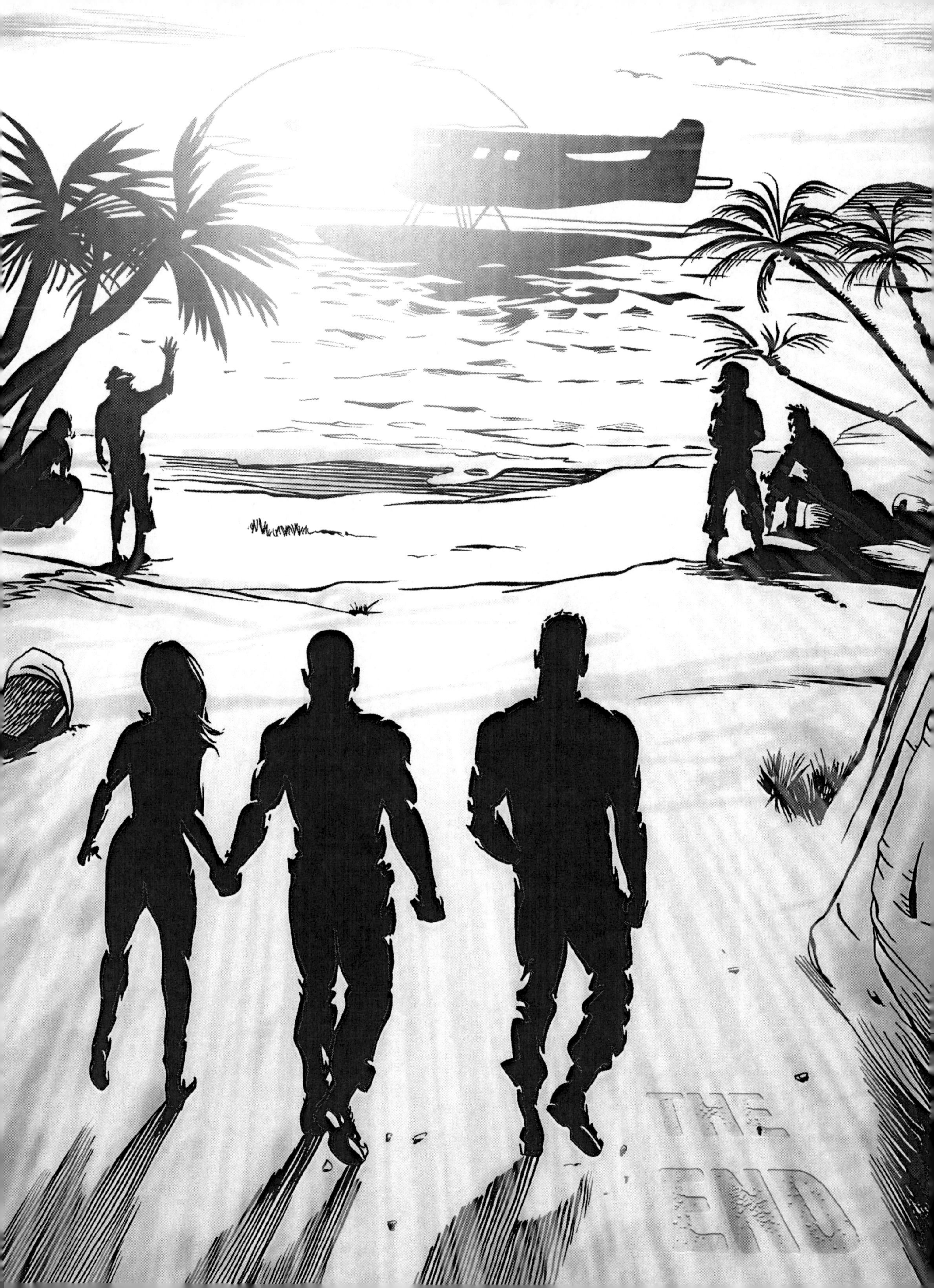
THE END

Written & Directed by
David J. Desjardin
Based on the non-existent film
"Strike Commando 3: Heavy Weapon"

Artistic Design
Michela Da Sacco

Inks & Special Effects
Andrew Dodd

Lettering
Jaymes Reed

Retro Cover Art
Sam Denmark

Alternate Covers
Ray Dillon
Michela Da Sacco

Russian / Chinese Translators
Mikhail Kiselgof
Chak Tsang

CAST

John Magnum	....	Terry J. White
Marion Deckard	....	Sam E. Selleck
Vladimir Kinski	....	Terence Harris
Ting Sun Wei	....	Lucy Gong Chung
Alonzo Richter	....	Raymond Vargas
Koh	....	Dalip Momoa
Longino	....	Mario Maung Khin
McClaine	....	Hunter Levesque
Hawkins	....	Reilly "Rex" Cobb
Chris Bowling	....	Himself
Penny Jameson	....	Scarlett Cuthbert
Robber	....	CeeGee
Asst. Robber	....	C.G.
Homeless Robber	....	Dan Desjardin
Miller	....	Lance H. Eastwood
Johnson	....	David McGill

Piss-Ant Soldiers

Erin Tripp	James Baker	Michael Oakes
Mike Landis	Raina Stroman	Toshiaki Yamazaki
Derrick Hunter	Brian Smith	Kevin Adams
Daniel Butler	David McGill	Ben Cornelius
Brandon Batista	Josh Nyenhuis	Jeffrey Schamber

Stunt Performers

Aron Riener	Rob Magruder	Kendal Brown
Rodolfo Ybarra	Mike Iacovoni	Kevin Dawson
Percy Butler	Rich Benson	Todd McKenna

Policeman	Nate Goodman
Helicopter Pilot	Johnathan Harrington
Vietnam Soldiers	William Tsueng
	Dennis Boulanger
	Justin Straussmeier
Russian Mercenaries	Ryan Smith
	John Bowlin
	Edward Terwilliger
Costa Rican Mercenaries	Jacob Urbschat-Satterfield
	Gustav Fitzpatrick
	Sid Caeser
Fight Choreographer	James Baker
Stunt Coordinator	Erin Tripp
Cinematography	Cinemageddon
Lighting Effects	Andrew Dodd
Lighting Effects Assistant	David Desjardin
Art Director	David Desjardin
Costume Designer	Sherly Novela Nur Imania
Ninja Weapons Specialist	Adrian Desjardin
Assistant One-Liners	Trevor Anderson
	Mike "Utah" Iacovoni

Associate Editor	David Desjardin
Assistant Editors	Sid Caeser
	Ryan Smith
	William Tsueng
	David McGill
	Edward Terwilliger
	Gustav Fitzpatrick

Jerkoff Consultant	Sir Richard "BoB" Jackson
Certified Lion Tamer	Sunjay Kelkar
Boom Operator	Kerri Brown

Special Thanks

Chad Irwin	John Bowlin
Christopher Bowling	William Tsueng
Derek Denmark	Ryan Smith
Claudio Magani	Tamara Fontenot
Aaron Robinson	Anthony Chilelli

Thanks

Batbaatar Tsolmonbayar		Elvyn Santos Sanchez	
Gutterpuppy	Groo	theyrhere	KissMyAsthma
PeteKelly	Ronin	JFJguy	Rouxbik
Dasgessabel	mdh	BucketofJustice	hobbes21
MistressOfRain	KCPenguins	Felty	TheDoctor
youruglyclone	epyon396	SEspo	MrRedlegs21
thunderdonkey	chiwii	synthetic1	BigBoss540
Kommie	cloudstrife	beavis	bill

Munition Edition Asst. Producers

Chad Irwin

Josh Lovejoy

Sunjay Kelkar

David Wyble Jr

Bjørn Martin Hestnes

Jason Gaitanis

Mika Köykkä

Kirk & Mindy Spencer

William Tsueng

Carlos "Ace" Deaton

Pete Kelly Jr.

Thomas Gustav Fitzpatrick

Gutterpuppy

Scott Early

Dal Bhatia

Frank D'Aloia

Jeremy Busch

Michael I Mcintosh

Joshua Gray

Robert Baxter Gray Jr.

John Goggan

Gilbert Deltres

Christopher Friedrich

Jocelyn Fenton

Kelly "SEGAMew" Van

Adam "8T" Tannir

Fredrick Thomas

Thomas Adam Lundy

James Moss

Derek Denmark

James Sonny Howard

Mikhail Kiselgof

Tranzor

Christopher Bowling

Metal Thug

Trevor "ThunderDonkey" Sparreboom

Stanley Yeung

William Patton

Zachary Knight

Caleb Rudd

John "VirtuAdept" Bowlin

James Straughan

Production Aides

Ryan Lucas	Bill Marrs	W.D. Selecman
Chriss	Matixmer	Nick Schmidt
Cassandra W.	Julien Simon	Luke Peters
Garrett Stump	Robert Rosenthal	Daniel Holden
Brandon Andrews	Reza Tootoonchian	Tiido Priimägi (TmEE)
Albert Chang	Aidan Easson	Mark Himmelsbach
Chase Pashkowich	Alexander Schulz	Patrick Awesome
Andrew Bowyer	Peter Sun	Soldier Systems Daily
Jason McNamara	David D'Emilio	George Ölund
Brandon Batista	David Francis	Ignacio Alcuri
Platinum Studios	Nathan Seabolt	Shean Mohammed
Joel Wismer	Samuel Gardener	Semeicha Mohammed
Kevin Babineau	Nick May	Sapphira Mohammed
Ethan Hubbard	Michael T. Kramer	Josh McArdle
Paul Vonasek	Scott Mitchell Rosenberg	Brendan G.
Cris Jensen	Sean CW Korsgaard	Wesley Mehler
SwordFire	Omnicool Caley Rossanova	Dutchess
BlackEagleBR	Jim Donnellan	Renelle Desjardin
Mike Serritella	Stefon Cromartie	Kevin Kainula
Rian Heist	Martin Gregory	William Thode
Marquac	Isaac 'Will It Work' Dansicker	Cheese

King Felty, Protector of the Earth

"HEARTS ON FIRE"
Written by **Vince DiCola, Ed Fruge & Joe Esposito**
Performed by **JOHN CAFFERTY**

"SOMEDAY, SOMEHOW, SOMEONE'S GOTTA PAY"
Written by **John Taylor**
Performed by **POWER STATION**

"BURNING HEART"
Written by **Jim Peterik & Frankie Sullivan**
Performed by **SURVIVOR**

"FAR FROM OVER"
Written by **Frank Stallone & Vince DiCola**
Performed by **FRANK STALLONE**

"NO EASY WAY OUT"
Written by **Robert Tepper**
Performed by **ROBERT TEPPER**

"CROCKETT'S THEME"
Written by **Jan Hammer**
Performed by **JAN HAMMER**

Production Equipment and Facilities supplied by
MAGNUM HOME VIDEO

The events, characters, and firms depicted in this novel are ficticious. Any similarity to actual persons living, or dead or to actual firms is purely coicidental.

No animals were harmed, except a hand-drawn deer.

STRIKE COMICS™

STRIKE COMICS ASSOCIATION OF AMERICA, INC.

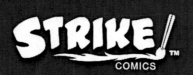

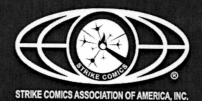

HEAVY WEAPON™
A PRECURSOR OF WAR

"Where am I? I'm on my way home. Why? Your old war buddy interrupted my operations, killed my army of mercenaries, and destroyed my camp in Costa Rica. He must be dealt with. You will find him, and we will come for him, wherever he may be. I will eat his still beating heart while his friends and family watch, helpless. This is far from over, and you will help me get my revenge... McClaine."

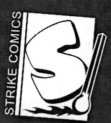

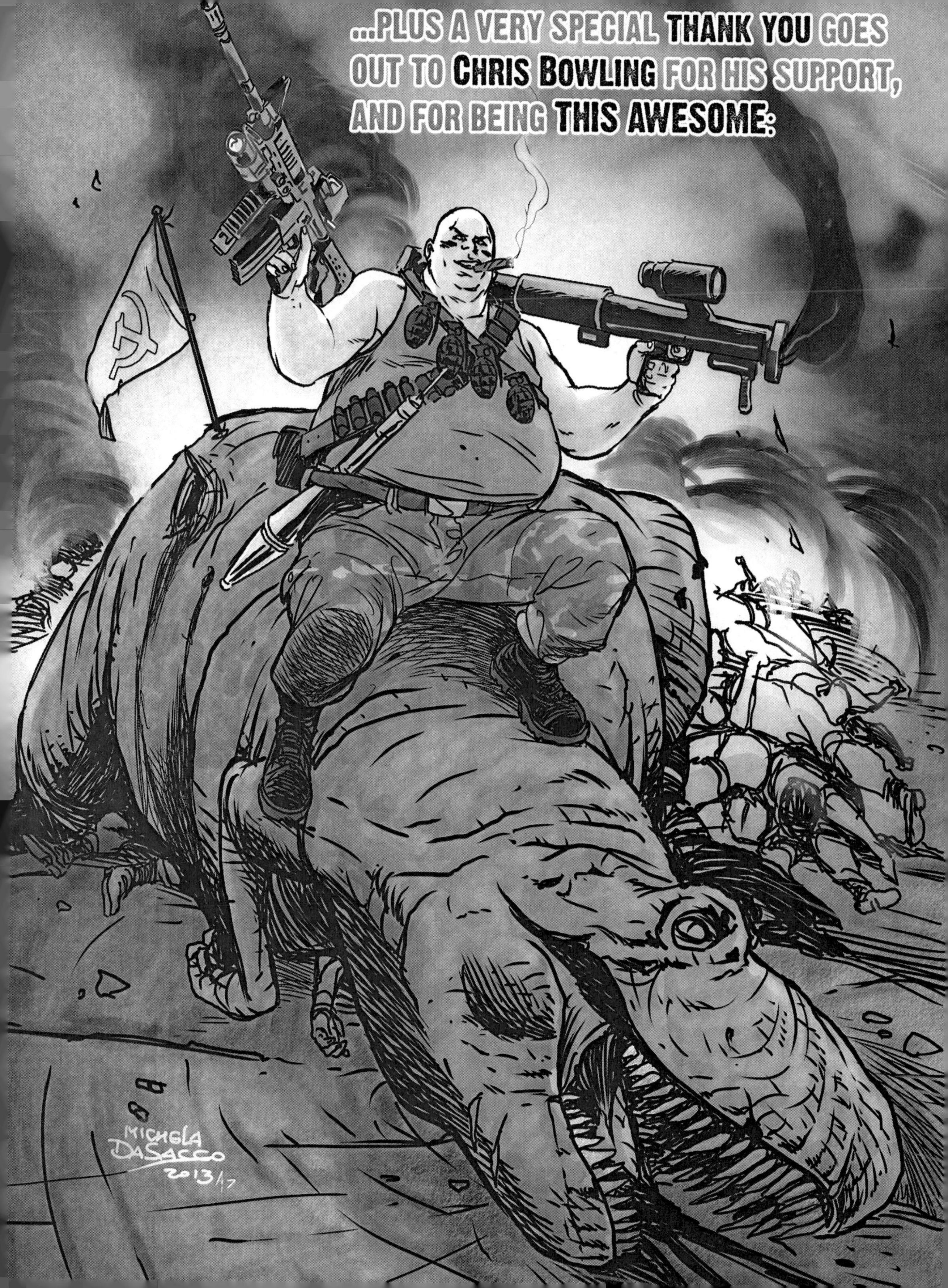
...PLUS A VERY SPECIAL THANK YOU GOES OUT TO CHRIS BOWLING FOR HIS SUPPORT, AND FOR BEING THIS AWESOME:
MICHELA DASACCO

ALTERNATE COVERS

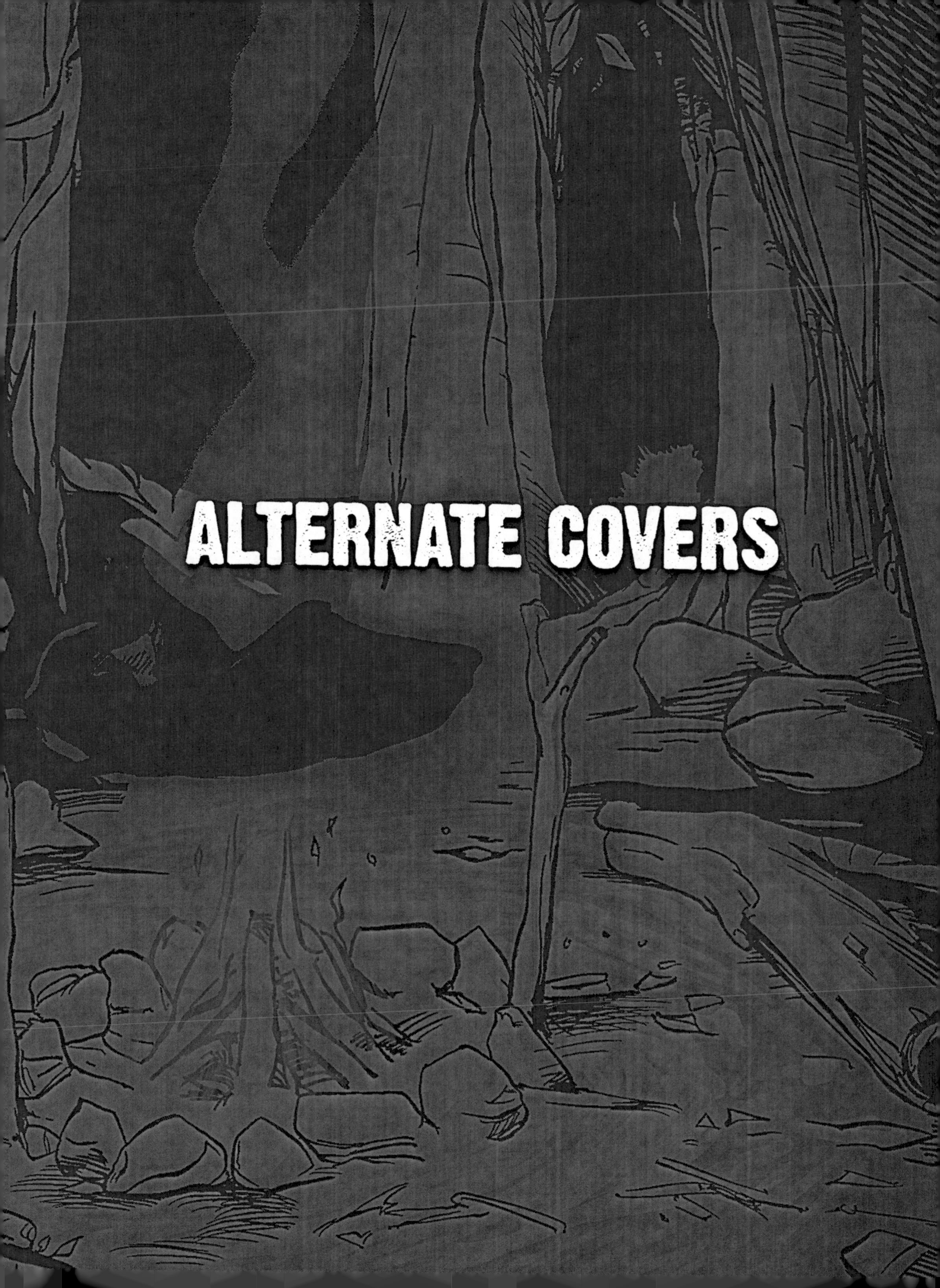

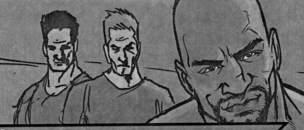

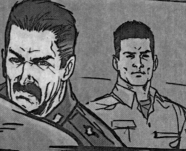

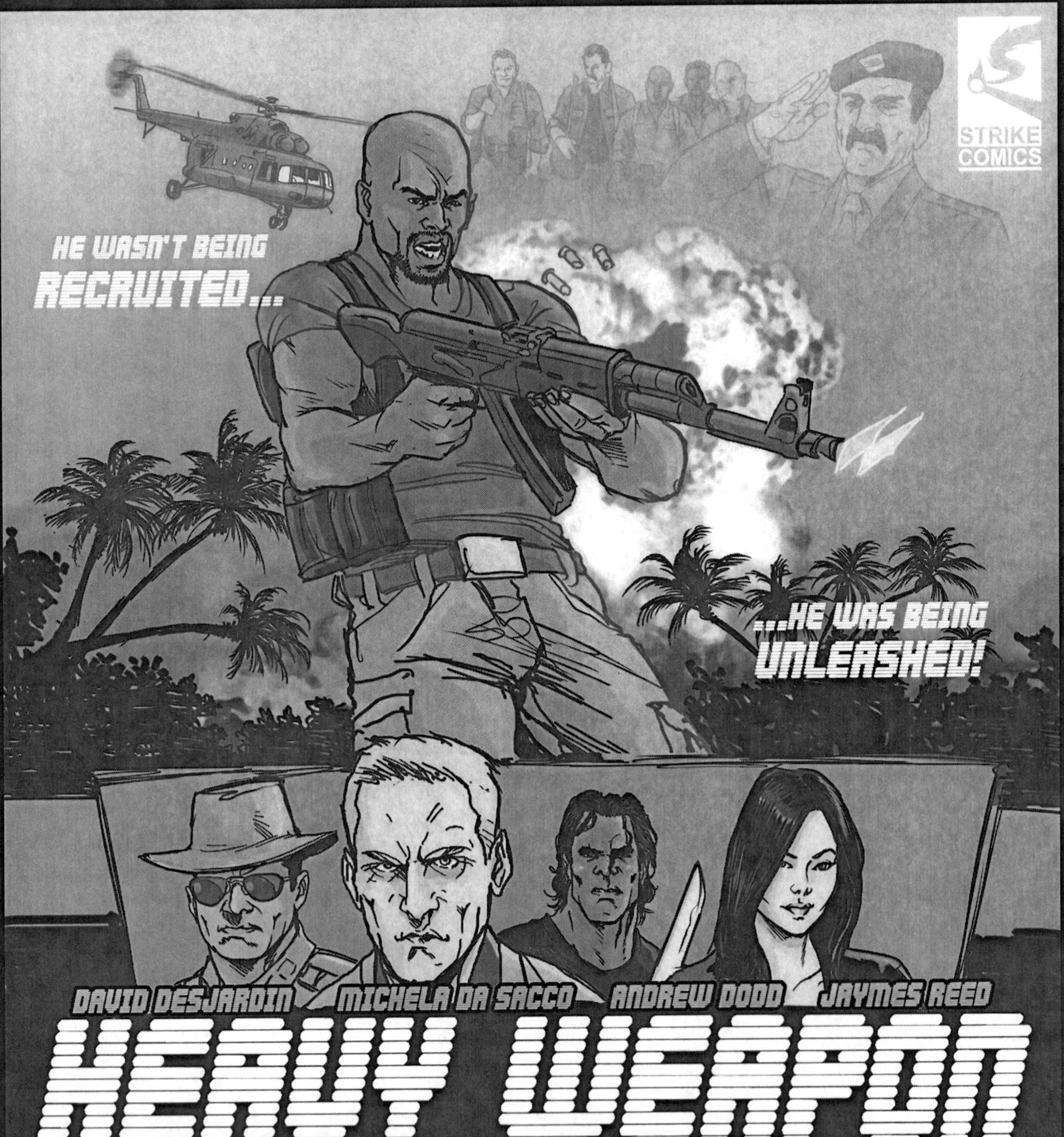
STRIKE COMICS
HE WASN'T BEING RECRUITED...
...HE WAS BEING UNLEASHED!
DAVID DESJARDIN
MICHELA DA SACCO
ANDREW DODD
JAYMES REED
HEAVY WEAPON
A GRAPHIC NOVEL BY DAVID DESJARDIN
MICHELA DASACCO

UNLEASHED
COVER ART BY MICHELA DA SACCO

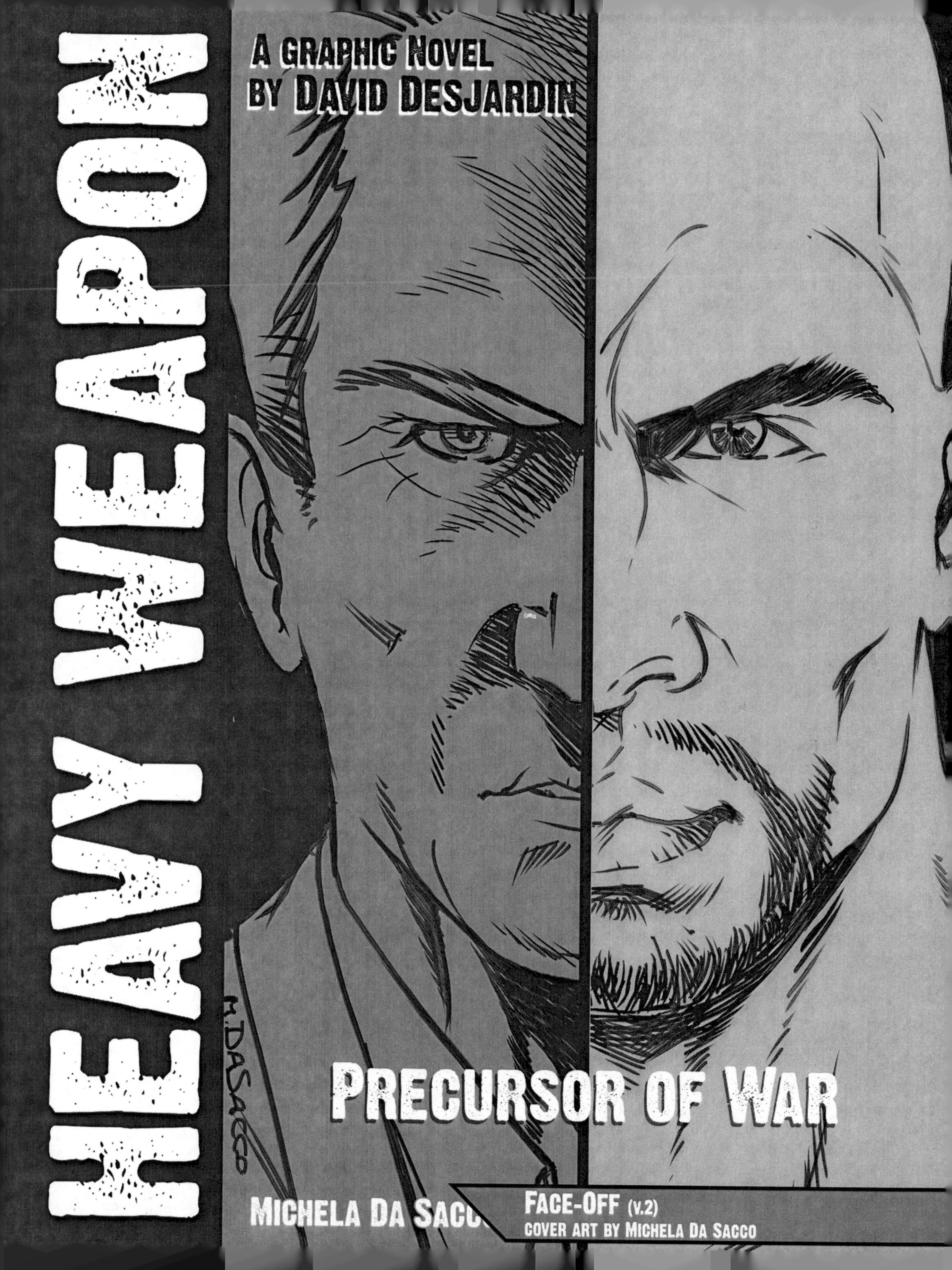
HEAVY WEAPON
A GRAPHIC NOVEL
BY DAVID DESJARDIN
PRECURSOR OF WAR
MICHELA DA SACCO

FACE-OFF (v.2)
COVER ART BY MICHELA DA SACCO

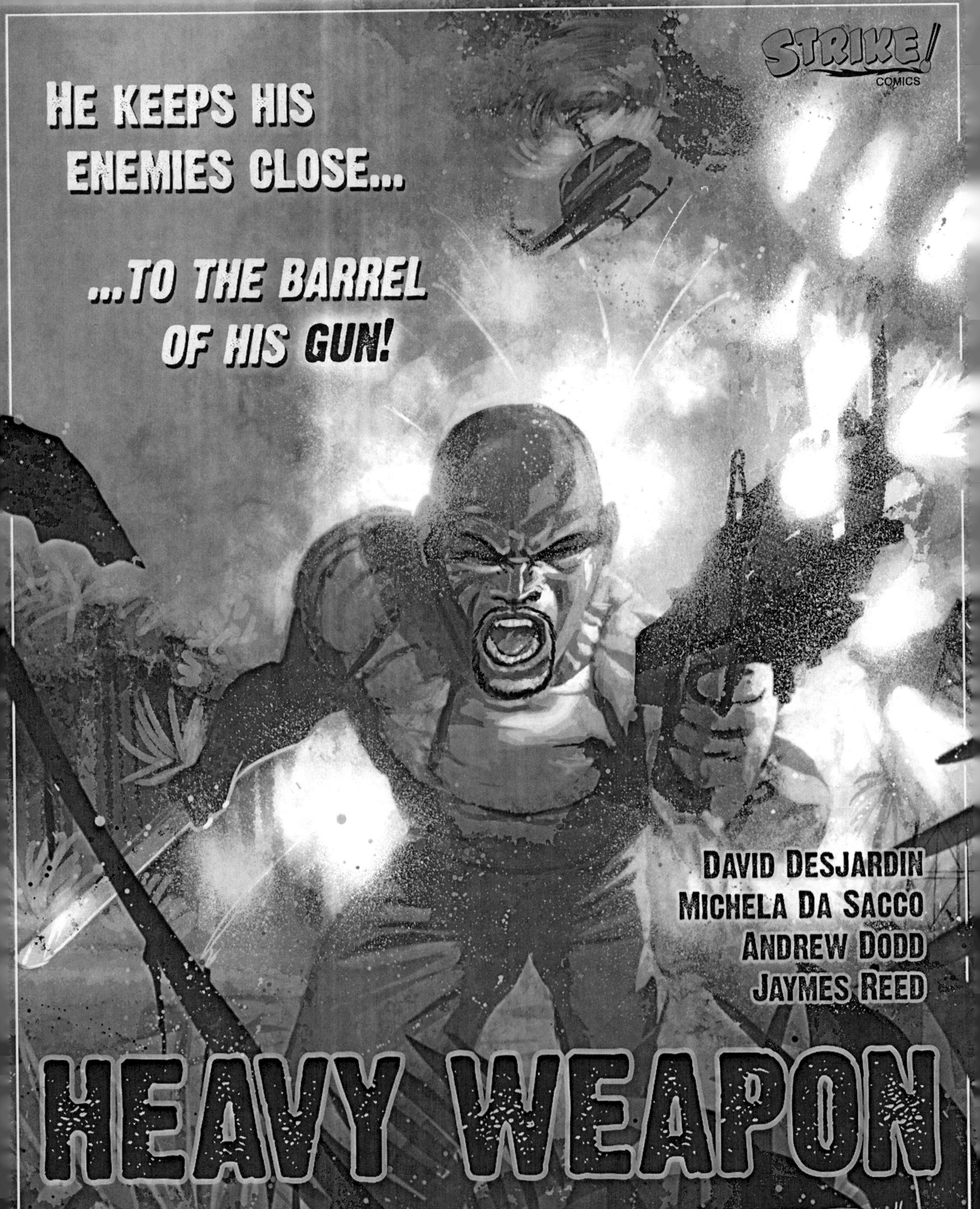
STRIKE! COMICS
HE KEEPS HIS ENEMIES CLOSE...
...TO THE BARREL OF HIS GUN!
DAVID DESJARDIN
MICHELA DA SACCO
ANDREW DODD
JAYMES REED
HEAVY WEAPON
2011
SHOOT FIRST...
COVER ART BY RAY DILLON

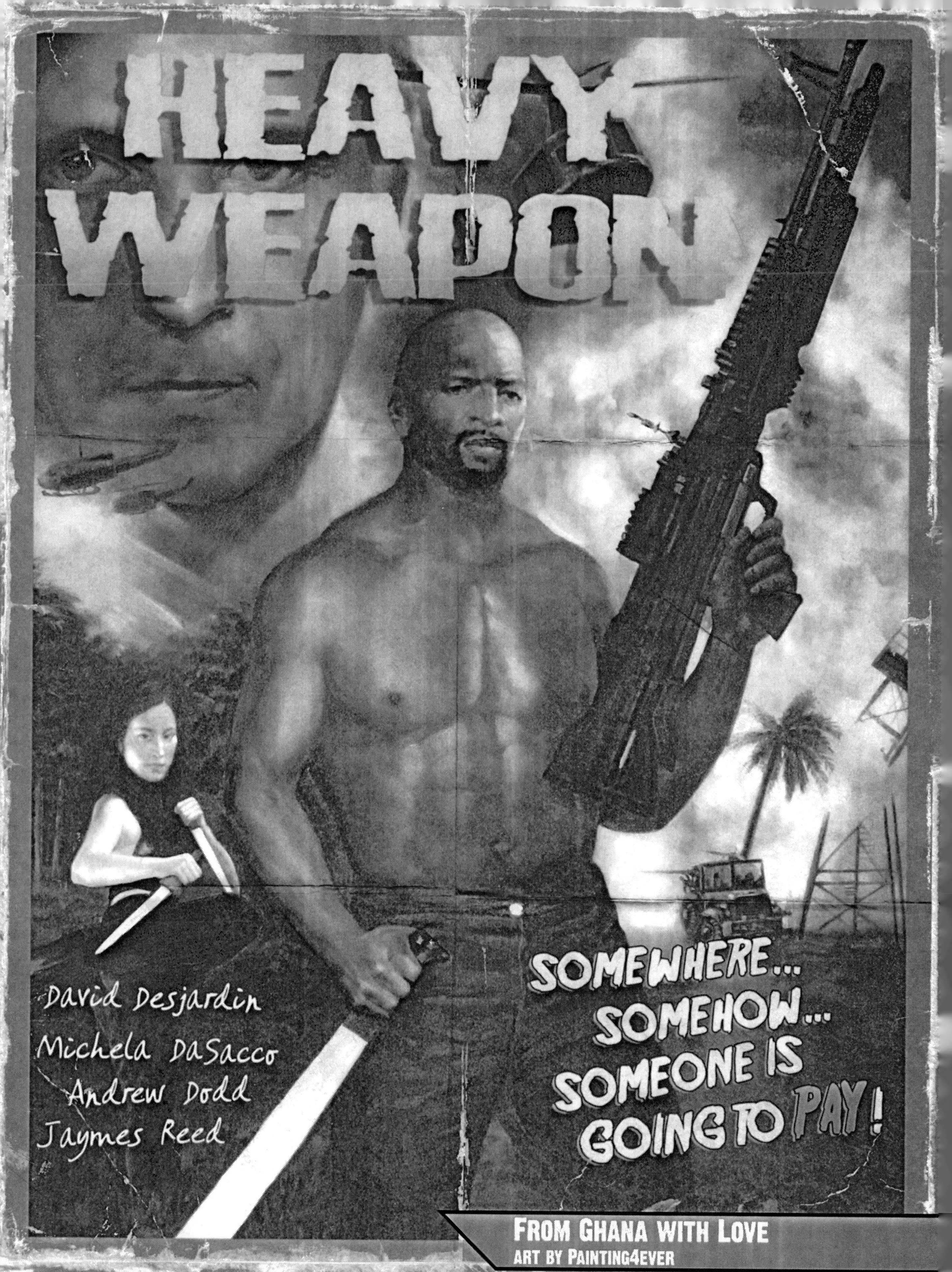
HEAVY WEAPON
David Desjardin
Michela DaSacco
Andrew Dodd
Jaymes Reed
SOMEWHERE...
SOMEHOW...
SOMEONE IS
GOING TO PAY!

FROM GHANA WITH LOVE
ART BY PAINTING4EVER

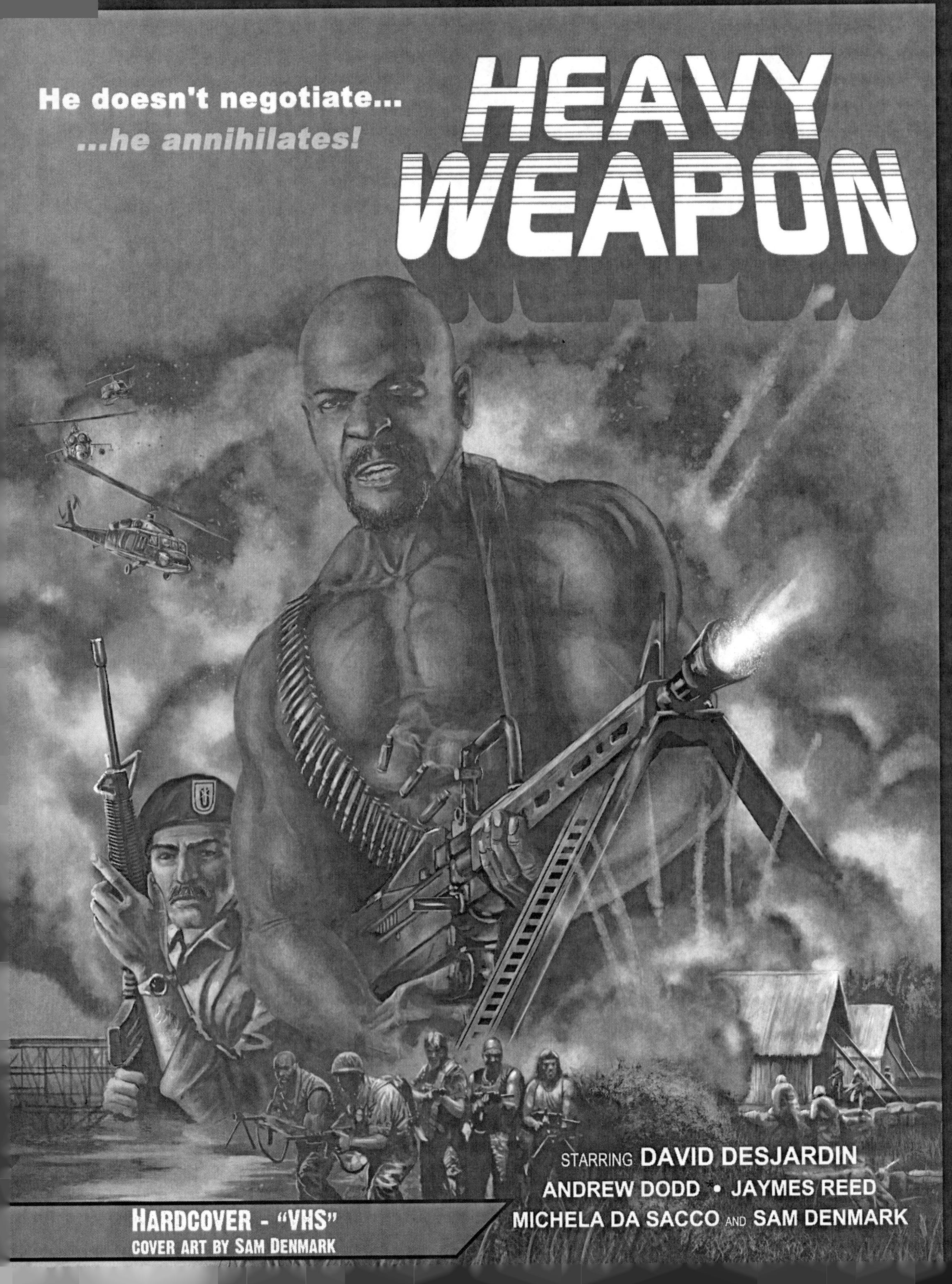
He doesn't negotiate...
...he annihilates!
HEAVY WEAPON
STARRING DAVID DESJARDIN
ANDREW DODD • JAYMES REED
MICHELA DA SACCO AND SAM DENMARK
HARDCOVER - "VHS"
COVER ART BY SAM DENMARK

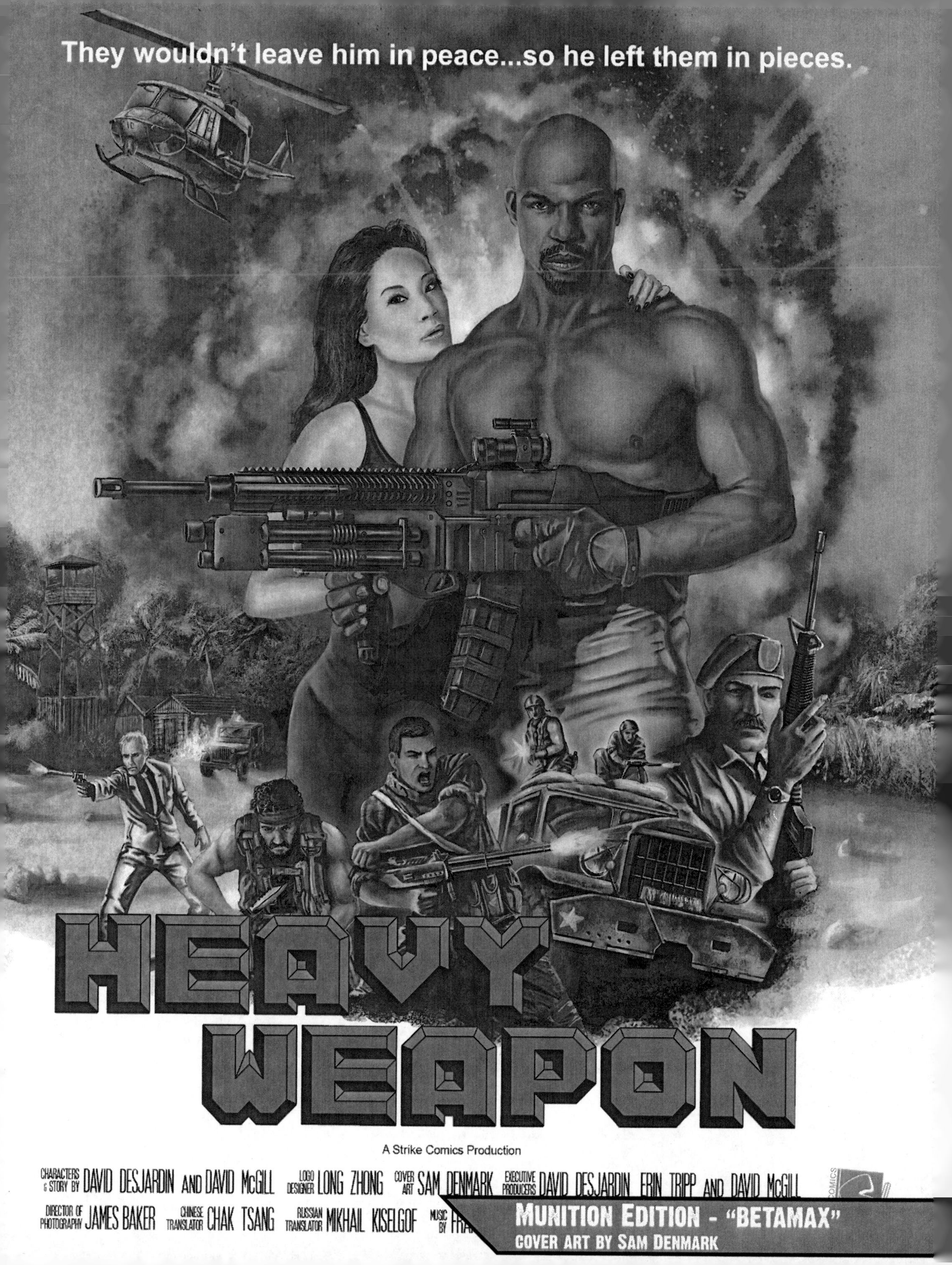
They wouldn't leave him in peace...so he left them in pieces.
HEAVY WEAPON
A Strike Comics Production
CHARACTERS & STORY BY DAVID DESJARDIN AND DAVID McGILL LOGO DESIGNER LONG ZHONG COVER ART SAM DENMARK EXECUTIVE PRODUCERS DAVID DESJARDIN ERIN TRIPP AND DAVID McGILL
DIRECTOR OF PHOTOGRAPHY JAMES BAKER CHINESE TRANSLATOR CHAK TSANG RUSSIAN TRANSLATOR MIKHAIL KISELGOF MUSIC BY
MUNITION EDITION - "BETAMAX"
COVER ART BY SAM DENMARK

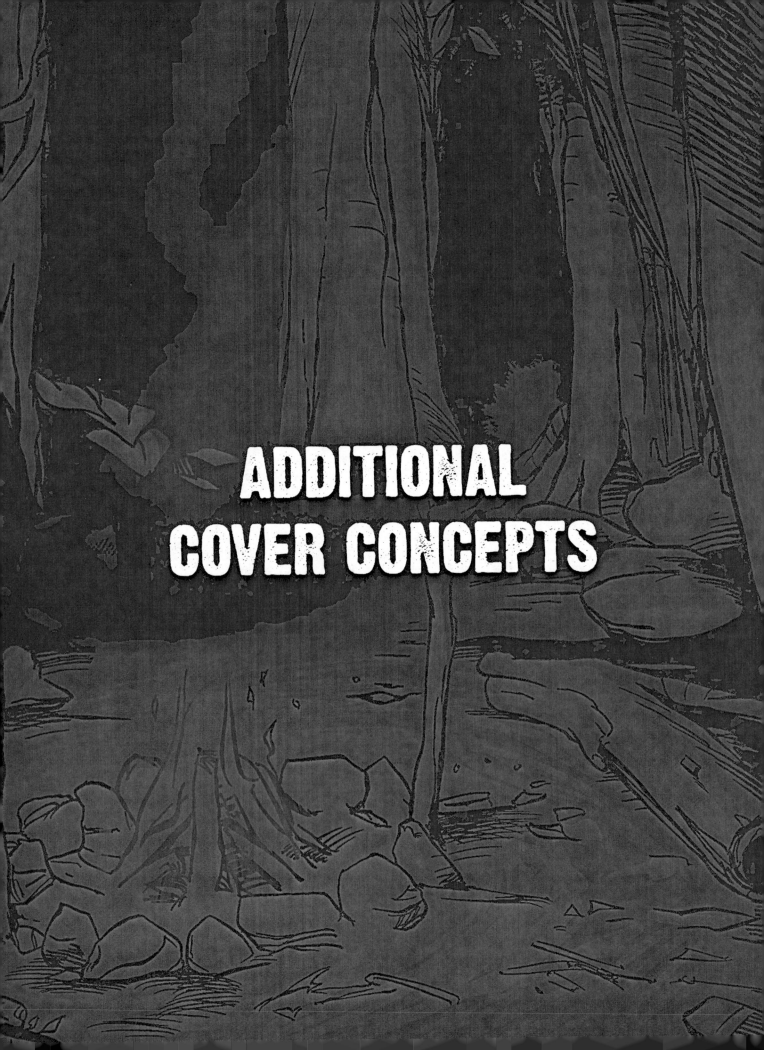

ADDITIONAL
COVER CONCEPTS

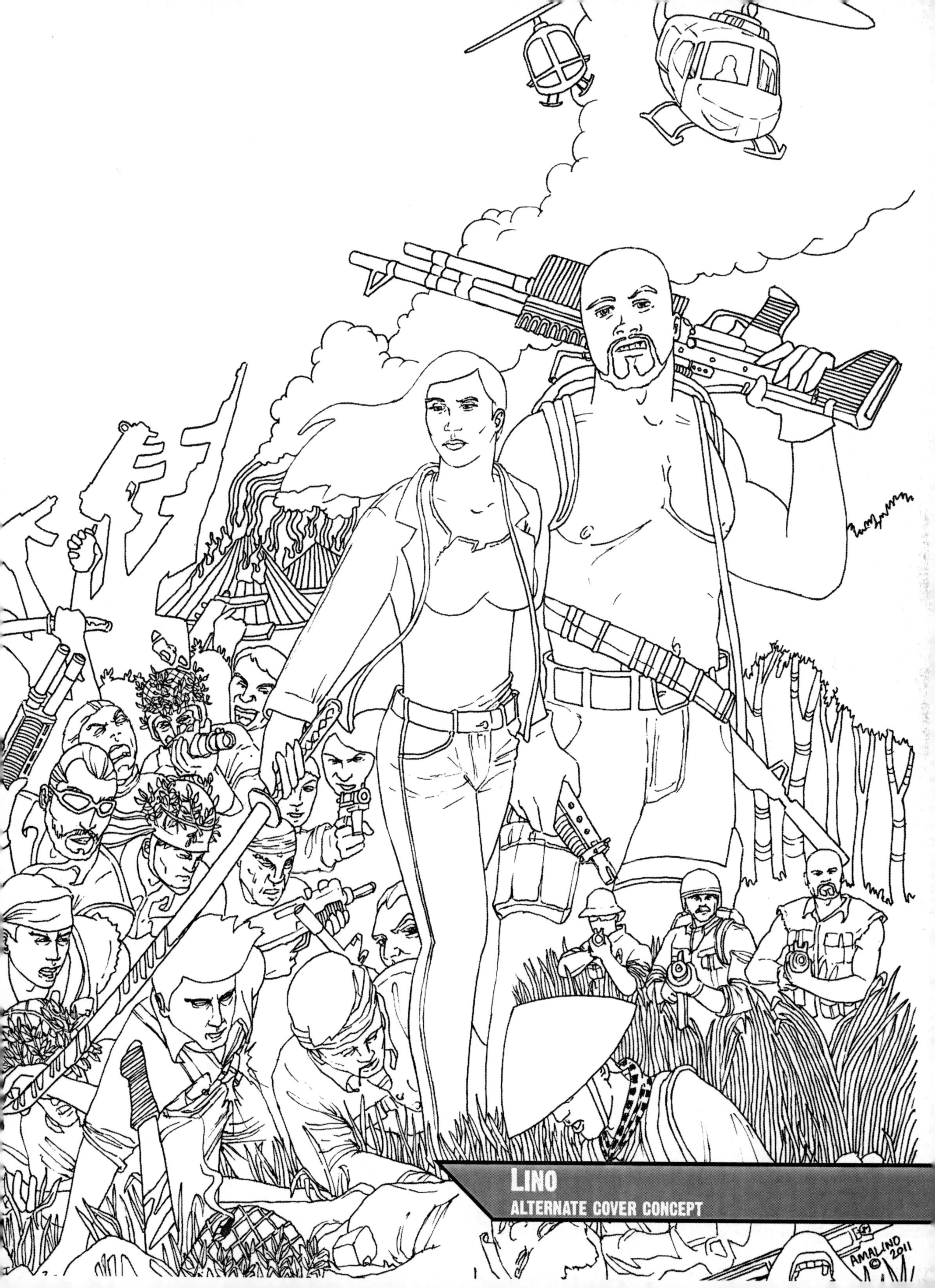
AMALINO
© 2011

LINO
ALTERNATE COVER CONCEPT

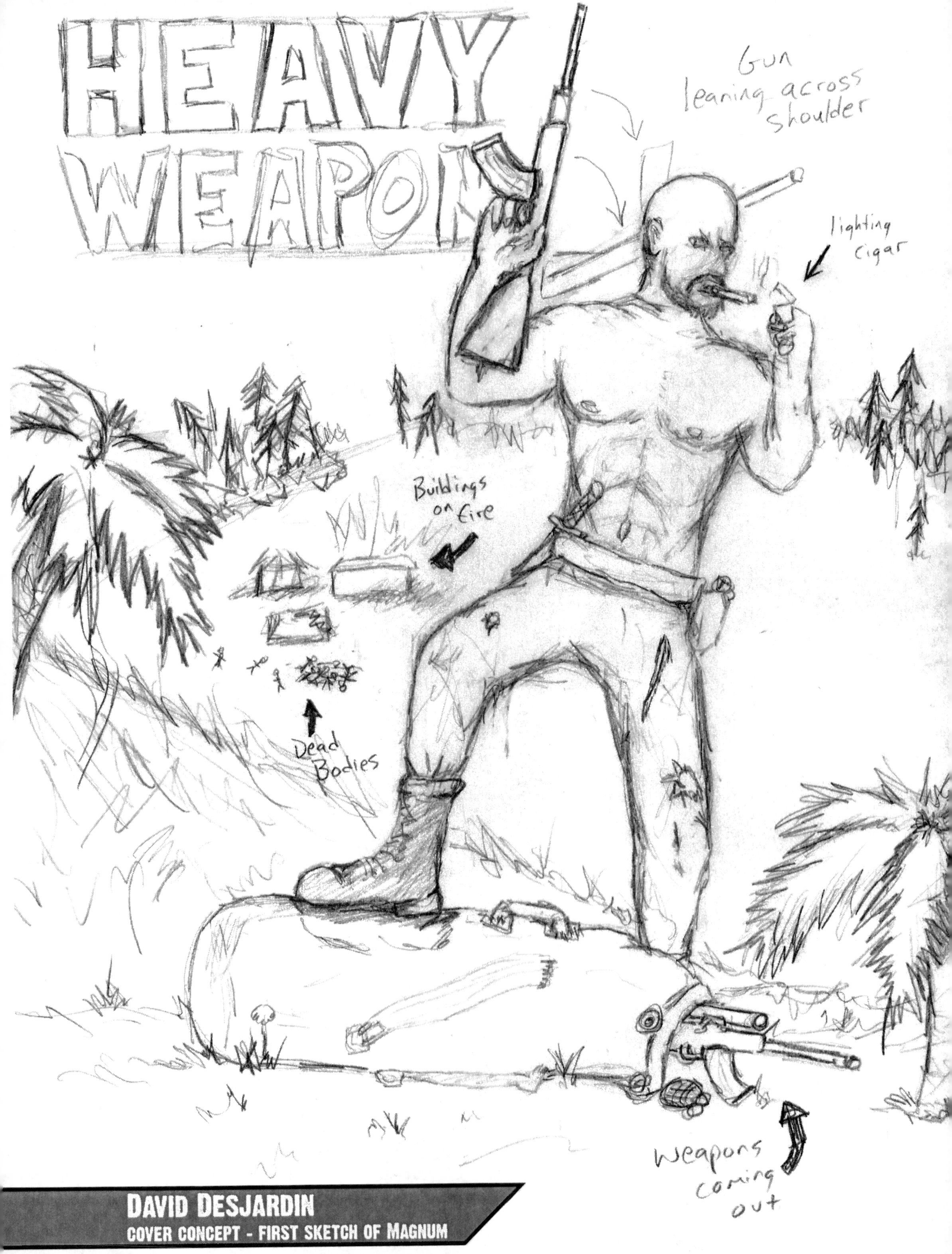
HEAVY
WEAPON
Gun leaning across shoulder
lighting cigar
Buildings on fire
Dead Bodies
Weapons coming out

DAVID DESJARDIN
COVER CONCEPT - FIRST SKETCH OF MAGNUM

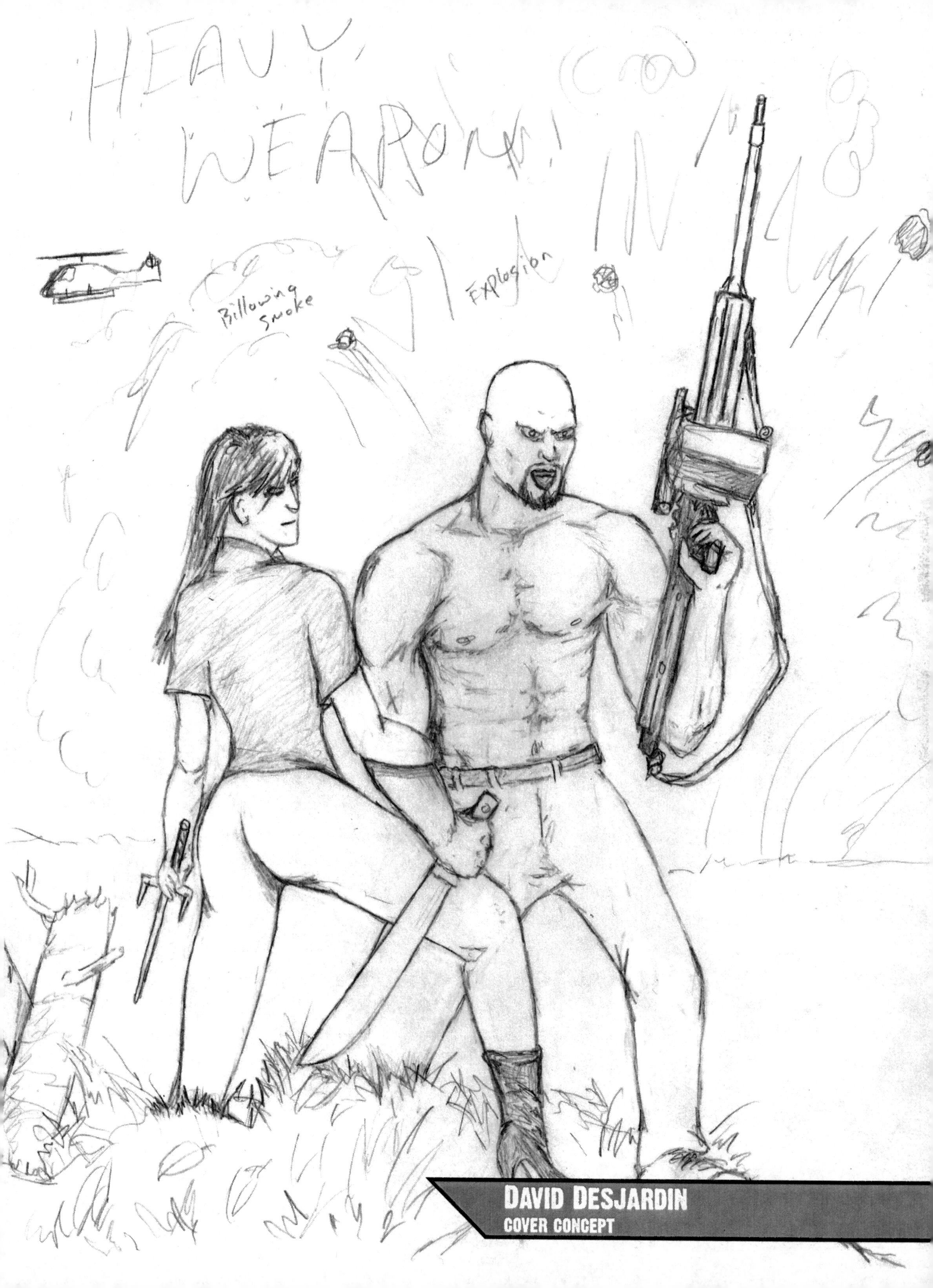
HEAVY WEAPON!
Billowing Smoke
Explosion

DAVID DESJARDIN
COVER CONCEPT

CONCEPT ART

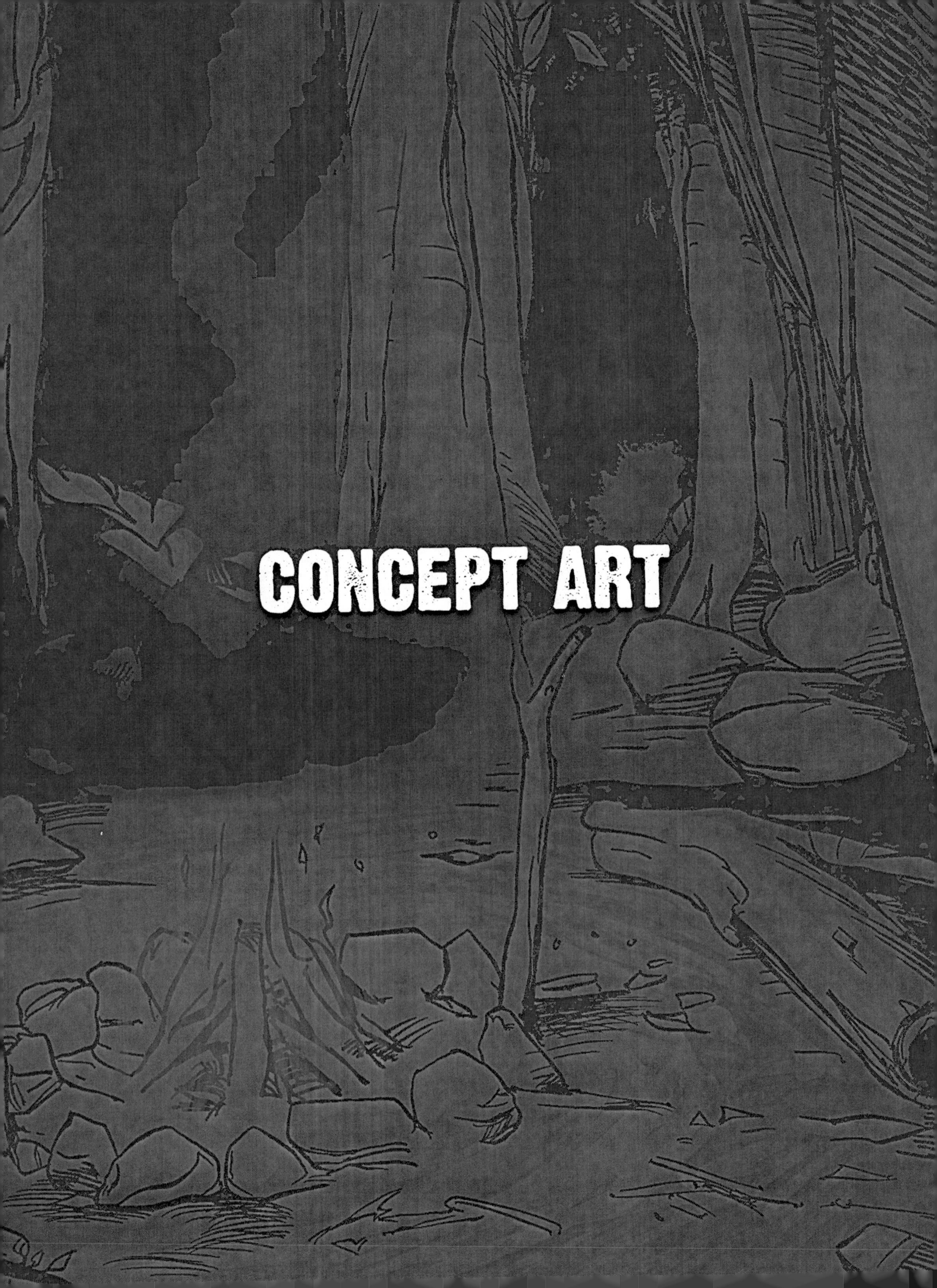

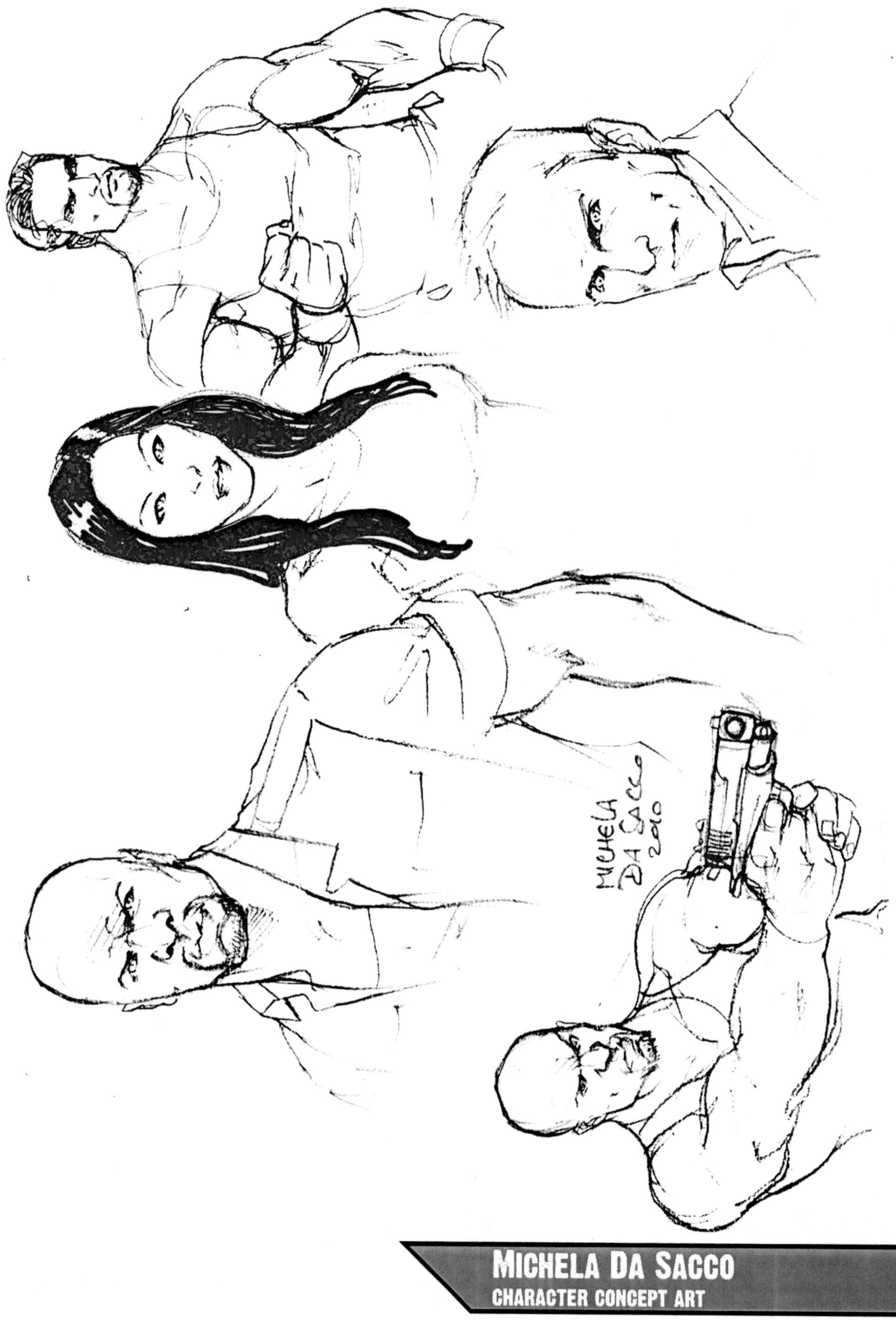
MICHELA DA SACCO 2010

MICHELA DA SACCO
CHARACTER CONCEPT ART

JOHN MAGNUM

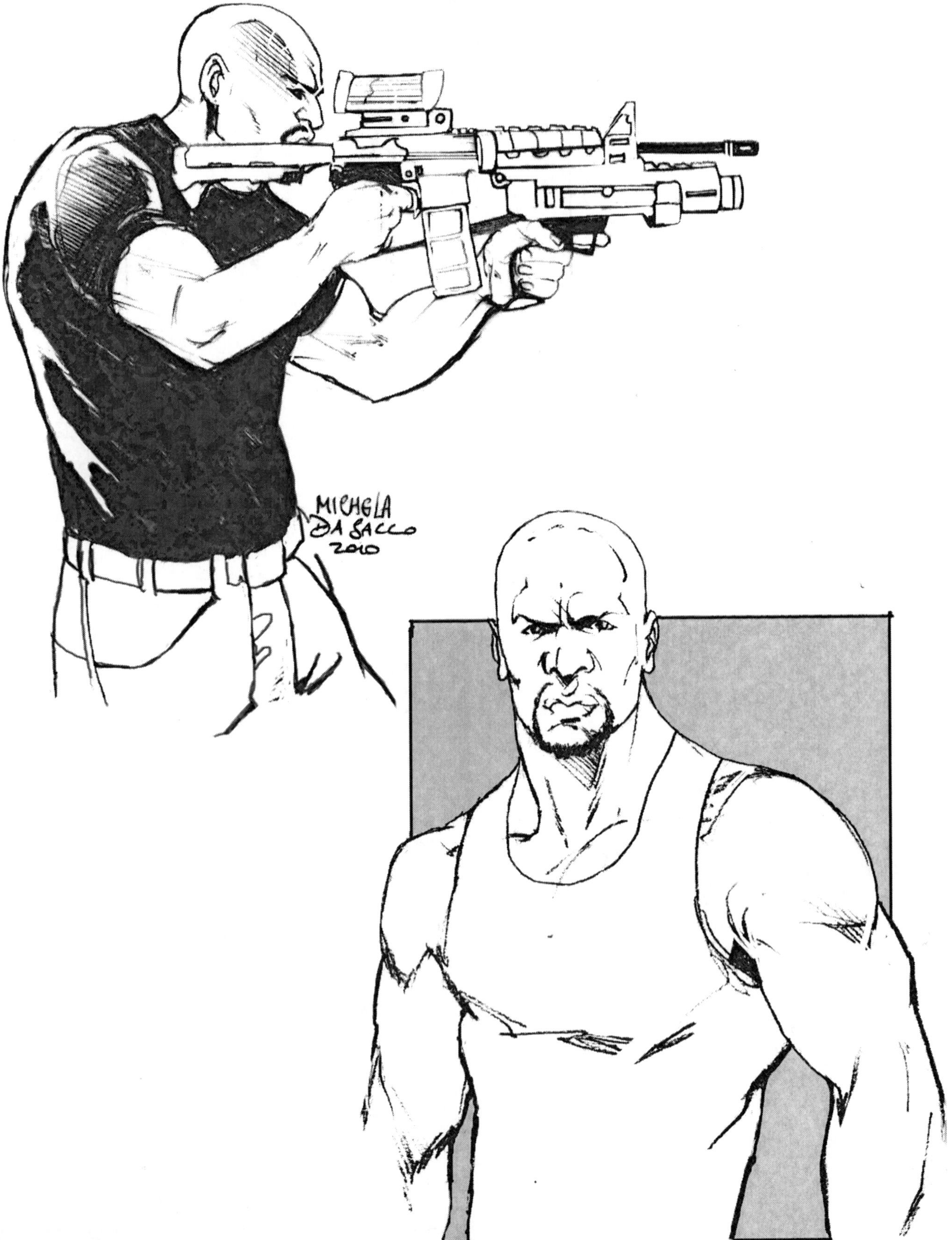
MICHELA
DA SACCO
2010

MARION DECKARD

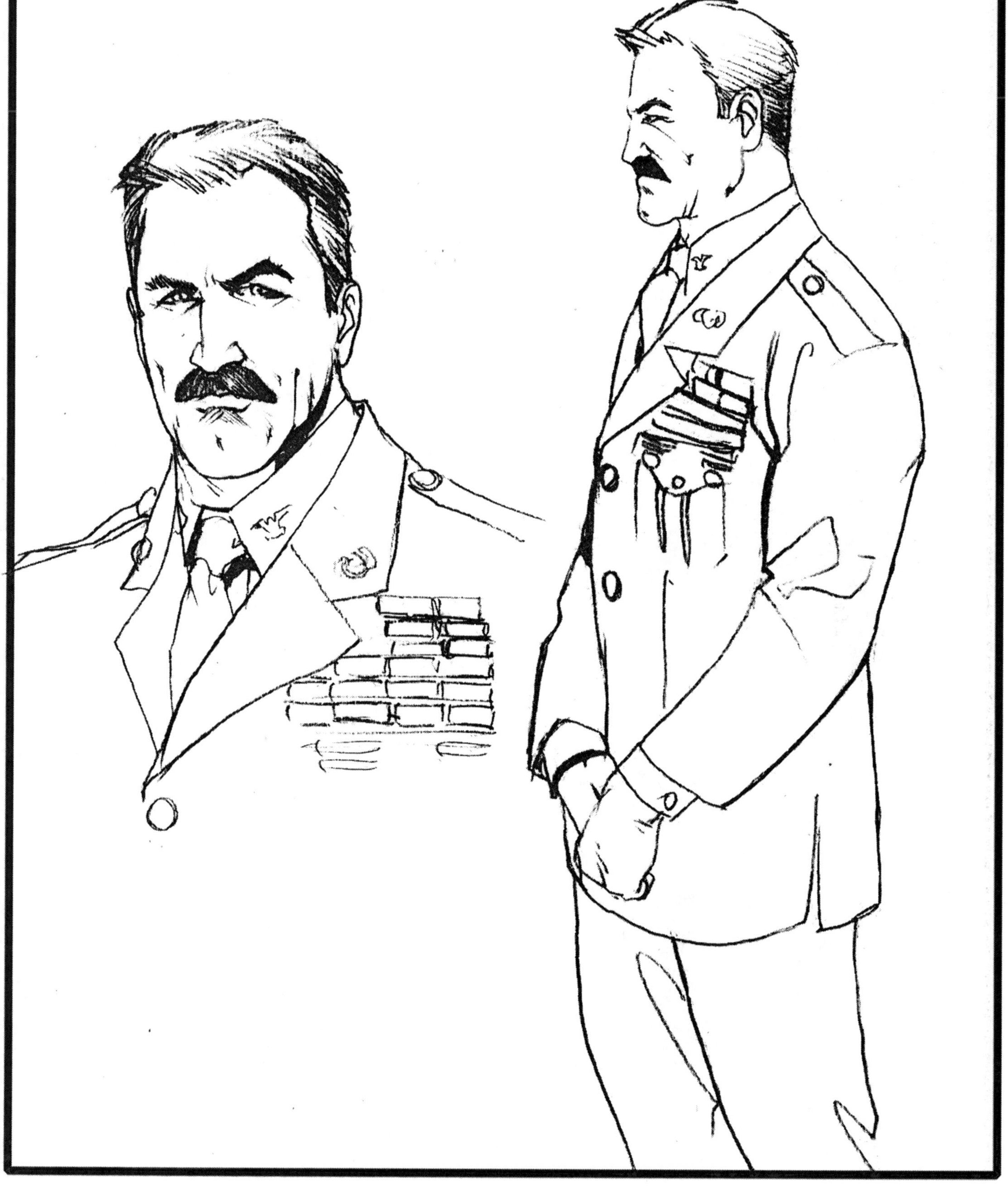

ALONZO RICHTER

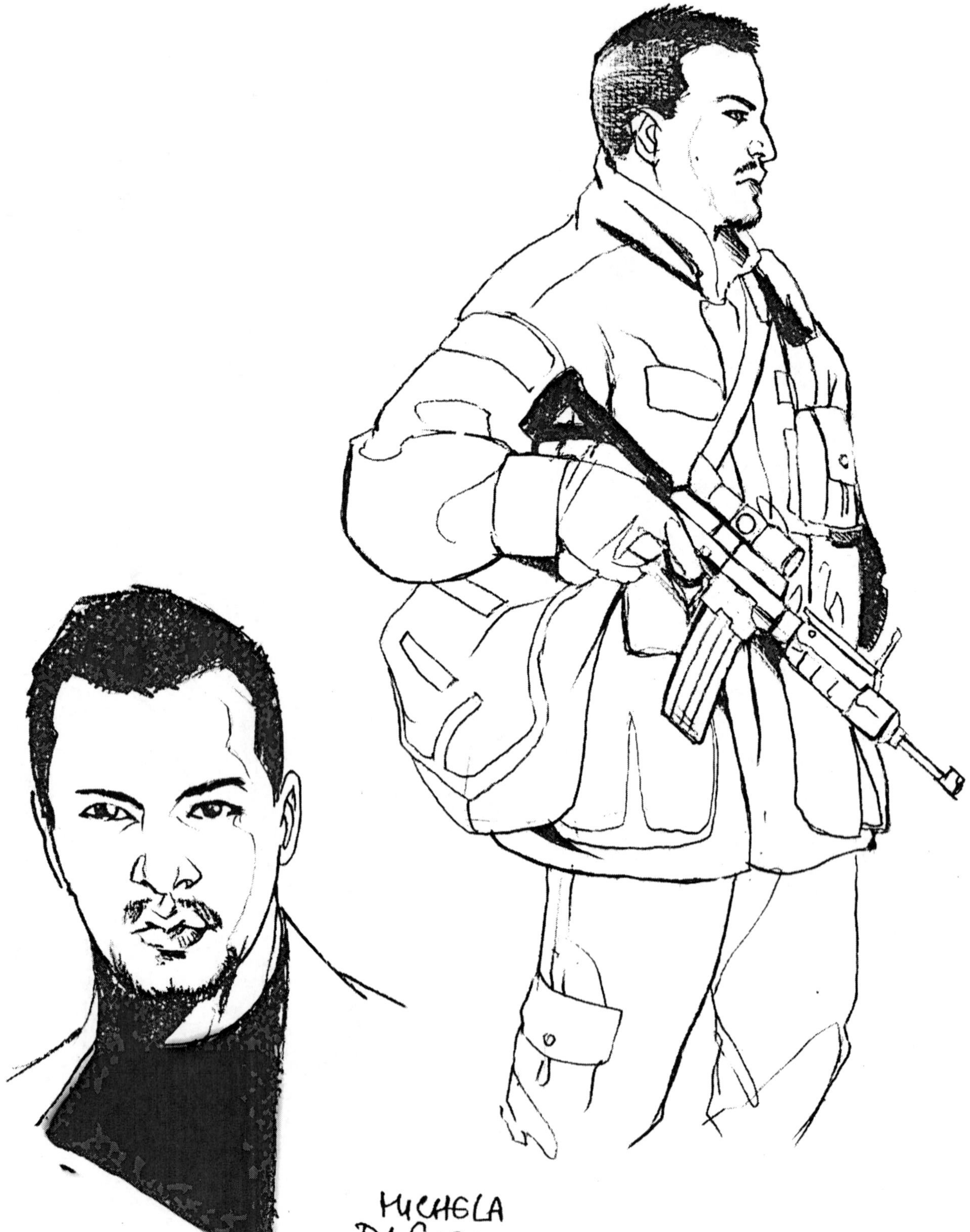
MICHELA
DA SACCO
2010

VLADIMIR KINSKI

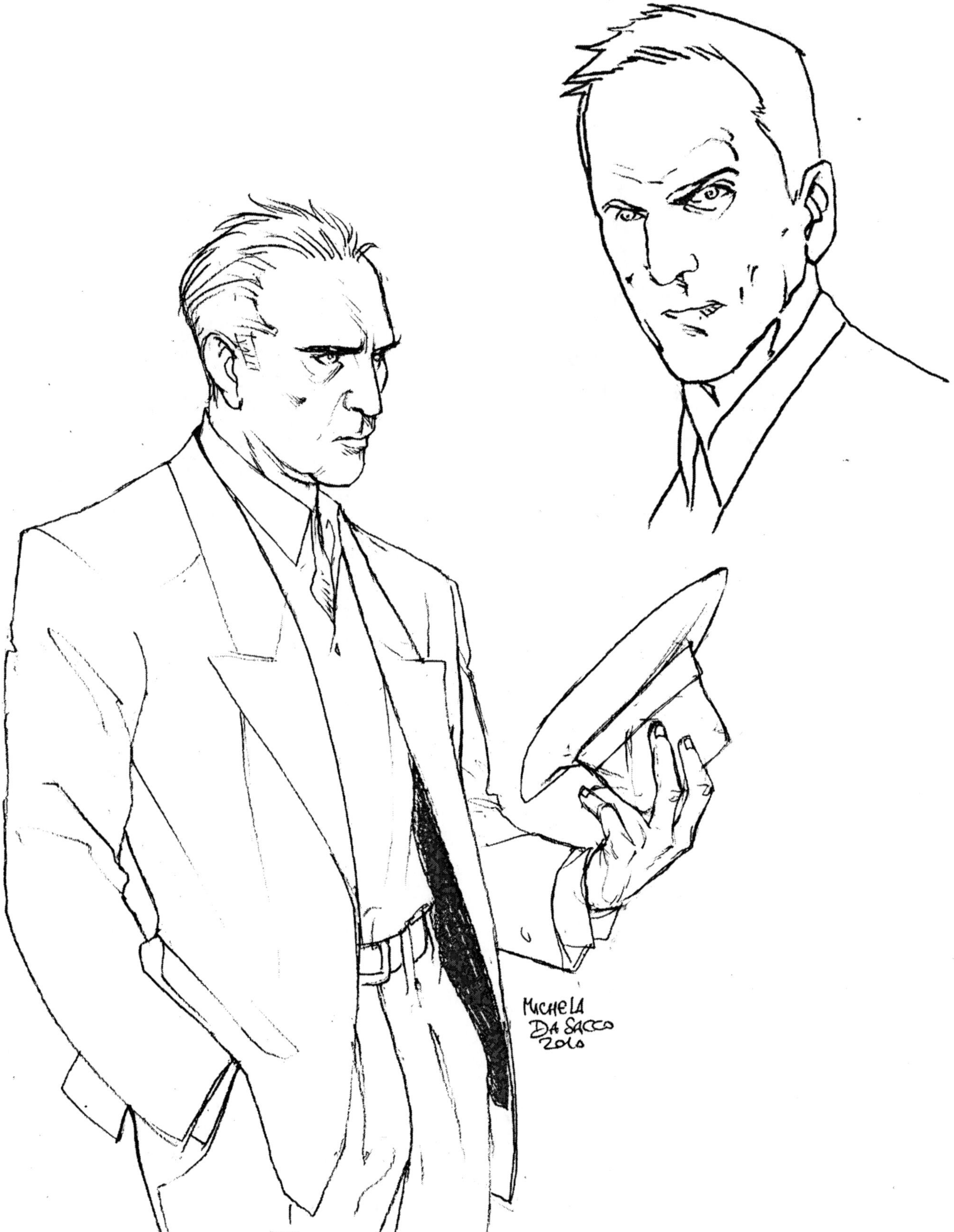
MICHELA
DA SACCO
2010

TING SUN WEI

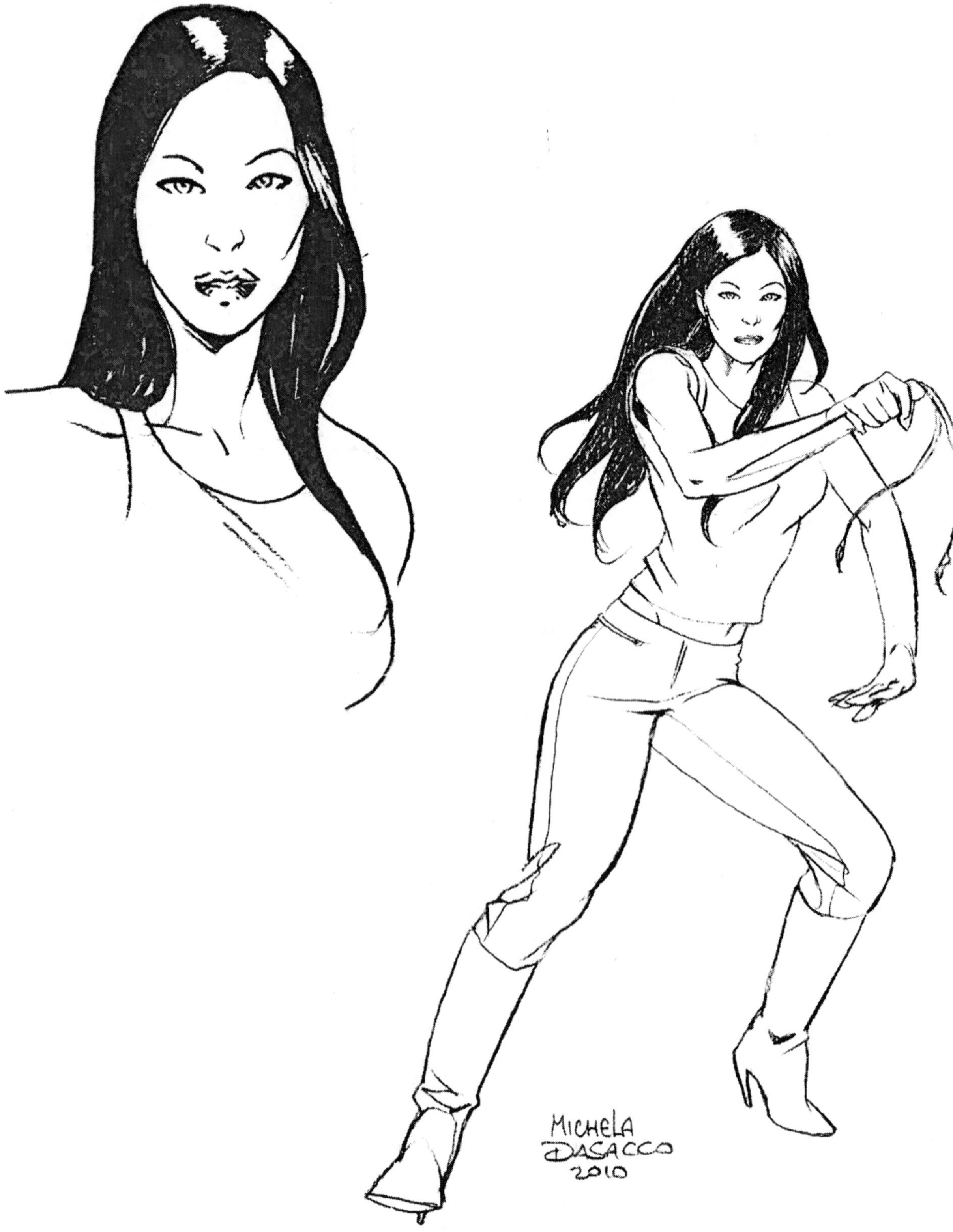
MICHELA
DASACCO
2010

KOH

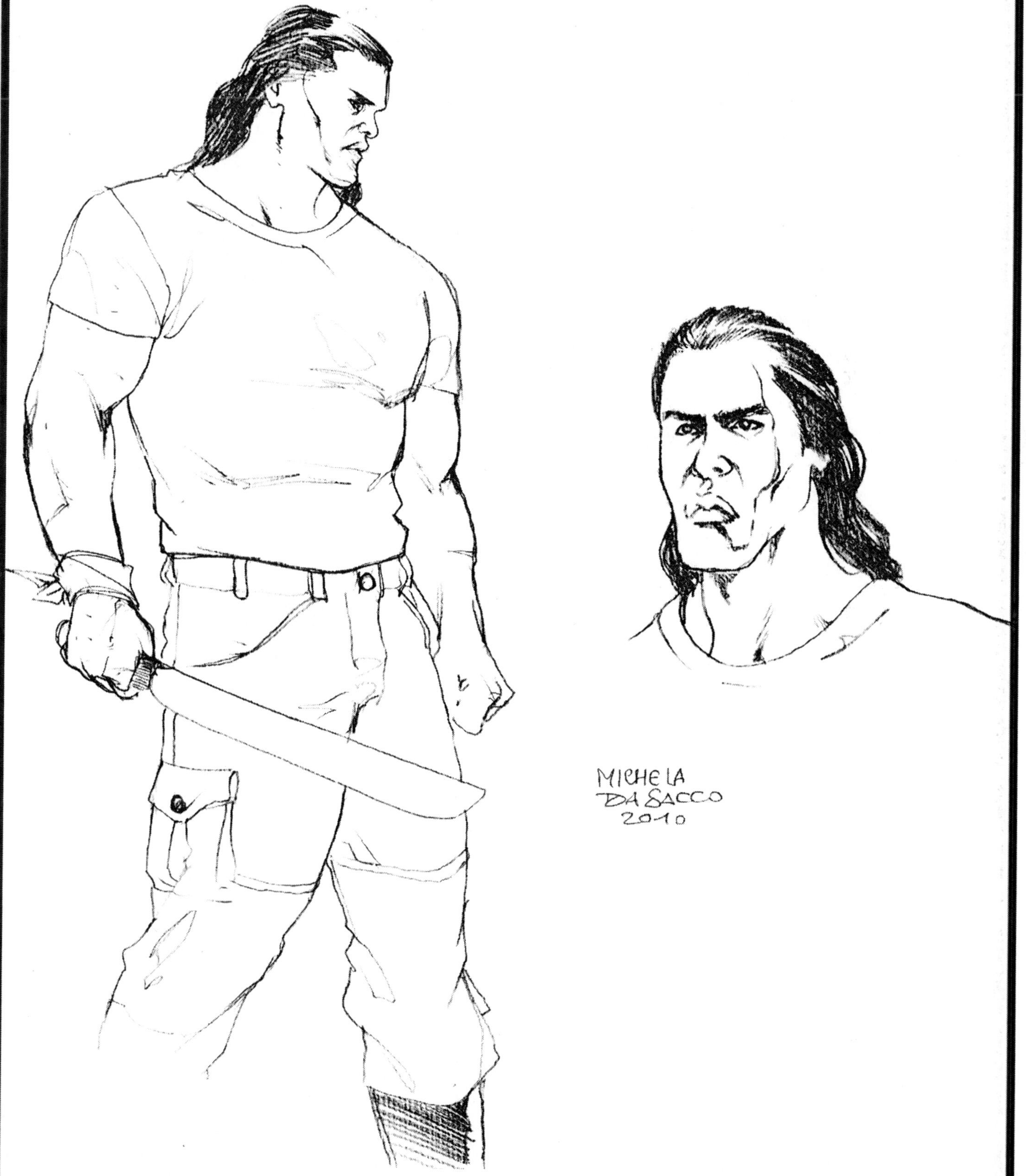
MICHELA
DA SACCO
2010

LONGINO

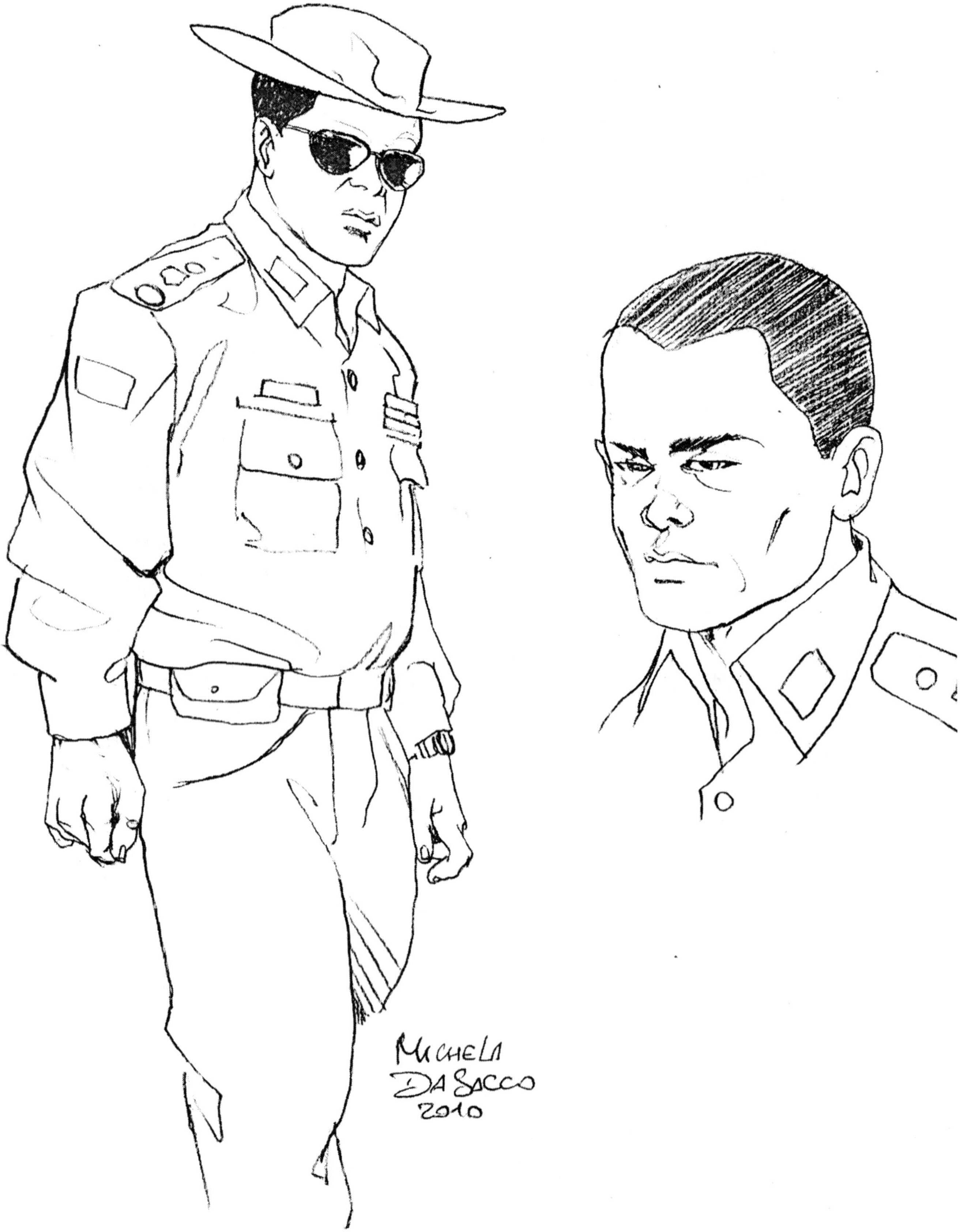
MICHELA
DA SACCO
2010

PENNY JAMESON

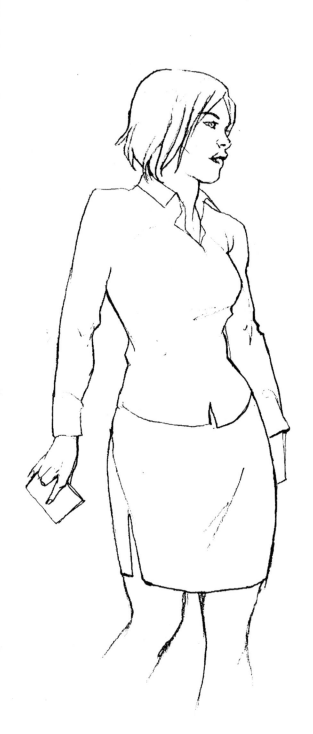

Michela
DaSacco
2010

PISS-ANT SOLDIERS

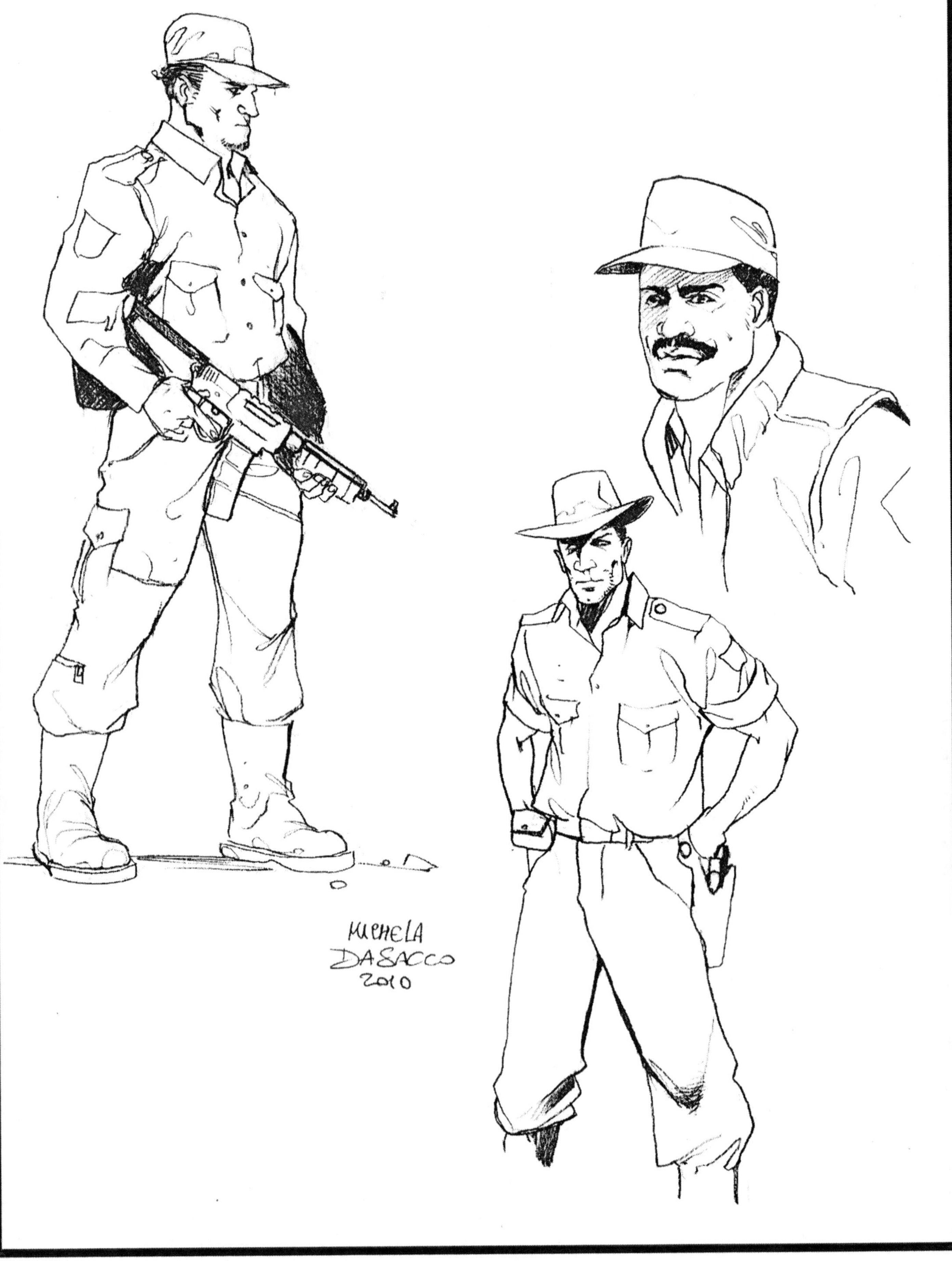
MICHELA
DASACCO
2010

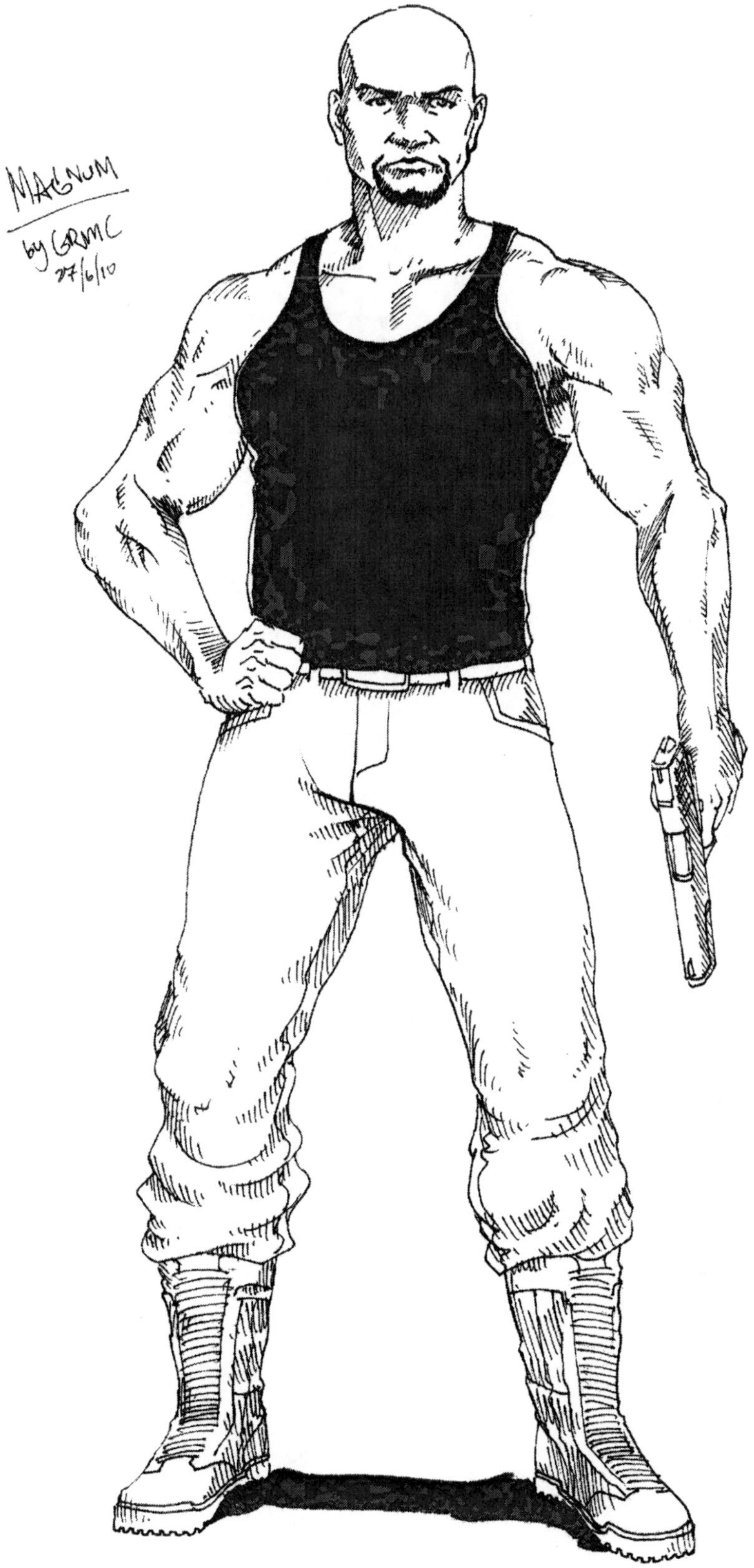
MAGNUM
by GRMC
27/6/10

BATBAATAR TSOLMONBAYAR
CHARACTER CONCEPT ART

Colonel Deckard
by [signature] 29/6/10

Richter
by GRMC
27/6/10

VLADiMiR
by GRMC
27/6/10

TING
by GRMC
27/6/10

Koll
by dRMc
2016.6.27

congfno

head of soldier

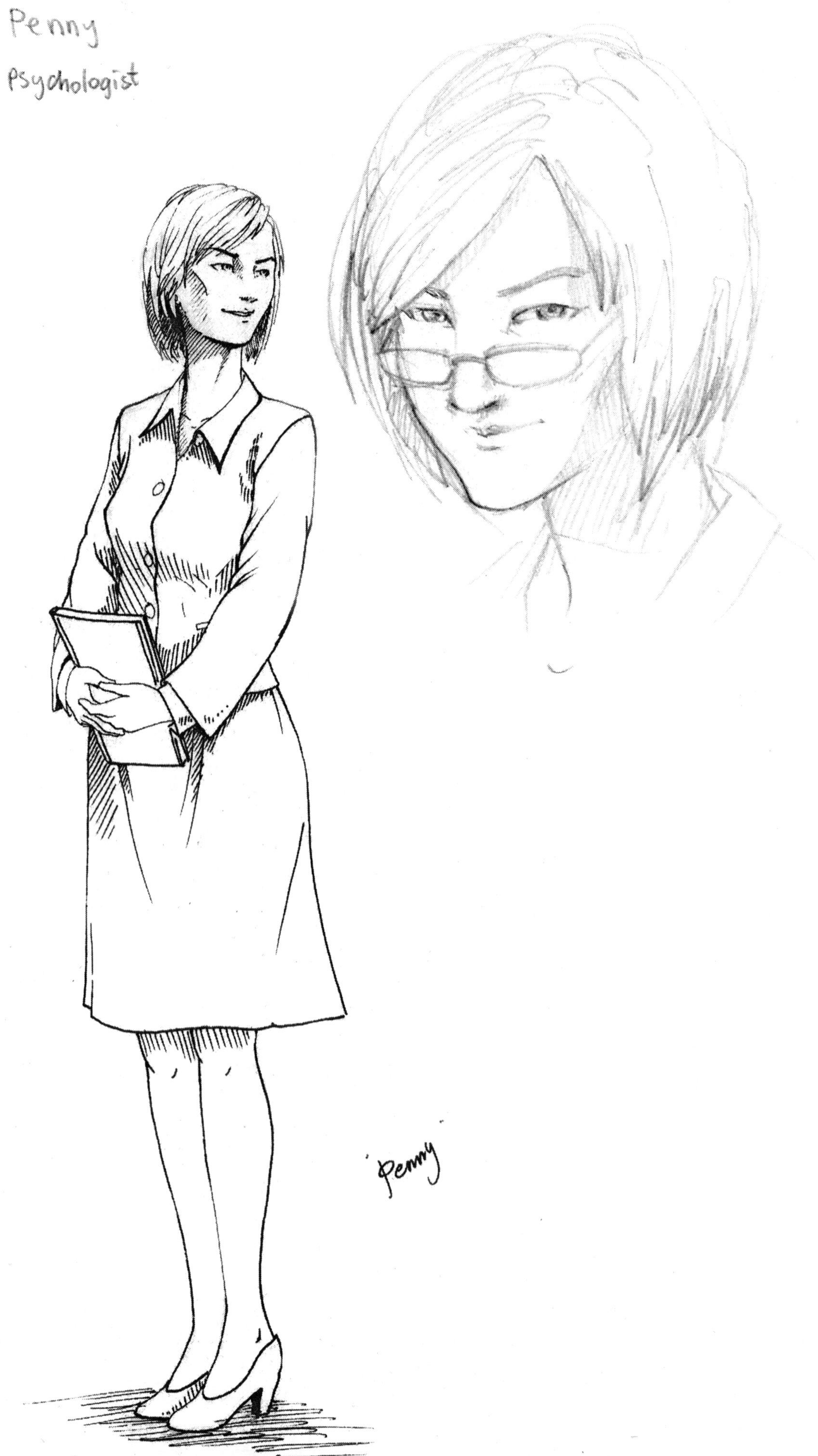
Penny
psychologist
Penny

The noname badguy Soldiers

- Brazilian southAmerican

poor - man's army

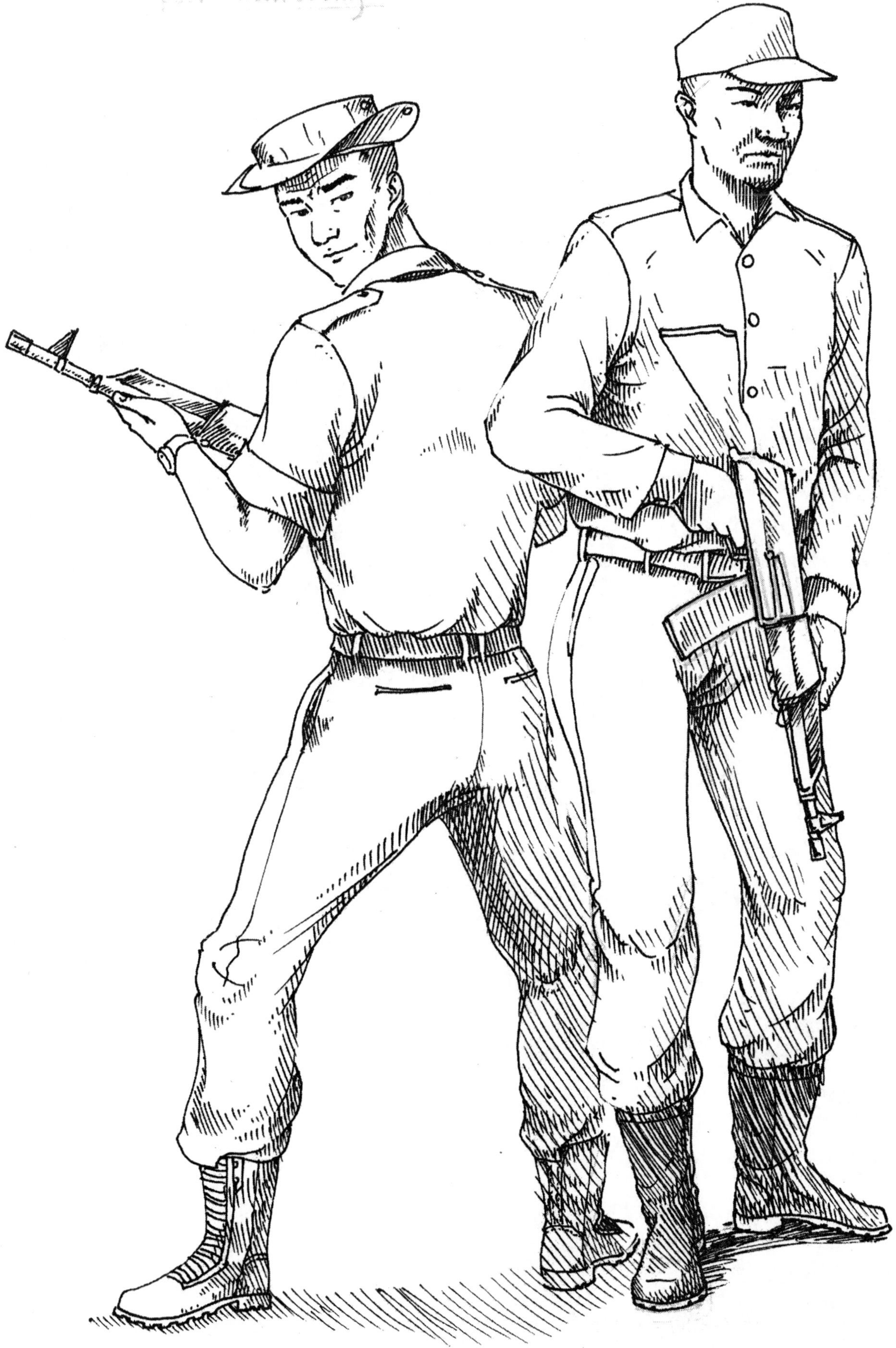

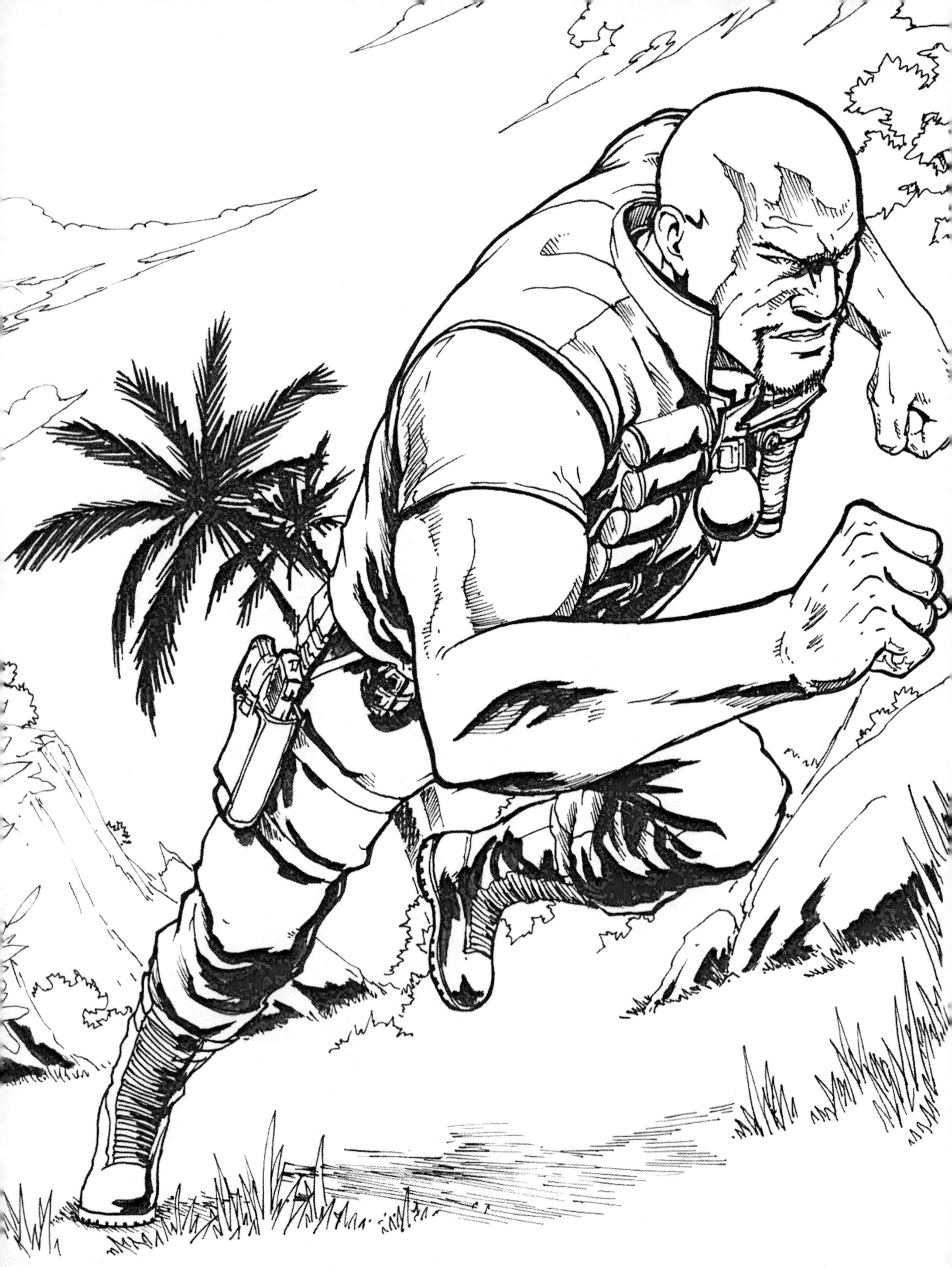

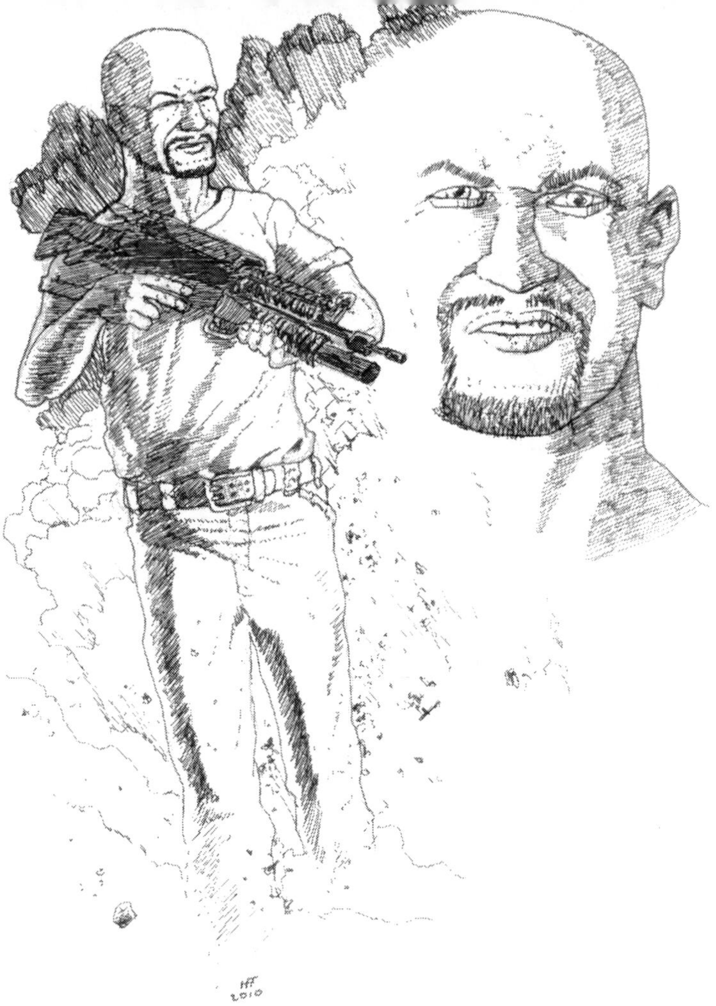

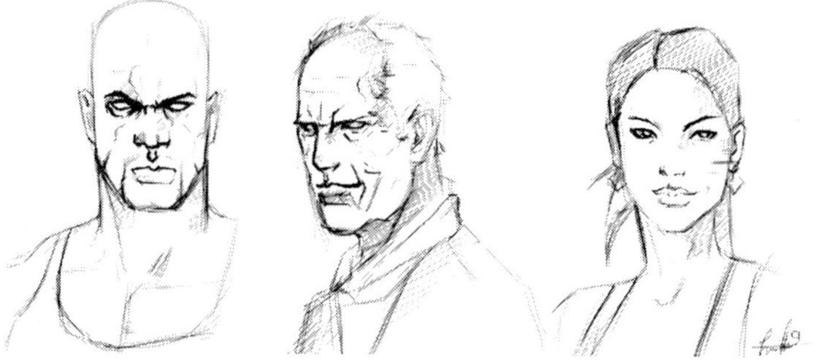

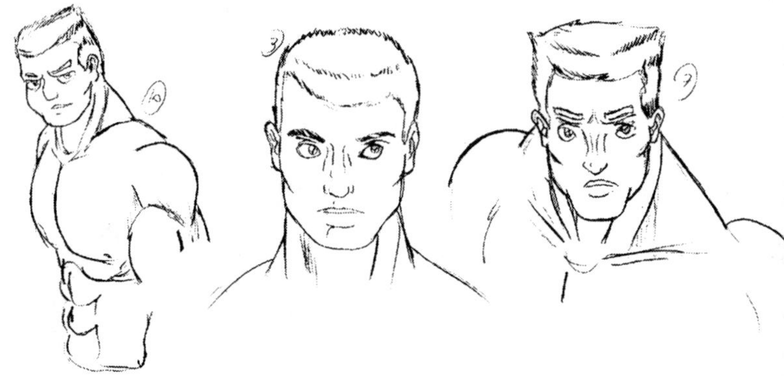

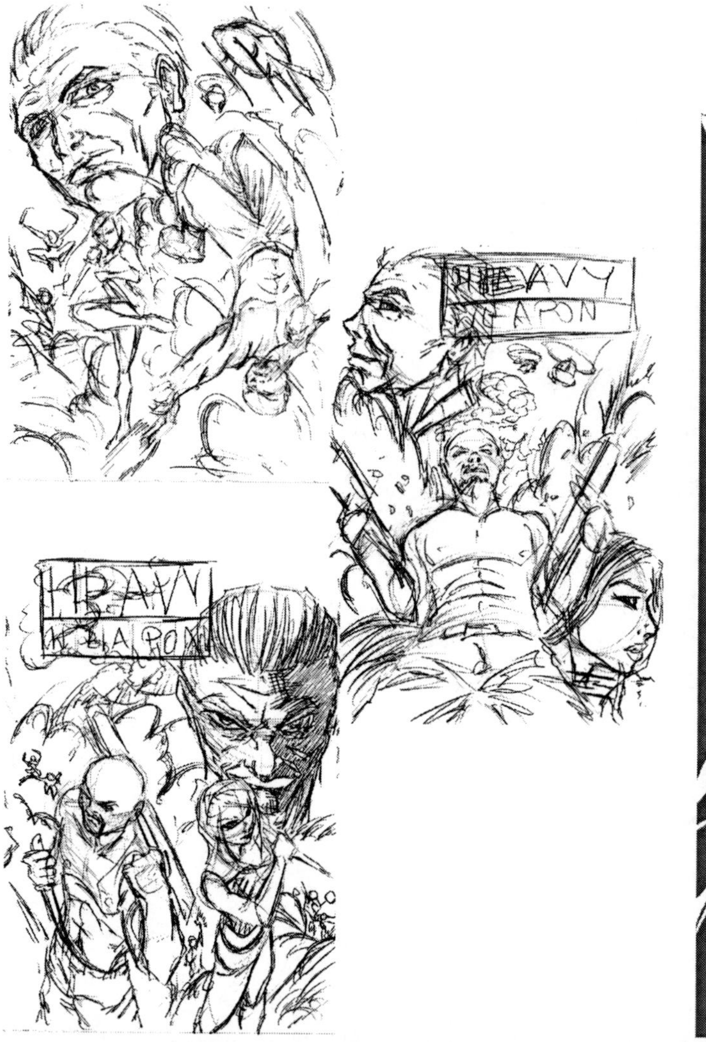

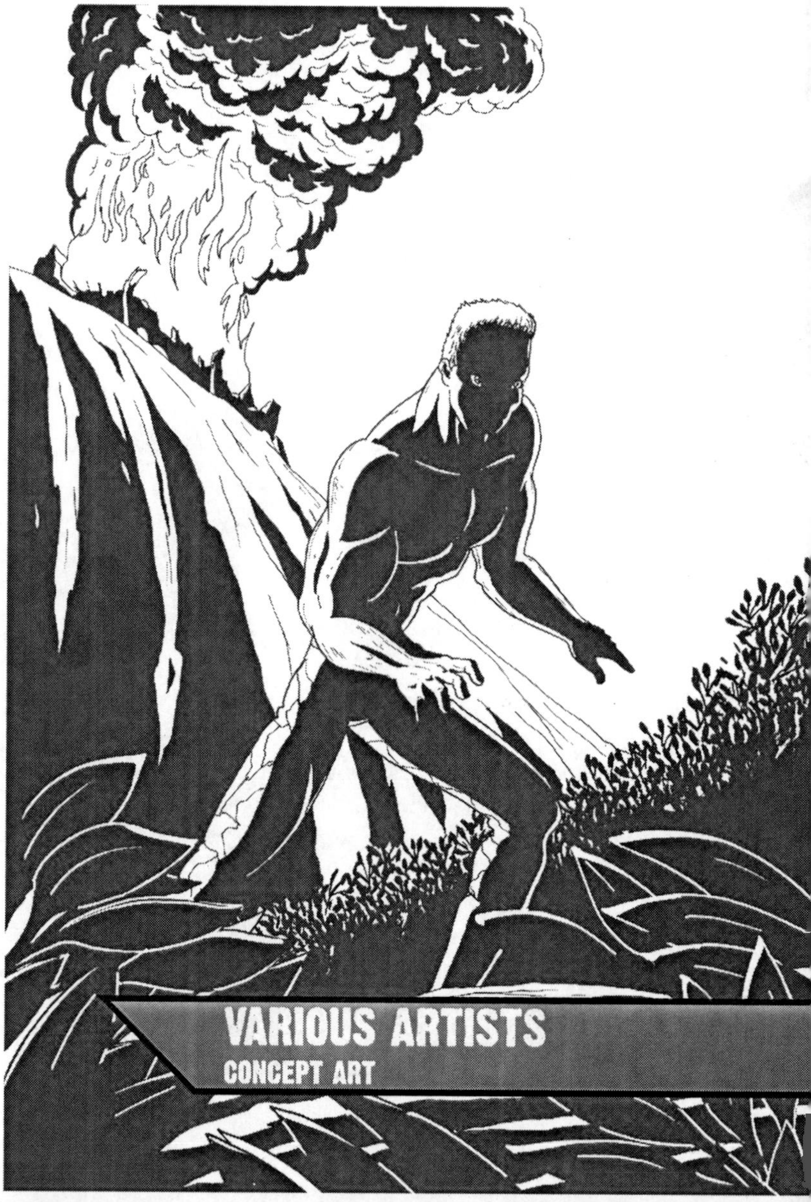

VARIOUS ARTISTS
CONCEPT ART

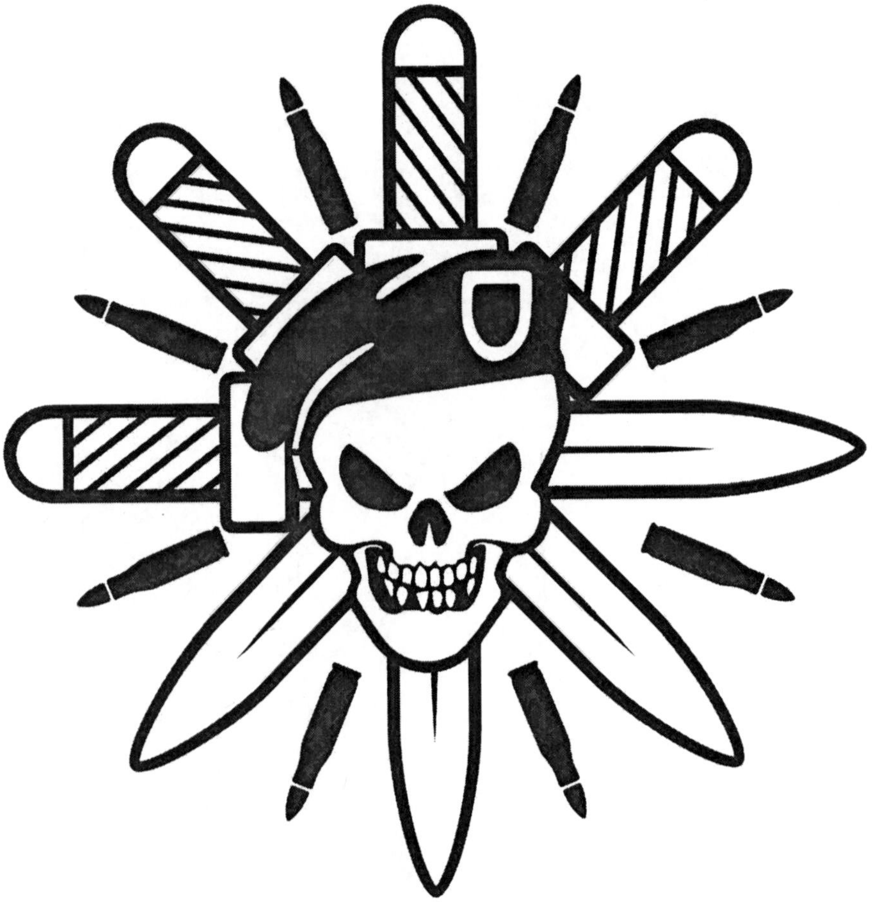

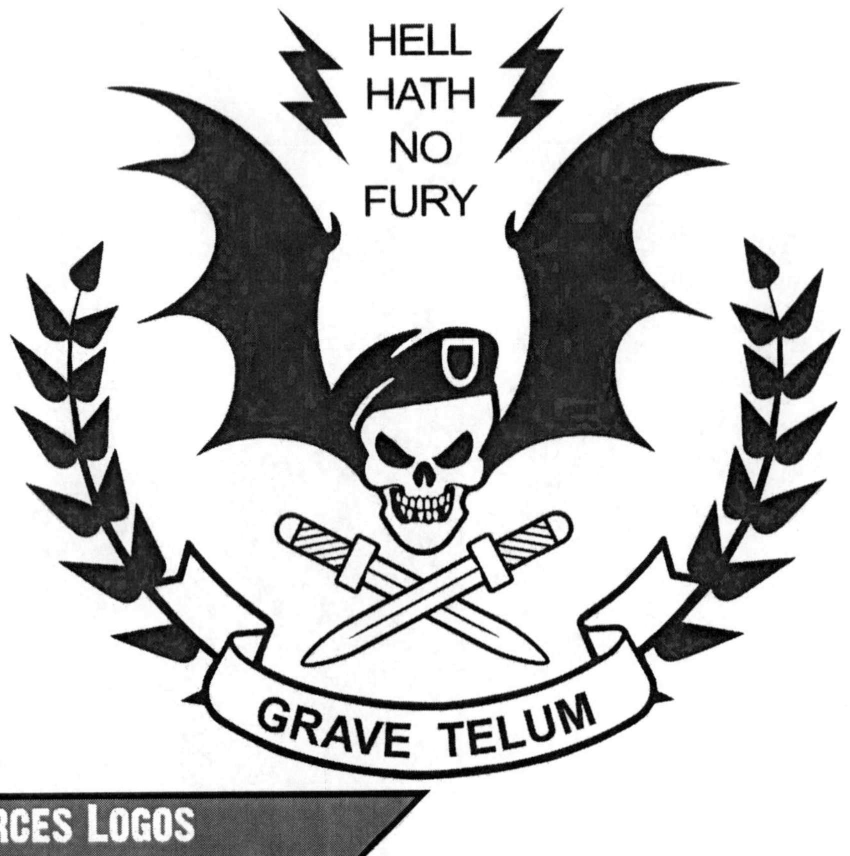
HELL
HATH
NO
FURY
GRAVE TELUM

SPECIAL FORCES LOGOS

ART BY SHANE ZHONG

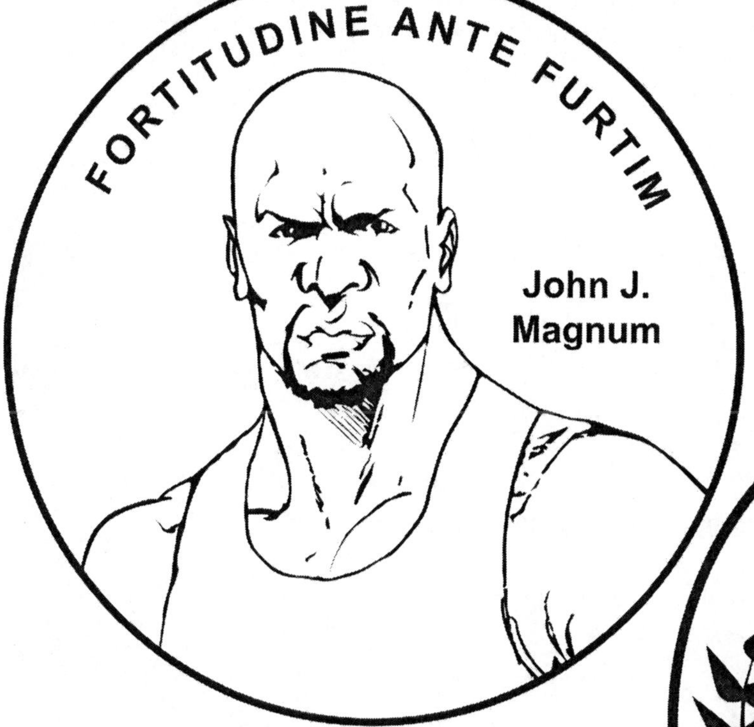
FORTITUDINE ANTE FURTIM
John J.
Magnum

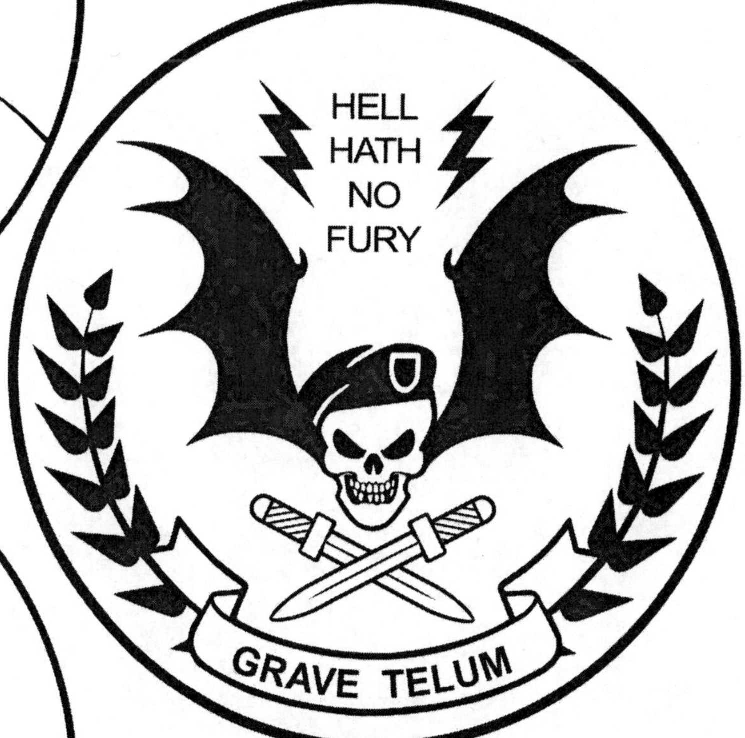
HELL
HATH
NO
FURY
GRAVE TELUM

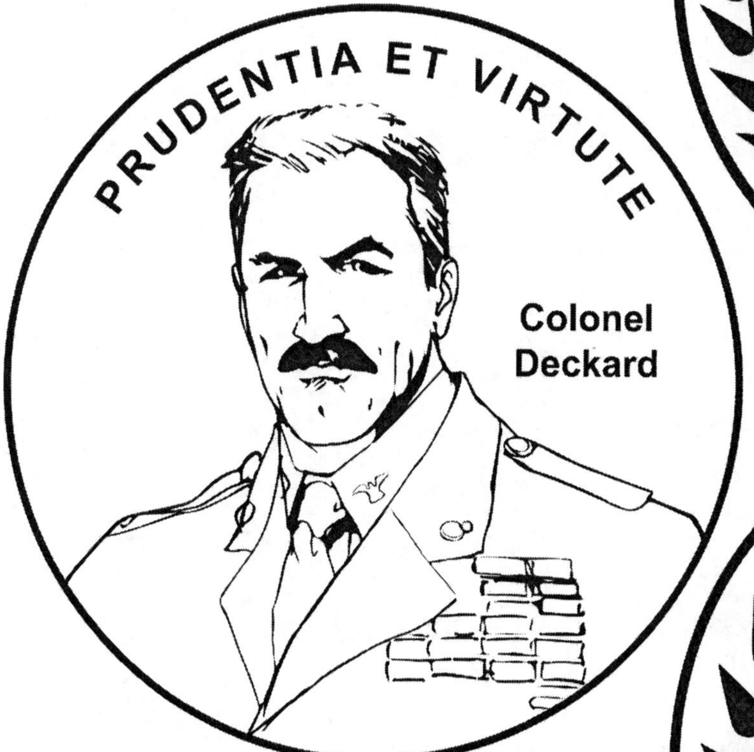
PRUDENTIA ET VIRTUTE
Colonel
Deckard

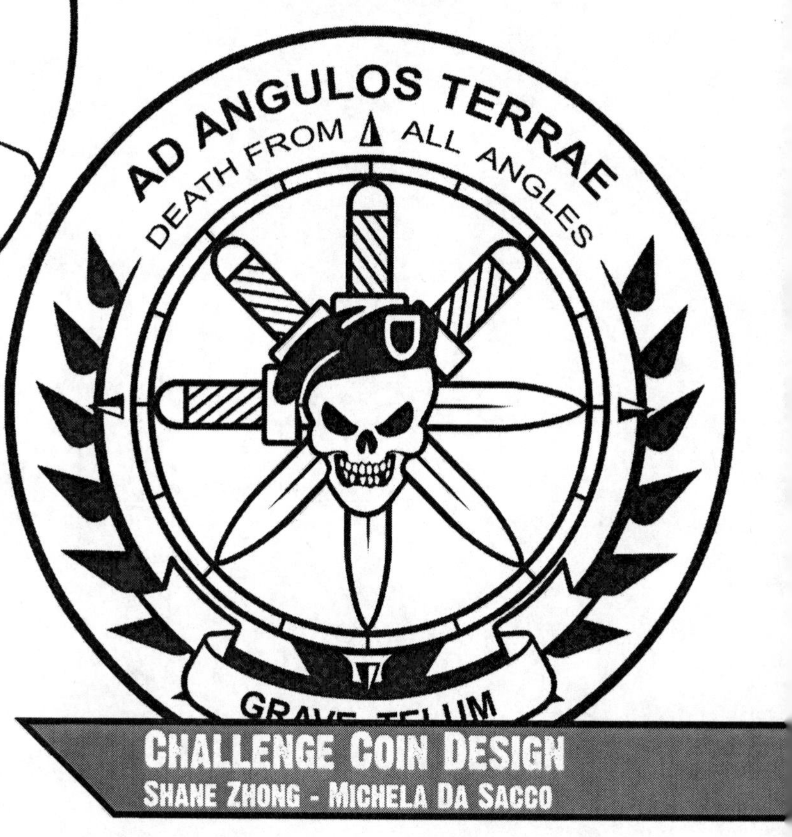
AD ANGULOS TERRAE
DEATH FROM ALL ANGLES

CHALLENGE COIN DESIGN
SHANE ZHONG - MICHELA DA SACCO

WANT MORE EXTRAS?
CHECK OUT THESE PREMIUM EDITIONS:

HEAVY WEAPON
HARDCOVER

- OVER 50 PAGES OF AN ALTERNATE VERSION OF HEAVY WEAPON THAT *ALMOST* HAPPENED!!
  ART BY BATBAATAR TSOLMONBAYAR.

- AN EXTENSIVE "MAKING OF HEAVY WEAPON" COLLECTION FROM THE SCRIPT TO COMPLETION!

- FULL-PAGE FAKE 80'S ADVERTISEMENTS GALLERY!

HEAVY WEAPON
MUNITION EDITION

- EXCLUSIVE HARDCOVER WITH ALTERNATE COVER LIMITED TO ONLY 250 COPIES!!

- RARE COLLECTOR'S ITEMS INCLUDING: DOG TAGS, COINS, CLOTH MAP, BOOKMARKS, AND MORE!!

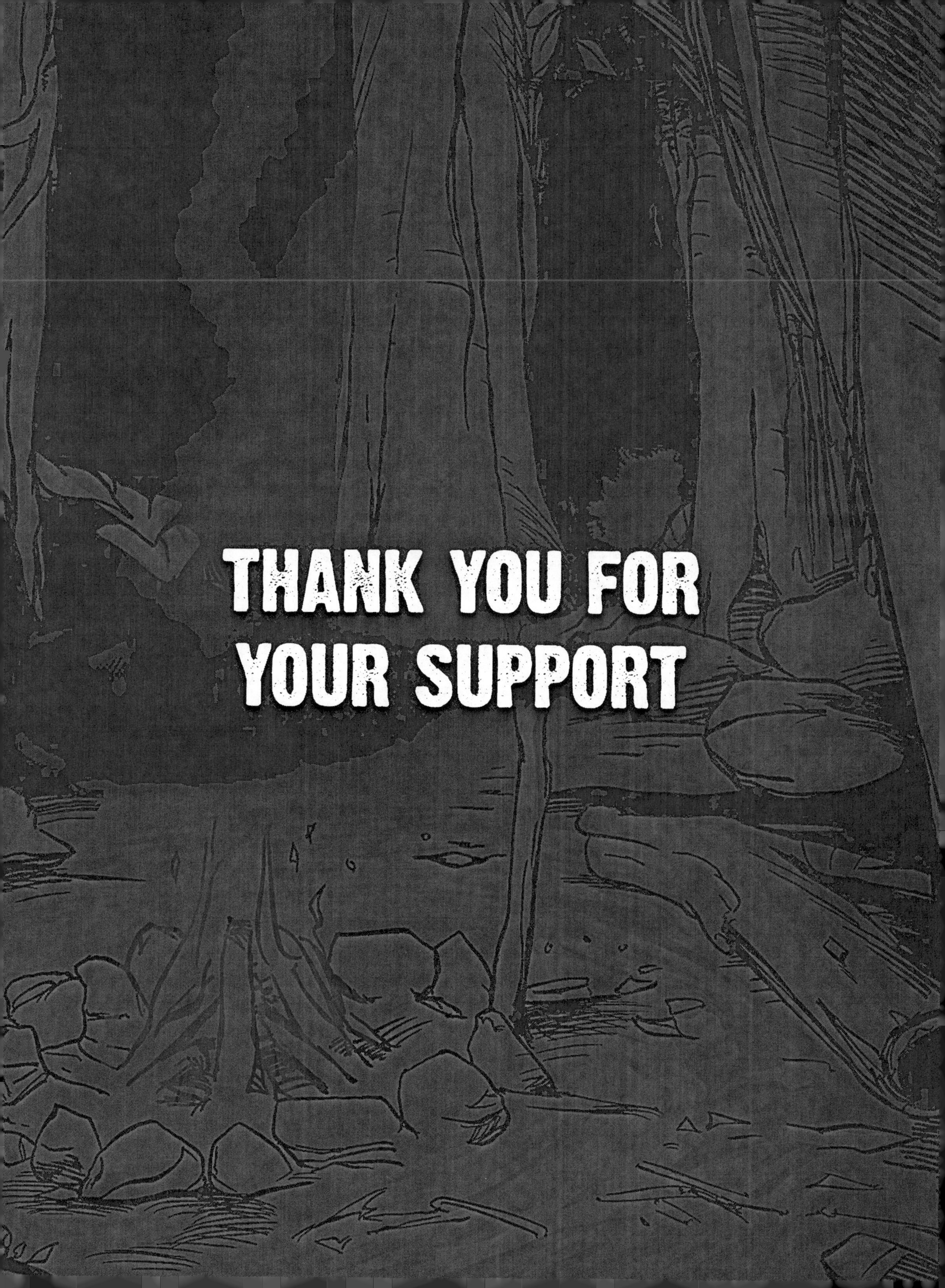
THANK YOU FOR
YOUR SUPPORT

STRIKE
COMICS

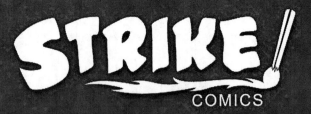

CPSIA information can be obtained at www.ICGtesting.com
Printed in the USA
LVOW09s0552051214

417210LV00012B/169/P